HOW to TALK
to a LIBERAL

(If You Must)

HOW to TALK
to a LIBERAL

(If You Must)

The World According to
ANN
COULTER

THREE RIVERS PRESS · NEW YORK

Published in the United States by Three Rivers Press, an imprint of the
Crown Publishing Group, a division of Random House, Inc.
www.crownpublishing.com

Three Rivers Press and the Tugboat design are registered trademarks
of Random House, Inc.

Originally published in hardcover in a slighly different form by
Crown Forum, an imprint of the Crown Publishing Group,
a division of Random House, Inc., New York, in 2004.

Portions previously published in slightly different form in
Human Events, the Universal Press Syndicate, and *George* magazine.

DESIGN BY BARBARA STURMAN

Library of Congress Cataloging-in-Publication Data

Coulter, Ann H.
How to talk to a liberal (if you must) : the world according to
Ann Coulter / Ann Coulter.
p.   cm.
1. Liberalism—United States.   2. United States—Politics and government—
1989–   3. Mass media—Political aspects—United States.   I. Title.
JC574.2.U6C67   2004
320.51.'3'0973—dc22   2004014791

ISBN-13 978-1-4000-5419-0
ISBN-10 1-4000-5419-2

2   4   6   8   10   9   7   5   3   1

First Paperback Edition

For my mother,

Nell Martin Coulter

Contents

1

How to Talk to a Liberal 1

2

This Is War 22

How 9/11 Happened 22

This Is War 26

The Hun Is at the Gate 29

Attack France! 32

May I Turn Down Your Bed, Mohammad? 35

Build Them Back 38

This Whistle-Blower They Like 40

My Name Is Adolf 43

Beauty Pageants Can Be Murder 46

War-Torn Democrats 48

"Will of Allah" Preempts Iraq Invasion 51

Kissing Cousins: New York Literati and Nazis 54

The Enemy Within 56

At Least Saddam Wasn't at Tailhook! 59

Liberals Meet Unexpected Resistance 61

We Don't Care 64

Taking Liberties 67

How to Lose a War 70

"The Plan" 73

It's Like Christmas in December! 76

Al Qaeda Barks, the Spanish Fly 78

Tit for Tet 81

This Is History Calling—Quick, Get Me Rewrite! 83

3

A Muslim by Any Other Name
Blows Up Just the Same 87
   John Davis: American Hero 87
   Where's Janet Reno When We Need Her? 91
   HillaryCare for the Airports 94
   The New Roman Arena: Airports 97
   Would Mohammed Atta Object to Armed Pilots? 100
   Thank You for Choosing United, Mr. Bin Laden 103
   Arab Hijackers Now Eligible for Preboarding 106
   Even with Hindsight Liberals Can't See Straight 110

4

At Least They Didn't Run
Jimmy Carter This Time 113
   *American Women to Kerry: We Don't Think You're
      So Hot Either* 114
   General Democrat 116
   The Party of Ideas 119
   The Jesus Thing 123
   What Happened to Your Queer Party-Friends? 126
   Just a Gigolo 129
   Boobs in the News 132
   In Desperate Move, Kerry Adopts Puppy 134

5

Barbra Streisand Feels Your Pain
(According to Her Publicist) 138
   I Like Black People Too, Julia! 138
   Dumb Hires Dumber 141
   Checks and Balances, but Mostly Checks 144

The Robert C. Byrd Bridge to Poverty 147

Chair-Warmer on the Hot Seat 150

6

When Bad Ideas (Liberalism) Happen
to Good People (You) 153

The New York Times's *Crusade Against Capitalism* . . 153

It's Just About Money 156

This Just In: Price Controls Cause Shortages 158

The Democrats' Laboratory: The Host Organism Dies . . 161

Nine Out of Ten Caribou Support Drilling 163

*All the News We Heard from a Guy at Handgun
Control, Inc.* 166

7

More Liberal Ideas! Sex, Segregation, Gay
Marriage, and Banning the G-Word (God!) . . . 170

Chicks with D**** 170

Democrats: A Lott of Trouble 173

Ashcroft and the Blowhard Discuss Desegregation 176

*Bizarre Political Sect Ousted from Judicial
Nomination Process* 179

Liberals Shocked—Rush Not Jesus Christ 184

It's the Winter Solstice, Charlie Brown! 187

Massachusetts Supreme Court Abolishes Capitalism! . . 190

The Passion of the Liberal 194

W.W.J.K.?: Who Would Jesus Kill? 196

Let's Rewrite One for the Gipper! 199

8

The Battle Flag 203

9

Give Us Twenty-two Minutes,
We'll Give Up the Country 212

Great Gray Lady in Spat with Saloon Hussy 219
How a White Male from Alabama Learned the Craft
   of Journalism from a Young Reporter Named
   Jayson Blair 221
The Weather's Great, Wish I Were Here 224
Here's a Traitor! 226
CBS Could Show Augusta How to Really
   Discriminate 230
Give Us Twenty-two Minutes, We'll Give Up
   the Country 233
Journalism: Where Even the Men Are Women 235
I Guess You're Right: There Is No Liberal Media Bias . . 239

10

Say, Does Anyone Know If Max Cleland
Lost His Limbs in Combat? 246

Cleland Drops a Political Grenade 246
My Readers Respond! 249
File Under: "Omission Accomplished" 251
My Readers Respond! (Part II) 254

11

The Only Cop the *New York Times*
Likes Is the One in the Village People 262

They Weren't Overzealous This Time 262
Murdering the Bell Curve 265
The New York Times *Goes Wilding on the*
   Central Park Jogger 268

DNA Evidence Exonerates Hitler! 271

*Media Support Citizenship Awards for
    Central Park Rapists* 275

12

What the Clintons' Ghostwriters
Should Have Written 280

At Least with Monica He Only Bit His Own Lip . . . 280

Hillary: Pro-Dung 283

We're Number Two! 289

These Charges Are False—Reel No. 857 291

Liberals Shocked: Impeached Felon Took Ottoman 295

Tell Him There's a Stopover in Bangkok 301

True Grit 303

Moby's Dick 306

13

Elián González: The Only Immigrant
Liberals Ever Wanted to Deport 310

14

The Democrats' New Symbol: Two Sets
of Standards 329

Elections in Clintonville 339

*New Equal Protection Clause: One Man,
    Several Votes* 343

The Liar Next Time 345

*This Is What the Electoral College Is Supposed
    to Prevent* 348

The Law, Not the Court, Has the Last Word 351

Certify the Electors, Then the Judges 355

Things Only a Democrat Will Say with a Straight Face . . 358
National Lampoon's *Florida Supreme Court Vacation* . 361
My Court Is Bigger Than Your Court 364

15

Hello, Room Service? Send Up a Bottle, a Blonde, and a Gun 368

Ruger Is a Girl's Best Friend 368
I'd Burn My Neighbor's House Down 372
Drug Shills 375
Capitol Punishment 379
A Republican Tribute to John 383

16

What You Could Have Read If You Lived in a Free Country 387

Call Me Ms. 392
*This Congressman Bought for You by the
New York Times* 400
Sally Does Monticello 408
If You Sup with the Devil, Use a Long Spoon 413

Afterword for the Paperback Edition

Gigolos, Document Forgers, Food Throwers, Sodomy Worshipers, and Other Distinguished Liberals 419

It's Only Funny Until Someone Loses a Pie 420
Put the Speakers in a Cage 424
Brothers Band Together Against Kerry 429
Dan Rather: Fairly Unbalanced 432
2004: Highlights and Lowlifes 435

Liar, Liar, Now You're Fired 439

Ever Have One of Those Millennia? 444

Where's That Religious Fanatic We Elected? 447

Starved for Justice 450

Drag Liberals into the Light 453

Seven "Extraordinary" Idiots 456

Come Back, Liberals! 459

ACKNOWLEDGMENTS 463

INDEX 465

HOW to TALK
to a LIBERAL
(If You Must)

1

How to Talk to
a Liberal

———————◼———————

Historically, the best way to convert liberals is to have them move out of their parents' home, get a job, and start paying taxes. But if this doesn't work, you might have to actually argue with a liberal. This is not for the faint of heart. It is important to remember that when arguing with liberals, you are always within inches of the "Arab street." Liberals traffic in shouting and demagogy. In a public setting, they will work themselves into a dervish-like trance and start incanting inanities: "BUSH LIED, KIDS DIED!" "RACIST!" "FASCIST!" "FIRE RUMSFELD!" "HALLIBURTON!" Fortunately, the street performers usually punch themselves out eventually and are taken back to their parents' house.

Also resembling the Arab street, liberals are chock-full of conspiracy theories. They invoke weird personal obsessions like a conversational deus ex machina to trump all facts. You think you're talking about the war in Iraq and suddenly you start getting a disquisition on Nixon, oil, the neoconservatives, Vietnam (Tom Hayden discusses gang violence in Los Angeles as it relates to Vietnam), or whether Bill O'Reilly's former show, *Inside Edition*, won the Peabody or the Peanuckle Award. This is because liberals,

as opposed to sentient creatures, have a finite number of memo-
rized talking points, which they periodically try to shoehorn into
unrelated events, such as when Nancy Pelosi opposed the first
Gulf war in 1991 on the grounds that it would cause environmental damage in Kuwait. Oddly enough, about half of liberal conspiracy theories involve the Jews. So be prepared for that.

A major impediment to arguing with liberals is: They refuse to
argue. Liberals' idea of a battle of wits is to say "Bush lied!" in front
of adoring college audiences and be wildly applauded for their
courage. They're like hack road comics who coax a cheap round of
applause out of audiences by declaring, "I just quit smoking!" or
"My wife just had a baby!" Without a Roman Coliseum–style audience to give them standing ovations for every idiotic utterance,
you get the liberal disappearing act.

At a loss whenever anyone argues back, liberals have a number
of stratagems to prevent conservatives from talking. They shout
conservatives down; unplug reporters' microphones; edit conservatives' answers in pretaped TV shows (*Hardball*) to make the conservative look like a monkey; burn student newspapers; and heckle
conservative speakers. When John Stossel went to Brown University for a report on "date rape," he was mobbed by angry protesters
chanting, "Rape is not TV hype!"—and then his microphone cord
was unplugged by an angry student. College dropout Michael
Moore put a microphone in Republican Congressman Mark Kennedy's face and asked for his help in getting more members of
Congress to send their own family members to fight the war on
terror. Kennedy replied that he would love to and that he already
had two nephews in the military, one on his way to Afghanistan.
Moore's documentary shows Kennedy's image—but cuts his answer from the film.

There is probably no conservative student newspaper in the
country that has not been trashed or burned by liberals. Meanwhile, there is no known instance of College Republicans burning
or trashing liberal student newspapers. To the contrary, conserva-

tives get a kick out of watching liberals try to thrash their way to a coherent argument ("BUSH LIED, KIDS DIED!"). In fact, if it weren't for conservatives with a taste for schadenfreude, literally no one would be listening to Air America—assuming it's still on the air by the time this book hits the stores.

Life was much better for liberals when there were only three TV stations airing precious little news. Back in the pre–cable news days, public political debate consisted exclusively of liberal Democrats debating radical Democrats. Now that conservatives are physically present on cable news, liberals are terrified they might have to respond to a conservative point, so liberals filibuster and interrupt, hoping to never hear it. Turn on your TV right now and you'll see a liberal—probably Julian Epstein—trying to filibuster his way out of having to respond to a conservative.

If you can somehow force a liberal into a point-counterpoint argument, his retorts will bear no relation to what you said—unless you were, in fact, talking about your looks, your age, your weight, your personal obsessions, or whether you are a fascist. In the famous liberal two-step, they leap from one idiotic point to the next, so you can never nail them. It's like arguing with someone with Attention Deficit Disorder.

Inasmuch as liberals can only win arguments when no one is allowed to argue back, they enjoy creating fictional worlds in movies and on TV where liberals finally get to win. Remember the Andy Hardy movies? Mickey Rooney and Judy Garland would be headed for disaster—until Andy shouted out, "I tell you what! Let's put on a play!" With liberals, it's "We're losing on the facts! Let's make a movie!"

In movies, liberals are invariably morally and intellectually superior. They are also good-looking, witty, compassionate, and always right—basically Bob Byrd, Jerry Nadler, Al Franken, and Hillary Clinton rolled into one adorable bunch. Only in Hollywood is Robert Redford considered a dead ringer for Bob Woodward, Emma Thompson for Hillary Clinton, Dustin Hoffman for

Carl Bernstein, and Andy Garcia for Al Franken. Typically, Republicans are played by hard-boiled B-list types whose only other roles are as cruel high school football coaches or rogue army drill instructors. Reflect on the fact that Anthony Hopkins played both Nixon and Hannibal Lecter.

The only policemen in the universe who are not aware that "cop-killer bullets" have never killed a cop are the ones on *Law & Order*. Only in liberal fantasy movies like *Coming Home* is a patriotic hawk the impotent klutz who shoots himself in the foot, and the liberal dove the sexually potent one. Only in Hollywood could a sitcom that parodies a U.S. president and is titled *There's My Bush* be about George Bush rather than Bill Clinton. (The show was unceremoniously and quietly canceled because of low ratings.) In movies, we always learn that there is NO REASON, EVER, to fight a war. Unless the Earth is invaded by aliens from outer space with huge scary spaceships and death rays and men of all races and nationalities can unite against a common enemy—like in *Independence Day*. So if the Earth is ever invaded by hostile aliens from outer space, you won't have to ask liberals twice to take up arms in defense of Planet Earth.

It was inevitable, given what liberals value, that on the popular sitcom *Friends* beautiful actresses would be depicted hyperventilating over George Stephanopoulos's fictional manhood when he drops his fictional towel. Only in the bizarro world of Hollywood can such a harmless little chap as George exude massive sexual potency. On HGTV, the female host of *What Not to Wear* leeringly jokes about seeing Bill Clinton in a Speedo. In real life, Monica Lewinsky can be heard on tape describing Clinton's executive branch thus: "Think of a thumb." No wonder liberals prefer the world of make-believe.

In addition to all Oliver Stone movies and all Michael Moore documentaries (Oliver Stone Without the Talent!), an extremely abbreviated list of liberal fantasy movies includes:

The Day After Tomorrow (not to be confused with *Next Friday*, starring Ice Cube)—message: LIBERALS ARE RIGHT ABOUT GLOBAL WARMING! The hyper-silly disaster epic is based on a book coauthored by UFO/black-helicopter/the-CIA-is-beaming-microwaves-into-my-teeth-fillings guru and late-night AM radio maven Art Bell.

The Cider House Rules—message: LIBERALS ARE RIGHT ABOUT ABORTION! Kindly small-town abortionist (Michael Caine) just wants to help unwed pregnant girls. Disaster strikes when it turns out the young lad taking over Caine's practice (Tobey Maguire) is opposed to abortion because it's "wrong." The lad soon learns the error of his ways after a black teenaged girl from a family of apple pickers is raped and impregnated by her own father and needs an abortion. (You can't remind people too often that most women having abortions were raped by their own fathers.) This film was a veritable ode to moral relativism and the hideous notion that there are no rules save the ones we make up ourselves as we go along. Shockingly, it only won a single Oscar.

The American President—message: DEMOCRATS WILL VOTE THEIR CONSCIENCES EVEN IF IT HURTS THEM POLITICALLY AND ALL REPUBLICANS EVER DO IS CALL PEOPLE NAMES. In this movie, Michael Douglas plays Bill Clinton as Clinton would like to be—handsome, thin, courageous, liberal, and widowed. The president's top Republican adversary goes on national TV and calls the president's girlfriend a "whore." So it's a plausible story.

Dave—message: LIBERALS ARE RIGHT ABOUT FEDERAL SPENDING ON THE HOMELESS! Only the president can put an end to homelessness, and he's got to cut $500 million in pork from the discretionary budget to do so. He finds the money by poring over the entire federal budget (during an "all-nighter") with the help of his tax guy, played by Charles Grodin. (Of course, to do that, the president would need a line-item veto. Now which party, do you suppose, supports a line-item veto and which opposes it?)

Of the dozens and dozens of nonfiction books to come out about the Clinton presidency, only one was made into a movie: *The*

Hunting of the President, by fanatical Clinton apologists Joe Conason and Gene Lyons. (Message: LIBERALS WERE RIGHT ABOUT CLINTON, EVEN IF THERE ARE ONLY TWO LIBERALS LEFT DEFENDING HIM!) The intriguing plotline is this: A lot of mean people tried to bring down a great president.

Leaving aside which account most closely resembles the truth, which one of these sounds like a better movie plot:

Movie Plot A: Through the freak accident of a third-party candidacy, a lying, horndog Jimmy Swaggart type somehow ends up as president of the United States. As his Eva Perón–style wife tries to socialize all industry, the president gallivants with Hollywood starlets, has repeated affairs, accepts illegal campaign donations from foreign enemies, and uses the vast powers of the federal government to frighten and intimidate the people who get in his way. Some end up dead, some have their secret FBI files pored over by a former bar bouncer, some are audited by the IRS. He is finally brought down when he ejaculates on an intern's dress and lies about it under oath—and it turns out the intern has kept the dress!

Movie Plot B: For no reason whatsoever, a few oddball private citizens develop a deep personal antipathy for a "Third Way," moderate Democratic president.

Amazingly, Hollywood actually made a movie, *Bob Roberts,* in which the slick, cosmetic tricks of the sophisticated right-wing political machine hoodwink the American people. (So that's why liberals are losing all the arguments in real life!)

Since cable news has begun forcing liberals to confront opposing points of view in real life rather than movie scripts where the Republicans' only argument is to call the president's girlfriend a "whore," liberals have been trying to drop emotionalism as their main argument. Their new posture is mock hardheaded realism. Now they begin sentences with phrases like, "The fact of the matter is," or "Experts say"—followed by comically false assertions. Liberals flex their spindly little muscles and announce that everything that used to make them cry—gun ownership, racial profiling, missile defense, school vouchers, torturing terror suspects—simply "doesn't work." *The fact is, it doesn't work, this is according to several studies, and no, you can't see them, why would you ask?*

After nineteen nearly identical-looking Muslim men hijacked four airplanes and murdered 3,000 Americans, people weren't in much of a mood for liberal preachiness about racial profiling. So instead of crying and trying to make Americans feel guilty, liberals pretended to be hardheaded realists. Asked if there was anything wrong with ethnic profiling at airports after 9/11, Harvard Law professor Alan Dershowitz said, "Yes, it doesn't work." Other, better ideas, he said, were face-recognition technology and national ID cards. These would work great—if only we knew who the terrorists were. But if we knew who the terrorists were, the only plane they'd be boarding would be headed to Guantánamo and we wouldn't need to search anyone at all.

On CNN, Juliette Kayyem, from the John F. Kennedy School of Government at Harvard, assured viewers that "no one is disagreeing" with extra scrutiny for potential terrorists. But profiling, she said, "won't work." It wouldn't work, allegedly, because al Qaeda "exists in places from Algeria to Zimbabwe." True, but since we're in America, wouldn't it be a big help if we could screen out most of the Americans? Liberals think "it doesn't work" has such a nice ring to it that the patent absurdity of what they're saying should not detract from their argument.

After Senator Teddy Kennedy tried to block federal funding for the government's program to fingerprint and photograph people entering the country from twenty-five Muslim nations, his sleazy back-door maneuver was defended on Fox News Channel's *O'Reilly Factor* by Sarah Eltantawi of the objective, nonpartisan, well-groomed Muslim Public Affairs Council. Eltantawi said it was a "huge mischaracterization" to think she was going to complain about racial profiling. "That's not the argument I'm here to make." To the contrary, her objection—and Kennedy's objection— was that fingerprinting immigrants from terrorist-producing countries is "completely inefficient." And we all know Teddy Kennedy cannot abide inefficiency!

Elizabeth Rindskopf Parker—former legal counsel to the CIA, the National Security Agency, and the State Department—has been quoted as saying, "We don't use torture because it doesn't work." (And it only took a little arm-twisting to get her to say that.) Torturing randomly chosen people on the off chance that they might be up to something—as was routinely done in liberals' favorite country, the USSR—clearly doesn't work. Torturing the guy you know for a fact is withholding information actually works quite well. There may be good and sufficient moral reasons for not torturing people for information, but efficacy is not among them.

After decades of womanly crying about guns, liberals finally admitted their earlier hysteria had been much ado about nothing. The real problem with guns was that they don't make people any safer. Fox News Channel's Alan Colmes said to Larry Pratt of Gun Owners of America, "Let's talk about some hard and cold facts, Larry. The fact of the matter is, Larry"—there's that "the fact of the matter is" qualifier I promised you—"that the odds that a home will be the scene of a homicide are much greater if there's a gun in the home." Soccer moms across America shot straight up and said, *I did not know that!* The study behind this flagrantly dishonest "cold hard fact" assumed that anyone killed by a gun in the vicinity of a home where anyone owned a gun was killed by "a gun in the home." The specious study merely attests to the fact that people who live in high-crime neighborhoods tend to own guns. As the inestimable economist John Lott says, on that theory of causation, hospitals must cause people to die, because lots of people die after being admitted to a hospital.

It's as if liberals held focus groups on how to best present their ridiculous ideas and were told, *Passion you've got. But what respondents say you lack is intellection, thinking things through, understanding elementary human nature, and a basic awareness of what people are like.* If conservatives have not yet persuaded liberals to give up on socialism and treason, we have at least gotten them to fake linear thinking.

Liberals' other new hobby is to call people "liars." After years of defending Clinton, they love the piquant irony of calling Bush a "liar." *Bush said he was a "reformer with results"—LIAR!* For fifty years liberals have called Republicans every name in the book— idiots, fascists, anti-Semites, racists, crooks, Constitution shredders, and masterminds of Salvadoran death squads. Only recently have they added the epithet "liar." Even noted ethicist Al Franken has switched from calling conservatives "big fat idiots" to calling them "liars." This is virgin territory for Democrats—they never before viewed lying as a negative. Their last president, Bill Clinton, was called "an unusually good liar" by a senator in his own party, and their last vice president, Al Gore, couldn't say "pass the salt" without claiming to have invented salt. Having only recently discovered the intriguing new concept of "lies," the Democrats are having a jolly old time calling Bush a liar. But they can't quite grasp the concept of a lie as connoting something that is intentionally untrue—or untrue at all.

About the time Baghdad was erupting in celebrations after receiving the news that Uday and Qusay were dead, liberals were still hopping mad that in January 2003 President Bush uttered the indisputably true fact that British intelligence believed Saddam Hussein had tried to acquire uranium from Africa. That was, and still is, believed by British intelligence. It also was, and still is, the conclusion in our own National Intelligence Estimate. The CIA, however, discounts this piece of intelligence. The CIA did such a bang-up job predicting 9/11, the Democrats have decided to put all their faith in it. They believe the nation must not act until absolutely every agency and every American is convinced we are about to be nuked. (Would that they had such strict standards for worrying about nuclear power plants at home!)

Sharing a chummy laugh about Republicans on *Meet the Press*, NBC's Tim Russert asked Senator Joe Biden what the Republicans would have done if a Democratic president had uttered sixteen mistaken words about national security in a State of the Union speech. Senator Biden said, "This is going to be counterintuitive for Biden to show his Irish instinct to restrain myself. You know the answer, I know the answer, the whole world knows the answer. They would have ripped his skin off." At least Bush put it in his *own* words—if you know what I mean. (Perhaps Biden is annoyed that Bush merely cited the head of the British Labor Party rather than plagiarized him.) Back to Russert's challenge, I shall dispense with Clinton's most renowned lies. (Every Democrat commits adultery and lies about it—fine, they've convinced me.) Clinton also lied every time he said "God bless America," and I don't recall any Republican ever ripping his skin off about that.

But how about a lie in a major national speech slandering your own country? In Clinton's acceptance speech at the 1996 Democratic National Convention, he said, "We still have too many Americans who give in to their fears of those who are different from them. Not so long ago, swastikas were painted on the doors of some African-American members of our Special Forces at Fort Bragg. Folks, for those of you who don't know what they do, the Special Forces are just what the name says; they are special forces. If I walk off this stage tonight and call them on the telephone and tell them to go halfway around the world and risk their lives for you and be there by tomorrow at noon, they will do it. They do not deserve to have swastikas on their doors."

Clinton was referring to an alleged act of racism in which the prime suspect was one of the alleged victims—a black soldier known for filing repeated complaints of racism. The fact that the leading suspect in an apparently racist incident was himself black had already been widely reported in the press. The soldier, not a member of the Special Forces, by the way, was later discharged. And yet Clinton lied about the swastika episode in speech after speech—including his speech at the Democratic National Convention—publicly citing a phony hate crime in order to accuse white Special Forces members of racism. (And he used a lot more than sixteen words to do it.)

Democrats didn't mind a president telling lies in order to defame his own country. They reserve their outrage for a president who defames the name of an honorable statesman like Saddam Hussein. (Note to the Democrats: Just because you defended Bill Clinton doesn't mean you have to defend every government official credibly accused of rape.) How dare Bush suggest Saddam was seeking uranium from Africa on the flimsy evidence of: the findings of British intelligence, the findings of our own NIE, the fact that Israel blew up Saddam's last nuclear reactor in 1981, and the fact that we learned about Saddam's reconstitution of his nuke program only in 1996, when his son-in-law briefly defected to Jordan. The Mr. Magoos from the UN Weapons Inspection Team had missed this fact while scouring the country for five years after Gulf War I. Apparently it's okay to get the facts wrong, but only in the service of slandering America—the country we're supposed to believe liberals love.

Most of this book will explain how to argue with liberals by example, not exegesis. But there are some useful pointers. Here are ten simple rules to keep in mind.

First, don't surrender out of the gate. This is a highly controversial approach among Republican politicians, obviously—otherwise we wouldn't already have a bipartisan consensus for the proposition that you should send half of what you earn to the government. Liberals always want to shame Republicans into making core concessions before the debate begins. *You raise taxes and then we'll discuss cutting spending. You admit the war in Iraq was a failure and then we'll argue about how to get out of it. You give us abortion on demand, then we'll discuss parental notification.* Never has any good come out of surrendering before negotiations begin.

Second, unless you were in the Ku Klux Klan like *Vanity Fair*'s "Profiles in Courage" winner Senator Bob Byrd, or you killed a woman like Senator Ted Kennedy, or you are credibly accused of rape by Juanita Broaddrick on NBC News within weeks of being impeached like You-Know-Who—you don't need to be defensive. Come to think of it, since our side does not accept Klansmen, murderers, or rapists, this rule may be simplified to: Don't be defensive.

Third, you must outrage the enemy. If the liberal you're arguing with doesn't become speechless with sputtering, impotent rage, you're not doing it right. People don't get angry when lies are told about them; they get angry when the truth is told about them. If you are not being called outrageous by liberals, you're not being outrageous enough. Start with the maximum assertion about liberals and then push the envelope, because, as we know, their evil is incalculable. They stand for the godless rule of dictators. They apologize for abortion, adultery, and everything bestial in society. They support al Qaeda and the Taliban as they once supported Stalin and Mao. They put Stalin apologist Paul Robeson on a stamp. Robeson is David Duke in blackface: This Stalin Peace Prize winner turned his back on Jewish refuseniks in the Soviet Union; after Joseph Stalin's death, he wrote a tribute to the dictator titled "To You Beloved Comrade." Most unforgivable of all, liberals have extended the public career of Martin Sheen by at least a full decade. The latest fashions dictated from European capitals ensure that Hating America is haute couture. Gwynnie Paltrow and Madonna—with their European homes, European husbands, and European accents—are demonstrating the same unblinking devotion to America's enemies that we have seen in the past. (Interestingly, the fake British accent Madonna uses in real life is better than the one Paltrow uses in her movies.) This crowd is always in search of approval from people who want to harm America. Nothing too extreme can be said about liberals, because it's all true. (That's why I almost called this book "You Don't Know the Half of It.")

Fourth, never apologize, at least not for what liberals want you to apologize for. These are the people who think Linda Tripp should apologize to the nation, but Bill Clinton was a hapless victim. After Dick "I Broke the News About al Qaeda to Condi" Clarke had the audacity to apologize to the McWidows on behalf of the U.S. government, liberals started demanding President Bush apologize for 9/11, too. Suddenly public apologies had become trendy; the thing to do, like getting drunk and having unprotected public sex with Colin Farrell. Instead of fighting the war on terrorism, liberals would prefer a Cabinet-level Department of Closure to handle issues like "presidential apologies," with headquarters in a building shaped like a giant hug and Dr. Phil as Secretary of Closure.

Fifth, never compliment a Democrat. Unfortunately, when dealing with liberals, you have to set aside everything your mother told you about giving compliments. Mother is wise about many things, and when you go over to Mrs. Jaworski's house, you should still compliment her on her rosebushes. But that doesn't mean you should ever say anything nice about a Democrat. For one thing, it's such a colossal waste of time racking your brain trying to think up nice things to say to a liberal. "Gee, your head doesn't seem quite as large and misshapen as usual today, Senator Kennedy!" But, more important, compliments to Democrats are always returned with insults.

On any television political roundtable you will see Republican politicians droning on about what a fine human being some heinous Democrat is and what a pleasure it was to work with him, only to have the heinous Democrat turn around and accuse the Republicans of near-complicity in genocide.

Consider the first statements out of the mouths of three senators on *Larry King Live* on May 7, 2004:

Senator John Warner (Republican of Virginia): "First, if I may say of my colleagues on the committee, and twenty-four senators out of the twenty-five were present at that hearing, I think we comported ourselves individually and collectively as best I've ever seen it in the Senate. . . ."

Senator Jon Kyl (Republican of Arizona): "I agree with Senator Warner that the senators comported themselves well for the most part. . . ."

Senator Tom Harkin (Democrat of Iowa): "Well, [Rumsfeld should resign] for a couple of reasons."

A few days later, Republican senator Lindsey Graham used about half his allotted time on *Meet the Press* to make clear he had absolutely no criticisms of the Democrats:

"I didn't come here to beat on Senator Kerry or to defend any political position. This is not about Republican and Democratic politics. . . . [Let's] show the world that Republicans and Democrats may disagree on the policy and the war in Iraq, but we have the ability to make sure those accountable are going to be held accountable. . . . Republicans and Democrats need to come together to prove to the world that our system works."

The Democrats on the panel returned the love by accusing President Bush of responsibility for the Abu Ghraib prison abuse (Senator Carl Levin [Democrat of Michigan]: "I think he helped to create the atmosphere") and saying the mission in Iraq would probably fail (General Wesley Clark: "I think there's a greater than 50/50 chance, let's say a 2:1 chance, of a catastrophic early end to this mission").

Sixth, never show graciousness toward a Democrat. (Rules Nos. 5, 6, and 7 may seem similar, but I want to be sure I've covered all the bases.) Not only will any kindness not be returned, but it will be used against you. President Bush has repeatedly learned the hard way what happens when you are nice to Democrats. After it leaked that the dignified staff of the dignified former president had trashed the White House on its way out, Bush downplayed the property damage, saying, "There might have been a prank or two. Maybe somebody put a cartoon on the wall, but that's okay." If you happened to know anyone moving into the Bush White House who had seen the damage firsthand, you knew it was a lot more than a "prank or two." But instead of stopping while they were ahead, pocketing Bush's graciousness and moving on, the Democrats aggressively attacked other Republicans for having falsely impugned the honor of the Clinton White House staff—citing Bush's magnanimity as proof that Republicans had lied about the damage. *USA Today* ran a snippy article titled "Ex-Clinton Staffers on Vandalism: Got Proof?" Former Clinton press secretary Jake Siewert insinuatingly asked why there were no records of the alleged damage—creating the uniquely ironic scenario of a Clinton spokesman demanding proof of a statement's veracity. *Washington Post* columnist William Raspberry noted that the damage was never catalogued and asked, "Can it be because the alleged vandalism never happened either?" And then a year later, the full GAO report came back: The Party of the People had done $15,000 worth of property damage to the People's House. And that didn't even include the cost of cleaning and sterilizing the rugs from Clinton's office.

Seventh, never flatter a Democrat. When Bush was first elected, he invited Senator Teddy Kennedy to the White House for movie night—to watch the hagiographic Kennedy snoozefest *Thirteen Days.* He named a federal building after one of Kennedy's brothers and gushingly praised the other. He brought Kennedy over to discuss education several times. Hell, he did everything but split a bottle of Chivas Regal with the guy—which, come to think of it, might have actually won Kennedy over. Asked about Bush's overtures, the Fredo of the Kennedy family said, "It takes more than good intentions to make a difference." When specifically asked whether he thought Bush was smart—a meaningless concept in the case of college admissions, but a hard fact in the case of Republican presidents—Kennedy pointedly said he found Bush only "engaging and personable." Yes, there's that trademark Kennedy wit and boyish charm.

After Bush named the Department of Justice building after Robert Kennedy, Kerry Kennedy Cuomo displayed the celebrated Kennedy graciousness by viciously attacking the Bush administration at the prededication ceremony. Speaking from the podium to her daughter in the audience, Kennedy Cuomo said, "Kara, if anyone tries to tell you this is the type of justice system your grandpa embraced, you just don't believe it." (Oddly enough, she didn't add, "Actually, Kara, Grandpa's justice was more like the justice system your great uncle Teddy turned to after he drowned that girl.") This is as we have come to expect from a family of heroin addicts, statutory rapists, convicted and unconvicted female-killers, cheaters, bootleggers, and dissolute drunks known as "Camelot." Extend an olive branch to Democrats and they'll smack the living daylights out of you with it—while hugging the tree itself, naturally.

Eighth, do not succumb to liberal bribery. Faustian bargains are still not a good deal. Liberals are a seductive group of minxes. They recruit conservatives the way colleges recruit star athletes, deploying celebrity starlets as comfort women. Become a liberal and you will be lavished with great wealth and adulation. Nationally renowned liberal female journalists have been known to offer oral sex to elected officials just for keeping abortion on demand legal. Liberals have scores of money-laundering schemes to pay off anyone who attacks a conservative—foundation jobs, radio stations, websites, movie "options," university professorships, and jobs writing for the *New York Times*. Lots of goodies are available to any conservative willing to give up all his principles. Imagine Satan's temptation of Daniel Webster if the old beastmaster had been able to dangle "a development deal with Tristar," "one of those phony Harvard Ph.D.s," or even "a power lunch with Harvey Weinstein" in front of Mr. Webster. Go with liberals and they will give you a lifetime of wine, women, and song.

The more public and respected a conservative you are, the more goodies will be offered to you, starting with the cover of the *New York Times Magazine.* Even a halfwit can get a pretty good life out of liberal enticements, rather like a bureaucrat in the old Soviet Union. If a conservative giant like Rush Limbaugh or Sean Hannity ever became liberal, there would be parades down Fifth

Avenue. At the freshman-liberal induction ceremony, Bill Moyers would MC, Bono would sing an original song, Maya Angelou would recite a poem, and Sean Penn would throw out the first punch.

Apparently it's difficult for some people to resist that kind of bribery. Weak and frightened conservatives crave liberal approval and will do anything to get it. The telltale sign is how quickly a conservative will publicly attack another conservative. These masters of the featherweight insight especially enjoy deploring evangelical Christians. (To do it right, every time you denounce a devout Christian or Jew for being a superstitious, intolerant ignoramus, you must praise radical Islam as "a religion of peace.")

It should have set off warning bells when David Brock, professional reformed conservative, was committed to the psychiatric ward of Sibley Memorial Hospital in Washington, D.C. It's never a good sign when you have to wipe the spittle from your champion's mouth before he goes on TV—as Ed Asner's handlers are discovering even as we speak. But Brock was a former conservative attacking conservatives, so before long, liberals were dragging him out of "The Quiet Room" at Sibley so they could give him $2 million to start a liberal website. You cannot starve in America as a liberal. For $2 million, liberals now have a website exposing the shocking fact that conservative opinion columnists have opinions that are . . . *conservative!* I could have told them that for, say, a hundred grand.

Ninth, prepare for your deepest, darkest secrets to become liberal talking points. Liberals' idea of a good retort to a conservative argument is to investigate your personal life and find out if you're into S&M. So if you have anything to hide—say, if you were married to a gay guy, but he was really, really rich and you knew you could talk him into running for the Senate—you'd best become a liberal. All will be forgiven. In fact, "something to hide" is often considered a résumé enhancer if you're a Democrat—just ask Bill Clinton, Barney Frank, Marion Barry . . .

But if you're a conservative, prepare to have your every foible unveiled as if you were caught raping kittens. Even if you've led a blameless life, liberals invent absurd stories about you. They will say you're afraid of Cheshire cats and ordered nude statues at the Department of Justice covered with drapery. You'll be sneered at for your former line of work, such as Tom DeLay, who is derisively called "the exterminator" because he used to run a massive pesticide company. (This is apparently not nearly as classy as having been an ambulance-chasing lawyer.) You will simultaneously be described as ugly—and accused of being on TV only because you're pretty. You will be called an anti-Semite—and a shill for the Jews. You will be called a homophobe—and a fag hag. (As with their political positions, logical consistency is not liberals' métier.) If it gets really ugly they may even call you a "neoconservative," by which liberals mean "dirty Jew." Not only will you not be lavished with jobs, money, and celebrity starlets—you will be unemployable, unpublished, and embarrassed. For good measure, magazines will never, ever run an attractive picture of you. Finally, after liberals have done everything they can to destroy your career, you will be accused of being a conservative only for career advancement.

On the bright side, you know you've arrived when liberals start calling you a fag. Curiously, these proponents of tolerance always choose "gay" as their most searing epithet. Joe McCarthy, J. Edgar Hoover, Matt Drudge, Starr's prosecutors, Linda Tripp's lawyer, Christopher Hitchens, Mel Gibson—all these have been denounced as homosexuals at some point by liberals. The *New York Times*'s Frank Rich (now there's someone who would never be called a homo) outed David Brock when he was still on the right. Rich favorably cited Christopher Hitchens—who himself was called a fag by liberals when he crossed them—for calling Gibson's movie *The Passion of the Christ* an exercise in "sadomasochistic male narcissism." Arguing with liberals instantly becomes a game of gay-baiting musical chairs. We just don't think they should get married. Liberals actually hate homosexuals.

Tenth, always be open to liberals in transition. Go all out—be at least as hospitable to them as Saddam was to al Zarqawi. As with al Qaeda, if you can create second thoughts in just a couple of them, it will be a lot less trouble for the rest of us down the road. Liberals in transition will tend to approach you in hushed tones, repeatedly looking over their shoulders, and explaining they have a family to feed. You might not want these guys watching your back in a bar fight, but at least they are trying to be good. People "coming out" as conservatives for the first time face being ostracized by friends, neighbors, coworkers, even family members. Refer them to a local support network such as "Parents and Friends of Conservatives and Their Partners." Nurture them—and make sure they aren't killed before they can move to the other side. That's when it's most dangerous.

When Christopher Hitchens decided not to lie to a congressional aide to protect his friend, Clinton consigliere Sidney Blumenthal, Hitchens was quickly denounced by his former friends as a drunk and a sexual pervert. (Imagine the indignity of having a Clinton defender call you a sexual pervert!) According to sworn statements from Hitchens and Hitchens's wife, early in the Monica Lewinsky scandal—before Monica produced the dress—Blumenthal told them that Clinton said Monica Lewinsky was a "stalker." But later, when asked by congressional investigators whether he had told anyone that Clinton called Lewinsky a stalker, Blumenthal had said, "I didn't mention it to my friends. . . . I certainly never mentioned it to a reporter." Hitchens told the investigators otherwise.

For the treachery of declining to perjure himself, Hitchens's erstwhile close friend Alexander Cockburn wrote that Hitchens "gets a frisson we'd guess to be quasi-sexual in psychological orientation out of the act of tattling or betrayal. . . . The booze has finally got to him. . . . His behavior exhibits all the symptoms of chronic alcoholism." He said Hitchens's statement was probably uttered "while [a] pint of alcohol and gallons of wine . . . [were]

coursing through his bloodstream." Oddest of all, Cockburn called Hitchens "a terrific fibber." All this for the "despicable" act of telling the truth. (Yes, Cockburn and Blumenthal are two of those liberal "friends" I warned you about earlier.)

To end on an optimistic note, remember there is some good in everyone. Hitler didn't smoke, for example. British traitor and spy Kim Philby had a pet fox. Even among the staunchest members of the Communist Party, there turned out to be a few good ones. Similarly, the vast majority of liberals are not intentionally sabotaging the nation. In fact, I don't think as many as 20 percent give a damn about the nation. That 20 percent, of course, deeply hates America. But the majority of liberals are just trying to sell books, get a TV show, be called "brave" in the *New York Times,* sound hip, or get a woman's phone number at an afternoon reception at the Westchester Kabbalah center. Intentions, of course, do not mitigate disastrous outcomes. If your doctor removes the wrong kidney because he was jet-lagged from a Doctors Without Borders flight with actor Noah Wyle, it makes precious little difference to you. This is why my philosophy on arguing with liberals is: Tough love, except I don't love them. In most cases I don't even like them. In other words, my "tough love" approach is much like the Democrats' "middle-class tax cuts"—everything but the last word.

I decided to write this book because I have liberals to thank for my career and I wanted something substantial to throw in their faces—oops, I mean I wanted to give something back. The majority of this book will be new to even my most devoted readers (who are able to locate the rare brave newspapers that carry my column). I've included columns too hot to be published until now—along with the editors' rejections. These columns, as well as any columns that caused more than the usual ruckus (like my 9/11 "kill their leaders" column), I preserved in their original form—so you can see what the fuss was about. Some columns I added a little to and some I added so much to that they grew from short columns to entire chapters (e.g., the Elián González and Confederate flag chapters). Even the unretouched columns are *my* unretouched columns, as they live on my computer—which was not always the same as the published version. I've occasionally run into editors with heavy hands, and I didn't necessarily care for their edits. These are bootlegs, never-released columns, NC-17 versions, lost classics, remixes, extended-play versions, and the director's cut.

There are many advantages to plumbing my old columns for a Coulterpalooza. For one thing, I am one of the most unpublished writers in America—except for my books, which sell pretty well. But unless you are on the Internet or a subscriber to *Human Events*—which everyone should read—all but a few intrepid newspaper editors have withheld these columns from you. Also, I have an ad hoc group of fanatical researchers doing fact-checking for me immediately after my columns go up on the Internet. If I get someone's middle initial wrong, it will be widely publicized on hundreds of reasonable, calm, objective, nonpartisan websites with names like www.I-hate-anncoulter.with.a.hot.hot.hate.com. (This is in addition to my fabulous official editor, Greg Melvin at Universal Press Syndicate, who does not consider it a "lie" to opine that taxes are too high.) Also, when you write for a small-circulation newspaper like *Human Events*, your columns are apparently considered community property by other journalists, who shamelessly poach your work without the briefest little credit. (At least I know who's been reading my stuff!) Now you can read the originals. Finally, I like my columns. Unlike liberals, who would rather have their old columns defending Ho Chi Minh just go away, I would prefer that my columns be more widely read. This includes columns from over a decade ago and columns deemed unpublishable—in fact *especially* the columns deemed unpublishable.

2

This Is War

◆

Want to make liberals angry? Defend the United States. Below are my columns on the war on terrorism. It's interesting to review how the carping from the Treason Lobby has evolved during the course of the war. My position hasn't changed since the column I wrote the night of 9/11. For reasons I cannot understand, I am often asked if I still think we should invade their countries, kill their leaders, and convert them to Christianity. The answer is: Now more than ever!

☞ How 9/11 Happened

We don't need a "commission" to find out how 9/11 happened. The truth is in the time line:

President Carter, Democrat

In 1979, President Jimmy Carter allowed the Shah of Iran to be deposed by a mob of Islamic fanatics. A few months later, Muslims stormed the U.S. Embassy in Iran and took American Embassy staff hostage.

Carter retaliated by canceling Iranian visas. He eventually ordered a disastrous and humiliating rescue attempt, crashing helicopters in the desert.

President Reagan, Republican

The day of Reagan's inauguration, the hostages were released.

In 1982, the U.S. Embassy in Beirut was bombed by Muslim extremists.

President Reagan sent U.S. Marines to Beirut.

In 1983, the U.S. Marine barracks in Beirut were blown up by Muslim extremists.

Reagan said the United States would not surrender, but Democrats in Congress threw a hissy fit, drafting a resolution demanding that our troops be withdrawn. All seven Democratic presidential candidates called for our troops to be withdrawn. Reagan caved in to Democrat caterwauling in an election year and withdrew our troops—bombing Syrian-controlled areas on the way out. Democrats complained about that, too.

In 1985, an Italian cruise ship, the *Achille Lauro*, was seized and a sixty-nine-year-old American was shot and thrown overboard by Muslim extremists.

Reagan ordered a heart-stopping mission to capture the hijackers after the "allies" promise them safe passage. The daring plan to intercept the hijackers' flight was conceived by Oliver North—later crucified by Democrats over Iran-Contra—and executed by Admiral Frank Kelso, later savaged by Representative Patricia Schroeder for saying hello to his boys at Tailhook. Kelso's boys captured the hijackers and turned them over to the Italians, who then released them to safe harbor in Iraq.

On April 5, 1986, a West Berlin discotheque frequented by U.S. servicemen was bombed by Muslim extremists from the Libyan Embassy in East Berlin, killing an American.

Ten days later, Reagan bombed Libya, despite our dear ally France refusing the use of their airspace. Americans bombed Qaddafi's residence, killing his daughter, and dropped a bomb on the French Embassy "by mistake."

Reagan also stoked a long, bloody war between heinous regimes in Iran and Iraq. All this was while winning a final victory over Soviet totalitarianism.

President Bush I, Moderate Republican

In December 1988, a passenger jet, Pan Am Flight 103, was bombed over Lockerbie, Scotland, by Muslim extremists.

President-elect George Bush claimed he would continue Reagan's policy of retaliating against terrorism, but did not. Without Reagan to gin her up, even Prime Minister Margaret Thatcher went wobbly, saying there would be no revenge for the bombing.

In 1990, Saddam Hussein invaded Kuwait.

In early 1991, Bush went to war with Iraq the way liberals like—with approval from the UN and "the allies." Still, a majority of Democrats opposed the war. Democrats demanded that our troops stop at Baghdad, but then after 9/11, absurdly complained that Bush didn't "finish off the job" with Saddam.

President Bill Clinton, Democrat

In February 1993, the World Trade Center was bombed by Muslim fanatics, killing five people and injuring hundreds.

Clinton did nothing.

In October 1993, eighteen American troops were killed in a savage firefight in Somalia. The corpse of one American was dragged through the streets of Mogadishu as the Somalian hordes cheered.

Clinton responded by ordering our troops home. Osama bin Laden later told ABC News, "The youth . . . realized more than before that the American soldier was a paper tiger and after a few blows ran in defeat."

In November 1995, five Americans were killed and thirty wounded by a car bomb in Saudi Arabia set by Muslim extremists.

Clinton did nothing.

In June 1996, a U.S. Air Force housing complex in Saudi Arabia was bombed by Muslim extremists.

Clinton did nothing.

Months later, Saddam attacked the Kurdish-controlled city of Erbil.

Clinton lobbed some bombs into Iraq, hundreds of miles from Saddam's forces.

In November 1997, Iraq refused to allow UN weapons inspectors to do their jobs and threatened to shoot down a U.S. U-2 spy plane.

Clinton did nothing.

In February 1998, Clinton threatened to bomb Iraq, but called it off when the United Nations said no.

On August 7, 1998, U.S. embassies in Kenya and Tanzania were bombed by Muslim extremists.

Clinton did nothing.

On August 20, Monica Lewinsky appeared for the second time to testify before the grand jury.

Clinton responded by bombing Afghanistan and Sudan, severely damaging a camel and an aspirin factory.

On December 16, the House of Representatives prepared to impeach Clinton the next day.

Clinton retaliated by ordering major air strikes against Iraq, described by the *New York Times* as "by far the largest military action in Iraq since the end of the Gulf War in 1991."

The only time Clinton decided to go to war with anyone in the vicinity of Muslim fanatics was in 1999—when Clinton attacked Serbians who were fighting Muslim fanatics.

In October 2000, our warship the USS *Cole* was attacked by Muslim extremists.

Clinton did nothing.

President George Bush, Republican

Bush came into office telling his national security adviser, Condoleezza Rice, he was "tired of swatting flies"—he wanted to eliminate al Qaeda.

On September 11, 2001, after Bush had been in office for seven months, three thousand Americans were murdered in a savage terrorist attack on U.S. soil by Muslim extremists.

Since then, Bush has won wars in Afghanistan and Iraq, captured Saddam Hussein, probably killed and certainly immobilized Osama bin Laden, destroyed al Qaeda's base, and begun to create the only functioning democracy in the Middle East other than Israel. Democrats opposed it all—except their phony support for war with Afghanistan, which they immediately complained about and said would be a Vietnam quagmire. Now they claim to be outraged that in the months before 9/11, Bush did not do everything Democrats opposed doing after 9/11.

What a surprise. ■

☞ This Is War

SEPTEMBER 12, 2001

Barbara Olson kept her cool. In the hysteria and terror of hijackers herding passengers to the rear of the plane, she retrieved her cell phone and called her husband, Ted, the solicitor general of the United States. She informed him that he had better call the FBI— the plane had been hijacked. According to reports, Barbara was still on the phone with Ted when her plane plunged in a fiery explosion directly into the Pentagon.

Barbara risked having her neck slit to warn the country of a terrorist attack. She was a patriot to the very end. This is not to engage in the media's typical hallucinatory overstatement about anyone who is the victim of a horrible tragedy. The furtive cell phone call was an act of incredible daring and panache. If it were not, we'd be hearing reports of hundreds more cell phone calls. (Even people who swear to hate cell phones carry them for commercial air travel.)

The last time I saw Barbara in person was about three weeks ago. She generously praised one of my recent columns and told me I had really found my niche. Ted, she said, had taken to reading my columns aloud to her over breakfast. I mention that to say three things about Barbara. First, she was really nice. A lot of people on TV seem nice but aren't. (And some who don't seem nice are.) But Barbara was always her charming, graceful, ebullient self. "Nice" is an amazingly rare quality among writers. In the opinion business, bitter, jealous hatred is the norm. Barbara had reason to be secure.

Second, it was actually easy to imagine Ted reading political columns aloud to Barbara at the breakfast table. Theirs was a relationship that could only be cheaply imitated by Bill and Hillary—the latter being a subject of Barbara's appropriately biting best-seller *Hell to Pay*. Hillary claimed preposterously in a *Talk* magazine interview that she discussed policy with Bill while cutting his grapefruit in the morning. But when asked about Monica Lewinsky, Hillary kept insisting she was waiting for the facts to come out. Couldn't she have asked her husband about the facts while cutting his grapefruit? Ted and Barbara really did talk politics—and really did have breakfast together. It's "Ted and Barbara" just like it's Fred and Ginger, and George and Gracie. They were so perfect together, so obvious, that their friends were as happy as they were on their wedding day. This is more than the death of a great person and patriotic American. It's a human amputation.

Third, since Barbara's compliment, I'd been writing my columns for Ted and Barbara. I'm always writing to someone in my head. Now I don't know who to write to. Ted and Barbara were a good muse.

Apart from hearing that this beautiful light has been extinguished from the world, only one other news flash broke beyond the numbingly omnipresent horror of the entire day. That evening, CNN reported that bombs were dropping in Afghanistan—and then updated the report to say they weren't our bombs. They should have been ours. I wanted them to be ours.

This is no time to be precious about locating the exact individuals directly involved in this particular terrorist attack. Those responsible include anyone anywhere in the world who smiled in response to the annihilation of patriots like Barbara Olson. We don't need long investigations of the forensic evidence to determine with scientific accuracy the person or persons who ordered this specific attack. We don't need an "international coalition." We don't need a study on "terrorism." We certainly didn't need a congressional resolution condemning the attack this week.

The nation has been invaded by a fanatical, murderous cult. And we welcome them. We are so good and so pure we would never engage in discriminatory racial or "religious" profiling. People who want our country destroyed live here, work for our airlines, and are submitted to the exact same airport shakedown as a lumberman from Idaho. This would be like having the Wehrmacht immigrate to America and work for our airlines during World War II. Except the Wehrmacht was not so bloodthirsty.

"All of our lives" don't need to change, as they keep prattling on TV. Every single time there is a terrorist attack—or a plane crashes because of pilot error—Americans allow their rights to be contracted for no purpose whatsoever. The airport kabuki theater of magnetometers, asinine questions about whether passengers "packed their own bags," and the hostile, lumpen mesomorphs ripping open our luggage somehow allowed over a dozen armed hijackers to board four American planes almost simultaneously on Bloody Tuesday. (Did those fabulous security procedures stop a single hijacker anywhere in America that day?)

Airports scrupulously apply the same laughably ineffective airport harassment to Suzy Chapstick as to Muslim hijackers. It is preposterous to assume every passenger is a potential crazed homicidal maniac. We know who the homicidal maniacs are. They are the ones cheering and dancing right now. We should invade their countries, kill their leaders, and convert them to Christianity. We weren't punctilious about locating and punishing only Hitler and his top officers. We carpet-bombed German cities; we killed civilians. That's war. And this is war. ■

☞ The Hun Is at the Gate

NOVEMBER 29, 2001

This week's winner for best comedy line about the war is New York Democratic senator Charles Schumer. Referring to—well, it doesn't really matter what he was referring to, but it was military tribunals—Schumer said, "To come up with the best way to do this, Congress ought to be involved." Congress came up with the Internal Revenue code, right? And the Department of Education? Midnight basketball? The now-bankrupt Social Security "trust fund"? The entire welfare state? Yes, that's just what we need: Congress involved in emergency national security measures!

Democrats are channeling their frustration with America's imminent military victory in Afghanistan into hysterical opposition to reasonable national security measures at home. (Incidentally, the war in Afghanistan ought to prove once and for all what a bunch of paper tigers the Russians were. What were they doing over there for ten years? It hasn't taken us ten weeks.)

Under the strange delusion that their input is necessary during wartime, various congressmen are trying to haul Attorney General Ashcroft before them to answer questions about the detentions of suspected terrorists. Fortunately, Congress has no role in prosecuting this war either abroad or domestically. They are relieved of duty, free to "get back to normal," as the president has recommended—which in their case means enacting massive spending bills to fund comically useless government programs. That should make them happy.

Senator Patrick Leahy (Democrat of Vermont), chairman of the Senate Judiciary Committee, has blustered that there "has been no formal declaration of war and, in the meantime, our civilian courts remain open and available to try suspected terrorists." He said it was questionable "whether the president can lawfully authorize the use of military commissions to try persons arrested here." Though I am sublimely confident that the public will recognize Leahy for the sputtering fool that he is, I note that: We are at war. We have been at war since 8:48 A.M. Tuesday, September 11, 2001. After a massive attack on our nation, we do not need to wait for some precise talismanic formulation by Congress to inform us of the fact that we are at war.

Wars can exist even if Congress does not declare them—if, for example, thousands of American civilians are slaughtered in a surprise attack on U.S soil. On the off chance anyone didn't know that we were at war when we were attacked, Bush said so in his address to a joint session of Congress the week after the attack: "On September the 11th, enemies of freedom committed an act of war against our country." A formal declaration of war has certain consequences only under international law, which is not relevant to domestic security measures taken under the president's war powers.

And that's making the rather large assumption that it is ever relevant at all. International law is like Santa Claus. The only difference is that Santa Claus exists only in the imaginations of small children, whereas international law exists in the imaginations of law school professors. In the real world, international law is whatever the United States and Great Britain say it is.

Because we are at war, Bush, the commander in chief, had authority on September 11 to give orders to shoot down a civilian plane and he had authority to bomb Afghanistan. He didn't need congressional approval for those actions any more than he needs congressional approval right now to try suspected belligerents on U.S. soil in military tribunals. If Congress doesn't like it, the Constitution gives it two choices: It can cut off funding or it can impeach the president. Knock yourselves out, fellas. (Has anyone else noticed there have been no polls taken on the issue of military tribunals for terrorists? This is the most heavily polled populace in the history of the universe; whenever certain polls are not being taken, you should smell a big fat commie rat.)

In 1942, six months after Pearl Harbor, the Supreme Court upheld the use of military tribunals for eight German spies captured on U.S. soil, two of whom were U.S. citizens. In that case, *Ex Parte Quirin*, the court found that military tribunals were appropriate for suspected enemies who have "entered or after entry remained in our territory without uniform," intending to engage in an act of belligerency against the United States. And consider that the Huns were accused only of planning attacks on war materials—not on U.S. citizens. The Supreme Court decided *Quirin* in less than twenty-four hours. Three days later, the military tribunal found the saboteurs guilty. Five days after that, six of the eight were executed, including Herbert Hans Haupt, a U.S. citizen. Only the two who ratted out the plot were given prison sentences instead of death.

The fact that the "courts are open"—the phrase absurdly invoked by Senator Leahy—refers to the Supreme Court's decision in *Ex Parte Milligan*, a Civil War–era case. The *Milligan* court said a citizen could not be tried in a military tribunal "where the courts are open and their process unobstructed"—i.e., in the absence of martial law. But the crucial part of the Court's decision was its determination that Milligan was a nonbelligerent. As the Supreme Court would explain nearly a century later in *Quirin*, the court in *Milligan* "concluded that Milligan, not being a part of or associated with the armed forces of the enemy, was a nonbelligerent, not subject to the law of war." Milligan had not committed any act of war—he was being tried in a military tribunal only because of Abraham Lincoln's suspension of habeas corpus during the Civil War.

It was irrelevant to the Court's decision that Milligan was also a citizen: We know citizens can be tried in military tribunals, otherwise Haupt—Nazi spy–cum–American citizen—would not have been tried and executed by the military. The difference in the two cases is based on the law to be applied, not on the citizenship status of the defendants. Quirin and company were enemy belligerents and thus tried under military law; Milligan was not an enemy belligerent, and thus was to be tried under civilian law—as long as "the courts are open." Michael Moore may wish for Americans to die every bit as much as Jose Padilla does, but he has not conspired, plotted, or committed acts of war sufficient to make him an "enemy belligerent." Mere treason is tried in civilian courts.

Though Bush has ordered military tribunals only for noncitizens thus far, the *Quirin* court did not exempt citizens from military tribunals—far from it. If "unlawful belligerency" is the offense, the Court held, then U.S. citizenship provides no shelter. Citizens who associate with the enemy—taking its aid, guidance, or direction—are "enemy belligerents." When Ashcroft is forced to waste his time in Senate hearings this week taking him away from protecting the nation from more terrorist attacks, he should remind the committee that there's no exemption for senators either. ∎

☞ Attack France!
DECEMBER 20, 2001

As pundits mull whether America's next target in the war on terrorism should be Iraq or a smaller quarry first—such as Sudan or Somalia—it's time to consider another petri dish of ferocious anti-American hatred and terrorist activity. The Bush doctrine is: We are at war not only with the terrorists but also with those who harbor them. We've got to attack France.

Having exhausted itself in a spirited fight with the Nazis in the last war, France cannot work up the energy to oppose terrorism. For decades now, France has nurtured, coddled, and funded Islamic terrorists. (Moreover, the Great Satan is getting a little sick of our McDonald's franchises being attacked on behalf of notoriously inefficient French dairy farmers.) At the 1972 Olympics, Muslim terrorists assassinated eleven Israeli athletes and one German policeman. Five years later, acting on intelligence from Israeli secret police, French counterespionage agents arrested the reputed mastermind of the massacre, Abu Daoud. Both Israel and West Germany sought the extradition of Daoud. Afraid of upsetting Muslim terrorists, France refused on technical grounds and set him free.

In 1986, Libyan agents of Muammar Qaddafi planted a bomb in a West Berlin discotheque, killing an American serviceman and a Turkish woman. Hundreds more were injured. President Reagan ordered air strikes against Libyan military targets—including Qaddafi's living quarters. Quaking in the face of this show of manly force, France denied America the use of its airspace. As a consequence, American pilots were required to begin their missions from air bases in Britain. When the pilots finally made it to Tripoli, tired from the long flights and showing a puckish sense of humor, they bombed the French Embassy by mistake. Oops! Butterfingers!

France has repeatedly decried economic sanctions against Iraq and has accused the United Nations of manufacturing evidence against Saddam Hussein. The UN—not even the Great Satan! The French UN ambassador dismissed aerial photographs of Iraqi military trucks fleeing inspections sites just before UN weapons inspectors arrived as—I quote—"perhaps a truckers' picnic."

Along with the rest of the European Union, France sends millions of dollars to the Palestinian Authority every year. Sucking up to the P.A. has really paid dividends to the craven butterbellies. While visiting Arafat in Gaza last year to announce several million more dollars in aid, Prime Minister Lionel Jospin was attacked by angry, stone-throwing Palestinian students.

Earlier this year, France connived with human-rights champions China and Cuba to toss the United States off the UN Human

Rights Commission. Sudan took America's place, and if its dip-
lomats are not too bogged down with human torture and slave
trading, they are very much looking forward to attending the
meetings.

This summer, Paris made Mumia Abu-Jamal an honorary citizen of Paris. In America's cowboy, blood lust, rush-to-judgment
approach to the death penalty, this convicted Philadelphia cop-
killer has been sitting on death row—giving radio interviews and
college commencement addresses—for twenty years. Luckily
"Mumia" sounds like a Muslim name, so Parisians can keep using
the same bumper stickers for the war on terrorism.

Two weeks into America's war in Afghanistan, *Le Figaro* began
calling for "American restraint." In polls, 47 percent of the French
said they believed the U.S. military action was failing and only 17
percent thought it was working (which was, admittedly, 17 percent
more than on the *New York Times* editorial page). Flaunting
France's well-established reputation as a fearsome fighting machine, the French foreign minister, Hubert Vedrine, immediately
called on the United States to stop bombing Afghanistan.

The first indictment to come out of the September 11 attacks
was of a French national, Zacarias Moussaoui. He is believed to
be the intended twentieth hijacker on Bloody Tuesday. France
quickly moved to extend consular protection for Moussaoui. In-
triguingly, French justice minister Marylise Lebranchu has demanded that Moussaoui not be executed. Mlle. Lebranchu seems
to have forgotten, but . . . WE ARE THE GREAT SATAN! We also
have Moussaoui. It's annoying enough when these celebrated Nazi
slayers refuse to extradite terrorists on the grounds that America
does not observe the pristine judicial formalities of their pals,
China, Cuba, and Sudan. But under what zany theory of international law does France think it can tell us what to do with a terrorist we caught right here on U.S. soil?

The Great Satan is wearying of this reverse hegemony, in
which little pipsqueak nations try to impose their little pipsqueak

values on us. Aren't we the ones who should be arrogantly oppressing countries that unaccountably do not have the death penalty? And now, as America goes about building support for an attack on Iraq—guess who's complaining again? The turtlenecked chickens are terrified of offending fanatical Muslims. Meanwhile we are asking Arab leaders to face down the vastly larger populations of crazies living in their countries. While France whines, predominantly Muslim Turkey is preparing its airstrips for a possible U.S. attack on Iraq. If this is a war against terrorism and not a Eurocentric war against Islam, the conclusion is ineluctable: We must attack France. What are they going to do? Fight us? ■

☞ May I Turn Down Your Bed, Mohammad?

FEBRUARY 1, 2002

In the event of a surprise attack by North Korea, Secretary of State Colin Powell urged President Bush to ensure that the Office of Homeland Security have full resources and authority to respond to any anti-Korean hate crimes at home. Since you can't tell these days: That's a joke. Powell's real beef concerns the technical procedure by which the United States concludes that the terrorists held at Guantánamo are not "prisoners of war." (Also, Korean-Americans are great Americans and would be the last people to whine about ethnic profiling.)

What Powell really says is that we should apply the Geneva Convention to the Guantánamo detainees. As he admits, under the convention, the detainees are not prisoners of war, inasmuch as they masquerade as civilians, stage sneak attacks, slaughter innocent civilians, pretend they are surrendering before they come out shooting, take hostages, hide arms in mosques, and generally do not abide by the laws or customs of war. Other administration officials have concluded that the Geneva Convention doesn't apply in the first place—because the detainees masquerade as civilians, stage sneak attacks, slaughter innocent civilians, pretend they are surrendering . . . etc. etc.

The subtle distinction is this: If I showed up at the Super Bowl this Sunday demanding to play for the Patriots, I would be turned away on the grounds that I am not within the definition of people known as "the Patriots." Powell's argument is that we should appease our completely useless "allies" by playing a make-believe game that I am a Patriot. Then the Patriots would make a painstaking finding of fact that I am scrawny 99-pound weakling and, on the basis of that finding alone, conclude that I cannot play in the Super Bowl. Either the Taliban and al Qaeda fighters are not covered by the Geneva Convention or they are but still do not qualify for prisoner-of-war status. So the main problem with Powell's position is that it lacks what we used to call "a point."

What determines whether the Geneva Convention applies in the first place is whether we are at war with a signatory nation to the convention. To be sure, some decades ago, a different government of Afghanistan played for the Patriots—that is, was a signatory to the Geneva Convention. But we are not at war with Afghanistan. To the contrary! We are Afghanistan's biggest best buddy in the whole world right now. (Though they seem to think the name of our country is "The Pentagon.") We are at war with al Qaeda. The 158 Guantánamo detainees come from at least twenty-five different countries. To pretend that the Taliban is bound by a convention signed by an earlier Afghan government because the al Qaeda fighters happened to have been captured in Afghanistan would be like trying to collect a bill from a family that bought your debtor's house, razed it, and happened to occupy the same property twenty years later.

The most popular argument for the Powell view is that we have to be nice to the detainees because otherwise people won't be nice to captured American soldiers. Who are we trying to impress by this largesse exactly? I promise you, any Americans captured by al

Qaeda will be tortured, disemboweled, and beheaded right before the traditional dancing on the American corpse begins. Indeed, it is difficult to conceive of the United States actually going to war against any country that would honor the Geneva Convention. Despite the enormous groundswell of support for an attack on France, for example, we probably won't invade France. The only people America ever goes to war against are utter savages.

In World War II, the Japanese tortured American prisoners of war. In the Vietnam War, the North Vietnamese tortured American prisoners of war. In the Gulf War, Iraq tortured U.S. prisoners of war—including a female officer who was sexually assaulted by her captors. So this Geneva Convention thing isn't really working out for us. The argument boils down to the claim that we have to treat the detainees the way humanrightsniks say we should in order to secure the approval of humanrightsniks. Even the late Justice William J. Brennan had more imaginative arguments than that.

Thus far in the war on terrorism, human-rights organizations have complained about: the detention of terrorism suspects, military tribunals for terrorists, a trial for John Walker, and (nonexistent) ethnic profiling at airports. No one in America cares. It must be galling to the UN human-rights commissioner. But for some reason, the human-rights organizations imagined that we would be impressed with their complaining about Guantánamo. The country is just shrugging that off, too. Afraid of seeming impotent and irrelevant, even Tony Blair immediately backed down from his criticisms of Guantánamo. Whether Muslim terrorists in Guantánamo are getting enough Froot Loops is not where the country is right now. We're too busy worrying about averting any potential hate crimes against Muslims. ∎

☞ Build Them Back

JUNE 7, 2002

Since September 11, we have been authoritatively informed that skyscrapers as tall as the World Trade Center will never be built again. A "consensus" quickly emerged among city officials to replace the soaring Twin Towers with some potty little buildings and a park. But then at a meeting to discuss the future of the site last week, hundreds of New Yorkers showed up and shocked the experts by demanding that the towers be rebuilt. One man, who had worked on the 77th floor of 1 World Trade Center, said, "Please do not diminish the memory of all of the people who died there by building fifty-, sixty-, or seventy-story mediocre buildings on the site." A little grassy park where people go to weep does lack something in the way of defiance. Instead of us crying, evidently many Americans feel, there should be a lot of Arabs crying.

The reason liberals prefer a park to luminous skyscrapers is that they are not angry. Liberals express sympathy for the victims, but they're not angry. Instead of longing to crush and humiliate the enemy, they believe true patriotism consists of redoubled efforts to expand the welfare state. Senator Hillary Clinton proposed a school for the World Trade Center site and Senator Charles Schumer, a park. Yeah, that'll show 'em! Meanwhile, the construction workers clearing away the rubble vowed they would work without pay to rebuild the World Trade Center. Of course, now that we have fourteen cows, that shouldn't be necessary. (In a genuinely touching story, a tiny cowherding village in Kenya only recently got word of the attack on America and this week made a special present of fourteen cows to the United States.)

The attack on the World Trade Center ripped America's soul not only for the thousands of lives it snuffed out. Even if the towers had been empty, the destruction of those buildings would have been heart-wrenching. Skyscrapers are the hallmark of civilization, monuments to human brilliance and creativity. I'm sure there are some nice trees, but I note that no one ever talks about the "heavenly suburb." Philosopher Jacques Ellul said cities exhibit "all the hopes of man for divinity." St. Augustine said the "house of God is itself a city."

It has become common wisdom that no one would rent property in a rebuilt World Trade Center. This is absurd. September 11 was a sucker punch. That trick doesn't work twice. We have the technology to make the buildings safe from incoming missiles. Moreover, by the time a new World Trade Center is built, Muslim fanatics will be about as threatening as Japanese kamikazi pilots. Who would have imagined after Pearl Harbor that the Japanese were governable? Yet Japan hasn't shown a disposition to fight in sixty years. Muslims feel humiliated now? We'll show them humiliated.

Aesthetes complain that the buildings were ugly. Perhaps. But the important thing is, they were really big. Whatever goes up on that site ought to be even bigger than the buildings the savages destroyed. Erecting enormous skyscrapers to replace the Twin Towers limns the distinction between us and the barbarians. We can ride elevators a quarter-mile into the sky and have a chocolate mousse. What can they do? Multimillionaire Osama bin Laden lived in a cave (and is now D-E-D dead under a Daisy Cutter in Tora Bora). Here in America, ordinary Americans consider seventy-story buildings "mediocre." As Donald Rumsfeld said of al Qaeda, their specialty is "destroying things they could never have built themselves using technologies they never could have developed themselves."

The urge to destroy may not come from Islam, but creation is not Islam's strong suit either. In his seminal book *The Creators*, historian Daniel Boorstin explains the Islamic approach to innovation. While Judaism and Christianity begin with the Creation, Islam reveres a God who creates nothing. It is a central tenet of Islam that God did not even create the Koran. According to

Boorstin, mullahs teach that since "the speech of God is uncreate, the words must be eternal uncreate." The world comes into being not by God's energy and initiative, but by fiat—much like Supreme Court rulings. As Boorstin says, "For a believing Muslim, to create is a rash and dangerous act." I guess that would explain why they don't have chairs.

Mohammed Atta loathed skyscrapers. *Newsweek* reported that he viewed the emergence of tall buildings in Egypt as an odious surrender to Western values. The most fitting memorial to the victims of the World Trade Center attack is to build the world's most breathtaking skyscraper in the world on top of Mohammed Atta's corpse. ■

☞ This Whistle-Blower They Like

JUNE 13, 2002

In their enthusiasm to bash the Bush administration for its handling of the war—which Democrats consider an annoying distraction from the real business of government, which is redistributing income—the left has embraced FBI agent Coleen Rowley as a modern Joan of Arc. From liberal headquarters at the *New York Times,* Maureen Dowd fawns over Rowley, calling her "the blunt Midwesterner" who painted a "stunning and gruesome portrait of just how far gone the bureau is." Frank Rich calls her "a forthright American woman."

At least liberals seem to have gotten over their disdain for government whistle-blowers. Back when the world's most famous whistle-blower produced tapes proving the president of the United States had committed a slew of felonies, the Left was somewhat muted in its enthusiasm for female truth-tellers. Dowd called Linda Tripp a "witch" with a "boiling cauldron." Rich said Americans "despise" a "snitch." Fortunately for Rowley, she is only a snitch against the FBI. One shudders to think what names liberals would be calling the unglamorous agent if she were testifying against Bill Clinton.

Also fortunately for Rowley, liberals aren't listening to her. It is striking how the media have studiously ignored Rowley's specific indictment of the FBI, preferring to prattle on about her raw courage in the abstract. Dowd exclaimed that Rowley painted "a stunning and gruesome portrait of just how far gone the bureau is." Okay—but what did she say exactly? Bewildering news accounts leave the impression that Rowley's act of dauntless valor was to fly to Washington to tell the Senate that the FBI has really old computers.

In fact, the gravamen of Rowley's 13-page memo is essentially that FBI headquarters botched the Zacarias Moussaoui case by refusing to racially profile Muslims. Boiled to its essentials, Rowley's theory is that being a Muslim should constitute probable cause. Rowley condemned FBI brass for refusing to authorize a search warrant for Moussaoui based on the following information: (1) he refused to consent to a search of his computer; (2) he was in flight school; (3) he had overstayed his visa; and (4) he was a Muslim.

Let's see, which of these factors constitutes probable cause?

- Refusal to consent to a search? It is your right to refuse. Any other rule would allow cops to bootstrap their way into a warrant. "Hi, Zacarias, may we search your computer? No? That's suspicious! Grounds for a warrant!" I don't think so.
- In flight school? NO.
- Overstayed visa? NO.
- Is a Muslim? NOT ALLOWED.

As Rowley admits, "reasonable minds may differ as to whether probable cause existed" on the basis of the above facts. But, she says, once French Intelligence confirmed Moussaoui's affiliations with "radical fundamentalist Islamic groups," probable cause was "certainly established." Not under the law it wasn't. Being in league with known terrorists may be suspicious, but it is not probable cause to believe that a particular crime has been committed by a specific individual. (Were the law otherwise, cops could get a warrant to search anyone who associates with the Clintons.)

Moreover, any Muslim who has attended a mosque in Europe—certainly in England, where Moussaoui lived—has affiliated with "radical fundamentalist Islamic groups." A few months after the September 11 attack, 80 percent of British Muslims said they opposed the war in Afghanistan. The Muslim Council of Britain called for an immediate end to the war. A poll by the *Daily Telegraph* found that 98 percent of Muslims between the ages of twenty and forty-five said they would not fight for Britain, but almost half said they would fight for Osama bin Laden. A Gallup poll taken in nine Muslim nations last year found that only 18 percent of the people believed the yarn about Arabs flying planes into buildings on September 11. (Many subscribed to the Zionist plot theory.) This was based on almost ten thousand face-to-face interviews in Saudi Arabia, Iran, Pakistan, Indonesia, Turkey, Lebanon, Kuwait, Jordan, and Morocco. Seventy-seven percent said America's military action in Afghanistan was "morally unjustified." (Just to give you some idea how extreme that is, even liberals pretended to support war with Afghanistan!) In other words, if you associate with Muslims abroad, you are associating with Muslim fanatics. Rowley's position is that "probable cause" existed to search Moussaoui's computer because he was a Muslim who had lived abroad.

I happen to agree with her, but liberals don't. So how did Rowley become the Left's new Norma Rae? Given their nutty ideas, liberals should be applauding FBI headquarters for refusing to consider the fact that Moussaoui was a Muslim, and condemning this incipient Mark Fuhrman. Rowley is my hero, not theirs. FBI headquarters rebuffed Rowley's callous insensitivity to Muslims and denied a warrant request to search Moussaoui's computer— and thus failed to uncover the September 11 plot. The FBI allowed thousands of Americans to be slaughtered on the altar of political correctness. What more could liberals ask for? ■

☞ My Name Is Adolf

SEPTEMBER 12, 2002

Among the patriotic lesson plans for 9/11 was one proposed by the National Council for Social Studies, which recommends a short story titled "My Name Is Osama." Calculatedly inciting hatred toward white American boys, the story is about a nasty little boy, "Todd," who taunts an Iraqi immigrant named "Osama":

> "Your mom is a rag head."
> He doesn't know my mother has a Ph.D. in pharmacology. She taught my pediatrician at Baghdad University.
> Todd says, "Your father forces your mother to wear a bag on her head. Your father must be a bully."
> My mother wears a hijab because she likes to. (http://www.ncss.org/resources/moments/nameisosama.shtml)

This is the lesson to commemorate the biggest hate crime in history—committed by someone named "Osama" against people with names like "Todd." Liberals are incapable of embarrassment—they're like Arabs without the fighting spirit. How about a 1942 lesson plan titled "My Name Is Adolf"? And while we're on the subject, might the 9/11 lesson plan inquire into what little "Osama" thinks about the terrorist attack? May we ask? (Question from the actual lesson plan: "Why, do you think, did Osama's family leave Iraq?" Incorrect answer: Because his father wanted to attend flight school in America.)

To be sure, there have been a number of hate crimes committed since 9/11. But they were committed by Muslims. Hesham Mohamed Hadayet murdered two and wounded many more at Los Angeles International Airport. Suleyman al-Faris, aka "John Walker Lindh," joined an attack in Afghanistan that left Michael Spann dead. Abdel Rahim, aka "Richard Reid," tried but failed to murder a planeload of people on an American Airlines jet headed to Miami. Meanwhile, there has been precisely one confirmed hate crime committed in retaliation for the monstrous 9/11 attack. Some nut in Arizona murdered a Sikh thinking he was a Muslim. Current hate crime tally: Muslims: over 3,000 (and counting); White Guys: 1.

In the spirit of specifically targeting only the worrisome Muslims, I note that the media have inadvertently identified several of them with blinding clarity. In case you missed these stories, I bring them to your attention so you will be forewarned: Do not fly with any of these kids. Soon after the terrorist attack, the *New York Times* chatted with students at the Al Noor School, a private Islamic academy in Brooklyn—evidently the Arab equivalent of the Horace Mann High School (Anthony Lewis, '44). None of the students said they had experienced any harassment since September 11. To the contrary, their school had been deluged with support from local Catholic schools, hospitals, state education officials, and political leaders.

But the love was entirely one-sided. The students stated point-blank that they would not fight for America against a fellow Muslim. They denied that Osama bin Laden was behind the attacks. They criticized the United States for its cruel treatment of Muslims. "Isn't it ironic," one Islamic student sneered, "that the interests of America are always against what Muslims want?" That's why the last several major American interventions—in Kuwait, Somalia, and the Balkans—were all in defense of Muslims. Of course, there was the attack on Osama bin Laden, but according to them, he wasn't practicing "true Islam." I wish they'd get their stories straight: Do most Muslims support bin Laden or not? Though uniformly refusing to believe bin Laden was behind the terrorist attack, the students showed a remarkable lack of curiosity about who was behind it.

Students from the Al Noor School were interviewed again a few weeks later, this time by CBS's *60 Minutes*. The students instantly and enthusiastically agreed with the proposition that a "Muslim who becomes a suicide bomber goes to Paradise for that action." One student answered, "Definitely" and called a female suicide bomber "very brave." Others said they earnestly hoped the suicide bombers went to Paradise. "I mean, they're doing it for a good cause," one boy explained. "I pray that they go to Paradise," another said. Most comforting, one student said, "I think we'd all probably do the same."

Weeks later, at the urging of the principal, the students modified their answers. But according to CBS, "None of them changed their view that suicide bombers in Israel would go to Paradise." The Islamic studies teacher at Al Noor claimed the students misunderstood true Islam: "If you go to chapter 4, verse 29, it says so clear, 'Do not kill yourself.'" It's always so comforting when Muslims cite the precise verse from the Koran that tells them killing is wrong. Don't all empathic human beings understand instinctively that suicide and murder are wrong? What if they lost their Koran that day and couldn't remember the specific verse condemning murder?

In any event, and more to the point, the Koran does not strictly inveigh against killing *someone else* for Allah. In the eye-opening book *Unveiling Islam,* Christian-convert authors Ergun Mehmet Caner and Emir Fethi Caner say the Koran "promises Paradise to those who die in battle for Islam more certainly than it promises salvation to anyone else." Muhammad says, "Fighting is prescribed upon you. . . . Tumult and oppression are worse than slaughter." The Koran instructs, "Fight those who believe not in Allah nor the Last Day . . . until they pay compensation with willing submission, and feel themselves subdued." It promises, "If you are slain or die in the way of Allah, forgiveness and mercy from Allah are far better than all they could amass."

Among the most famous victims of Islam's will to slaughter as practiced on 9/11 was a man named "Todd"—just like the nasty little boy in the social studies lesson. When Todd Beamer and the other passengers on United Airlines Flight 93 realized the Muslim hijackers were on a mission of death, they fought back. The real Todd did not shout "God is great!" before ripping out an innocent man's entrails. Todd Beamer prayed, "The Lord is my shepherd; I shall not want. He maketh me to lie down in green pastures: He leadeth me beside the still waters. He restoreth my soul: He leadeth me in the paths of righteousness for His name's sake. Yea, though I walk through the valley of the shadow of death, I will fear no evil: for Thou art with me." ■

☞ Beauty Pageants Can Be Murder

NOVEMBER 28, 2002

The Religion of Peace suffered another PR setback this week when Muslims in Nigeria welcomed the Miss World beauty pageant by slaughtering Christians in the street and burning churches to the ground. At last count, more than two hundred people were dead, hundreds more were injured, and thousands were left without homes. Also, the Nigerian contestant's chances of winning "Miss Congeniality" were cruelly dashed.

Leaping at the one chance they had to attract positive press to their pissant country and begin the process of dragging themselves out of the thirteenth century, Nigerian Muslims instead chose to hack innocent people to death in the name of Allah. Pageant officials pulled up stakes and immediately took the show to London. One assumes the director of the Nigerian Department of Tourism isn't pleased. Winning the pageant site had been an uphill battle from the beginning. Some of the more closed-minded Miss World participants were already carping about the upcoming stoning of a Nigerian woman, in accordance with Islamic Sharia law.

The president of Nigeria, Olusegun Obasanjo, tried to downplay the Muslims' murderous rampage by cheerfully explaining,

"The beauty queens should not feel that they are the cause of the violence. It could happen at any time irresponsible journalism is committed against Islam." Well, that's a relief. It seems an article in a Nigerian newspaper had mused that the Prophet Muhammad "would probably have chosen a wife" from among the Miss World contestants. This upset the practitioners of the Religion of Peace. (And for good reason. Their polygamous prophet actually preferred his wives a little younger—one of Muhammad's wives was six years old.) Muslims reacted to the article by bludgeoning, stabbing, and burning Christians to death. Some enforcers of the Religion of Peace in Nigeria ordered Muslims to kill the author of this blasphemy. (Overheard at the Miss World contest: "Does this make me look fatwa?")

As long as liberals are going to keep demanding that Americans refer to Islam as a "religion of peace," it would be a big help if Muslims would stop killing people. The *New York Times* simply refuses to admit that their little darlings—angry, violent Muslims—could ever be at fault for killing people. That makes no sense because Islam is a Religion of Peace. The *Times* reviewed the facts of the slaughter during the Miss World contest, processed them through a PC prism, and came to the conclusion that Islam is peaceful but religion causes violence. Thus, according to the *Times* headline, "Religious Violence in Nigeria Drives Out Miss World Event." It wasn't Muslims killing people; it was nonspecific "religious violence." The article explained that Muslims pouring out of mosques to kill Christians and torch churches in Nigeria resulted from "the tinderbox of religious passions in the country." The police step in to try to quell rioting Muslims, and the *Times* reports this as "fighting between Christians and Muslims." Ah, the cycle of violence.

Religion causes violence and never mind that the most bloodthirsty cult in the twentieth century was an atheistic sect known as "communism." It was not "true communism"! And Muslim terrorists are not practicing "true Islam." Ironically, liberals would hate Muslims who practiced "true Islam." Without the terrorism, Muslims are just another group of "antichoice" fanatics.

Winning "Best in Show" was the *Times*'s headline on an article about the Christian missionary shot dead in Lebanon by a Muslim: "Killing Underscores Enmity of Evangelists and Muslims." This is like referring to the enmity between a woman and her rapist. She hates him, he hates her. It's a cycle of violence! Except the funny thing about the Christians is, they still love the Muslims. The Muslims' main beef with the Christians was—I quote— Christians "destroy the fighting spirit of the children, especially of the Palestinian youth, by teaching them not to fight the Jews, [teaching] the Palestinians to forgive the Jews and leave them Jerusalem."

The *Times* seemed to agree the Muslims had a point with the evangelical. Just as no new data can shake the *Times*'s belief that Islam is a religion of peace, nothing can disabuse them of the idea that Christians, as a general matter, deserve to be shot. In a news analysis, the *Times* said the missionaries *claimed* they were merely exposing people to Jesus Christ. "But," the *Times* said in a *j'accuse* tone, "a somewhat more direct goal emerges amid the Web site postings." The *Times* had caught the Christians red-handed committing irresponsible web postings against Islam! They were asking for it. (On the bright side, at least this means the *Times* is holding the gun innocent in this one instance.) Luckily for the *Times,* Christians do not rip out people's entrails in response to "irresponsible journalism" committed against Christianity. ■

☞ War-Torn Democrats

JANUARY 29, 2003

Last week Senator John Kerry gave a speech saying: "Mr. President, do not rush to war!" Rush to war? We've been talking about this war for a year. It's been three months since Kerry duly recorded his vote in favor of a war resolution to forcibly remove Saddam Hussein from power.

In 1991, Kerry voted against the Gulf War, saying the country was "not yet ready for what it will witness and bear if we go to war." Having been taunted for that vote and that prediction ever since, this time Kerry made sure to vote in favor of war with Iraq. This will allow the *New York Times* to describe him as a "moderate Democrat" forevermore. Indeed, a surprisingly large number of Democrats voted for the war resolution last October. But as soon as the November elections were over, Democrats like Kerry began aggressively attacking the very war they had just voted for.

These Democrats want to have it both ways. If the war goes well—a lot of them voted for war with Iraq, didn't they? But if the war does not go well, many of the very Democrats who voted for the war resolution will have emerged as leading spokesmen for the antiwar position. A vote for the war, surrounded by Neville Chamberlain foot-dragging, is a fraud.

The Neville Chamberlain Democrats are now claiming they didn't realize what they were voting for. John Kerry says he thought a resolution authorizing the president to use force against Iraq meant that the United Nations would have to approve. Dianne Feinstein said she voted for the resolution assuming it meant we would invade only if "our allies" approved. Joe Biden made the terrific argument that if we don't wait for UN approval, it would "make a mockery of the efficacy of the UN." The Democrats appear to be the only people who still believe there is any "efficacy" to the UN. In any event, I believe the United Nations should be more worried about that consequence than we should.

Kerry claims he is still foursquare behind disarming Saddam Hussein, but not "until we have exhausted the remedies available, built legitimacy, and earned the consent of the American people, absent, of course, an imminent threat requiring urgent action." As George Bush pointed out in his State of the Union address, dictators are not in the habit of "politely putting us on notice before they strike." By the time a threat is "imminent," the Capitol will be gone.

That's the short version. The long version of Kerry's position is this: "[I]f you have a breach that, by everybody's standard, at least in the United States, those of us in the House and Senate, and the president, join together and make a judgment, this is indeed a material breach, and then others—some of them can't be persuaded—if we have evidence, sufficient to show the materiality of the breach, we should be able to do what Adlai Stevenson did on behalf of the administration, Kennedy administration, and sit in front of the Security Council and say, 'Here is the evidence. It's time for all of you to put up. We need to all do this together.' And that's what I think the resolution that was passed suggests."

There's a call to arms to unite the Democrats! If there has been a material breach "by everybody's standard," then and only then, we can boldly go . . . to the United Nations! This is the fundamental problem of the anti-war movement. They can't bring themselves to say it's a mistake to depose Saddam Hussein, and "don't hurry" is not much of a rallying cry.

Why not hurry? Democrats claim they haven't seen proof yet that Saddam is a direct threat to the United States. For laughs, let's suppose they're right. In the naysayers' worst-case scenario, the United States would be acting precipitously to remove a ruthless dictator who tortures his own people, gassed the Kurds, and allows his sons to operate rape rooms. As Bush said, after detailing some of Saddam Hussein's charming practices: "If this is not evil, then evil has no meaning." It's not as if anyone is worried that through some horrible miscalculation we could be removing the Iraqi Abraham Lincoln by mistake.

Either we're removing a dictator who currently has plans to fund terrorism against American citizens or—if Bush is completely wrong and Eleanor Clift is completely right—we're just removing a dictator who plans to terrorize a lot of people in the region, but not Americans specifically. Even for someone like me, who doesn't want America to be the world's policeman, the risk of precipitous action against Saddam Hussein doesn't keep me up at night.

The Democrats' jejune claim that Saddam Hussein is not a threat to our security presupposes they would care if he were. Who are they kidding? Democrats adore threats to the United States. Bush got a raucous standing ovation at his State of the Union address when he announced that "this year, for the first time, we are beginning to field a defense to protect this nation against ballistic missiles." The excitement was noticeably muted on the Democrats' side of the aisle. The vast majority of Democrats remained firmly in their seats, sullen at the thought that America would be protected from incoming ballistic missiles. To paraphrase George Bush: If this is not treason, then treason has no meaning. ∎

☞ "Will of Allah" Preempts Iraq Invasion

FEBRUARY 6, 2003

I knew the media were up to something with their wall-to-wall coverage of the Columbia space shuttle explosion. The full story is: Shuttle disintegrated during reentry; all astronauts killed, including some very remarkable people; very sad; NASA picking up the debris to figure out what happened. It was a plane crash story, only a lot more expensive. So why was the shuttle explosion being covered like the 9/11 attack?

A quick review of the *Treason Times* laid bare the seditious objective. The shuttle presented a new argument for appeasement. *Warning, Great Satan: Your money and technology and little gadgets cannot insulate you from disaster!* The *New York Times* proclaimed, "As Iraq War Looms, a New Sense of Vulnerability." American hubris blunted again! Breathless news accounts of the shuttle blast were merely a more demure version of Islamic terrorists cheering in the street in reaction to the explosion. If the *Times* weren't afraid of violating the "wall of separation," it would have run an editorial titled "It was the will of Allah!"

The *Times* quoted a series of random Americans saying things like "Now I'm hearing a lot of people say if we go to war, we're going to endanger a lot more than seven lives." Another classic *Times* Man on the Street said that it reinforced his belief "that we should find diplomatic solutions instead of threatening other countries with war." For one year, in a nation ablaze with war fever, I don't believe the *Times* has managed to interview a single person who supports war with Iraq. Their Man on the Street always seems to be standing on a street suspiciously close to Central Park West.

The Gettysburg Address of liberal idiocy was a letter to the editor from a Jim Forbes of San Francisco two days after the crash. The *Times* titled his contribution to Liberalthink "A Time of Mourning for Shattered Dreams: A Period of Healing." In full-dress sanctimony, Forbes wrote, "The loss of the space shuttle Columbia and its crew of seven is a national tragedy. Time is needed for Americans to mourn. I hope that President Bush will do the right thing by slowing down his march to war and focusing instead on the healing that such a blow to national pride requires."

Here was a pithy concentration of the multiple idiotic things liberals were saying about the space shuttle, the insincerity, the audacity, the smarminess—he even worked in "the healing process." How Jim Forbes of San Francisco must have polished that little gem! The idea that liberals feel the shuttle explosion was a tragedy is patent nonsense. They were ecstatic at this new excuse to condemn the "march to war." The nation is marching to war at such breakneck speed, it will be two years from 9/11 before we finally attack Iraq.

Morose that their relentless nay-saying is having no effect on the president's war plans, *New York Times* columnists are now positing imaginary scenarios in which war with Iraq leads to a stock market crash and brings the nation to the brink of nuclear war. Nicholas Kristof has gone the Maureen Dowd route of using the op-ed page of the *Times* for a dream-sequence column. But instead of dreaming about Bush being retarded, as Dowd does, Kristof dreams of catastrophe for America. In Kristof's fantasy, Bush eventually apologizes to Secretary of State Colin Powell for invading Iraq. The strain of not having a Democrat in the Oval Office to lose wars for America is driving liberals to fevered fantasies of America's defeat somewhere in the world.

In other appeasement news, former UN arms inspector Scott Ritter has completely vanished from the antiwar scene since news of his sex arrest broke. Three weeks ago, it was revealed that Ritter was nabbed soliciting sex from underage girls on the Internet in 2001. He was charged with attempted endangerment of a child and the case was adjourned in contemplation of dismissal, with directions for him to stay out of trouble for six months. Until news of his sex arrest became public, the *New York Times* had been treating Ritter's reincarnation as a peacenik as the greatest act of patriotism since Nathan Hale told the British he regretted only that he had but one life to give for his country. It's now Day 17 and counting of the *Times*'s refusal to mention Ritter's arrest. (As we go to press on the book, it's Day 562 of the *Times*'s refusal to mention Ritter's arrest.) Though the peace movement lost Ritter, it seems to have picked up Jerry Springer. Perhaps Springer is hoping he can get Scott Ritter's wife on the show to confront Ritter and the underage girl.

But Ritter was a freelance peacenik. At least the *Times* could count on stability and permanence from John Hartpence Kerry. Poor Kerry was just on the verge of figuring out whether he was for war with Iraq or against it when he was told he hadn't figured out his own last name. Kerry was shocked to be told that, despite years of allowing himself to be passed off as an Irish Brahmin, both his paternal grandparents were Jewish and his real name is Kohn. When confronted with the news, Kerry said there were signs he missed, such as his longtime, twice-requited desire to marry a rich shiksa. Now Kerry will need time for the healing process. We must halt the march to war. ■

☞ Kissing Cousins: New York Literati and Nazis

MARCH 20, 2003

It became clear the nation was finally going to war with Iraq this week when the *New York Times* pulled two dozen reporters off the Augusta National Golf Club story. On Monday, President Bush gave Saddam Hussein forty-eight hours to get out of Baghdad or the U.S. military would remove him forcibly. Many still held out hope that Saddam would abandon power without a fight—primarily so we could listen to liberals explain how a peaceful resolution was brought about by their urgent demands that we work through the United Nations, and had nothing to do with the fact that Saddam was surrounded by 200,000 American troops.

In response to Bush's ultimatum, Saddam's son, Uday Hussein, said Bush was stupid. He said Bush wanted to attack Iraq because of his family. And he said American boys would die. At least someone is finding the *New York Times* helpful these days!

In angry harangues largely indistinguishable from the one by Uday Hussein, the Democrats were outraged at Bush. Senator Joe Lieberman (Democrat of Connecticut) spent forty minutes detailing Saddam Hussein's manifest cruelties and violations of all human norms. Without breaking a sweat, Lieberman then said he could understand why the French were not bothered by these indisputable barbarisms: It was Bush's failure of "diplomacy." Bush, the clod, had failed to convince the inconvincible.

Senator Tom Daschle (Democrat of South Dakota) said, "I'm saddened, saddened that this president failed so miserably at diplomacy that we're now forced to war. Saddened that we have to give up one life because this president couldn't create the kind of diplomatic effort that was so critical for our country." Mostly, the Democrats were saddened that America was about to win a war.

With the nation on the verge of a glorious military triumph, liberals have had to put their predictions of a Vietnam "quagmire" on the back burner for a few weeks. Instead, they have turned with a vengeance to attacking "American arrogance." The day after President Bush's speech, *Washington Post* columnist David Ignatius spoke of self-defeating "American arrogance." The *Post* quoted "a senior U.S. official" (that's newspaper jargon for: "a janitor at the Pentagon who picked up the phone") warning of "a degree of hubris unprecedented in American history." The *New York Times*'s lead editorial the day after Bush's speech also bemoaned American "hubris." One front-page article called Bush trigger-happy and another bitterly accused him of breaking a campaign pledge to preside over a "humble" America. In the nineteen months since the 9/11 attack, the *Times* has used the phrase "American arrogance" nearly as many times (seventeen) as in the entire 96 months of the Clinton presidency (twenty-four). Instead of American arrogance, the *Times* yearns to return to Clintonian flatulence.

There was no more eloquent testimony to what liberals mean by "American arrogance" than an article in the March 10 *New Yorker*, which nonchalantly quoted a Nazi in support of the proposition that Americans are jingoistic, imperialist rednecks. Amid page after gleeful page of European venom toward Americans, Columbia University professor Simon Schama quoted the anti-American bile of Norwegian writer and renowned Nazi-sympathizer Knut Hamsun.

Schama admiringly cited Hamsun's contempt for American patriotism, neglecting to mention that Hamsun went for Nazi patriotism in a big way. Beginning in the early thirties and until his death in 1952, Hamsun was absolutely smitten with Adolf Hitler. When the Nazis invaded Norway, Hamsun wrote a newspaper column saying, "NORWEGIANS! Throw down your rifles and go home again. The Germans are fighting for us all." He exchanged gifts and telegrams with Goebbels and Hitler. Indeed, so enamored of Joseph Goebbels was Hamsun that he gave Goebbels his Nobel Prize medal. Inconsolable upon news of the Führer's death, Hamsun was quoted in an obituary on Hitler saying, "I am not worthy to speak his name." He never equivocated and he never apologized.

Between issuing tributes to Hitler, Hamsun wrote the ironically titled book *The Cultural Life of Modern America*, which, as professor Schama sniggeringly writes, was "largely devoted to asserting its nonexistence." Hamsun called America "a strapping child-monster whose runaway physical growth would never be matched by moral or cultural maturity." For "cultural maturity," Hamsun turned to Nazi Germany.

Hamsun hated America for all the same reasons liberals hate America. To the delight of New York sophisticates, Hamsun sneered at Americans who march in veterans' parades, "with tiny flags in their hats and brass medals on their chests marching in step to the hundreds of penny whistles they are blowing." America's little patriotic parades apparently compared unfavorably to a stirring Nazi war rally. This is the essence of liberal admiration for Europeans and their pompous cultural snobbery: For proof that Americans are jingoistic hicks, they cite a Nazi. ∎

☞ The Enemy Within

MARCH 28, 2003

Just five days into the war in Iraq, the *New York Times* was optimistically reporting that despite a strong start, American troops had gotten bogged down. This came as a surprise to regular readers of the *Times* who remembered that the *Times* thought we were bogged down from the moment the war began. The day after the first bombs were dropped on Baghdad, the *New York Times* ran a front-page article describing the mood of the nation thus: "Some faced it with tears, others with contempt, none with gladness."

Apparently some people were gladdened: The stock market had its best week in twenty years. What people do with their money is a rather more profound barometer of public sentiment than any stupid poll—much less bald assertions by *New York Times* reporters. *Times* news stories are beginning to have the ring of Arab-style proclamations in defiance of the facts. As with Saddam Hussein, the truth for them has no meaning. They say whatever honor commands them to say.

Five days after the *Treason Times* was morosely reporting that no one viewed the war with gladness . . . things had gotten even worse! In a single editorial, the *Times* said our troops were "faced with battlefield death, human error and other tragedies." The task "looks increasingly formidable." There were "disturbing events," and American forces were engaged in a "fierce firefight—an early glimpse of urban warfare." There were "downsides," "disheartening events," and "grievous blows." *We're losing this war! The Elite Republican Guard is assembling outside New York City! Head for the hills!* In fact, the "fierce firefight" referred to in the editorial concerned a battle in Nasiriyah in which American troops took an entire city with nine casualties. That's what most people call a "triumphal a**-kicking."

CNN's favorite general, Wesley Clark, has also been heard to opine that our troops are getting bogged down in Iraq. His competence to judge American generals is questionable, inasmuch as his command was limited to NATO. We prefer to hear from American generals, thanks. When Clark was NATO commander in the Balkans, his contribution to international peace consisted of mistakenly bombing the Chinese embassy in Belgrade and ordering U.S. pilots to fly at such high altitudes that even the pilots complained they were being forced to incur unnecessary civilian casualties. On MSNBC, Forrest Sawyer compared Iraqi forces killing our troops to American revolutionaries and said the war was likely to turn into a "nightmare."

Liberals never quit. American forces have taken two-thirds of Iraq and are fast advancing on Baghdad. Saddam's lieutenants are so demoralized that they have turned to lashing out at the Jews. Saddam's vice despot Tariq Aziz says the war is being fought only to "create something called greater Israel." (If the dictator business doesn't work out for him, at least Aziz is well positioned to run for Congress as a Democrat.) Thousands of Iraqi soldiers have surrendered or disbanded, thousands more have been captured, and still thousands more have been killed. Meanwhile, American forces have suffered fewer than two dozen deaths. And if that's not enough to convince you the war is going splendidly, just look at the increasingly gloomy expression on Dan Rather's face.

Most auspiciously, the Arab League has appealed to the United Nations Security Council to stop the war. One can only hope the Security Council will agree to intervene. I'd like to see them try to stop us. Would France threaten us with war? Young men across America would have to enlist as a matter of honor. The army could use it as a recruiting slogan: "Are you too chicken to fight the French?" Even liberals would enlist as a way to pick up credit for military service with no risk of injury.

Not surprisingly, the New York Times gave Saddam's recent speech more exultant coverage than they did Bush's State of the Union address. Since the first bomb hit Baghdad, everyone at the Times had been itching to use the word "quagmire." Somewhat surprisingly, Saddam beat even Maureen Dowd to the punch. According to Saddam, the invading forces are "in real trouble." The Times agrees. Liberals aren't afraid we'll do badly in Baghdad. They're afraid we'll do well.

After the Arab television network al-Jazeera repeatedly ran footage of U.S. prisoners of war over the weekend, the New York Stock Exchange threw al-Jazeera reporters off the trading floor.

This raises the question: When are they going to remove the *Times* reporters? ■

☞ At Least Saddam Wasn't at Tailhook!

APRIL 17, 2003

Despite liberals' calm assurance that Iraq wasn't harboring terrorists, this week Abul Abbas, mastermind of the 1985 *Achille Lauro* hijacking, was captured in Baghdad. This is the second time the United States has caught Abbas. The last time, the Europeans let him go. (Which may explain why liberals are so eager to have Europeans "help" with the war on terrorism—they've done such a bang-up job in the past.)

In 1985, Muslim terrorists hijacked the Italian cruise ship *Achille Lauro* and threatened to kill the passengers and crew unless fifty imprisoned Palestinians were released by Israel. The terrorists doused American and British women with gasoline and taunted them with matches. They forced passengers to hold live grenades. When their demands were not met, the terrorists shot a wheelchair-bound American, Leon Klinghoffer, and forced other passengers at gunpoint to throw him overboard in his wheelchair.

Even as the Americans were preparing a rescue mission, the Italian and Egyptian governments made a deal with the terrorists, offering the release of the Palestinians and safe passage to Tunisia to end the ordeal. The Europeans were delighted with this masterful act of diplomacy. The Americans were not so pleased.

So Oliver North conceived of an operation to get the terrorists back. Contrary to Egyptian president Mubarak's assurances that the terrorists had already left Egypt, North found out the terrorists were still there. Working with Israeli intelligence, North ascertained the precise EgyptAir flight that would carry the terrorists out of Egypt, right down to the flight number. He devised a plan to intercept the plane, modeled on the military's interception of Yamamoto, mastermind of Pearl Harbor during World War II.

President Reagan was briefed on the daring plan—along with copious warnings from timorous State Department officials that the Europeans might have their feelings bruised, America would look like a cowboy, and it would only strengthen the hard-liners in Egypt. Asked if the operation should proceed, Reagan said, "Good God! They've murdered an American here. Let's get on with it."

Admiral Frank Kelso, the officer in charge of America's Sixth Fleet in the Mediterranean, ordered his men to carry out the mission. In no time flat, Tomcat fighters had taken off from the U.S. aircraft carrier *Saratoga*. Guided by Hawkeyes, the Tomcats caught up with the EgyptAir flight. The fighters stealthily trailed their target in total darkness, their lights off, even in the cockpit. The American pilots flew so close to the EgyptAir flight, they used flashlights to read the plane's tail number. Then the Tomcats swooped in, surrounded the EgyptAir flight, and forced it to fly to a NATO base on Sicily controlled by the United States. The *New York Post* headline the next day was "GOT 'EM." And then Abul Abbas was released by the Europeans and given safe haven in Iraq under Saddam Hussein—whom liberals have assured us was not harboring terrorists. Republicans keep catching terrorists and liberals keep sending them back.

If there is a parable of how liberals support the enemy, this is it. Admiral Kelso, whose men carried out the dauntless EgyptAir interception, was cashiered out of the navy because of Tailhook. Feminists don't care about Saddam Hussein and his rape rooms. But they were hopping mad at Admiral Kelso for strolling through the Tailhook convention to say hello to his boys—among them, the ones who captured Leon Klinghoffer's murderers.

To jog the memory of the horror that was Tailhook, Lieutenant Paula Coughlin, the officer who made the most lurid allegations, accused a black Marine of molesting her. But then she kept identifying different black males as the perpetrator. Liberals managed to put their concern for racist accusations against blacks on the back burner in this case. (When liberals get going, the ironies never end.) Though Admiral Kelso was cleared of any wrongdoing after an official navy investigation, liberals still wanted him punished. Former Representative Patricia Schroeder (Democrat from Colorado) engaged in a hysterical witchhunt of Kelso, marching with her fellow termagants to the Senate to demand that their colleagues deny Kelso retirement with four stars. The *New York Times* editorialized against Kelso.

After a lifetime of honorable service to his country, Admiral Kelso barely managed to retire with four stars, in a 54–43 Senate vote. A majority of Democrats opposed Kelso, along with all the Republican women in the Senate—Kay Bailey Hutchison, Nancy Landon Kassebaum, and Arlen Specter. Had the Senate denied Kelso his retirement with four stars, this American hero would have received a pension of $67,000 per year, rather than the princely sum of $84,000 per year accorded a four-star admiral.

The Left's relentless attacks on Oliver North hardly require elaboration. He was investigated, charged with crimes, indicted by Lawrence Walsh, and his Senate campaign was destroyed. Al Gore compared North's supporters to Down syndrome children. Now Democrats are demanding that the Europeans be let into Iraq so they can release some more terrorists, while liberals do their part at home, carving up the colonels and admirals who capture the people who murder Americans. ■

☞ Liberals Meet Unexpected Resistance

MAY 1, 2003

Though many had anticipated a cakewalk for the media in undermining the war on terrorism, instead liberals are caught in a quagmire of good news about the war. Predictions that liberals would have an easy time embarrassing President Bush have met unexpected resistance. They're still looking for the bad news they said was there. Experts believe the media's quagmire results from severely reduced troops. The Left's current force is less than half the size of the coalition media that lost the Vietnam War.

It's been a tough few weeks all around for the antiwar crowd. On Sunday, the London *Telegraph* reported that documents had been discovered in Baghdad linking Saddam Hussein to Osama bin Laden. Hussein and bin Laden had a working relationship as far back as 1998, based on their mutual hatred of America and Saudi Arabia. The Osama files showed that the Iraqis were working feverishly to establish a "future relationship" with bin Laden and to "achieve a direct meeting with him." The meeting with Osama's envoy took place a few months before al Qaeda bombed two American embassies in East Africa.

As we go to print, it's Day 4 of the *New York Times*'s refusal to mention these documents. (And as we go to print on the book, it's Day 492 of the *New York Times*'s refusal to mention these documents.) Government documents have also been found in Iraq showing that a leading antiwar spokesman in Britain, Member of Parliament George Galloway, was in Saddam Hussein's pay. Galloway says the documents are "forgeries" and the Iraqis set him up. Scott Ritter, former UN arms inspector turned peacenik, erstwhile suspected pederast, immediately defended Galloway in a column in the London *Guardian*. With any luck, Tariq Aziz will now step in to defend Ritter.

At least Tariq Aziz knows he lost the war. American liberals are still hoping for a late-inning rally. But the war was so successful, they don't have any arguments left. Liberals can't even sound busy. In their usual parody of patriotism, liberals are masters of the long-winded statement that amounts to nothing. They can't go on TV and say nothing, but all they can find to complain about are some broken figurines.

Liberals said chemical weapons would be used against our troops. That didn't happen. They predicted huge civilian casualties. That didn't happen. They said Americans would turn against the war as our troops came home in body bags. That didn't happen. They warned of a mammoth terrorist attack in America if we invaded Iraq. That didn't happen. Just two weeks ago, they claimed American troops were caught in another Vietnam quagmire. That didn't happen. The only mishap liberals can carp about is that some figurines from an Iraqi museum were broken—a relief to college students everywhere who have ever been forced to gaze upon Mesopotamian pottery. We're not talking about Rodins here. So the Iraqis looted. Oh well. Wars are messy. Liberalism is part of a religious disorder that demands a belief that life is controllable.

At least we finally got liberals on the record against looting. It seems the looting in Iraq compared unfavorably with the "rebellion" in Los Angeles after the Rodney King verdict. When "rebels" in Los Angeles began looting, liberals said it was a sign of frustration—they were poor and hungry. (As someone noted at the time, apparently they were thirsty, too, since they hit a lot of liquor stores.) At least the Iraqis were careful to target the precise source of their oppression: They looted Saddam's palace, official government buildings—and the French cultural center.

However many precious pots were stolen, it has to be said: The Iraqi people behaved considerably better than the French. After Americans liberated Paris, thousands of Frenchmen were killed by other Frenchmen on allegations of collaboration with the Nazis. Subsequent scholarship has shown that charges of "collaboration" were often nothing more than a settling of personal grudges and family feuds—which was made easy by the fact that so many Frenchmen really did collaborate with the Nazis. The French didn't seem to resent the Nazi occupation very much. Nazi occupation is their default position. They began squirming only after Americans came in and imposed democracy on them.

Despondent over the success of the war in Iraq, liberals tried to cheer themselves up with the politics of personal destruction—their second favorite hobby after defending Saddam Hussein. Responding to the question of whether the Supreme Court should hold sodomy to be a fundamental constitutional right, Republican senator Rick Santorum made the indisputably true point that a general right to engage in consensual sex would logically include adultery, polygamy, and any number of sex acts prohibited by the states.

For the limited purpose of attacking Santorum, liberals agreed to stipulate that adultery is bad. After spending all of 1998 ferociously defending adultery as something "everyone" does and "everyone" lies about, liberals claimed to be shocked to the core that anyone would compare homosexuality to such a morally black sin as adultery. (While we're in a sensitive mood, how about the name "the DIXIE Chicks"? Isn't that name provocative to African-Americans?)

When you get liberals to come out against both looting and adultery in the same week, you know the Left is in a state of total disarray. They shouldn't feel so bad. Their boys put up a good fight in Iraq for seventeen days. ■

☞ We Don't Care

JUNE 4, 2003

Liberals have started in with their female taunting about weapons of mass destruction. The way they carry on, you would think they had caught the Bush administration in some shocking mendacity. (You know how the Left can't stand a liar.) For the sake of their tiresome argument, let's stipulate that we will find no weapons of mass destruction—or, to be accurate, no more weapons of mass destruction. Perhaps Hussein was using the three trucks capable of assembling poison gases to sell ice cream under some heretofore undisclosed UN "Oil for Popsicles" program.

Should we apologize and return the country to Saddam Hussein and his winsome sons? Should we have him on *Designer's Challenge* to put his palaces back in all their eighties Vegas splendor? Or maybe Uday and Qusay could spruce up each other's rape rooms on a very special episode of *Trading Spaces*? What is liberals' point?

No one cares. The question was never whether Saddam Hussein had weapons of mass destruction. We know he had weapons of mass destruction, because he used weapons of mass destruction against the Kurds, against the Iranians, and against his own people. The United Nations weapons inspectors repeatedly found Saddam's weapons of mass destruction in Iraq after the 1991 Gulf War, right up until Saddam threw them out in 1998. Justifying his impeachment-day bombing, Clinton cited the Iraqi regime's "nuclear, chemical and biological weapons programs." (Indeed, to date this constitutes the only evidence that Saddam didn't have weapons of mass destruction: Bill Clinton said he did.)

Liberals are now pretending that their position all along was that Saddam had secretly disarmed in the last few years without telling anyone. But that wasn't liberals' position—though it would finally explain the devilish question of why Saddam thwarted inspectors every inch of the way for twelve years, issued phony reports to the UN, and wouldn't allow flyovers or unannounced inspections: It was because he had nothing to hide!

Liberals also have to pretend that the only justification for war given by the Bush administration was that Iraq was knee-deep in nukes, anthrax, biological weapons, and chemical weapons—so much so that even Hans Blix couldn't help but notice them. But that wasn't the Bush administration's position.

Rather, it was that there were lots of reasons to get rid of Saddam Hussein and none to keep him. When President Bush gave the Hussein regime forty-eight hours' notice to quit Iraq, he said, "All the decades of deceit and cruelty have now reached an end." He told the Iraqi people there would be "no more wars of aggression against your neighbors, no more poison factories, no more executions of dissidents, no more torture chambers and rape rooms. The tyrant will soon be gone. The day of your liberation is near."

Liberals kept saying that's too many reasons. The *New York Times*'s leading hysteric, Frank Rich, complained, "We know Saddam Hussein is a thug and we want him gone. But the administration has never stuck to a single story in arguing the case for urgent pre-emptive action now." Since liberals never print retractions, they can say anything. What they said in the past is always deemed inadmissible and unfair to quote.

Contrary to their current self-advertisements, it was liberals who were citing Saddam's weapons of mass destruction—and with gusto—in order to argue *against* war with Iraq. They said America would suffer retaliatory strikes, there would be mass casualties, Israel would be nuked, our troops would be hit with Saddam's chemical weapons, it would be a Vietnam quagmire. Their position was "all" we needed to do was disarm him—which would have required a military occupation of Iraq and a systematic inspection of a thousand or so known Iraqi weapons sites without interference from the Hussein regime. In other words, pretty much what we're doing right now.

That's why liberals were so smitten with the idea of relying on UN weapons inspectors. As their title indicates, "weapons inspectors" inspect weapons. They don't stop torture, abolish rape rooms, feed the people, topple Saddam's statues, or impose democracy.

In January this year, the *New York Times*'s Nicholas Kristof cited the sort of dismal CIA report that always turns up in the hands of *New York Times* reporters, warning that Saddam might order attacks with weapons of mass destruction as "his last chance to exact vengeance by taking a large number of victims with him." Kristof said he opposed invading Iraq simply as a matter of the "costs and benefits" of an invasion, concluding we should not invade because there was "clearly a significant risk" that it would make America less safe.

In his native tongue, weaselese, Kristof claimed he would be gung-ho for war if only he were convinced we could "oust Saddam with minimal casualties and quickly establish a democratic Iraq." We've done that, and now he's angry that his predictions of calamity didn't come true. That's Bush's fault, too. Kristof says Bush manipulated evidence of weapons of mass destruction—an act of duplicity he calls "just as alarming" as a brutal dictator who has weapons of mass destruction.

If Americans were lied to, they were lied to by liberals who warned we would be annihilated if we attacked Iraq. The Left's leading intellectual light, Janeane Garofalo, was featured in an antiwar commercial before thewar, saying, "If we invade Iraq, there's a United Nations estimate that says, 'There will be up to half a million people killed or wounded.'" Now they're testy because they realize Saddam may never have had even a sporting chance to kill hundreds of thousands of Americans. ∎

☞ Taking Liberties

JULY 16, 2003

After Pearl Harbor, President Roosevelt rounded up more than one hundred thousand Japanese residents and citizens and threw them into internment camps. Indeed, both liberal deities of the twentieth century, FDR and Earl Warren, supported the internment of Japanese-Americans. In the twenties, responding to the bombing of eight government officials' homes, a Democrat-appointed attorney general arrested about six thousand people. The raids were conducted by A. Mitchell Palmer, appointed by still-revered segregationist Democrat Woodrow Wilson, who won the 1916 election based on lies about intelligence and war plans.

In response to the worst terrorist attack in the history of the world right here on U.S. soil, Attorney General John Ashcroft has detained fewer than a thousand Middle Eastern immigrants.

Ashcroft faces a far more difficult task than FDR did: Pearl Harbor was launched by the imperial government of Japan, not by Japanese-Americans living in California. The 9/11 Muslim terrorists, by contrast, were not only in the United States but, until the attack, had not broken any laws (aside from a few immigration laws, which liberals don't care about anyway). And yet, without internment camps or mass arrests, Ashcroft's carefully tailored policies have prevented another terrorist attack for almost two years since the 9/11 attack.

Naturally, therefore, the Democrats have focused like a laser beam on the perfidy of John Ashcroft. Representative Dick Gephardt recently said, "In my first five seconds as president, I would fire John Ashcroft as attorney general." (In his first four seconds, he would establish the AFL-CIO wing of the White House.)

Senator John Kerry has vowed, "When I am president of the United States, there will be no John Ashcroft trampling on the Bill of Rights." Experts are still trying to figure out why Kerry didn't mention his service in Vietnam during that last statement.

Senator John Edwards said that "we must not allow people like John Ashcroft to take away our rights and our freedoms." Apparently, we must, however, allow Janet Reno to run over our rights and our freedoms with a tank.

As usual, the Democrats have come up with a lot of bloody adjectives, but are a bit short in the way of particulars as to how Ashcroft is trampling on anyone's rights. Their case-in-chief seems to be Tarek Albasti. Albasti's story has now run in more than seventy overwrought news reports. His tale of torment led a *New York Times* report on terrorism suspects whose lives have been uprooted. He was the featured story on a PBS special about the civil-liberties crisis sweeping America.

Tarek Albasti is an Egyptian immigrant who married an American woman, brought seven of his Egyptian friends to America, and was enrolled in flight school when America was hit on

9/11. Based on a tip from the ex-wife of one of the men that they were plotting a suicide mission, the eight Egyptian immigrants were held for one week in October 2001—one week. The men were questioned and released. Since then, the government has issued copious apologies to the men and has expunged their records.

What are liberals claiming law enforcement was supposed to do with information like that? We're sorry for any Arabs whose dearest dream was to go into crop dusting, but this really isn't a good time. (Perhaps we could institute a five-day waiting period for Muslims who apply to U.S. flight schools for a background check.) Albasti told PBS—that's right, PBS, the television network owned, operated, and funded by the very same federal government Albasti now claims is oppressing him—that during his one-week confinement he was worried he would be hanged without anyone ever knowing what happened to him. For that remark alone, he should be deported. Is that what he thinks of America? But at least detained Arabs—and more to the point, their lawyers—have a monetary incentive to make absurd claims of persecution. What is the Democrats' excuse?

Based on the wails from our stellar crop of Democratic presidential candidates, you would think every Muslim in the country is cowering in fear of John Ashcroft. But their case-in-chief proving the existence of a civil-rights crisis in America is that eight Egyptian immigrants—one in flight school, no less—were detained for one week after the ex-wife of one of the men tipped off the FBI to a possible terrorist plot in the making.

Apparently, a lot of the false tips to law enforcement are coming from ex-wives. (Maybe Muslim men should have thought of that before introducing the burka.) Esshassah Fouad, a Moroccan student, was detained in Texas after his former wife accused him of being a terrorist. She is now serving a one-year prison sentence for making a false charge.

But someday, small children will be reading somber historical accounts about the dark night of fascism under John Ashcroft. Of course, thanks to Ashcroft, at least they'll be reading them in English rather than Arabic. If liberals applied half as much energy to some business endeavor as they do to creating the Big Lie, they would all be multimillionaires. What are we to make of people who promote the idea that America is in the grip of a civil-liberties emergency based on a hundred hazy stories of scowls and bumps and one-week detentions? Manifestly, there is no civil-liberties crisis in this country. People who claim there is must have a different goal in mind. ■

☞ How to Lose a War

SEPTEMBER 10, 2003

Vermont governor Howard Dean has been issuing diatribes against the Bush administration that would beat Tariq Aziz with severe menstrual cramps. This strategy has made him the runaway favorite of the Democratic Party. Even Mr. War Hero, John Kerry, is getting shellacked by Dean. At times Kerry seems almost ready to surrender, making him look even more French. (If only Kerry had a war record or an enormously rich spouse to fall back on!) In the wake of Dean's success, the entire Democratic Dream Team is beginning to talk like Dr. Demento. On the basis of their recent pronouncements, the position of the Democratic Party seems to be that Saddam Hussein did not hit us on 9/11, Halliburton did.

Explaining his vote for a war that he then immediately denounced, Kerry recently said his vote was just a head-fake, leading some to wonder how many of Kerry's other votes in the U.S. Senate this would explain. He voted for war only to bluff Saddam Hussein into letting in the UN weapons inspectors. "It was right to have a threat of force," Kerry said, "because it's only the threat of force that got Hans Blix and the inspectors back in the country." But he never imagined that Bush would interpret the open-ended war resolution as grounds to start an actual war! "The difference is," Kerry said, "I would have worked with the United Nations."

None of the Democrats has the guts to come out and demand that the United States turn tail and run when the going gets tough. If only one of them had the courage to demand cowardice like a real Democrat! Instead, they stamp their feet and demand that Bush go to the United Nations. Apparently it is urgent that we replace the best fighting force in the world with an "international peacekeeping force"—a task force both feared and respected worldwide for its ability to distribute powdered cheese to poor children. Inconsolable that their pleas to "work through" the UN did not stop Bush from invading Iraq and deposing Saddam Hussein, now the Democrats are eager for the UN to get involved. Since we didn't let the UN lose the war for us, the least we can do is let them screw up the peace. The idea that we would involve those swine in the postwar occupation of Iraq is so preposterous that it's under serious consideration as next week's slogan for the Howard Dean campaign.

I hesitate to raise it to the level of a serious argument by offering a rebuttal, but as luck would have it, we have two models for how to occupy a country after a war. At the risk of giving away the ending, getting "the allies" involved is not the successful model. After World War II, the United States ran the Japanese occupation unilaterally. Without the meddling of other nations, the Japanese occupation went off without a hitch. Within five years, General Douglas MacArthur had imposed a constitutional democracy on Japan with a bicameral legislature, a bill of rights, and an independent judiciary. Now the only trouble Japan causes us is its insistence on selling cars and small trucks to Americans at good prices.

By contrast, the German occupation was run as liberals would like to run postwar Iraq: a joint affair among "the Allies"—the United States, Britain, France, and the Soviet Union. It took forty-five years to clean up the mess they created. The Soviets bickered with the French, refusing to treat them as "allies" (on the admittedly sensible grounds that they didn't fight). While plundering their zone, the Soviets refused to relinquish any territory to France. Trying to be gallant, the Americans and the British carved a French zone out of their own sectors. The Soviets then blockaded Berlin and built the Berlin Wall, and Germany was split for the next half century. The British made Germany's war-torn economy worse by trying to impose socialism in their zone (as well as in their country). Predictably, economic disaster ensued. Over the next five years, the United States was required to spend the equivalent of about $200 billion annually in today's dollars to bail out Western Europe under the Marshall Plan. I note that there was no need for a Marshall Plan in Japan.

And the disastrous German occupation is the best-case scenario for "international peacekeeping." The less successful version includes our "international peacekeeping" in Somalia in 1993, leading to the corpses of American servicemen being defaced and one corpse being dragged through the streets by dancing, cheering savages. Showing that America is not a country to be toyed with, our draft-dodging, pot-smoking commander in chief responded by withdrawing our troops.

So naturally the Democrats are rooting for an international force in Iraq. The Democratic logic on national defense is: As soon as anyone in the military gets his hair mussed, we must pull out and bring in "international peacekeeping" forces. Our boys are in harm's way! People are dying! Bush lied when he said major combat operations were over! Let's run. That'll show 'em. It was not lost on Osama bin Laden that it only took eighteen dead in Somalia for the Great Satan to pull out. It should not be lost on Americans that this is what the Democrats are again demanding we do in Iraq. ■

☞ "The Plan"

NOVEMBER 5, 2003

The Democrats' new method of opposing the war on terrorism while pretending not to oppose the war on terrorism is to keep demanding that Bush produce a "plan." Senator John Kerry said the difference in how he would have prosecuted the war in Iraq is: "I would have planned." Yes, the invasion of Iraq was the usual unplanned, spur-of-the-minute thing that took eighteen months of discussion.

Wesley Clark recently complained that Bush had put American troops in harm's way, "without a plan." Of course, Clark's "plan" would have been to create a quagmire, just like he did in Bosnia.

Senator John Edwards noted for the record that when he voted for war with Iraq, "I said at the time that it was critical for us to have a plan. . . . This president has no plan of any kind that I can see." Maybe it's that Beatlemania mop-top that's blocking Edwards's view.

Senator Joe Lieberman—the one Democratic presidential candidate too conservative for Barbra Streisand—said that President Bush gave the American people "a price tag, not a plan." He said, "We in Congress must demand a plan." You know, like that incredibly detailed plan the Democrats have in place to spend $400 billion buying prescription drugs for elderly millionaires.

Senator Edward Kennedy said, "The administration had a plan to fight the war, but it had no plan to win the peace." Kennedy's idea of "a plan" consists of choosing a designated driver before heading out for the evening. The Democrats' urgent need for an "exit strategy" apparently first arose sometime after 1993, when Bill Clinton sent all those U.S. soldiers to Bosnia—who are still there.

Interviewing Vice President Dick Cheney on *Meet the Press*

about a month ago, Tim Russert echoed the theme, asking, "What is our plan for Iraq? How long will the 140,000 American soldiers be there? How many international troops will join them? And how much is this going to cost?" *Are we there yet, Daddy? Can I go to the bathroom? Are we there yet? How much longer?*

The same questions were asked of FDR over and over again by the American people after the Japanese attacked Pearl Harbor. *"How much will this cost?" "My husband's a sailor—how long will he be gone?" "What's your exit strategy, you warmonger?"* Wait—no. My mistake. That didn't happen.

The Democrats' incessant demand for a "plan" tends to suggest there is something called "The Plan," which would magically prevent bad things from ever happening—especially something as totally unexpected as violence in the Middle East. Violence in the Middle East constantly comes as a bolt out of the blue to liberals. We're at war with Islamic lunatics. They enjoy blowing things up and killing people. What further insights do liberals have to impart about this war? Bush said deposing Saddam Hussein and building a democracy in Iraq was an essential part of the war on terrorism. He did not say that invading Iraq would instantly end all Muslim violence and rainy days that make liberals blue.

A war is not as predictable as, say, a George Clooney movie (although generally more entertaining). Historian Stephen Ambrose described General Dwight Eisenhower's genius as a soldier, noting that "he often said that in preparing for battle, plans were essential, but that once the battle was joined, plans were useless." Transforming a blood-soaked police state dotted with mass graves into a self-governing republic might take slightly longer than this week's makeover on *Queer Eye for the Straight Guy.*

This is not the first time an evil tyrant was deposed only to have bloody elements of his regime remain. For example, it's been nearly five months since Howell Raines was removed as editor of the *New York Times.* What is Bill Keller's "plan" to turn the *New*

York Times around, and how long will it take? And when will liberals give us an "exit" strategy for their utterly failed forty-year "War on Poverty"? The U.S. military has had considerably more success in turning Iraq around than liberals have had in turning the ghettos around with their "War on Poverty." Indeed, so far, fewer troops have been killed by hostile fire since the end of major combat in Iraq than civilians were murdered in Washington, D.C., last year (239 deaths in Iraq compared with 262 murders in the U.S. capital). How many years has it been since we declared the end of major U.S. combat operations against Marion Barry's regime? How long before we just give up and pull out of that hellish quagmire known as Washington, D.C.?

The Democrats' conception of a "plan" is like the liberal fantasy that there's a room somewhere full of unlimited amounts of "free" money that we could just give to teachers and hospitals and poor people and AIDS sufferers and the homeless if only the bad, greedy Republicans would give us the key to that wonderful room. Republicans should claim the "plan" is in that room, in a lockbox.

It's interesting that after we've finally gotten liberals to give up on seven decades of trying to plan an economy, now they want to plan a war. Extra-credit question for the class: Comparing a peacetime economy with a war, which do you think is more likely to shoot back at the planners and require subsequent readjustments? No, no, not the usual hands from the eager YAFers in the front row. Are there any liberals in the back rows who want to take a stab at answering this one? Paul Krugman?

Needless to say, the Democrats have no actual plan of their own, unless "surrender" counts as a plan. They just enjoy complaining about every bombing, every attack from Muslim terrorists, every mishap. Back in the 1870s, General William Tecumseh Sherman told a group of graduating cadets, "There are many of you here who think that war is all glory. Well, war is all hell." We didn't start it, but we're going to win it. ∎

DECEMBER 14, 2003: Saddam Hussein is captured.

☞ It's Like Christmas in December!

DECEMBER 17, 2003

Say, has anyone asked Dick Gephardt if this falls under "miserable failure"? Obviously we'll have to wait for all the politics to play out, but at this stage it's hard to say which was worse for Howard Dean this week: the capture of Saddam Hussein or Al Gore's endorsement. Until Sunday, Governor Mean's big applause line in speeches has been to sneer about the Bush administration's failure to catch Saddam Hussein. It seems the governor is better at prescribing bitter pills than at swallowing them. In a speech to the Pacific Council the day after Saddam was captured, Dean nearly choked on the words, "The capture of Saddam is a good thing," before quickly adding, "but the capture of Saddam has not made America safer." (Possible headline: "Dean Says Saddam's Capture Good Thing, Just Not Really Good Thing.") If George W. Bush announced that a cure for cancer had been discovered, Democrats would complain about unemployed laboratory rats.

On Fox News Sunday, Senator John F. Kerry said of Saddam's capture, "This is a great opportunity for this president to get it right for the long term. And I hope he will be magnanimous, reach out to the UN, to allies who've stood away from us." It's as if he were reading my mind! After listening to all the bellyaching from European leftists for the past eight months, I think I speak for all Americans when I say I've been waiting for just the right opportunity to grovel to the French. And now we have it—a major win is the perfect opportunity! That Kerry, he has an uncanny sense for what the average American is thinking.

Actually, to tell the truth, he lost me with that one. Maybe it's a good opportunity for the French and the United Nations to reach out to us, but by what logic is this an opportunity for us to reach out to them? As I understand it, the situation is: We caught Saddam. So the obvious next move is . . .

    (a) Put him on trial.
    (b) Get information from him.
    (c) Torture him.
    (d) Turn him over to the Iraqis.
    (e) Appeal to the French.

What was interesting about Kerry's suggestion was that it was the exact same suggestion liberals were making when they claimed the war was going badly. The day before Saddam's capture, the *New York Times* editorialized, "The way to deal with all that is going wrong in Iraq remains as clear as it was on the day that Mr. Bush declared an end to major combat operations. . . . Instead of driving away France, Germany, Russia and Canada with financial sanctions, the president should be creating the room for compromise." Damn that Bush. He squandered the good will of a bunch of people who hate our guts.

I guess, this is what liberals mean by "a plan":

Military setback:	Appeal to the French.
Military victory:	Appeal to the French.
Saddam captured:	Appeal to the French.
Osama captured:	Appeal to the French.
Osama catches Saddam:	Appeal to the French.

In twenty-four months, Bush has perceptibly degraded terrorist operations throughout the world. The rebuilding in Iraq is going better than could possibly have been expected. Liberals don't care. They just want to turn everything over to the French. (And apparently, the recent capture of Saddam presents us with a golden opportunity to do so!) The Birchers were right about these people. They believe in world government more than they believe in the United States.

One strongly suspects that the White House sat on the story of Saddam's capture for a day so the *Times* could put out its regular Sunday bad news: "A Baghdad Neighborhood, Once Hopeful, Now Reels as Iraq's Turmoil Persists," "Saboteurs, Looters and Old Equipment Work Against Efforts to Restart Iraqi Oil Fields," "It's Going to Be a Bloody Christmas." The *New York Times* hasn't looked this foolish . . . well, I guess since the day before. Liberals should perk up. It's not all bad news. True, Saddam Hussein has been captured. But Norman Mineta is still at large. ■

☞ Al Qaeda Barks, the Spanish Fly
MARCH 17, 2004

After a terrorist attack by al Qaeda that left hundreds of their fellow countrymen dead, Spanish voters immediately voted to give the terrorists what they want—a socialist government that opposes America's war on terrorism. Al Qaeda has changed a government.

Until the bombings last week, the center-right Popular Party of outgoing Prime Minister José Maria Aznar had been sailing to victory. But then the al Qaeda bombs went off and Spaniards turned out in droves to vote against the government that had been a staunch Bush ally in the war on terrorism. (I guess it's okay for a Spanish socialist to "politicize" a terrorist attack just to get elected.)

In a videotaped message, the al Qaeda "military commander" for Europe claimed credit for the bombings, saying that the terrorist attack was meant to punish Spain for supporting the war in Iraq. The message came as a total shock to liberals, who have been furiously insisting that Iraq had absolutely nothing to do with al Qaeda. Apparently al Qaeda didn't think so. After the Madrid bombings, it looks like liberals and terrorists will have to powwow on whether there was an Iraq/al Qaeda link. Two hundred dead Spaniards say there was.

The *New York Times* called the Spanish election "an exercise in healthy democracy." And an ATM withdrawal with a gun to your head is a "routine banking transaction." Instead of vowing to fight the people who killed their fellow citizens, the Spanish decided to vote with al Qaeda on the war. A murdering terrorist organization said, "Jump!" and an entire country answered, "How high?" One Spaniard who decided to switch his vote in reaction to the bombings told the *Times:* "Maybe the Socialists will get our troops out of Iraq and al Qaeda will forget about Spain so we will be less frightened." That's the fighting spirit! If the violent Basque separatist group only killed more people, Spain would surely give them what they want, too.

After his stunning upset victory, Socialist Party leader José Luis Rodríguez Zapatero said he would withdraw Spanish troops from Iraq if the United States does not turn over Iraq to the United Nations. He also vowed that all of Spain's remaining trains will run on time. Zapatero said the war with Iraq had "only caused violence" and "there were no reasons for it." One reason for the war, which would be a sufficient reason for a more manly country, is that the people who just slaughtered two hundred Spaniards didn't like it. But like the Democrats, the Spanish hate George Bush more than they hate the terrorists. Zapatero said the war in Iraq was based on "lies" and called on President Bush and Tony Blair to "do some reflection and self-criticism." So don't think of the Spanish election as a setback for freedom—think of it as a preview of life under President John Kerry!

What kind of lunatic would blame Bush for two hundred Spaniards killed by al Qaeda bombs? Oh wait—Howard Dean just did. Summarizing the views of socialists everywhere, Dean said, "The president was the one who dragged our troops to Iraq, which apparently has been a factor in the death of two hundred Spaniards over the weekend." Yes, with 1,700 dead or injured Spaniards, George Bush certainly has some explaining to do. What have the terrorists ever done besides kill and maim thousands of innocent civilians? Bush isn't fully funding No Child Left Behind, for God's sake!

Before he was put into office because he supported policies favored by al Qaeda terrorists, appeasement candidate Zapatero said, "I want Kerry to win." Kerry is also supported by North Korean dictator Kim Jong II, who broadcasts Kerry speeches over Radio Pyongyang with favorable commentary. So now Kerry really does have two foreign leaders on record supporting him: a socialist terrorist-appeaser and a Marxist mass murderer who dresses like Bea Arthur.

Zapatero predicted that his own victory would help the antiwar party "in the duel between Bush and Kerry." *Would you mind repeating that, sir? I was distracted by that large white flag you're waving.* However Spain's election affects Americans, we can be sure that Spain's surrender to terrorism hasn't been lost on the terrorists. It's difficult to imagine the American people responding to a new terrorist attack by deciding to placate the terrorists, as the Spanish did. A mollusk wouldn't react that way to an attack. Only a liberal could be so perverse.

No matter how many of our European allies may surrender to the terrorists, America will never be alone. This is a country founded in a covenant with God by people who had to flee Europe to do it. Sailing to the New World in 1630 on the ship *Arabella,* the Puritans' leader and governor, John Winthrop, said Americans were entering a covenant with God to create a "city upon a hill." He said we would be judged by all the world if we ever broke that covenant. But if we walked with God, "We shall find that the God of Israel is among us, when 10 of us shall be able to resist a thousand of our enemies." He has intervened in our affairs before, such as in 1776, 1861, and 1980. With the Spanish election, we are witnessing a capitulation to savagery that makes full-scale war inevitable. The Democratic candidate wants to represent godless Europeans. The Republican candidate wants to represent Americans. As Winthrop said, "The eyes of all people are upon us." ∎

☞ Tit for Tet

MAY 25, 2004

Abu Ghraib is the new Tet offensive. By lying about the Tet offensive during the Vietnam War, the media managed to persuade Americans we were losing the war, which demoralized the nation and caused us to lose the war. And people say reporters are lazy.

The immediate consequence of the media's lies about the Tet offensive was a 25 percent drop in support for the war. The long-term consequence for America was twelve years in the desert until Ronald Reagan came in and saved the country.

Now liberals are using their control of the media to persuade the public that we are losing the war in Iraq. Communist dictators may have been ruthless murderers bent on world domination, but they displayed a certain degree of rationality. America may not be able to wait out twelve years of Democrat pusillanimity now that we're dealing with Islamic lunatics who slaughter civilians in suicide missions while chanting "Allah Akbar!"

And yet the constant drumbeat of failure, quagmire, Abu Ghraib, Bush-lied-kids-died has been so successful that merely to say the war in Iraq is going well provokes laughter. The distortions have become so pervasive that Michael Moore teeters on the brink of being considered a reliable source.

If President Bush mentions our many successes in Iraq, it is evidence that he is being "unrealistically sunny and optimistic," as Michael O'Hanlon, of the liberal Brookings Institution, put it.

O'Hanlon's searing indictment of the operation in Iraq is that we need to "make sure they have some budget resources that they themselves decide how to spend that are not already pre-allocated." So that's the crux of our challenge in Iraq: Make sure their "accounts receivable" columns all add up. Whenever great matters are at stake, you can always count on liberals to have some pointless, womanly complaint.

We have liberated the Iraqi people from a brutal dictator who gassed his own people, had weapons of mass destruction, invaded his neighbors, harbored terrorists, funded terrorists, and had reached out to Osama bin Laden. Liberals may see Saddam's mass graves in Iraq as half-full, but I prefer to see them as half-empty.

So far, we have found chemical and biological weapons— brucella and Congo-Crimean hemorrhagic fever, ricin, sarin, aflatoxin—and long-range missiles in Iraq.

The terrorist "stronghold" of Karbala was abandoned last week by Islamic crazies loyal to cleric Moqtada al-Sadr who slunk away when it became clear that no one supported them. Iraqis living in Karbala had recently distributed fliers asking the rebels to please leave, further underscoring one of the principal remaining problems in Iraq—the desperate need for more Kinko's outlets. Last weekend, our troops patrolled this rebel "stronghold" without a shot being fired.

The entire Kurdish region—one-third of the country—is patrolled by about three hundred American troops, which is fewer than it takes to patrol the Kennedy compound in Palm Beach on Easter weekends.

But the media tell us this means we're losing. The goalpost of success keeps shifting as we stack up a string of victories. Before the war, *New York Times* columnist Nicholas Kristof warned that war with Iraq would be a nightmare: "We won't kill Saddam, trigger a coup or wipe out his Republican Guard forces." (Unless, he weaseled his way out, "we're incredibly lucky.")

We've done all that! How incredibly lucky.

Kristof continued, "We'll have to hunt out Saddam on the ground—which may be just as hard as finding Osama in Afghanistan, and much bloodier."

We've captured Saddam! And it wasn't bloody! Indeed, the most harrowing aspect of Saddam's capture was that he hadn't bathed or been de-liced for two months.

Kristof also said, "Our last experience with street-to-street fighting was confronting untrained thugs in Mogadishu, Somalia. This time we're taking on an army with possible bio- and chemical weapons, 400,000 regular army troops and supposedly seven million more in Al Quds militia."

And yet, somehow, our boys defeated them in just a few weeks! Incredibly lucky again! And just think: all of this accomplished without even having a "plan."

Now we're fighting directly with Islamic loonies crawling out of their ratholes from around the entire region—which liberals also said wouldn't happen. Remember how liberals said the Islamic loonies hated Saddam Hussein—hated him!—because he was a "secularist"? As geopolitical strategist Paul Begala put it, Saddam would never share his weapons with terrorists because "those Islamic terrorists would use them against Saddam Hussein because he's secular."

Well, apparently the crazies have put aside their scruples about Saddam's secularism to come out in the open where they can be shot by American troops rather than fighting on the streets of Manhattan. (Where the natives would immediately surrender.)

The beauty of being a liberal is that history always begins this morning. Every day liberals can create a new narrative that destroys the past as it occurred. *We have always been at war with Eastasia.*

To be sure, Iraq is not a bed of roses. As the Brookings Institution scholar said, we have yet to give the Iraqis "budget resources" that "are not already pre-allocated." I take it back: It is a quagmire. ■

☞ This Is History Calling— Quick, Get Me Rewrite!

JUNE 3, 2004

The invasion of Iraq has gone fabulously well, exceeding everyone's expectations—certainly exceeding the doomsday scenarios of liberals. The Bush-haters' prewar predictions—hundreds of thousands dead, chemical attacks on our troops, retaliatory terrorist attacks in the United States, an invasion by Turkey, oil facilities in flames, and apocalyptic environmental consequences—have proven to be about as accurate as Bill Clinton's "legally accurate" statements about Monica Lewinsky.

Inasmuch as they can't cite any actual failures in Iraq, liberals busy themselves by claiming the administration somehow "misled" them about the war.

As I understand it, there would be no lunatics shouting "Bush lied, kids died!" if Paul Wolfowitz had admitted before the war that Saddam "probably hadn't rebuilt his nuclear program"—the one that was unilaterally blown up by the Israelis in 1981, thank God. What Wolfowitz should have said is that "proof beyond a reasonable doubt is the way you think about law enforcement, and I think we're much closer to being in a state of war than being in a judicial proceeding."

Liberals would be all sugar and sweetness if only—instead of blathering about nukes, nukes, nukes—Wolfowitz had forthrightly conceded back in 2002 that "there's an awful lot we don't know, an awful lot that we may never know, and we've got to think differently about standards of proof here."

Also, I assume we wouldn't be hearing that the administration is frustrated by its failure to instantly create a Jeffersonian democracy in Iraq if Wolfowitz had said something like "Well, Japan isn't Jeffersonian democracy, either." If only Wolfowitz had lowered expectations by saying that "even if [Iraq] makes it only Romanian style, that's still such an advance over anywhere else in the Arab world."

Also, the media would have no grounds for complaint if Wolfowitz had said Iraqi democracy "is not the president's declared purpose of 'regime change' in Iraq, which is to get rid of a very bad man." If only he had mentioned that Saddam Hussein "has been known to have children tortured in front of their parents."

But guess what? That is exactly what Wolfowitz did say! All these quotes are from a September 22, 2002, article in the *New York Times Magazine* written by Bill Keller, now editor-in-chief at the seditious rag. The last paragraph, about Saddam's torture of children, is Keller paraphrasing Wolfowitz; the rest are direct quotes from the wily neoconservative himself.

But you'd have to put liberals in Abu Ghraib to get them to tell the truth about what people were saying before the war—and then the problem would be that most liberals would enjoy those activities. No torture has yet been devised that could get a liberal to mention the poor, beleaguered Kurds dancing in the streets because Saddam is gone.

To refresh everyone's recollection, before the war began, the Democrats' argument was that Iraq was not an "imminent" threat to the United States. The Republicans' argument was: By the time the threat is imminent, Chicago will be gone. Bush's January 2003 State of the Union address specifically responded to the Democrats' demand that we wait for nuclear and biological threats to be "imminent" before we act, saying that if we waited for this threat to "fully and suddenly emerge, all actions and words, and all recriminations would come too late." But now liberals want to have their Nigerian yellow cake and eat it, too.

In January 2003—or three months after Senator Tom Daschle voted for the Iraq war resolution hoping to fool the voters of South Dakota this November—he was horrified that Bush seemed to be actually contemplating war with Iraq! According to Daschle, Bush should have waited for Iraq to grow into a problem of crisis proportions before deciding to do anything—citing the Cuban Missile Crisis as a model to be emulated. "If we have proof of nuclear and biological weapons," Daschle asked, "why doesn't [Bush] show that proof to the world as President Kennedy did forty years ago when he sent Adlai Stevenson to show the world U.S. photographs of offensive missiles in Cuba?"

The answer is: Because by the time Saddam had nuclear

weapons, we wouldn't be able to do anything. That's why it's known as the "Cuban Missile Crisis," not the "Cuban Missile Triumph."

Before the war, Democrats were carping about the Bush administration's inability to predict the future and tell us everything that would happen in Iraq after the war. On MSNBC in September 2002, for example, Robert Menendez (Democrat of New Jersey) was complaining that Secretary of Defense Donald Rumsfeld "didn't have an answer for what happens in a post-Saddam Iraq." But now liberals are acting as if the Bush administration said they knew exactly what would happen after liberating a country from a thirty-year barbaric dictatorship—and got it wrong.

The good news is: Liberals' antiwar hysteria seems to have run its course. I base this conclusion on Al Gore's lunatic antiwar speech last week. Gore always comes out swinging just as an issue is about to go south. He's the stereotypical white guy always clapping on the wrong beat. Gore switched from being a pro-defense Democrat to a lefty peacenik—just before the 9/11 attack. He grew a beard—just in time for an attack on the nation by fundamentalist Muslims. He endorsed Howard Dean—just as the orange-capped Deaniacs were imploding. Gore even went out and got really fat—just before America officially gave up carbs. This guy is always leaping into the mosh pit at the precise moment the crowd parts. Mark my words: Now that good old Al has come lunging in, the antiwar movement is dead. ■

3

A Muslim by Any
Other Name Blows Up
Just the Same

■

☛ John Davis: American Hero

JULY 29, 1999

My life is almost complete. Tonight I was on a TV show on "extreme catfighting"—the closest I'll ever get to Jerry Springer—*and* I shook hands with John Davis, hero to frequent flyers everywhere. Now if I can just manage to rear-end Kate Michelman of NARAL I can call it a day.

Mild-mannered Davis was attempting to fly Continental Airlines to Florida with his wife and toddler child a couple of weeks ago. (For frequent flyers, your stomach is already in a knot.) After the standard two-hour delay, Davis's child broke from his parents and ran onto the jetway leading to the aircraft, presumably hoping to start a trend. The accounts of the resulting altercation begin to differ at this point, so, to be fair, I'll go with the version that reflects most poorly on my hero.

As John Davis and his wife were running for their pre-preboarding toddler on the jetway, the Continental Airlines ticket-taker blocked Mr. Davis's way, stood between father and child, and informed Mr. Davis that he could not enter the jetway without a boarding pass.

Remember, all this Continental Airlines readily admits.

The father responded the way fathers are wont to do in such situations, which is violently. Davis is a slight man; the damage he did to the ticket-taker reminds one of biology class lessons on adrenaline that involve mothers lifting Volkswagens to release pinned children.

The lesson of this and many other happy travel stories is that humans are fascists by nature. Give some humans control over other humans and they will seamlessly transform into brownshirts, patting you down, ripping apart your belongings, breaking your valuables, and telling you where to stand, to drink, and to smoke and when to go to the bathroom. And if you complain they will arrest you. Worse, they will bump you or your luggage or take away your nice aisle seat and give you a center seat.

But the head of Continental Airlines reacted as if his faithful employee had brilliantly averted another toddler-down-the-jetway scam. He called for a federal law, not banning hairless simians from total control over other people's lives at airports, but banning "violent" passengers from the airways. Interestingly, he said "air rage" cannot be tolerated—no matter what the reason.

No matter what the reason? Even in case of rape or incest, or if the mother's life is in danger? A No-Matter-What-the-Reason standard could come only from a person who flashes a "Chief Executive, Continental Airlines" card when he flies.

Admittedly, I have seen plenty of dumb and nasty passengers—some Hollywood celebrities don't even have the common courtesy to wait their turn to defecate on a beverage cart—and also plenty of patient, saintly airline employees, who have completely suppressed the human instinct to fascism. And that's not just the Stockholm syndrome talking.

But if we're passing federal laws, a really useful federal law would be one that prohibits pilots from talking. There is nothing that makes you feel like you are in Orwell's *1984* so much as being trapped on an airplane with a pilot who thinks he's Shecky Greene. You can't leave the plane, obviously. You generally can't even leave your seat or turn on your Walkman. The only other places in this country where you can be forced to listen to someone talk are prison and grade school. And prison guards and teachers have more interesting information than "If you look out your right window, you can see Cleveland."

Several years ago, one of my father's business colleagues was trapped on a plane when the pilot began to play out his fantasy of being a tour guide. The colleague called a flight attendant over, handed her a section of his paper, and asked her to give it to the pilot so he'd stop with his incessant jabbering. When the plane landed, the businessman was arrested. That's a true story.

Americans may vote for creeping socialism, but deep in their beings they sense that they are still free, that this is not yet Orwell's *1984*. As long as there are some people who are not willing to roll over for the airline fascists and be docile sheep—*Stand in line, open your bag, walk through the metal detector again, take off your belt, take off your coat, take off your jewelry, stand in line, turn on your computer, present your ID, has anyone given you anything?, no drinking, no smoking, you'll have to check that, stand here, sit down, don't get up, put your seatback up, turn off your computer, we're at 30,000 feet and if you look to your left you can see Pittsburgh . . .* whoops! and another plane down not because of the Waterford crystal the X-ray goon just broke in your carry-on luggage, but because of pilot error—there will be John Davises.

Most of the fascistically controlling airline regulations are the result of—surprise!—government regulations. I would risk terrorist sabotage not to have to be mauled by the X-ray crew, who see their sole life's work as trying to cause passengers to miss planes. That would be a completely rational trade-off, by the way, but the government won't allow consumers to make it.

On average, there is one fatality for every 3 million people who fly on a commercial aircraft. You are more likely to drown in your bathtub than die in an airplane. Ten times more likely. In any six-month period, more people will die in car accidents than have ever died in airplanes—in the history of flight.

But the government doesn't require anyone to shake you down before you take a bath. You don't get the third degree every time you get behind the wheel of a car. So why are the consumers of airline travel patted down and interrogated like denizens of a crack house?

Most of those rare air flight fatalities are the result of accidents, not terrorists, anyway. Accidents are caused by pilots, government bureaucrats, and airline personnel—not passengers. But every time there's an airline crash due to pilot error the government immediately springs into action by piling on yet more intrusive passenger interrogations.

Moreover, if the airlines weren't required by the government to engage in moronic exercises like asking every passenger if he packed his own bags (what are the odds that a terrorist would answer, "Why no, the bomb squad back at terrorist headquarters did"?), they would undoubtedly come up with actually plausible methods to keep their planes accident- and terrorist-free. In-flight bombings are terrible PR.

Airlines could, for example, put undercover armed guards on all their flights. They could allow passengers to fly armed. This would not only make air travel safer, it would prove once and for all the most compelling argument for gun rights by posing the rhetorical question, "Would you ever try to hijack a plane if you knew that every passenger aboard might be armed?" Imagine how much more pleasant airline travel would be if the airport security moron were required to ask every passenger, "And did you load your concealed weapon yourself today, sir?" The government already carves out a little exception for itself on the no-guns rule. FBI agents are allowed to pack heat on commercial airlines, and let me hasten to add, it wasn't armed civilians who mistakenly shot down Randy Weaver's wife, child, and dog.

Alternatively, airlines could allow frequent flyers to submit to personal investigations in return for a special airline passport allowing them to skip the Make-Them-Miss-Their-Flights X-ray crew. (These would be just like the ones flight attendants and pilots already have.)

But creative, consumer-friendly solutions are not possible, because the government has given itself monopoly control of air safety.

Let's just hope they don't find out about bathtub drownings. ■

☞ Where's Janet Reno When We Need Her?

SEPTEMBER 20, 2001

Just as I predicted, the new "security procedures" adopted by the U.S. Department of Transportation in response to the most deadly hijackings in history will be incredibly burdensome for millions of American travelers but, at the same time, will do absolutely nothing to deter hijackers. The single most effective thing we could do in this country to protect travelers from terrorist attacks would be to abolish the Department of Transportation.

The government's logical calculus on flight security has long been: Really Annoying = Safe Plane. (Does anyone not know how to use a seat belt? Say you were an alien from a distant galaxy and had never in your entire life seen a seat belt before—couldn't you figure it out?) The FAA's new hijacker repellant is this: Passengers will now have to show boarding passes to get to the gates. This wily stratagem will stop cold any hijackers on suicide missions who forgot to buy airline tickets! It's times like this that I get down on my knees and thank God we have a federal Department of Transportation.

The genius security procedures laboriously implemented by the government over the past decade certainly served this country well on Bloody Tuesday. The real puzzler is how the hijackers managed to evade the "Did you pack your own bags?" trap. Only further investigation will solve that mystery. If only we'd implemented the tough new "Cross your heart and hope to die?" follow-up question in time!

Last week a CNN anchor raised the "Did you pack your own bags?" dragnet and somberly remarked—this is a quote—"No one will answer those questions so cavalierly again." We certainly won't. We will all remember that if those asinine questions hadn't been asked of millions of travelers day in day out year after year, enragingly stupid every time, nineteen murderous hijackers might have boarded four separate commercial jets in America almost simultaneously one morning. Oh—no, wait. The hijackers weren't foiled. But somehow the manifest irrelevance of the "Did you pack your own bags?" question has become its principal selling point.

We are also grateful for the magnetometers. The McDonald's rejects who man the machines are so efficient and courteous, you hardly notice them anymore. That's sarcasm. Despite addled TV commentators claiming that, heretofore, travelers had breezed right through the metal detectors, these are obviously people who haven't flown since the fifties.

Back on Earth, the sullen, dictatorial security personnel invariably stop all passengers who are not likely to punch them (girls), rifle through their belongings, slowly wipe some wand over their computers (a procedure that takes just long enough for you to almost miss your plane), carefully examine their persons—down to the tiny metallic bra-strap hook—and then methodically break any crystal vases the passenger is carrying. So don't tell me they're lazy.

It may be annoying, but the rash of hijackings by Connecticut WASP girls surely explains the time-consuming—but still somehow completely useless—examination of my personal effects. We all have to make sacrifices for airline safety.

Even with the shakedowns, I personally have carried a deadly plastic shiv and FBI Mace through metal detectors dozens of times. Dozens. I wasn't even trying. I just forgot I was carrying them. Unless the government is going to require passengers, crew, and pilots to travel naked and with no luggage, there is no spot search devisable that can keep the skies safe—no matter how irritating.

Consequently, I propose an all-new standard for airline safety procedures. Bear with me here, but my idea is this: We should be looking for procedures that make the airplane safer. With this new standard as my guide, I have a five-point plan.

1. Pilots should be the first to board the plane and the cockpit door should be locked like Fort Knox behind them, impenetrable by anyone until the plane lands. The cabin crew should be able to communicate with the pilots only to request an emergency landing. But nothing that needs to be spoken over an intercom, such as "Fly to Kabul or every passenger gets his throat slit."

2. Every flight should carry at least two undercover agents capable of discharging hollow-point bullets, poison darts, and electric shocks. The armed guards have to be incognito so that hijackers can't knock them off—and also to improve in-flight courtesy.

3. We should require passports to fly domestically. Passports can be forged, but they can also be checked with the home country in case of any suspicious-looking swarthy males. It will be a minor hassle, but it's better than national ID cards. It's also far less annoying than being told how to use a seat belt.

4. All nineteen hijackers in last week's attack appear to have been noncitizens. As far as the Constitution is concerned, visitors to this country are here at the nation's pleasure. Congress could pass a law tomorrow requiring that all aliens from Arabic countries leave. Congress could certainly pass a law requiring that all aliens get approval from the INS before boarding an airplane in the United States.

5. Of course, any security procedure imaginable can be breached by well-financed fanatics willing to commit suicide for their cause. The main deterrent to terrorists is to create despair and hopelessness by destroying their home sponsors. Donald Rumsfeld is just the man for the job. But on the off chance that he is insufficiently ruthless, someone should tell Janet Reno that Islamic fundamentalism is an offshoot of the Branch Davidians. ■

☞ HillaryCare for the Airports
NOVEMBER 8, 2001

The main sticking point between the Senate and House versions of the aviation security bill now headed for conference is whether airport magnetometers will be run with private-sector values or the smooth efficiency of the Department of Motor Vehicles. In the event that Congress chooses the latter, anyone planning to travel by air during this calendar year is hereby advised to leave for the airport now.

This is lesson #1,475,607,033 on the point that the free market is a counterintuitive concept. Only liberals still associate the words "government employee" with "efficiency" and "competence." Without constant reminders of the material bounty produced by the glorious Soviet Union, people, by which I mean "liberals," will list toward socialist solutions time and again.

Even the lily-livered Europeans, usually cited warmly by the Left for their progressive views on adultery, have abandoned the idea of government bureaucrats running security at airports. If there's one thing the Europeans know it's how efficient a government employee who can't be fired can be. But the *New York Times* has been editorializing daily against private security firms in deference to—and I quote—"a highly trained federal force." The only rhetorical flourish the *Times* avoided was to call private sector workers "shiftless." When was the last time you heard someone say, "The help here is way too slow and incompetent. Why don't they hire some civil service people"?

Far be it from me to defend airport security personnel, but making them government employees, I assure you, will not improve matters. We're not going to call out the Marines to rifle through little old ladies' handbags before they board flights to Cleveland. This is HillaryCare for the airports.

The reason airports already resemble the torture chambers in Orwell's *1984* is that they are natural monopolies. If you live in Chicago, you can't decide you really prefer to fly out of Dallas because you like the airport better. You're stuck in Chicago, and O'Hare knows you're stuck with Chicago airports. (There is no other explanation for why there even is an airport in Chicago. Planes are only allowed to fly in or out of O'Hare for approximately twenty minutes every week.) The absence of competition among airports leads to phenomenally stupid inconveniences that would be unfathomable in a competitive environment.

Only a monopoly would ban the world's most popular soft drink, Coca-Cola, from being sold on its premises or sell a tasteless tuna salad sandwich for about what you'd pay for a kobe beef steak dinner in Tokyo. Only a monopoly would have bathrooms that still employ those ridiculous Potemkin hand dryers in lieu of something that might possibly dry your hands . . . like, say, paper towels. Only a monopoly could force people to stand in two-hour lines in order to answer phenomenally stupid questions with a straight face or risk being denied service. Natural monopolies everywhere adopt a philosophy on customer service best summed up with the words, "Take it or leave it."

The liberal's solution to a monopoly is invariably to create an even bigger monopoly by turning it over to the federal government. Not surprisingly, the only experiences nearly as unpleasant as commercial air travel are those enterprises run by the government. If you had to get up tomorrow morning and get a driver's license or a lamp, which would you dread more? At least natural monopolies only lead to bathrooms with no paper towels. Government monopolies have been known to lead to the Khmer Rouge.

The only effective solution to a natural monopoly is for the government to create artificial competition by setting standards (off the top of my head, for example: no box cutters on airplanes) and fining airports that fail random spot checks. In other words, conform to these national standards or we'll penalize you monetarily. We could call it the No Airport Left Behind Act. Even for major criminal offenses like cigarette-smoking in Los Angeles bars, the government doesn't send in a government workforce to tend bar. It fines bars that fail to comply with the law. Moreover, I wish the security guards luck, but keeping weapons off planes is not the linchpin to safe skies anyway. It better not be: We can't keep weapons out of prisons; we certainly can't keep them off airplanes.

The airport shakedowns do, however, comply with the government's primary criterion for airport safety, which is that all travelers be inconvenienced with absolutely no increase in airline safety. Thus, one of the FAA's recent safety innovations is to demand photo IDs from passengers at various checkpoints throughout the airport. For maximum annoyance, this includes the moment at which you are about to board the plane, when you are balancing carry-on luggage, a newspaper, and a Starbucks coffee, and clenching a boarding pass between your teeth. Studies have shown that demanding photo ID is a highly effective method of keeping vampires off airplanes.

There's only one small flaw in the photo ID requirement: There is absolutely no reason to imagine terrorists don't have photo IDs. Indeed, the 9/11 terrorists not only had ID cards but blessed their ID cards. Instruction #12 of the terrorists' pre-attack manual was "bless your ID, your passport, and all of your papers."

The instructions give another clue to the hijackers' state of mind that, in the hands of creative safety professionals, might lead to a practical safety check: Instruction #1 was to put on cologne; Instruction #2 was to shower. See—it doesn't work if you put on cologne and *then* take the shower. (Instruction #3: "For a definition of the word 'shower,' consult the glossary.")

If the government demanded results, airports wouldn't have time to engage in man's truly oldest profession, oppressing his fellow man. Instead, this natural monopoly would finally be forced to stop harassing passengers for the fun of it and to adopt safety procedures that would have the novel attribute of making planes safe. ∎

☞ The New Roman Arena: Airports
NOVEMBER 22, 2001

If the airlines had hired the most expensive consultants in the country to help them figure out a way to make the flying experience even more unpleasant than it was before September 11, the consultants would have given up in despair. But chalk one up to American ingenuity: The airlines have done it on their own!

Getting a head start on the holiday season, airport security guards have already begun their Christmas shopping by stealing travelers' belongings. Unless they pilfer possessions worth more to you than making your plane and getting to wherever you are going, there's nothing you can do. And the guards know there's nothing you can do, which adds to the innate charm of airport security personnel. A security guard took a piece of my jewelry at the Spokane Airport last Saturday with approval from his Olympic Security supervisor. The alert supervisor called airport police when I asked for her name.

I want it back. It was a silver charm from Aspen in the shape of a bullet with a great deal of sentimental value. But in a strange coincidence, a few hours later it was missing from the Olympic Security box of confiscated loot. It's probably already wrapped. I'm now carrying gift certificates from Zales in my carry-on bag just to save the guards time during the busy holiday season.

If you are not a halfwit—and not Christmas shopping from other people's stuff—you will instantly recognize that a silver charm is a silver charm, and it doesn't matter if it's in the shape of the anthrax virus. Even a real bullet can't cause any harm without a gun. A silver charm soldered to a key chain is less threatening than a tube of lipstick. Of course, my lipstick would undoubtedly also have been deemed a grave security risk by Olympic Security if it had been in the supervisor's color. Since September 11 alone, that silver-charm key chain has been through airport security dozens of times. But security guards are on high alert. There are only twenty-nine more shopping days till Christmas!

There has been more caterwauling about the Bureau of Prisons listening to the conversations of prison inmates suspected of plotting terrorist attacks on America than to the universal physical inspections of Americans trying to board airplanes. If law-enforcement officers ever dared paw through the belongings of an Egyptian immigrant named Mustafa with the fascistic intensity of airport security patting down little old ladies suspected of flying to Iowa, liberals would explode in righteous indignation.

As long as the airlines insist on going through the manifestly absurd exercise of treating all passengers alike in some obscure desire to impress the *New York Times* editorial page, they ought to abandon the personal inspections altogether. It's absurd to imagine that personal inspections are going to keep weapons off airplanes—even by turning airports into the pleasant and welcoming environment of a federal penitentiary. You'd keep more weapons off planes just by banning Christian Slater from commercial air travel.

After airport security confiscates any jewelry that might make a nice Christmas gift, the airlines hand out weapons on the planes.

They still serve wine in glass goblets that can be smashed to create jagged glass daggers. They serve soda in cans that can be twisted apart to create razor-sharp knives. Not to worry, though. If you think about it for up to three seconds, it will occur to you that terrorists don't want to knife a few passengers. If terrorists just wanted to kill a bunch of people in one place, they could go to shopping malls, restaurants, movie theaters—anywhere, really. So why aren't there security guards at the Cineplex pawing through our purses and stealing our jewelry?

Airports are attractive to terrorists for one reason: There are airplanes at airports! And what is alluring about airplanes is that they can be turned into cruise missiles or blown up in the air. The only safety precaution that will make the planes safer would be impenetrable cockpit doors and bomb checks for all cargo—two security measures airlines doggedly refuse to implement.

While still completely vulnerable to another terrorist attack, Americans submit like good Germans to these purposeless airport shakedowns—which are about as useful as those national guardsmen hanging around in airports right after 9/11 carrying unloaded rifles. Most sickening is the relish other Americans are taking in their new roles as fascist storm troopers. In a famous study conducted at Yale in the sixties by professor Stanley Milgram, members of the public willingly administered what they thought were fatal electric shocks to another human being—simply because they were told to do so by an authority figure.

Believing they were participating in a study on memory, the volunteers watched a "pupil" being strapped to a chair and wired with electrodes. The volunteers were then taken to an adjacent room, where they were told to read questions to the pupil and to administer increasingly powerful electric shocks for every incorrect answer. The electric-shock buttons seemed to go up to one administering a jolt of 450 volts on a button labeled "Danger: Severe Shock."

As the shocks were administered, the mock pupils acted as if they were being subjected to increasingly greater pain. Even as the pupils writhed and screamed in pain, the volunteers readily administered the shocks. Finally, the pupil would emit a bloodcurdling scream and then suddenly fall totally silent, apparently dead. Two-thirds of the volunteers continued to administer the shocks. The study was scandalous: If asked to do so by an authority figure, a majority of people will kill another human being completely unknown to them. It would be interesting to know if professor Milgram advised the airlines on their security procedures. ∎

☞ Would Mohammed Atta Object to Armed Pilots?

MAY 30, 2002

In a new safety initiative, the Department of Transportation has instituted an affirmative-action program for Arabs interested in pursuing careers in aviation. Transportation Secretary Norman Mineta explained the security advantages of the program, saying, "Surrendering to discrimination makes us no different than the terrorists." Since you can't tell these days: This is not, in the strict sense, true.

It is true that the department has prohibited pilots from carrying guns and has rejected the idea of a "trusted traveler" program. In fact, it's not doing anything to make the airlines any safer. This should come as no surprise, inasmuch as Mineta recently said he was unaware of any specific threat against aviation. They hate us. They're trying to kill us. They use airplanes as weapons. If Mineta doesn't read intelligence reports, can't he at least read the newspapers?

In congressional testimony last week, Mineta mercifully spared the senators a recap of his experience in a Japanese internment camp and allowed his assistant, longtime Bush crony and ATF apologist John Magaw, to explain the department's key security improvements. The reason Magaw decided to prohibit pilots from having guns is—I quote—"they really need to be in control of that aircraft."

This is literally the stupidest thing I've heard in my entire life. It is like saying women walking home late at night in dangerous neighborhoods shouldn't carry guns (or Mace, for my liberal friends) because they "really need to be walking home." If the undersecretary for transportation security thinks we have to debate whether pilots "really need to be in control of that aircraft," someone other than him really needs to be in control of airline security.

The scenario under which a pilot might need a gun is this: Islamic crazies have penetrated the locked cockpit, thwarting air marshals, passengers, and crew. It's going to be a little difficult for the pilot to "be in control of that aircraft" when he's fighting off an angry mob of sweaty Arabs. There is nothing that could go wrong at that point—a wounded passenger, a hole in the side of the plane, terrorists wresting control of the gun—that would be worse than the alternative.

Ah, but Magaw is worried that the terrorists will now be in possession of a firearm. Think of the havoc they could wreak with a gun! Of course, they'll also be in possession of a Boeing 767 careering at 480 miles per hour toward the nearest landmark building. Magaw seems to think the real danger is that terrorists will shoot at the White House from the cockpit window, not that they'll fly the plane into it.

Magaw is the worst kind of government bureaucrat. He defends fascistic government abuses, but the citizenry is no safer as a consequence. Fascism has its bad points, but at least trains are supposed to run on time. As the head of the Bureau of Alcohol, Tobacco and Firearms, Magaw famously defended an unprovoked government assault against Randy Weaver and his family, culminating in the murder of Weaver's wife. In testimony before a Senate committee investigating the raid at Ruby Ridge, Magaw stubbornly refused to admit the ATF had done anything wrong.

Indeed, he even refused to acknowledge a jury verdict finding that the government had entrapped Weaver. Of the jury's verdict, Magaw said, "Do you believe Randy Weaver—or do you believe the federal agents who have sworn to tell the truth and are carrying out a career in this government?"

If only airline pilots worked for the ATF. Then Magaw would not only allow them to carry guns, he would also allow them to shoot law-abiding passengers at random. (The Senate report found Magaw's testimony not credible and recommended abolition of his entire agency.)

Magaw's other airline safety improvement was to reject the idea of a "trusted-traveler" program, which would allow passengers to avoid three-hour airport security lines in return for submitting to an intrusive background check. As reported by the *New York Times,* Magaw spurned the trusted-traveler idea on the ground that "he is not sure who could safely be given the card." I don't know, how about . . . NO ARABS? (Religion-of-Peace Update: As Pakistanis prepare to stone a rape victim to death, the latest suicide bombing in Israel claimed the lives of a grandmother and her eighteen-month-old granddaughter.)

Amazingly, President Bush has actually found someone even dumber than Norman Mineta to be Mineta's assistant. The secretary of transportation is the only person on the face of the globe who thinks the airlines face no terrorist threat, and his deputy—by his own admission—hasn't the first idea how to figure out which airline passengers can be "trusted."

If these guys were doing their jobs right, civil libertarians would be screaming bloody murder, Congress would be reining them in, and professional ethnic victims would be holding candlelight vigils and singing "We Shall Overcome." Instead, Congress is forced to pass laws overruling Mineta and Magaw, civil libertarians are scratching their heads wondering why profiling is prohibited, and professional complainers are sending these guys flowers. Maybe somebody else should be doing this job.

POSTSCRIPT: On July 18, 2002, the Bush administration fired Magaw. On November 25, 2002, Bush signed legislation that would allow pilots to carry guns. ∎

☞ Thank You for Choosing United, Mr. Bin Laden

APRIL 14, 2004

Last week, 9/11 commissioner John Lehman revealed that "it was the policy [before 9/11] and I believe remains the policy today to fine airlines if they have more than two young Arab males in secondary questioning because that's discriminatory." Hmmm . . . Is nineteen more than two? Why, yes, I believe it is. So if two Jordanian cabdrivers are searched before boarding a flight out of Newark, Osama bin Laden could then board that plane without being questioned. I'm no security expert, but I'm pretty sure this gives terrorists an opening for an attack.

In a sane world, Lehman's statement would have made headlines across the country the next day. But not one newspaper, magazine, or TV show has mentioned that it is official government policy to prohibit searching more than two Arabs per flight.

Meanwhile, another 9/11 commissioner, the greasy Richard Ben-Veniste, claimed to be outraged that the CIA did not immediately give intelligence on 9/11 hijackers Nawaf Alhazmi and Khalid Almihdhar to the FBI. As we now know—or rather, I alone know because I'm the only person in America watching the 9/11 hearings—Ben-Veniste should have asked his fellow commissioner Jamie Gorelick about that.

In his testimony this week, John Ashcroft explained that the FBI wasn't even told Almihdhar and Alhazmi were in the country until weeks before the 9/11 attack—because of Justice Department guidelines put into place in 1995. The famous 1995 guidelines were set forth in a classified memorandum written by the the deputy attorney general at the time—Jamie Gorelick. The memo was titled "Instructions for Separation of Certain Foreign Counterintelligence and Criminal Investigations" and it imposed a "draconian" wall between counterintelligence and criminal investigations.

What Ashcroft said next was breathtaking. Prohibited from mounting a serious search for Almihdhar and Alhazmi, an irritated FBI investigator wrote to FBI headquarters, warning that someone would die because of these policies—"since the biggest threat to us, OBL [Osama bin Laden], is getting the most protection." FBI headquarters responded, "We're all frustrated with this issue. These are the rules. NSLU [National Security Law Unit] does not make them up. But somebody did make these rules. Somebody built this wall."

The person who built that wall, Ashcroft said, "is a member of the commission." If this had been an episode of *Matlock*, the camera would have slowly panned away from Ashcroft's face at this point and then quickly jumped to an extreme close-up of Jamie Gorelick's horrified expression. Armed marshals would then escort the kicking, screaming Gorelick away in leg irons as the closing credits rolled. The 9/11 Commission has finally uncovered the proverbial "smoking gun"! But it was fired by one of the 9/11 commissioners. Maybe between happy reminiscences about the good old days of Ruby Ridge, Waco, and the Elián Gonzáles raid, Ben-Veniste could ask Gorelick about those guidelines. Democrats think it's a conflict of interest for Justice Scalia to have his name in the same phonebook as Dick Cheney. But there is no conflict of interest having Gorelick sit on a commission that should be investigating her.

Bill O'Reilly's entire summary of Ashcroft's testimony was to accuse Ashcroft of throwing sheets over naked statues rather than fighting terrorism. No mention of the damning Gorelick memo. No one knows about the FAA's No-Searching-Arabs counterterrorism policy. Predictions that conservatives have finally broken through the wall of sound coming from the mainstream media may have been premature.

When Democrats make an accusation against Republicans, newspaper headlines repeat the accusation as a fact: "U.S. Law Chief 'Failed to Heed Terror Warnings,'" "Bush Was Told of Qaida Steps Pre-9/11; Secret Memo Released," "Bush White House Said to Have Failed to Make al-Qaida an Early Priority." But when Republicans make accusations against Democrats— even accusations backed up by the hard fact of a declassified Jamie Gorelick memo—the headlines note only that Republicans are making accusations: "Ashcroft Lays Blame at Clinton's Feet," "Ashcroft: Blame Bubba for 9/11," "Ashcroft Faults Clinton in 9/11 Failures."

It's amazing how consistent it is. A classic of the genre was the *Chicago Tribune* headline that managed to use both constructs in a single headline: "Ashcroft Ignored Terrorism, Panel Told; Attorney General Denies Charges, Blames Clinton." Why not: "Reno Ignored Terrorism, Panel Told; Gorelick Denies Charges, Blames Bush"?

Democrats actively created policies that were designed to hamstring terrorism investigations. The only rap against the Bush administration is that it failed to unravel the entire 9/11 terrorism plot based on a memo titled "Bin Laden Determined to Attack Inside the United States." I have news for liberals: Bin Laden is *still* determined to attack inside the United States! Could they please tell us when and where the next attack will be? Because unless we know that, it's going to be difficult to stop it if we can't search Arabs. ■

☞ Arab Hijackers Now Eligible
for Preboarding

APRIL 25, 2004

In June 2001, as Mohammed Atta completed his final "to do" list before the 9/11 attacks (". . . amend will to ban women from my funeral . . . leave extra little Friskies out for Mr. Buttons . . . set TiVo for Streisand on *Inside the Actors Studio* . . ."), Secretary of Transportation Norman Mineta was conducting a major study on whether airport security was improperly screening passengers based on ethnicity. As Mineta explained, "We must protect the civil rights of airline passengers." Protecting airline passengers from sudden death has never made it onto Mineta's radar screen.

A few months later, nineteen Muslim men hijacked U.S. airplanes and turned them into weapons of mass destruction on American soil; suddenly, Mineta was a whirlwind of activity. On September 21, as the remains of thousands of Americans lay smoldering at Ground Zero, Mineta fired off a letter to all U.S. airlines forbidding them from implementing the one security measure that would have prevented 9/11: subjecting Middle Eastern passengers to an added degree of preflight scrutiny. He sternly reminded the airlines that it was illegal to discriminate against passengers based on their race, color, national or ethnic origin, or religion. Mineta would have sent the letter even sooner, but he wanted to give the airlines enough time to count the number of their employees and customers who had just been murdered by Arab passengers.

On September 27, 2001, the ACLU sent out a press release titled "ACLU Applauds Sensible Scope of Bush Airport Security Plan," which narrowly won out over the headline "Fox Approves Henhouse Security Plan." As a rule of thumb, any security plan approved by the ACLU puts American lives at risk. Former ACLU Associate Director Barry Steinhardt praised Bush's Transportation Department for showing "an admirable degree of restraint by not suggesting airport security procedures that would deny civil liberties as a condition of air travel." As usual the ACLU had zeroed in on the true meaning of 9/11: Americans needed to be more tolerant of and sensitive toward ethnic minorities.

Flush with praise from the ACLU, Mineta set to work suing airlines for removing passengers perceived to be of Arab, Middle Eastern, or Southeast Asian descent and/or Muslim. If we're going to start shifting money around based on who's rude to whom, my guess is Muslims are going to end up in the red. But that's not how Mineta's Department of Transportation sees it.

Despite Mineta's clearly worded letter immediately after the 9/11 terrorist attacks and another follow-up letter in October, the Department of Transportation found that in the weeks after the 9/11 terrorist attacks carried out by Middle Eastern men, the airlines were targeting passengers who appeared to be Middle Eastern. To his horror, Mineta discovered that the airlines were using logic and deductive reasoning to safeguard their passengers— in direct violation of his just-issued guidelines on racial profiling!

The Department of Transportation filed a complaint against United Airlines, claiming United removed passengers from flights in "a few instances" based on their race, color, national origin, religion, or ancestry. Mineta gave United no credit for so scrupulously ignoring ethnicity on September 11 that it lost 4 pilots, 12 flight attendants, and 84 passengers (not including the 9 Arab hijackers). In November 2003, United settled the case for $1.5 million.

In another crucial antiterrorism investigation undertaken by Norman Mineta, the Department of Transportation claimed that between September 11, 2001, and December 31, 2001, American Airlines—which lost 4 pilots, 13 flight attendants, and 129 passengers (not including 10 Arab hijackers) on September 11 by ignoring the ethnicity of its passengers—removed 10 individuals who appeared to be Middle Eastern from American Airline flights as alleged security risks. On March 1, 2004, American Airlines settled the case for $1.5 million.

The Department of Transportation also charged Continental Airlines with discriminating against passengers who appeared to be Middle Eastern after the September 11 terrorist attacks. In April 2004, Continental Airlines settled the complaint for $500,000.

Like many of you, I carefully reviewed the lawsuits against the airlines in order to determine which airlines had engaged in the most egregious discrimination, so I could fly only those airlines. But oddly, rather than bragging about the charges, the airlines heatedly denied discriminating against Middle Eastern passengers. What a wasted marketing opportunity! Imagine the great slogans the airlines could use:

"Now Frisking All Arabs—Twice!"

"More Civil-Rights Lawsuits Brought by Arabs Than Any Other Airline!"

"The Friendly Skies—Unless You're an Arab!"

"You Are Now Free to Move About the Cabin—Not So Fast, Mohammed!"

Worst of all, the Department of Transportation ordered the settlement money to be spent on civil-rights programs to train airline staff to stop looking for terrorists, a practice known as "digging your own grave and paying for the shovel." Airlines that have been the most vigilant against terrorism are forced by the government into reeducation seminars to learn to suppress common sense. Airlines are being forced, at their own expense, to make commercial air travel more dangerous.

Despite the deployment of fifty thousand government-paid screeners since 9/11, it's still fairly easy to sneak knives, box cutters, and even guns onto most commercial flights. But there's good news, too. It's now virtually impossible to hijack a plane using an oversized carry-on bag or a set of nail clippers.

Americans lull themselves into a sense of security by simply assuming the government is secretly screening airline passengers who look like the last two dozen terrorists. No, it isn't. To the contrary, the government aggressively punishes airlines that have not abandoned rationality. The government fines airlines that give a secondary security check to more than two Arabs per flight, and Norman Mineta is busy suing airlines for millions of dollars if the airline removes passengers who share any physical characteristics with the people who recently killed three thousand Americans using airplanes as their weapon. (Also, Mineta is pushing to broaden the definition of "on-time arrival" to include planes that crash into buildings ahead of schedule.) If any airline hijackings in the United States have been averted since 9/11, it is only because Attorney General John Ashcroft already has the terrorists in lockup. They're certainly not being stopped at the airport.

Mineta doggedly insists that aviation security does not justify "discrimination" against passengers. Why not? The entire concept of "security" consists of a rational, experience-based process of discriminating between likely attackers and unlikely ones. If you could bring someone back in a time machine from pre–Politically Correct America, he would survey the situation after September 11 and say, "Well, you've got one advantage in this war with al Qaeda—at least you know what the enemy looks like. They're all Muslim men, so just work over those guys. . . . Why is no one saying anything? Hello? Norman? Wow, you could hear a pin drop in this room."

Not coincidentally, the only airline terrorist stopped since 9/11 was stopped by passengers. Fortunately, the passengers on an American Airlines flight 63 from Paris were unburdened by Department of Transportation guidelines forbidding them to take Richard Reid's appearance into account. Not having been warned not to make judgments based on appearance because that might send a message of inferiority to Muslims, the passengers were able to take one look at Reid and know he was trouble. They wrestled Reid to the ground just before he detonated a shoe bomb that would have blown up a plane with 185 passengers.

An Australian newspaper titled its article on Reid "Would You

Let This Man Board a Plane?" Norman Mineta responded by ordering airport security to start checking all passengers' shoes. ∎

☞ Even with Hindsight Liberals Can't See Straight

MAY 5, 2004

Over in the alternative universe of the 9/11 Commission hearings watched only by me, Richard Ben-Veniste recently proposed an amazing new standard for investigating Arabs in this country. In the middle of haranguing Condoleezza Rice, Ben-Veniste demanded to know why the suspected twentieth hijacker, Zacarias Moussaoui, had not been more aggressively investigated, despite the fact that—I quote—he had "no explanation for the funds in his bank account, and no explanation for why he was in the United States."

So let me get this straight: Airport security can't acknowledge that a person is an Arab, but they should be allowed to audit his bank records? (Come to think of it, "Can't Explain His Bank Account or Why He's Here" is also a pretty good description of John Kerry.)

Can we use that as a standard going forward? The government prohibits airlines from searching more than two Arabs per flight, so it would be terrific if liberals would let us examine their financial statements. If Democratic Party shills like Ben-Veniste—who himself looks like someone who ought to be searched at airports—are going to make ludicrous, macho statements like that in order to win applause from weeping widows in the peanut gallery, can't we hold them to that policy when it matters?

Ben-Veniste thinks the key to stopping the 9/11 attack was for the FBI to have drawn the obvious conclusions from an Arab in-flight school. If only the FBI had searched Moussaoui's computer, they would have found a flight-simulator computer program, information about the Boeing 747, and extensive files on crop dusters. From this, apparently, Ben-Veniste imagines the FBI would have concluded that on September 11, nineteen Muslims were going to hijack airplanes out of Logan, Newark, and Dulles airports and fly them into buildings.

A somewhat more direct chain of causation traces its way back to the aviation-security commission chaired by Vice President Al Gore in 1997. If that commission had done its job, you wouldn't have to wait for one of my columns to find out that there was a commission on airline safety years before the 9/11 attacks. Isn't it curious that Democrats aren't bragging about Gore inventing air safety? The reason Al Gore hasn't added "antiterrorism" to the list of things he invented is that Gore's commission concluded that passenger profiling must ignore ethnicity and nationality. Or as Gore himself might have put it, "I took the initiative in making it easier for Muslims to use airplanes to slaughter innocent American citizens."

The Gore commission on air safety decided that profiling should be based on "reasonable predictors of risk, not stereotypes or generalizations." Amazingly, all those "reasonable predictors of risk" failed to stop a single Muslim terrorist on 9/11. One wonders whether a profiling system that included ethnicity and nationality would have been more helpful in stopping nineteen Muslim men, fifteen of whom were from Saudi Arabia, all speaking Arabic to one another, from boarding planes on September 11.

Recently—that is, about the time Ben-Veniste was shocked that the FBI hadn't uncovered the 9/11 plot based on the fact that Moussaoui had overstayed his visa—Senator Hillary Clinton and Senator Chuck Schumer were clamoring for the release of Ansar Mahmood, a twenty-six-year-old Pakistani immigrant detained in October 2001 after he was observed taking photographs at a water-treatment plant in upstate New York. Mahmood later pleaded guilty to committing a felony by giving financial aid to illegal immigrants from Pakistan. Schumer says Mahmood should be permitted to stay in the United States because he "was cleared of terrorist links," and he has already served his time for "a non-violent felony." Hillary simply calls Mahmood's detention "disturbing."

Where is Ben-Veniste when we need him? What happened to the "We Don't Know Why He's Here or His Sources of Money" standard for harassing Muslim immigrants? In contrast to Mahmood, Zacarias Moussaoui had committed no felonies; his only apparent offense was to have overstayed his visa. But Ben-Veniste is appalled that the FBI didn't beat Moussaoui for information. The French had linked Moussaoui to al Qaeda—based largely on the information that he took frequent trips to Afghanistan and Pakistan, Mahmood's home country. When FBI agents in Minneapolis requested a warrant to search Moussaoui's computer, FBI headquarters wrote back, "We don't know he's a terrorist"—the same argument Schumer is making for Mahmood's release right now.

Liberals always claim to know exactly what to do as soon as it's too late. After Muslims attack with airplanes, they want to investigate flight schools. After Muslims attack with shoe bombs, they want to investigate shoes. After a Muslim introduces *E. coli* into New York's water supply, liberals will be enraged that Muslim immigrants taking pictures of New York water-treatment plants weren't investigated more aggressively—as soon as they are done blaming Bush for not stopping the attack. Liberals are the only known species whose powers of reasoning are not improved by the benefit of hindsight. Not only are they always fighting the last war, in most cases they're surrendering. ■

4

At Least They Didn't Run Jimmy Carter This Time

———————◼———————

Inasmuch as John Kerry's campaign strategy is to hide until election day, and let his many positions on every issue speak for themselves, there isn't a lot to say about the gigolo. Kerry wants to let people know what he stands for, but first he has to decide what he stands for. (Just the other day a reporter asked Kerry, "Are you for or against gay marriage?" As usual, his answer was, "Yes.") So I'm including a few columns on the Democratic presidential candidates who are already appearing on *Hollywood Squares*. The idea that there are any meaningful differences among the Democratic contenders is absurd anyway. They're all the same—except Dennis Kucinich: only Kucinich could have held up a pie chart during a Democratic debate that was broadcast *only on radio*. (Even more embarrassing: Al Sharpton asked the moderator what kind of pie it was.)

☞ American Women to Kerry: We Don't Think You're So Hot Either

MAY 7, 2003

Senator John F. Kerry has been citing his valorous Vietnam record more often than General George Patton cursed. It's a good theme for him. Liberals keep loudly proclaiming that they support "the troops"—while simultaneously running sneering articles that portray the troops as coarse, semiliterate cads. So a tax-and-spend Massachusetts liberal like Kerry could finally provide them with one "troop" they really do like. (By contrast, for the first time ever, I find myself in favor of the war but against the troop.)

Kerry has been aggressively brandishing his military service with the bristling connotation that if you didn't fight, you can't quarrel with him on war and peace. In a catfight with former Vermont governor Howard Dean during the Democrats' first presidential debate in South Carolina, Kerry snarled at Dean, "I don't need any lectures in courage from Howard Dean." If John Kerry had a dollar for every time he bragged about serving in Vietnam— Oh wait, he does.

Though Kerry makes liberal ladies' bosoms heave with his self-advertisements about his Vietnam experience, the Democrats might not want to let Kerry pursue this particular line of argument. According to Thomas Ricks's book *Making the Corps,* the vast majority of officers currently serving in the military are conservative Republicans—"largely comfortable with the views of Rush Limbaugh." Citing a series of studies expressing alarm at what they viewed as a disquieting trend, Ricks says that "open identification with the Republican Party is becoming the norm— even, suggests former army major Dana Isacoff, part of the implicit definition of being a member of the officer corps." Why the officer corps would take a dim view of a party that has spent the last three decades systematically trying to emasculate the military in pursuit of every conceivable social cause is anybody's guess. Still, there it is. So, by Kerry's own logic, in a few years only right-wing Republicans will be eligible for the presidency.

But that's the Democrats' problem. For now, there are other, more urgent implications to Kerry's argument. As long as we're going to get uppity about our personal experiences, why is John Kerry allowed to have any opinion about taxes? He has spent his entire life marrying a succession of heiresses and living off the fortunes amassed by other men. (It must be the luck of the pseudo-Irish.) How can Kerry claim to understand the anguish of people who pay high taxes? What does this pompous, whining, morally superior, mincing habitué of Boston drawing rooms know about confiscatory taxes on hard-earned money? (Not that his nuptial path to wealth is not also hard-earned.) If Kerry doesn't need lectures on the military from Howard Dean, do the rest of us need lectures from this sponge on how much we should be willing to pay in taxes? What is this male Anna Nicole Smith's expertise in average people paying taxes? I don't have a rich wife supporting me. And I don't look French.

There was a firestorm of indignation when an unnamed Bush adviser recently remarked to the *New York Times* that Kerry "looks French." Up until five minutes ago, the entire Kerry family used adjectives like "European" as statements of the highest praise. Kerry's sister cited her brother's cultured refinement in a 1994 profile of Kerry in *Rhode Islander Magazine* by saying, "Our parents felt deeply that we needed to absorb the culture and know the Europeans as friends." In his 1996 Senate campaign, reporters were dazzled and awed when Kerry responded to a Canadian reporter in French, snootily noting that Kerry's French was much better than his opponent's.

In a profile of Kerry's current heiress wife, Teresa Heinz, in the June 2003 issue of *Elle* magazine, noted journalist Lisa DePaulo quotes Kerry oozing with admiration for his wife, saying she is "very earthy, sexy, European." "Earthy" and "European" sound like euphemisms for hairy armpits and body odor. But we get it. American girls aren't good enough for Frenchy. Well, we don't think he's so hot either. Even after Kerry was attacked for looking French, Heinz thought the best course would be to defend her husband by haughtily snipping that the Bush aides "probably don't even speak French." Take that, you boorish Americans! If the Democrats nominate Kerry, Bush should take the high road and pledge not to raise the issue of his opponent looking French. But the question of Kerry's fitness to discuss taxes while living off rich women is still on the table. ■

☞ General Democrat

OCTOBER 1, 2003

According to a new survey, six out of ten Americans can't name a single Democrat running for president. And that poll was actually taken among the ten current Democratic candidates. According to the survey answers, "the military guy" leads with 19 percent, followed by "that doctor—what's his name?" with 12 percent, and "the French-looking guy" with 9 percent. Since Wesley Clark entered the race, Democrats have been salivating over the prospect of a presidential candidate who is a four-star general—and has the politics of Susan Sarandon! Clark's entry into the race was seen as a setback for John Kerry, the only other Democratic contender with combat experience. (Although back in the 1970s, Dennis Kucinich served in the Kiss Army.)

Before Clark becomes the answer to a Trivial Pursuit question, consider that his main claim to fame is that he played a pivotal role in what most of his supporters passionately believe was an illegal, immoral war of American imperialism in Vietnam. How does that earn you points with Democrats?

Clark said he would have supported the war in Iraq if he had been in Congress last year, but now he opposes the way the war is being fought and he wants U.S. troops out of Iraq as soon as possible. This was very exciting for Senator Joe Biden, because for the first time ever he can now credibly accuse someone of plagiarizing him.

Clark's other credential to lead the free world was that he supervised the "liberation" of Kosovo by ordering our pilots to drop bombs from 15,000 feet at a tremendous cost in innocent civilian life in a 100 percent humanitarian war against a country that posed absolutely no threat to the United States—imminent or otherwise—and without the approval of the almighty United Nations. So you can see why Clark supported, then opposed, then supported, then opposed the current war in Iraq. (Say, is there a website where I can get up-to-the-minute updates on Wesley Clark's current position on the war in Iraq, kind of like a Nasdaq ticker?)

Possible Clark campaign slogans are already starting to emerge:

"I Was into Quagmires Before Quagmires Were Cool"

"Honk If You Got Bombed in Kosovo"

"Only Fired by the Pentagon Once!"

"The OTHER Bush-Bashing Rhodes Scholar From Arkansas"

"No, Really, Vice President Would Be Fine"

On *Meet the Press*, on June 15, 2003, Clark told Tim Russert that he got a lot of calls after 9/11 telling him to go on television and say, "This has to be connected to Saddam Hussein." Asked who had told him that, Clark said, "The White House; it came from people around the White House. It came from all over."

But under cross-examination by Sean Hannity on the Fox News Channel a few weeks later, Clark would say only that he had gotten a call from "a fellow in Canada who is part of a Middle Eastern think tank who gets inside intelligence information." So in two weeks' time, Clark had gone from "the White House" to "people close to the White House" to "some guy in Canada." Clark is for abortion, tax hikes, affirmative action, and he is against the war in Iraq. But he served in Vietnam. So he's basically Howard Dean with scarier flashbacks.

Howard Dean is not a general, but he is a doctor. Democrats are enthusiastic about Dean, since they figure that if this Democrat was ever caught with a naked intern, he could just say it was her annual physical. Dean has leapt beyond criticizing Bush and is now embracing terrorists. He has called Hamas terrorists "soldiers in a war" and said the United States should not take sides between Israel and Palestinian suicide bombers. This has won him a spot in the hearts of the Democratic Party base—middle-class white kids from Ben-and-Jerryville who smash Starbucks windows whenever bankers come to town for a meeting. If Dean doesn't get the Democratic nomination, perhaps he could throw his hat into the ring to replace Arafat.

The also-rans are trying to distinguish themselves by competing to see who can denounce George Bush with greater zeal. Senator John Kerry has said we need to "de-Americanize" the war—I guess on the theory that the "de-Americanizing" process has worked so well for the Democratic Party. He is furious at Bush for prosecuting a war Kerry voted for, saying the difference is "I would have been patient." He would have had to be extremely patient in the case of Germany, inasmuch as Gerhard Schroeder announced before the war began that he would never authorize war in Iraq under any circumstances.

Florida senator Bob Graham recently told the Council on Foreign Relations that in "answer to any questions about the Bush administration on the war on terror," the answer is "No, they are not doing a good job." This would explain Graham's commanding lead among members of his own household, although his maid is still "Undecided."

Dick Gephardt has taken to calling President Bush a "miserable failure"—as opposed to Gephardt, who is a "happy failure." Things have gotten pretty bad when you're being called a "failure" by a guy who spent thirty years sucking up to labor but still can't get the AFL-CIO's endorsement.

Dennis Kucinich recently proposed a new U.S. policy for Iraq, known in military circles as "unconditional surrender." He wants all U.S. troops to leave immediately and be replaced by UN troops. The head of the UN Human Rights Commission—Syria—would surely have things back to normal in no time. Kucinich has also offered his services as a consultant to any city in Iraq that's thinking about filing for bankruptcy. According to most polls, the Democrat who stands the best chance to beat Bush is a guy named "Generic." ∎

☞ The Party of Ideas

NOVEMBER 20, 2003

With economic growth and name recognition of the average Democratic presidential candidate both running at about 7 percent, the Democrats are in trouble. It turns out that given a choice between "shock and awe" and "run and hide," the American people prefer the former. Unable to rouse more than the Saddam-supporting left with their kooky foreign-policy ideas, the Democrats had been counting on a lousy economy. Now that the Bush tax cuts have already started to kick in and boost the economy, it was beginning to look as if the Treason Lobby would have nothing to run on.

But the Democrats have discovered a surprise campaign issue: It turns out that several of them have had a death in the family. Not only that, but many Democrats have cracker-barrel humble-origins stories and a Jew or lesbian in the family. Dick Gephardt's campaign platform is that his father was a milkman, his son almost died, and his daughter is a lesbian. Vote for me!

So don't say the Democrats aren't the party of ideas. As they keep reminding us, their ideas are just too darn complex to fit on a bumper sticker. Consequently, the Democrats can't tell us their ideas until after the election. Instead, their version of a political campaign is to stage a "Queen for a Day" extravaganza—which has special resonance in the case of the Democrats.

Al Gore famously inaugurated the family tragedy routine at the 1992 Democratic National Convention, where his idea of an inspiring political speech was to recount the story of his son being hit by a car. At the 1996 convention, Gore told a tearjerker about his sister's long, painful death from lung cancer. It got to the point that Gore's family members had to fear any more runs for higher office.

In the current campaign, Gephardt has taken to spinning out a long, pitiful tale of his son's near-death three decades ago. At dozens of campaign stops, Mrs. Gephardt weeps anew as her husband tells the same gut-wrenching story over and over again. The relevance of their son's illness to Gephardt's run for the presidency is this: It inspired Gephardt's call for national health insurance. With his wife softly weeping in the background, he intones, "I get it."

At least when Gephardt exploits a family tragedy, he doesn't expect praise for not exploiting a family tragedy. John Edwards injects his son's fatal car accident into his campaign by demanding that everyone notice how he refuses to inject his son's fatal car accident into his campaign. Edwards has talked about his son's death in a 1996 car accident on *Good Morning America*, in dozens of profiles, and in his new book—"It was and is the most important fact of my life." His 1998 Senate campaign ads featured film footage of Edwards at a learning lab he founded in honor of his son, titled the Wade Edwards Learning Lab. He wears his son's Outward Bound pin on his suit lapel. He was going to wear it on his sleeve, until someone suggested that might be a little too "on the nose."

If you want points for not using your son's death politically, don't you have to take down all those "Ask me about my son's death in a horrific car accident" bumper stickers? Edwards is like a politician who keeps announcing that he will not use his opponent's criminal record for partisan political advantage. *I absolutely refuse to mention the name of my dearly beloved and recently departed son killed horribly in a car accident, which affected me deeply, to score cheap political points.* I wouldn't want John Edwards to be president, but I think even Karl Rove would be willing to stipulate that the death of a son is a terrible thing.

Howard Dean talks about his brother Charlie's murder at the hands of North Vietnamese Communists. If a death in the familly is the main qualification for becoming a Democratic presidential candidate, what's Scott Peterson waiting for? Bizarrely, after working on the failed George McGovern campaign, Charlie Dean went to Indochina in 1974 to witness the ravages of the war he had opposed. Not long after he arrived, the apparently ungrateful Communists captured and killed him. *Hey fellas! I'm on your si—CLUNK!* Howard Dean wears his brother's battered 1960s belt every day. (By contrast, Ted Kennedy honors the memory of his deceased family members with several belts every day.) Dean told Dan Rather about his brother's death at some length on CBS News: "It gave me a sense that you ought to live for the moment with people; that you really—you really need to tell people you love them if you love them. It was certainly the most awful thing that ever happened to our family. It was terrible for my parents; it was even worse for them than it was for us."

Dammit, if a man wants to be my president, I have a right to know where he stands on the issue of when to tell the people you love that you love them! Couldn't the Democratic Party go back to plagiarizing British Labour Party leader Neil Kinnock the way Senator Joe Biden did, rather than plagiarizing *Lifetime: TV for Women*? Do any men at all vote for the Democrats anymore?

Carol Moseley Braun's personal tragedy is that she's being forced to run for president even though it turns out the Democrats won't need her to split the black vote anyway. *Please, can I drop out now? Al Sharpton is only polling at 2 percent. I hate this!*

Sharpton is the counterpoint to his sob sisters in the Democratic Party. Sharpton libeled innocent men in the Tawana Brawley case. He inflamed angry mobs in Brooklyn's Crown Heights, leading to the murder of Yankel Rosenbaum. He incited an anti-Semitic pogrom against a Jewish-owned clothing store in Harlem, Freddy's, ending in a blaze of bullets and a fire that left several employees dead. So while the other Democrats talk about their personal tragedies, Sharpton goes around creating personal tragedies.

In addition to having a number of family deaths among them, the Democrats' other big idea—too nuanced for a bumper sticker—is that many of them have Jewish ancestry. There's Joe Lieberman: Always Jewish. Wesley Clark: Found Out His Father Was Jewish in College. John Kerry: Jewish Since He Began Presidential Fundraising. Howard Dean: Married to a Jew. Al Sharpton: Circumcised. Even Hillary Clinton claimed to have unearthed some evidence that she was a Jew—along with the long-lost evidence that she was a Yankees fan. And that, boys and girls, is how the Jews survived thousands of years of persecution: by being susceptible to pandering.

Clark said that when he discovered he was half-Jewish, he remembered growing up in Arkansas and feeling "a certain kinship" with Jewish families in the dry-goods business. (I, too, have always felt a certain kinship with Calvin Trillin.)

The Democrats' urge to assert a Jewish heritage is designed to disguise the fact that the Democrats would allow the state of Israel to perish as Palestinian suicide bombers slaughter Jewish women and children. Their humble-origins claptrap is designed to disguise the fact that liberals think ordinary Americans are racist scum. Their perverse desire to discuss the deaths and near-deaths of their children is designed to disguise the fact that they support the killing of more than a million unborn children every year. (Oh, by the way, what did their milkman and millworker fathers think about abortion?) Be forewarned: If the Democrats start extolling you—get a gun. ■

☞ The Jesus Thing

JANUARY 7, 2004

When they were fundraising, the Democratic candidates for president all claimed to be Jewish. Now that they are headed for Super Tuesday down South, they've become Jesus freaks. Listening to Democrats talk about Jesus is a little like listening to them on national security: They don't seem terribly comfortable with either subject.

To ease Democrats into the Jesus thing, the Democratic Leadership Council is actually holding briefings for Democratic candidates teaching them how to talk about religion. As has been widely reported, the DLC gingerly suggests that Democrats start referring to "God's green earth." The participants were also warned that millions of Americans worship a supreme being whose name is not Bill Clinton. Democrats never talk about believing in something; they talk about simulating belief in something. *Americans believe in this crazy God crap that we don't, so how do we hoodwink them into thinking we believe in God?* It's part of the casual contempt Democrats have for the views of normal people.

What is arresting is the Democrats' fantastic habit of openly talking about how they plan to fake out the American people. The Democrats candidly say, *How do we make sure the Americans don't know what we're really thinking? Let's get a Southerner, let's talk about Jesus, let's talk about NASCAR—white Southern guys seem to like that. Let's see . . . if we could get a general on the ticket, Americans will forget how much we hate the military and long to see America humiliated.* Never has a major political party talked so openly about their plans to fool the voters. It's the damnedest thing I've ever seen. They seem not to realize the people they are talking about are listening.

In the current *New Republic* magazine, Peter Beinart points out that the capture of Saddam has hurt the antiwar cause and left the Democrats with nothing to say. He proposes that Democrats pretend to support the war on terrorism by calling for a massive campaign to catch Osama. Yeah, let's try that. That'll fool 'em. In the debate this week, John Kerry responded to a question about how he would appeal to Southerners by saying he could put a Southerner on his ticket. As Howard Dean has explained, they're stupid enough: It's just a bunch of white guys in pickup trucks with Confederate flags.

Dean himself has recently made the fascinating discovery that a lot of Americans believe in God. Hold the phones—the Democrats have a soothsayer in their midst! Next, Dean will be announcing that he's just discovered how important this sex thing is. Before the poll numbers came out on religious belief in America, Dean said, "We have got to stop having our elections in the South based on race, guns, God and gays." Higher taxes, gay marriage, abortion on demand, and surrender in Iraq—that'll do the trick in Mississippi!

Then about a month ago, the Pew Research Center for the People and the Press released a poll showing that people who regularly attend religious services supported Bush 63 percent to 37 percent, and those who never attend religious services opposed him 62 percent to 38 percent. When you exclude blacks (as they do in Vermont), who are overwhelmingly Baptist and overwhelmingly Democratic, and rerun the numbers, basically any white person who believes in God is a Republican. The only Democrats who go to church regularly are the ones who plan to run for president someday and are preparing in advance to fake a belief in God.

Though Dean is pursuing the Jesus thing with a vengeance, the results so far have been mixed. In Iowa last week, Dean said, "Let's get into a little religion here," and then began denouncing Christian minister Jerry Falwell. "Don't you think Jerry Falwell reminds you a lot more of the Pharisees than he does of the teachings of Jesus?" I don't even know what Dean means by that. I am sure his audience doesn't.

Rapping with reporters about God on the campaign plane, Dean said, "If you know much about the Bible, which I do"—and then proceeded to confuse the Old Testament with the New Testament.

Dean illiterately claimed his favorite book of the New Testament was the Book of Job. (He said his least favorite was the Book of Numbers and then explained how he planned to balance the budget.) Having already complained to DNC chairman Terry McAuliffe about other Democrats attacking him, Dean recently said, "I'm feeling a little more Job-like recently." That's comforting. A few snippy remarks from the likes of Dick Gephardt and Dean thinks it's the wrath of the God of Abraham. Yeah, that's definitely the guy we want leading the nation in perilous times.

Dean's epiphanic religious awakening occurred over a bike path—and that's his version of what happened. He was baptized Catholic and raised an Episcopalian, but left the Episcopal Church in a huff when he finally found his true religion: environmentally friendly exercise. The Episcopalians don't demand much in the way of actual religious belief. They have girl priests, gay priests, gay bishops, gay marriages—it's much like the *New York Times* editorial board. They acknowledge the Ten Commandments—or "Moses' talking points"—but hasten to add that they're not exactly "carved in stone." After Bush said that the most important philosopher to him was Jesus Christ, the Episcopal bishop in Des Moines, Iowa, C. Christopher Epting, said the answer was "a turnoff." So there isn't a lot of hair-shirt-wearing and sacrifice for the Episcopalians.

But the bike-path incident was too much for Dean. A key tenet of the Druidical religion of liberals is non–fossil-fuel travel. So Dean left the Church of the Proper Fork because the Episcopal

Church in Montpelier hesitated before ceding some of its land for a bike path.

On CNN, Judy Woodruff asked Dean in amazement, "Was it just over a bike path that you left the Episcopal Church?"

Dean: "Yes, as a matter of fact it was."

Dean waxed expansive on the theological implications of bike paths, saying, "I didn't think that was very public-spirited."

But recently, Dean has leapt even beyond the DLC-recommended "God's green earth" and begun talking about Jesus, saying, "He was a person who set an extraordinary example that has lasted 2,000 years, which is pretty inspiring when you think about it." Gosh, to hear Dean tell it, Jesus is even giving Oprah a run for her money! Also, Christ died for our sins, but let's not get into the hocus-pocus part of Christianity. The gist of the New Testament is about bike paths. Dean's relationship with Jesus is a little like David Lloyd George's relationship with the Slovaks. At the Treaty of Versailles conference, the British prime minister was heard to whisper, "Who are the Slovaks again? I can never place them." ∎

☞ What Happened to Your Queer Party-Friends?

JANUARY 21, 2004

The endless receding nightmare of the Iowa caucuses has finally produced something interesting: The Democrats have one hellacious catfight on their hands. After all the hoopla about Howard Dean's new mass movement of "Deaniacs," it appears that blanketing Iowa with self-righteous twenty-year-olds in orange wool caps may not have been the ideal campaign strategy. Dean's distant third-place finish makes you want to ask him the question Jack Nicholson put to his down-and-out gay neighbor in *As Good as It Gets*: "What happened to your queer party-friends?"

At the behest of the Democratic Party establishment, the

media dutifully destroyed Howard Dean, the legitimate leader of the opposition. Democratic voters are such lemmings. The *New York Times* told them to switch from Dean to John Kerry, so they all obediently switched from Dean to Kerry. But Dean still has the money and foot soldiers and endorsements to stay in the fight for the foreseeable future. And being from Vermont, Dean should do well in New Hampshire. I went to a public school, but if I remember my high school geography correctly, New Hampshire and Vermont are the same state.

Until Kerry won Iowa, Wesley Clark was viewed as the preeminent electable Democrat, principally because he's a Republican. Dean said he thinks Clark is a fine fellow but truly a Republican. In response, General Clark immediately put on a third sweater. Sadly, it may turn out that Clark's whole raison d'être is now gone. Never was so much money, media, chicanery, Gwyneth Paltrow, Madonna, conniving, and Kabbalah deployed to promote a quote-unquote "electable" Democrat. Clark was supposed to be the phony American to stop Dean, but Kerry is the even better phony American! And he's already stopped Dean in Iowa. Kerry and Clark now represent the two major wings of the Democratic Party—the Kennedy wing and the Clinton wing. One drowns you after the extramarital affair; the other one calls you a stalker.

Other than that, there isn't a hair's difference between any of the Democrats on any substantive issues. All the Democrats are for higher taxes. All of them favor Hillary's socialist health-care plan. All of them are for higher pay for teachers and nurses—and no pay at all for anyone in the pharmaceutical or oil industries, especially Halliburton executives, who should be sent to Guantánamo. All the Democrats believe the way to strike fear in the hearts of the terrorists is for the federal government to invest heavily in windmills.

All the Democrats oppose the war. And all the Democrats who took a position on the war before it began were for it, but now believe that everything Bush did from that moment forward has been bad! bad! bad! This is with the exception of Joe Lieberman who, as an observant Jew, is forbidden to backpedal after sundown on Fridays. Representing a large flabby chunk of the Kennedy wing, Ted Kennedy gave a speech last week in which he called the liberation of Iraq a "political product." Then again, Ted Kennedy calls Chivas Regal "that life-sustaining liquid." Finally, all the candidates are willing to sell out any of these other issues in service of the one burning desire of all Democrats: abortion on demand. If they could just figure out a way to abort babies using solar power, that's all we'd ever hear about.

For all his talk, even Dick Gephardt was willing to abandon blue-collar workers in a heartbeat. The Teamsters haven't asked for much, only two big votes in the past decade: (1) Oppose NAFTA, and (2) support drilling on a small, godforsaken patch of the Alaskan wilderness, as the people who actually live there have been begging us to do for decades. Like all the other Democrats, Gephardt voted against the Teamsters—but with Barbra Streisand—to oppose drilling in the godforsaken Alaskan wilderness. When Gephardt entered politics he was pro-life. But then—like Al Gore, Jesse Jackson, Dennis Kucinich, and scores of other Democrats with national ambitions—he quickly figured out that position wasn't, well . . . viable. In short order he had adopted the whole NARAL party line. That's how you woo old-time union Democrats.

On Monday night in Iowa, Gephardt was shocked to discover that blue-collar Democrats have gone the way of all patriotic Democrats: They're all Republicans now. (But thanks for that NAFTA vote a decade ago!) You knew Gephardt was toast when even responsible journalists started using words like "decent" and "solid" to describe the two-faced weasel from Missouri. Though I suppose "decent" has a pretty broad meaning in a party that still admires Bill Clinton.

The Iowa caucus was just another one of the Democrats' ongoing public debates about how to fake out the American people. Fifty percent of Iowa Democrats participating in the caucus said they "strongly disapprove" of the war with Iraq and another 25 percent "somewhat disapprove." But more important to Democrats than their pacifism was "electability." The entire Iowa electorate was committed to the proposition: How do we fool the neighbors? In the end, the caucus-goers chose a decorated war hero who voted in favor of the very war that 75 percent of them oppose. So much for the antiwar fever sweeping the country. The Democrats aren't even man enough to run a genuine coward for president. ■

☞ Just a Gigolo

JANUARY 28, 2004

After the New Hampshire primary, Dennis Kucinich's new slogan is ".001 Percent of America Can't Be Wrong!" John Edwards's new slogan is "Vote for Me or We'll See You in Court." Joe Lieberman's new slogan is "Sixth Place Is Not an Option" (bumper sticker version: "Ask Me About My Delegate") Wesley Clark's new slogan is "Leading America's War on Fetuses." Howard Dean's new slogan is "I Want to Be Your President . . . And So Do I!" Al Sharpton's new slogan is "Hello, Room Service?"

That leaves John Kerry (new slogan: "Nous Sommes Nombre Un!"), who is winning Democratic voters in droves on the basis of his superior ability to taunt George Bush for his lack of combat experience. Like every war hero I've ever met, John Kerry seems content to spend his days bragging about his battlefield exploits. Wait, wait . . . let me correct that last sentence: Like *no* war hero I've ever met . . .

As everyone has heard approximately one billion times by now, Kerry boasts that he has REAL experience with aircraft carriers, and if Bush wants to run on national security, then . . . BRING IT ON! I note that when George Bush directed that precise phrase at Islamic terrorists who yearn to slaughter American women and children, liberals were enraged at the macho posturing of it. But they feel "Bring it on!" is a perfectly appropriate expression when directed at a dangerous warmonger like George Bush. ("Bring it on!" won out over Kerry's first impulse, "Let's get busy, sister!")

Kerry was indisputably brave in Vietnam, and it's kind of cute to see Democrats pretend to admire military service. Physical courage, like chastity, is something liberals usually deride but are tickled about when it accidentally manifests itself in one of their own. One has to stand in awe of Kerry's military service thirty-three years ago. Of course, that's where it ends, including with Kerry—inasmuch as, upon his return from war in 1970, he promptly began trashing his fellow Vietnam vets by calling them genocidal murderers.

But if Bush can't talk to Kerry about the horrors of war, then Kerry sure as hell can't talk to anyone about the plight of the middle class. Kerry's life experience consists of living off other men's money by marrying their wives and daughters. For over thirty years, Kerry's primary occupation has been stalking lonely heiresses. Not to get back to his combat experience, but Kerry sees a room full of wealthy widows as "a target-rich environment." This is a guy whose experience dealing with tax problems is based on spending his entire adult life being supported by rich women. What does a kept man know about taxes?

In 1970, Kerry married into the family of Julia Thorne—a family estimated to be worth about $300 million. She got depressed, they separated, and soon he was seen catting around with Hollywood starlets, mostly while he was still married. (Apparently, JFK really was his mentor.) Thorne is well bred enough to say nothing ill of her Lothario ex-husband. He is, after all, the father of her children—a fact that never seemed to constrain him.

When Kerry was about to become the latest Heinz family charity, he sought to have his marriage to Thorne annulled, despite the fact that it had produced two children. It seems his second meal ticket, Teresa Heinz, wanted the first marriage annulled—and she's worth more than $700 million. Kerry claims he will stand up to powerful interests, but he can't even stand up to his wife. Heinz made Kerry sign a prenuptial agreement, presumably aware of how careless he is with other people's property, such as other people's Vietnam War medals, which Kerry threw on the ground during a 1971 antiwar demonstration.

At pains to make Kerry sound like a normal American, his campaign has described how Kerry risked everything, mortgaging his home in Boston to help pay for his presidential campaign. Technically, Kerry took out a $6 million mortgage for "his share" of "the family's home"—which was bought with the Heinz family fortune. (Why should he spend his own money? He didn't throw away his own medals.) I'm sure the average working stiff in Massachusetts can relate to a guy who borrows $6 million against his house to pay for TV ads. Kerry's campaign has stoutly insisted that he will pay off the mortgage himself, with no help from his rich wife. Let's see: According to tax returns released by his campaign, in 2002, Kerry's income was $144,091. But as the *Washington Post* recently reported, even a $5 million mortgage paid back over thirty years at favorable interest rates would cost $30,389 a month—or $364,668 a year. Paying it off "himself," is he?

The Democrats' joy at nominating Kerry is perplexing. To be sure, liberals take a peculiar, wrathful pleasure in supporting pacifist military types. And Kerry's life story is not without a certain feral aggression. But if we're going to determine fitness for office based on life experience, Kerry clearly has no experience dealing with problems of typical Americans, since he is a cad and a gigolo living in the lap of other men's money. Kerry is like some character in a Balzac novel, an adventurer twirling the end of his mustache and preying on rich women. This lowborn poseur with his thread-bare pseudo-Brahmin family bought a political career with one rich woman's money, dumped her, and made off with another heiress to enable him to run for president. If Democrats want to talk about middle-class tax cuts, couldn't they nominate someone who hasn't been a poodle to rich women for the past thirty-three years? ■

☞ Boobs in the News

FEBRUARY 4, 2004

Just to give you a snapshot of the current Democratic Party, in the North Dakota primary, Dennis Kucinich got three times as many votes as Joe Lieberman did. After that, Lieberman quit the race. In sympathy with Lieberman and facing similar odds—I quit the race too. To my supporters: Hey, we didn't go all the way, but just look how much we accomplished! In his concession speech, Lieberman thanked each one of the Democratic presidential can-didates for contributing to the race and thanked Al Sharpton in particular for inciting no additional violence against the Jews.

Former front-runner Howard Dean managed to make news by ridiculing the FCC's plan to investigate MTV's halftime show at the Super Bowl. Dean pronounced the proposed investigation "silly." He explained that since he's a doctor, a naked breast is "not exactly an unusual phenomenon" for him. That's an interesting standard. Presumably a prime-time exhibition of Janet Jackson having a full pelvic exam and pap smear would not be "exactly an unusual phenomenon" for Dean either. Let's just be grateful Dean's not a proctologist.

Meanwhile, the rest of the country was not so copacetic about being flashed with what the *New York Times* called Janet Jackson's "middle-aged woman's breast." Janet Jackson said she decided to add "the reveal" following the final rehearsal, which I found pretty shocking. Not the reveal—the fact that the number in question was actually rehearsed. Even CBS executives were enraged by MTV's halftime show, saying they could have gotten the identical show from *National Geographic* for a fraction of the price.

Speaking of boobs, after sustaining his first losses in two primaries Tuesday night, senator and trophy husband John Kerry has said he's going to concentrate on solidifying the support of his base. People like David Gest, Claus von Bulow, and Tom Arnold. Liberals laughed at George Bush for citing Jesus Christ as his favorite philosopher, but are impressed that John Kerry's favorite philosopher is Louis Prima ("Just a Gigolo"). Kerry thinks people are dying to hear his economic plan. In fact, the only economic plan most male voters want to hear about is how Kerry snookered two babes worth hundreds of millions of dollars into marrying him.

Kerry might as well start giving out dating tips. He's running out of other ideas. A few weeks ago, the *Washington Post* reported that Kerry has taken more money from paid lobbyists than any other senator over the past fifteen years. In a face-saving move, Senator Botox has quietly dropped the part of his stump speech where he inveighs against Washington special interests: "We're coming, you're going, and don't let the door hit you on the way out." (Interestingly, these were also Senator Kerry's words to his first wife after he hooked up with Teresa Heinz.)

Not only that, but according to Kerry's principal cheerleaders—Teddy Kennedy and the *New York Times*—Kerry absolutely refuses to talk about his Vietnam service. Kennedy insists that Kerry "just won't talk about" Vietnam. Apparently Vietnam was a brief, death-defying interlude that Kerry would simply prefer not to discuss. You might say it's his Chappaquiddick. In the objective part of a factual news story, the *New York Times* reported that Kerry "has been careful to avoid being seen as exploiting his service politically." He simply will not do it. This came as a shock to most Americans, who were discovering for the very first time that Kerry had served in Vietnam.

While there is indisputably nothing cooler than having fought for your country, John Kerry's status as a Vietnam veteran is unlikely to change a single vote. Military guys will support Bush, and liberals don't admire bravery. After starting the Vietnam war, the Democratic Party suddenly decided it was an illegal, immoral, undeclared war, and soldiers like John Kerry were baby-killers. Today, vast majorities of Democratic primary voters tell pollsters they opposed the war in Iraq—which their boy Kerry voted for. Kerry's sole appeal is that he gives pacifist cowards cover to fume about Bush.

Just a few years ago, the Democrats thought a pot-smoking draft-dodger would make a splendid president. But now they act as if they are inflamed at the thought that Bush didn't fight in Vietnam. In other words, it's honorable to march in anti-American protests in Europe when America is at war, but not to be a fighter pilot in the Texas Air National Guard.

Democrats know they can't beat Bush, but they intend to enjoy being hysterical about him throughout the campaign. Calling Bush a draft-dodger, which he is not, will join the Democrats' list of other cogent, reasoned arguments, such as "You're stupid" and "Halliburton!" Democrats think they invented war heroes, but being a war hero didn't help Bob Dole. It didn't help George Herbert Walker Bush. It didn't help John McCain. The Democrats didn't invent war heroes. What they invented is the scam of deploying war heroes to argue for surrender. ∎

☞ In Desperate Move, Kerry Adopts Puppy

JULY 7, 2004

I guess with John Kerry's choice of John Edwards as his running mate, he really does want to stand up for all Americans, from those worth only $60 million to those worth in excess of $800 million.

In one of the many stratagems Democrats have developed to avoid telling people what they believe, all Edwards wants to talk about is his cracker-barrel humble origins story. We're supposed to swoon over his "life story," as the flacks say, which apparently consists of the amazing fact that . . . his father was a millworker!

That's right up there with "Clinton's stepdad was a drunk" and "Ted Kennedy's dad was a womanizing bootlegger" on my inspirational-life-stories meter. In fact, I'm immediately renouncing my university degrees and going to work for the post office just to give my future children a shot at having a "life story," should they decide to run for president someday.

What is so amazing about Edwards's father being a millworker? That's at least an honorable occupation—as opposed to being a trial lawyer. True, Edwards made more money than his father did. I assume strippers make more money than their alcoholic fathers who abandoned them did, too. This isn't a story of progress; it's a story of devolution.

Despite the overwrought claims of Edwards's dazzling legal skills, winning jury verdicts in personal injury cases has nothing to do with legal talent and everything to do with getting the right cases—unless "talent" is taken to mean "having absolutely no shame." Edwards specialized in babies with cerebral palsy who he claimed would have been spared the affliction if only the doctors had immediately performed Caesarean sections.

As a result of such lawsuits, there are now more than four times as many Caesarean sections as there were in 1970. But curiously, there has been no change in the rate of babies born with cerebral palsy. As the *New York Times* reported, "Studies indicate that in most cases, the disorder is caused by fetal brain injury long before labor begins." All those Caesareans have, however, increased the mother's risk of death, hemorrhage, infection, pulmonary embolism, and Mendelson's syndrome.

In addition, the "little guys" Edwards claims to represent are having a lot more trouble finding doctors to deliver their babies these days as obstetricians leave the practice rather than pay malpractice insurance in excess of $100,000 a year.

In one of Edwards's silver-tongued arguments to the jury on behalf of a girl born with cerebral palsy, he claimed he was channeling the unborn baby girl, Jennifer Campbell, who was speaking to the jurors through him:

"She said at 3, 'I'm fine.' She said at 4, 'I'm having a little trouble, but I'm doing OK.' Five, she said, 'I'm having problems.' At 5:30, she said, 'I need out.'"

She's saying, "My lawyer needs a new Jaguar...."

"She speaks to you through me and I have to tell you right now—I didn't plan to talk about this—right now I feel her. I feel her presence. She's inside me, and she's talking to you."

Well, tell her to pipe down, would you? I'm trying to hear the evidence in a malpractice lawsuit.

To paraphrase Oscar Wilde on the death of Little Nell, one must have a heart of stone to read this without laughing. What is this guy, a tent-show preacher? An off-the-strip Las Vegas lounge psychic couldn't get away with this routine.

Is Edwards able to channel any children right before an abortionist's fork is plunged into their tiny skulls? Why can't he hear those babies saying, "Let me live! Stop spraying this saline solution all over me!" Edwards must experience interference in channeling the voices of babies about to be aborted. Their liberal mothers' hands seem to muffle those voices.

And may we ask what the pre-born Jennifer Campbell thinks about war with Iraq? North Korea? Marginal tax rates? If Miss Cleo here is going to be a heartbeat away from the presidency, I think the voters are entitled to know that.

While making himself fabulously rich by taking a one-third cut of his multimillion-dollar verdicts coaxed out of juries with junk science and maudlin performances, Edwards has the audacity to claim, "I was more than just their lawyer; I cared about them. Their cause was my cause."

If he cared so deeply, how about keeping just 10 percent of the multimillion-dollar jury awards, rather than a third? In fact, as long as these Democrats are so eager to raise the taxes of "the rich," how about a 90 percent tax on contingency fees?

For someone who didn't care about the money, it's interesting that Edwards avoided cases in which the baby died during delivery. Evidently, jury awards average only about $500,000 when the babies die, and there is no disabled child to parade before the jury.

Edwards was one of the leading opponents of a bill in the North Carolina legislature that would have established a fund for all babies born with cerebral palsy. So instead of all disabled babies in North Carolina being compensated equitably, only a few will win the jury lottery—one-third of which will go to trial lawyers like Edwards, who insists he doesn't care about the money.

Despite the now-disproved junk science theory about C-sections preventing cerebral palsy that Edwards peddled in the channeling case, the jury awarded Edwards's client a record-breaking $6.5 million. This is the essence of the modern Democratic Party, polished to perfection by Bill Clinton: They are willing to insult the intelligence of 49 percent of the people if they think they can fool 51 percent of the people.

So while Michael Moore, Al Franken, George Soros, Crazy Al Gore, and the rest of the characters from the climactic devil-worshipping scene in *Rosemary's Baby* provide the muscle for the Kerry campaign, Kerry picks a pretty-boy milquetoast as his running mate, narrowly edging out a puppy for the spot. Just don't ask the Democrats what they believe. Edwards's father was a mill-worker, and that's all you need to know.

5

Barbra Streisand Feels Your Pain (According to Her Publicist)

———— ■ ————

☞ I Like Black People Too, Julia!

MARCH 28, 2002

I tuned in late and consequently can speak only to the last three hours of Halle Berry's acceptance speech at the Academy Awards last Sunday. But inasmuch as she engaged in wild race-baiting to get her Oscar, Berry's expressions of shock were not very believable. She had spent weeks complaining about one time she did not get a role because of her color. It was the part of a forest ranger. Arnold Schwarzenegger probably has trouble getting roles as a ballet dancer, too. And yet still, somehow, white guilt worked on Hollywood liberals! Berry had successfully mau-maued her way to a Best Actress award—and then acted surprised.

It's interesting that Berry makes such a big deal about being black. She was raised by her white mother who was beaten and abandoned by her black father. But clearly, Berry has calculated that it is more advantageous for her acting career to identify with the man who abandoned her rather than the woman who raised her.

Demanding that everyone marvel at her accomplishment, Berry gushed, "This moment is so much bigger than me." Whenever people say something is not about them, it's always just about them. This is a turn of phrase meant to remind the audience of the importance and beauty of them. Berry said her triumph was a victory "for every nameless, faceless woman of color who now has a chance because this door tonight has been opened." Yes, at long last, the "glass ceiling" had been broken. Large-breasted, slightly cocoa women with idealized Caucasian features will finally have a chance in Hollywood! They will, however, still be required to display their large breasts for the camera and to discuss their large breasts at some length with reporters.

Thus, Berry has explained her philosophy on nude scenes, saying, "If it's what the character would do, then I'd use my body in any way that would best serve that character." This, she said, is her "strong belief." But what does it mean, exactly? Don't all people undress sometimes? All people pick their noses, but vapid Hollywood actresses don't insist on showing us that in every movie on the grounds that it is "what the character would do." In fact, Berry's unseemly enthusiasm for displaying "these babies," as she genteelly refers to her breasts, reduces the number of roles for any women who lack Berry's beauty-queen features.

If movies must include soft-porn scenes, the audience is entitled to demand performers with sexual characteristics they would like to see in a soft-porn movie. Somehow, characters played by Whoopi Goldberg are never the sort of characters who would do things in real life like undress or have sex. (And by the way, Billy Bob Thornton isn't cutting it for the female audience.) When they are young, nubile Hollywood actresses all utter the same idiotic clichés about the artistic value of nudity in movies. Then they expect us to feel sorry for them when parts dry up after they become old and start to sag. Live by the breast, die by the breast.

But Berry's self-aggrandizing pap was merely a footnote to the main event of the awards ceremony, which was: Julia Roberts loves all the black brothers! It was a point Roberts felt could not be made too often or with too much condescension. Her presentation of the Best Actor award began with the exciting revelation that she had just kissed Sidney Poitier! Having once dramatically proclaimed she did not want to live in a world in which Denzel Washington had not won an Oscar for Best Actor, Roberts preceded her announcement of Washington's award saying, "I love my life!" This was about her, not him. It was Julia Roberts's personal triumph over racism. The only patronizing remark Roberts skipped was to note that Washington and Poitier were "articulate."

After Washington accepted his award, Roberts leapt on him and would not let go. It was as if he had grown some sort of exotic Julia Roberts wart. Washington—and, more urgently, his wife— deserve great credit for their forbearance. Whatever indignities Hollywood has visited on blacks in the past, it would be hard to top Roberts's performance.

Apparently, Oscar night was Hollywood's shot at patronizing blacks to generate good will—perhaps as wartime penance for its long-standing hatred of America. Like clockwork, whenever white liberals are in trouble, they run to the blacks. After his abomination of a presidency, Jimmy Carter built housing in Harlem. Immediately after the Monica Lewinsky scandal broke, Monica went to a Washington Wizards game, where she hoisted some poor unsuspecting black girl onto her lap in full view of the TV cameras. Bill Clinton dropped the subtlety and dashed off to Africa. It's too bad Denzel Washington's Oscar was tainted by Hollywood's self-serving night of condescension. He deserved that award. And he deserves a special award for not punching Julia Roberts in the mouth. ■

☞ Dumb Hires Dumber

NOVEMBER 9, 1999

Just when you thought Al Gore could get no more comical, it turns out he's been taking masculinity lessons from a feminist. Since January, the Gore campaign had been covertly funneling $15,000 a month to "controversial feminist author Naomi Wolf"—as she is invariably described. The payments were funneled through other consulting firms, thus eliminating the embarrassing prospect of having to mention her name in the campaign's reports to the FEC. As has been widely reported, Wolf advised the vice president to shed his beta-male characteristics and become an alpha male like Bill Clinton—who is virile in the sense that a filthy, rabid stray dog humping your ankle is virile. The insight that first caught Al's attention was Wolf's article in the June 1998 *George* magazine titled "Al's Inner Alien." ("Gore should let his defenses down and allow his inner oddness out.") While it's true the citizens of this nation don't want a pervert and crook in the Oval Office, I don't know that we're clamoring for an idiot either.

There would have been enough guffaws to go around if Bill Bradley had been caught paying exorbitant fees to some bimbo babbling about alpha males and earth tones. But it was nearly perfect that it was Gore. This was Dumb hiring Dumber. Gore already gives off a strong impression of being mentally deficient. It has something to do with his habit of enunciating basic points as if he's talking to an extremely slow four-year-olds—to say nothing of his lunatic claims to having invented the Internet and been the inspiration for *Love Story*. But then he was caught paying a ludicrous salary to a mind-bogglingly stupid girl. To be sure, stupid isn't the worst thing in the world. The worst thing in the world is: Stupid trying to pass itself off as smart. Like Gore, Wolf insists on posing as a great intellect instead of just working at Hooters. (One wonders if, like Gore, Naomi's friends also claim she's much smarter and uproariously funny "in person.")

In her latest book, *Promiscuities*, Wolf argued—if that is the appropriate verb—that schools should teach teenagers masturbation and oral sex. If we don't act now, onanism could become a lost art! "Teaching sexual gradualism is as sensible as teaching kids to drive," Wolf says. Adding sexual "gradualism" to the high school curriculum: now that's what I call a workable "Stay in School" program. I'm all for the government teaching our kids how to have sex, provided they also have to be licensed by the DMV before they go at each other.

In fact, I don't know why we couldn't combine sex ed with driver's ed just for the sake of efficiency. Why not require an operator's license, issued by the DMV, for any kid who wants to have sex? I'm picturing millions of kids who think they're finally going to have sex, only to be told, "You don't have the right form. Go to the back of the line."

It is that kind of "out-of-the-box thinking"—as Gore press secretary Chris Lehane described Wolf's talent—that gets you paid $180,000 per year by the Gore campaign. Except teaching kids to masturbate really isn't that new an idea. Indeed, for quite some time liberals have been not only discussing but sometimes actually *teaching* small children things I can't discuss in a family newspaper. That's what got New York City schools chancellor Joseph Fernandez removed from office as long ago as February 1993 and Clinton's surgeon general Joycelyn Elders fired in 1995—to mention a few times this "out-of-the-box thinking" has been thought of before. Shhhhhhh. No one tell the Gore campaign. Now, I don't know much about that fancy "out-of-the-box thinking," but it seems to me such thinking must, at a minimum, consist of ideas that forty-seven people haven't thought of before.

Wolf's only serious advice to Gore was: Distance yourself from Clinton. Not to brag, but I've been giving the whole country that advice totally free for quite some time now. Fifteen thousand a month. The money was good, especially for the "breadwinner for a growing family," as Wolf claimed to be. (Her husband must have enjoyed hearing that.) Still, Wolf resented her anonymity in the Gore campaign. Indeed, *Time* magazine says Wolf's claims that she had been trying to disguise her role in the campaign came as "news to some Gore campaign officials." To the contrary, campaign officials said, Wolf had been "agitating for a more public profile." She made an "ostentatious appearance" at Gore's New Hampshire debate and "ignored suggestions to stay away from reporters." After her cunning plan of talking to reporters somehow failed to keep her role a secret, Wolf ignored the Gore campaign's request that she not go on TV and discuss her role any further. This was her "out-of-the-box thinking" for which I am most grateful.

On ABC's *This Week,* George Will asked Wolf what she meant about Gore being "a Blakeian deep inside" as she had said in her article "Al's Inner Alien." She may as well have been asked to do long division. While clearly having no idea, Wolf proclaimed delight that they were "talking about nineteenth-century romantic and mystical poets." No, they weren't actually, and not only because Blake was mostly an eighteenth-century poet. They were talking about *talking about* a nineteenth-century poet—who was actually an eighteenth-century poet. Whenever really stupid people try to sound intellectual, this is as far as they get: nonsubstantive recitations of important-sounding names. They love to exclaim that they are "talking about" poets, world leaders, or God, when all they're doing is saying the names. "I can't believe—I'm pleased, but I can't believe, at this early in the morning," she said, we are "talking about" poets.

When the seemingly interminable subject of the subject had at last been exhausted, Wolf "explained" how Gore was a "Blakeian" by unleashing a series of meaningless clichés: "What I'm talking about is a vision that incorporates many disparate parts for a whole that's more than the sum of its parts." The clichés ultimately led, somehow, to the stirring conclusion that Gore was a Blakeian because of his yearning to resolve this critical federal crisis: "How do you get working parents home in time so that they have a chance to read a bedtime story to their kids?" Another of Wolf's other self-described "wacky" and "larger picture" ideas were things like . . . school uniforms! George Will dryly asked the "larger picture" gal, "Who ever said school uniforms are wacky, by the way?"

In her tawdry book *Promiscuities,* Wolf unloads a tanker of "out-of-the-box" thoughts. She writes, for example, "If thirteen-year-old Juliet were to fall in love with Romeo today, she could get a condom in the ladies' room of the train station and instructions from *Cosmo* ('Your Sexual Style'), and Shakespeare would have to look elsewhere for his plot." Um. No. The problem fair Juliet had with Romeo was *not* that she could not find suitable birth control. But then Naomi and I went to different schools. Different planets, if you credit her account. It may explain a lot that she's the one teaching Al Gore to be a man. ■

☞ Checks and Balances, but Mostly Checks

JULY 31, 2002

Having dragged a group of Manhattan elites back from the Hamptons in the summer of 2002 to attend a fundraiser at a tony Chelsea nightclub, Al Gore criticized the Bush administration for "working on behalf of the powerful, and letting the people of this country get the short end of the stick."

Back when he was exhibiting the Democrats' renowned good sportsmanship after he lost the presidential election, Gore managed to fund his tantrum with donations sent in from such ordinary Americans such as dot-com multimillionaire Steven Kirsch ($500,000), former Slim-Fast Foods chief S. Daniel Abraham ($100,000), and Minneapolis multimillionaire Vance Opperman ($100,000). He got help from the Manhattan "working poor," such as Loews Hotels scion and tobacco company beneficiary Jon Tisch ($50,000); ex-wife of pardoned financier Marc Rich, Denise Rich ($25,000); and investment banker Jon Corzine ($25,000), who is now representing working families against "the powerful" in the U.S. Senate. Also moved by Gore's pledge to fight for "working families" were some of Hollywood's typical "working families." Notorious inseminator and Hollywood "producer" Stephen Bing ponied up $200,000. (In Democratic Party parlance, "producer" evidently means "a do-nothing who inherited a lot of money.") Actress and traitor Jane Fonda gave the Gore-Lieberman fund $100,000.

By contrast, George W. Bush limited donations to his Election Recount Fund to $5,000 or less. But normal Americans saw what the Democrats were up to, and thousands upon thousands of small contributions poured in to Bush from across the country. Bush raised four times as much money as Gore did. Even with individual donations of half a million dollars, Gore raised only $3.2 million. Small individual donors, none contributing more than $5,000, gave $13.8 million to Bush.

Two-thirds of Gore's Tantrum Fund came from just 38 rich liberals, who contributed $2.1 million. Eighty-four individuals donated $2.8 million of Gore's $3.2 million recount fund. This, in a country of 280 million people. Without Malibu, there would be no Democratic Party. Of the 84 rich liberals who nearly single-handedly bankrolled Gore's Tantrum Fund, 30 were from California and 23 from New York—and that doesn't include rich liberals who ought to be in Malibu but whose legal residence is Georgia, like Jane Fonda. Only $56,216 of the entire Gore-Lieberman fund came from donations of $200 or less—that is, about half the size of the check cut by Jane Fonda to Gore's fund. Bush raised more than the entire amount of Gore's fund in individual donations of $200 or less.

The tale of the two recount funds once again proved the division between the two parties as: Those Who Make Their Own Beds and Those Who Do Not. But that's not the story the media told. Amazingly, the media turned the facts upside down, absurdly implying that Bush had been bankrolled by billionaires while Gore made do with small donations from the working poor. The genuine and spontaneous outrage of ordinary Americans against a small band of Democratic royalists became another story about mythical Rich Republicans beating down the working class with their polo mallets.

Newspaper headlines simply ignored the size of the individual donations, and instead broadcast only the raw totals of the two funds—amid copious reminders that Republicans are the Party of the Rich. In an article titled "Bush Far Outspent Gore on Recount," the *Washington Post* referred to "the powerful fund-raising abilities of the Republican Party." The *Chicago Tribune*'s headline was "Bush Spent 4 Times as Much as Gore in Florida Recount" and the AP headline was "IRS: Bush Spent Four Times as Much as Gore on Florida Recount." How about: "Gore Bankrolled by 84," "Small Donors Flock to Bush, Billionaires to Gore," or "Malibu Pool Party Finances 7/8ths of Gore Recount Fund"?

A year later, the Democratic National Committee took in its largest single donation ever: $5 million from "producer" Stephen Bing—our featured Democrat this week. In the current *Vanity Fair*, Bing is described by other Hollywood billionaires as a self-effacing, modest man. As evidence, they note that he has only one maid. "Name anyone else with his wealth who has only one maid," Man of the People Rob Reiner says. "You'd be hard-pressed." I'd be hard-pressed to think of one of my friends who *has* a maid. Marie Antoinette did not flaunt her wealth the way "progressive" liberals in America do.

Other Hollywood progressives commented on how Bing helps strippers when they're down on their luck. (And, one may surmise, also down on their knees.) "I've helped so many," Bing says, "you'd have to get me the names." That's "self-effacing" for a liberal. Bing's admiration for the underclass is mainly shown by his predilection for siring children out of wedlock. This seems to be the new status symbol among liberals, with Bing currently leading Jesse Jackson 2-to-1 in disclosed illegitimate children. (Q: How do you empty a room full of rich liberals? A: Ask for a paternity test.) In a romance born of progressivism, the mother of one of Bing's illegitimate children, Elizabeth Hurley, crossed a Screen Actors Guild picket line—and Bing gallantly paid her fine to the union. So much for the little people. Also, he plays the blues on the piano. I take it back: He is a man of the people.

Interestingly, Bing doesn't make a fuss about the estate tax. His professional accomplishments amount to having dropped out of Stanford—which we can assume he did not enter on the basis of his SAT scores—and then spending a decade writing a single episode of *Married . . . with Children*. Bing's credentials as a producer are as credible as his belief that women are not attracted to him for his money. The current Democratic Party is a crowd of idle, rich degenerates, the likes of which hasn't existed since the czar's court. When not occupied with abortions or strippers, they busy themselves denouncing the cossacks as "the powerful." ∎

☞ The Robert C. Byrd Bridge to Poverty

FEBRUARY 14, 2002

The poor's sense of class superiority over the rich is getting out of hand. At a Senate Budget Committee hearing last week, Senator Robert Byrd (who was named after a bridge in West Virginia) viciously attacked Treasury Secretary Paul O'Neill for having made a success of himself. Claiming to speak for worthless layabouts, Byrd snippily informed O'Neill, "They're not CEOs of multibillion-dollar corporations. . . . In time of need, they come to us, the people come to us." And evidently, what the people-in-need are crying out for are a lot of federal projects named after Senator Byrd.

Some items paid for by taxpayers—but inexplicably named after "Robert C. Byrd"—are: the Robert C. Byrd Highway; the

Robert C. Byrd Locks and Dam; the Robert C. Byrd Institute; the Robert C. Byrd Life Long Learning Center; the Robert C. Byrd Honors Scholarship Program; the Robert C. Byrd Green Bank Telescope; the Robert C. Byrd Institute for Advanced Flexible Manufacturing; the Robert C. Byrd Federal Courthouse; the Robert C. Byrd Health Sciences Center; the Robert C. Byrd Academic and Technology Center; the Robert C. Byrd United Technical Center; the Robert C. Byrd Federal Building; the Robert C. Byrd Drive; the Robert C. Byrd Hilltop Office Complex; the Robert C. Byrd Library; the Robert C. Byrd Learning Resource Center; the Robert C. Byrd Rural Health Center.

And then it got late, and I had to stop searching Google. But it appears that every slab of concrete in West Virginia is named after Bob Byrd.

Really warming to his class-envy tirade, the King Tut of the Senate further informed O'Neill, "I haven't walked in any corporate boardrooms. I haven't had to turn any millions of dollars into trust accounts. I wish I had those millions of dollars." Instead, Byrd had to scrape by with billions of dollars forcibly extracted from the taxpayers to build grotesque banana-republic tributes to himself. At least the money O'Neill "turn[ed] into trust accounts" came from his own pocket. Coincidentally, the money Byrd turned into eponymous monuments also came from O'Neill's pocket. A humble display of gratitude to O'Neill might have been more appropriate.

An astonished O'Neill responded to the harangue: "I started my life in a house without water or electricity. So I don't cede to you the high moral ground of not knowing what life is like in a ditch." And then the hearing spun totally out of control as Senator Tut redoubled his own sob story: "Well, Mr. Secretary, I lived in a house without electricity, too, no running water, no telephone, a little wooden outhouse." (Though Byrd was manifestly enamored of all the tiny particulars of his life story, he unaccountably skipped the part about his youthful membership in the Ku Klux Klan.)

When did a lack of money and accomplishment become a

mark of virtue? Some rich people may be swine, but so are some poor people. A lot of rich people work harder, are more creative, and are a lot nicer than the poor—especially rich people who earned it themselves, unlike Democratic senators. Paul O'Neill was never in the Klan and Paul O'Neill never filched taxpayers' hard-earned money to build a vast complex of shrines to himself. More perplexingly, when did a scoundrel whose only source of capital comes from other people's paychecks assume the "high ground" over a rich man who gave people paychecks? Paul O'Neill is rich, I'm not. Oh well. At least he didn't steal half my paycheck.

Every society must have concentrations of wealth in order to build and create. Even the Soviet Union of beloved memory had concentrations of wealth—but it was in the government rather than in corporations. It's called capital. Capital is needed to launch society's most important projects—factories, bridges, skyscrapers, inventions, and telescopes named after Bob Byrd. O'Neill's concentration of money came to him through the voluntary decisions of investors and consumers. Byrd's far larger concentration of money came to him by force. Send half your paycheck to the government or go to jail.

The lie at the heart of liberals' mantra on tax cuts—"tax cuts for the rich"—is the ineluctable fact that unless taxes are cut across the board, nobody's taxes ever get cut. As loaded Hollywood liberals are always reminding us, they don't "need" a tax cut. Alas, the rich we shall always have with us, kind of like the poor. At least conservatives defend the right of middle-class people to keep their money, too.

The only rich people deserving of malice are rich liberals who express bemusement at the nonrich's desire for a tax cut. In their campaign to make the middle class pay more in taxes, liberals use the lumpen poor as a battering ram against these hated, acquisitive coupon-clippers. Despite his maudlin self-flattery, Robert Byrd and the rest of his party don't resent the rich on behalf of the poor. They resent the rich on behalf of the government. Poor Senator

Byrd can't rest knowing there may still be a toilet in West Virginia that is not named for Bob Byrd. ■

☞ Chair-Warmer on the Hot Seat

MARCH 24, 2004

Are you sitting down? Another ex–government official who was fired or demoted by Bush has written a book that . . . is critical of Bush! Eureka! The latest offering is Richard Clarke's new CBS-Viacom book, *Against All Enemies,* which gets only a 35 on "rate a record" because the words don't make sense and you can't dance to it. For those of you who haven't heard of Dick Clarke—that is to say, all of you—he's a career back-bencher who was passed over as National Security Adviser in favor of Condoleezza Rice, who later demoted him (speaking of hidden agendas).

As long as we're investigating everything, how about investigating why some loser no one has ever heard of is getting so much press coverage for yet another "tell-all" book attacking the Bush administration? Kiss-and-tell books about the Bush administration by disgruntled ex-employees looking to make a quick buck are coming out as fast as "Elvis and Me" books by distant relatives of the King after his death. This is not to compare the two: At least the authors of the Elvis books had more than "facial expressions" to report.

When an FBI agent with close, regular contact with President Clinton wrote his book, he was virtually blacklisted from the mainstream media. Upon the release of Gary Aldrich's book *Unlimited Access* in 1996, White House adviser George Stephanopoulos immediately called TV producers demanding that they give Aldrich no airtime. *Larry King Live* and NBC's *Dateline* abruptly canceled their scheduled interviews with Aldrich. Aldrich was mentioned on fewer than a dozen TV shows during the entire year of his book's release—many with headlines like this one on CNN: "Even Conservatives Back Away from Aldrich's Book." That's almost as much TV as Lewinsky mouthpiece William Ginsburg did before breakfast on an average day. (Let's take a moment here to imagine the indignity of being known as "Monica Lewinsky's mouthpiece.") In terms of TV exposure, Aldrich's book might well have been titled "No Access Whatsoever."

But a "tell-all" book that attacks the Bush administration gets the author interviewed on CBS's *60 Minutes* (two segments), CNN's *American Morning*, and ABC's *Good Morning America*— with an "analysis" by George Stephanopoulos, no less. In the first few days of its release, Clarke's book was hyped on more than two hundred TV shows.

In contrast to Aldrich's book, which was vindicated with a whoop just a few years later when the Monica Lewinsky scandal broke, many of Clarke's allegations were disproven within days of the book's release. Clarke claims, for example, that in early 2001, when he told Condoleezza Rice about al Qaeda, her "facial expression gave me the impression that she had never heard the term before." (If only she used Botox like Senator Kerry!) Sean Hannity has been playing a radio interview that Dr. Rice gave to David Newman on WJR in Detroit back in October 2000, in which she discusses al Qaeda in some detail. This was months before chair-warmer Clarke claims her "facial expression" indicated she had never heard of the terrorist organization.

But in deference to our liberal friends, let's leave aside the facts for now. A few months before Clarke was interpreting Dr. Rice's "facial expression," al Qaeda had bombed the USS *Cole*. Two years before that, al Qaeda bombed U.S. embassies in Kenya and Tanzania. In fact, al Qaeda or their allies had been responsible for a half dozen attacks on U.S. interests since Clinton had become president. (Paper-pusher Clarke was doing one heck of a job, wasn't he?) In the year 2000 alone, LexisNexis lists 280 items mentioning al Qaeda. By the end of 2000, anyone who read the paper had heard of al Qaeda. It is literally insane to imagine that Condoleezza Rice had not. For Pete's sake, even the *New York Times* knew about al Qaeda.

Rice had been a political science professor at Stanford University, a member of the Center for International Security and Arms Control, and a senior fellow of the Stanford Institute for International Studies. She had written three books and numerous articles on foreign policy. She worked for the first Bush administration in a variety of national security positions. All this was while Clarke was presiding over six unanswered al Qaeda attacks on American interests and fretting about the looming Y2K emergency. Of course, Madeleine Albright also had some fancy degrees and important positions, so let me add: Anyone who has listened to Rice for sixty seconds knows that she is very smart. But chair-warmer Clarke claims that on the basis of Rice's "facial expression" he could tell she was not familiar with the term "al Qaeda."

Isn't that just like a liberal? The chair-warmer describes Bush as a cowboy and Rumsfeld as his gunslinger—but the black chick is a dummy. Maybe even as dumb as Clarence Thomas! Perhaps someday liberals could map out the relative intelligence of various black government officials for us.

Did Clarke have the vaguest notion of Rice's background and education? Or did he think Dr. Rice was cleaning the Old Executive Office Building at night before the president chose her—not him—to be national security adviser? If a Republican ever claimed the "facial expression" on Maxine Waters—a woman whose face is no stranger to confusion or befuddlement—left the "impression" that she didn't understand quantum physics, he'd be in prison for committing a hate crime.

As we know from Dr. Rice's radio interview describing the threat of al Qaeda back in October 2000, she certainly didn't need to be told about al Qaeda by a government time-server. No doubt Dr. Rice was staring at Clarke in astonishment as he imparted this great insight: *Keep an eye on al Qaeda! We've done nothing, but you should do something about it. Tag—you're it.* That look of perplexity Clarke saw was Condi thinking to herself, "Hmmm, did I demote this guy far enough?" ■

6

When Bad Ideas (Liberalism) Happen to Good People (You)

———————— ■ ————————

☞ The *New York Times*'s Crusade Against Capitalism

JANUARY 24, 2002

Before the *New York Times* starts running "Portraits in Grief" of former Enron employees, it's worth remembering that even after the collapse, Enron stock is still worth more than the entire Social Security "trust fund." Liberals have suspended their typical class-envy paradigm long enough to weep huge crocodile tears for the almost-rich. Weren't these the precise people we were trained to hate in the nineties as they high-fived one another amid extravagant claims of retirement by age forty? In record time, we've gone from schadenfreude to lachrymose liberal pity. Poor ghetto blacks must be transfixed by the turn of events that supplanted them with erstwhile "yuppie scum" as the new class-war victims.

When this much bathos is expended on middle-class white

people with stock portfolios, liberals are up to no good. The only coherence to the *Times*'s wildly contradictory feelings toward rich yuppies is that they want to scare people away from the stock market. The *Times* is openly rooting for a prolonged recession, if not a depression. They are desperately trying to destroy people's faith in the market, in 401(k)s—in capitalism. When President Bush merely acknowledged that the economy was in a recession soon after he took office, liberals screamed that he was "talking down the economy." But now liberals are willing to wreck the whole country to help the Democratic Party. A continuing weak stock market would serve the Democrats' short-term interest of bashing Bush as well as their long-term interest of keeping Americans dependent on the government.

Thus, the *Times* cites Enron in order to sneer about the "view" that investing in the market would provide Americans with robust retirement funds amid snippy references to the "now dormant" idea of privatizing Social Security. Even the *Times*'s pet cause of campaign-finance reform is somehow more urgently needed in the wake of Enron's collapse. The morality play being showcased in the *Times* concerns "the plight of loyal workers who lost retirement savings while company officials cashed in $1.1 billion in stock." This puts a human face on the *Times*'s vicious attacks on "the integrity of markets."

Not so fast. Even if Enron executives had sold no stock whatsoever in 2001, Enron shares would still be worthless. Enron executives may well be guilty of criminal misconduct: That is a separate, discrete matter to be determined by the criminal laws. But just because your boss is a criminal doesn't make you a victim. Contrary to lugubrious news stories, there is no causal relationship between the boss selling his stock and the employees' losses.

The reason the employees lost money is that Enron had a faulty business model and the company went bankrupt. Whenever a company collapses, the people who own it (stockholders) lose money. That's why people always tell you not to put all your money in a single company's stock. Enron employees had eighteen investment options, but many decided to invest heavily in the high-flying company stock.

The only beef Enron employees have with top management is that management did not inform employees of the coming collapse in time to allow them to get in on the swindle, too. If Enron executives had shouted, "Head for the hills!," the employees might have been able to sucker other Americans into buying their wildly overinflated Enron stock, as their bosses apparently did. The employees were victims only in the sense that they were not able to get in on the rip-off, too.

Moreover, the billions of dollars Enron employees "lost" in paper profits they had gained only in the last few years. Between 1997 and 2000, Enron stock quadrupled in price, while the Standard & Poor's 500 index edged up only a few percentage points. In 2000, Enron stock was trading at an astronomical 66 times recent earnings. Until ten minutes ago, people who made a quick buck in the stock market were dot-com millionaire yuppie scum. Now when the market collapses before they cash out, they are, as the *Times* puts it, "the tale's most sympathetic characters, its victims." Compared with what the stock was worth in 1997, Enron employees lost an average of about $20,000 per employee in the largest company failure in U.S. history. I've lost more money on Social Security in that time, and no one's weeping for me.

Liberals have leapt on Enron's collapse to try to persuade Americans to avoid the market altogether. They would prefer that the middle class put all its money under the mattress. The stock market, the *Times* instructs, is not for the little people because—as the headline of the Week in Review proclaimed—"The Rich Are Different. They Know When to Get Out." Manifestly, the rich do not know when to get out. Otherwise, we wouldn't be hearing about the ripple effect of Enron's collapse hitting the likes of Citicorp—despite the lobbying efforts of billionaire Democrat Robert Rubin. The rich do, however, have more money, a point that is endlessly intriguing to liberals. The lesson liberals want the middle class to glean from this is: Do not invest in the market! End hope! Trust Big Brother. ■

☞ It's Just About Money
JULY 25, 2002

Liberals' comprehension of corporate scandals is like the Woody Allen joke about reading Tolstoy's *War and Peace* in twenty minutes after taking a speed-reading course. *Q: What's it about? A: It involves Russia.*

George Bush and Dick Cheney's connection to corporate corruption consists primarily of the media's capacity to mention their names in the same sentence as "corporate corruption" one million times a day. Liberals think their saying someone's name in an accusatory tone of voice is sufficient to impute criminality to Republicans. Since Republicans are intrinsically evil, merely mentioning their names suffices to make any point liberals want to make. Bush and Cheney have bought and sold stock! The swine!

Whenever the media start intoning darkly about "perceptions," "the full details," "unanswered questions," and—most pathetic— "the shadow of Enron"—that rustling you hear is the sound of wool being pulled over your eyes. In fact, there are no "unanswered questions" about Bush and Cheney. There are only insipid insinuations.

The facts are: Bush sold his stock in Harken Energy to purchase the Texas Rangers. The price of the stock later went down. (And then it went up to more than what he sold it for.) Amid hectoring from liberals that he do so, Cheney sold his interest in Halliburton before he assumed the vice presidency to eliminate the possibility of a conflict of interest. Later, the price of that stock went down—in large part because trial lawyers were filing asbestos suits against Halliburton. It's not illegal to sell or buy stock. It's illegal to sell stock based on insider information that the price is about to tank or to buy stock based on the insider information that the price is about to soar.

Thus, the Democrats' theory is that Bush bought the Texas Rangers and Cheney became vice president only as part of wily scams to conceal their real reason for selling stock: insider information! Of this, there is no evidence. Literally no evidence, in contradistinction to when liberals say there is "no evidence," meaning there hasn't been a conviction in a court of law but there is lots of evidence. The imputation of criminality to Bush and Cheney is so ludicrous that even in the girly-girl, eye-poking attacks on the *New York Times* op-ed page it has been roundly admitted that there is no question of "any criminality" (Frank Rich) and that "Mr. Bush broke no laws" (Nicholas Kristof). Representative Barney Frank, the only honest Democrat in the House, has repeatedly said that it is "not a case of Dick Cheney violating the law." Rather, the media explain their baseless sneering about the president and vice president as attempts to "add to our knowledge of the ethics, policies and personnel of a secretive administration," as Rich put it.

It's a little late for liberals to pretend they care about ethics. These are the people who angrily defended a president who perjured himself, hid evidence, suborned perjury, was held in contempt by a federal court, was disbarred by the Supreme Court, and lied to his party, his staff, his wife, and the nation. The ethics of that president included having staff perform oral sex on him in the Oval Office as he chatted on the phone with a congressman about sending American troops into battle. The secular saints of liberalism indignantly defended all this on the grounds that it's fine to lie and commit crimes if it's "just about sex."

Well, evidently some corporate chieftains took that lesson to heart and concluded that it's also fine to commit crimes if it's "just about money." Just as Ronald Reagan gave American culture a renewed patriotism and self-confidence that outlasted his presidency, Clinton has bequeathed America a culture of criminality and rationalization by the powerful. But still, somehow, Republicans are said to be more vulnerable whenever a businessman becomes a crook on the basis of their general support of capitalism. But if criminality and not capitalism is to blame, then Democrats are to blame for their general support of crooks. As part of the Left's long-standing fanatical defense of their favorite criminal, Bill Clinton, it will be screeched that conservatives want to blame everything on Clinton, including the wacky idea that a direct assault on honor and honesty led some people to behave dishonorably and dishonestly.

Not everything. But some of us called this ball and this pocket years ago:

"If Congress doesn't have the will to throw him out, Clinton will have set a new standard for the entire country. The new standard will be a total absence of standards. . . . If you get caught and don't have a good enough legal team to escape, you might have to pay a fine or go to prison. But there's no shame in it. The country doesn't really condemn this. We adore a lovable rogue. . . . It is fine to lie and cheat and manipulate because honor is just a word, just hot air and the country doesn't believe in it" (*High Crimes and Misdemeanors: The Case Against Bill Clinton*, 1998).

It took a bear market to inexorably repeal the Clintonian national motto of "Just Do It!" ∎

☞ This Just In: Price Controls Cause Shortages

FEBRUARY 2 , 2001

Another "Dog Bites Man" story has once again taken the American press corps by storm. California's electricity crisis is treated in the media as if it were some sort of natural disaster, like a hurricane. But the only fact of nature operating here is the hard-and-fast rule that whenever you come across a screw-up this big, you know the government is behind it. The California legislature created this problem about five years ago when it deregulated the wholesale market for electricity but fixed prices at the retail level, based on economic principles that have made Cuba the happy, prosperous country that it is today.

Needless to say, eventually wholesale prices soared, but the utilities were prohibited from passing their increased costs on to consumers. Buy high, sell low! (Isn't that what they teach you in business school?) Since the California utilities are about to go bankrupt on the governmentally imposed "Buy high, sell low" strategy, no one will sell them electricity. So now there's no electricity in California—but at least it's cheap!

You are probably wondering how it is that multibillion-dollar corporations with highly paid business school graduates populating their corporate risk-management departments could have failed to anticipate price fluctuations in the electricity market and entered into long-term contracts. The answer is: Remember what I said about screw-ups this big. California actually prohibited utilities from entering into long-term contracts. (The California legislature came up with many other idiotic ways to mess up the electricity market; this is just the highlight reel.) If California utilities had relied on evil, bloodsucking hedge-fund managers rather than the California Centralized Committee to Fix Prices and Plan Markets, they'd have plenty of electricity now.

To repeat: The California Legislature fixed prices at which electricity could be sold to consumers and prohibited utilities from entering into long-term contracts to hedge the electricity market, leading like night into day to wild fluctuations in the price of electricity, but the utilities couldn't recoup their costs because the government had fixed prices in the retail market. In the mainstream media, this is known as "deregulation."

In point of fact, the California electricity crisis resulted from government policies that are the opposite of deregulation, the antimatter of deregulation, as antithetical to deregulation as class and decorum are to Courtney Love. If the California legislature had helped the Soviet Union with its transition from Communism to a market economy, the farmers would be experiencing their eighty-fourth year of "bad weather" again this year. Instead, only California utilities had "bad weather." The utilities signed on to what was a politically attractive package at the time, and now it turns out they stepped on a rake and the rake hit them in the face.

Why is it so difficult for people to grasp the advantages of a free market? It's never going to get any easier than this. Only a little over a decade ago, the centralized planning of the Eastern bloc was exposed as having created a squalid, poverty-stricken abyss. Meanwhile, corrupt running-dog lackeys of the capitalist system here in America managed to produce a society in which the poorest citizens have televisions, refrigerators, telephones, and the opportunity to appear on the *Jerry Springer Show*.

But no matter how often capitalism manages to produce good products at low prices, and no matter how spectacular the failures of government intervention are, some segment of the population continually lists toward the old Soviet bread-distribution model. Evidently, the free market is a counterintuitive concept. People have to be constantly reminded how excellent the market is at distributing goods and services.

The basic idea of a free market is that the consumer and seller enter directly into mutually beneficial transactions. The consumer has the best information about what he wants and how much he is willing to pay; the seller has the best information about what he can provide and what it will cost him. That's how we end up with great products like reasonably priced Chia pets in the shape of Jerry Garcia's head.

The government bureaucrats' rallying cry is "Insert a middleman!" They simply cannot shake the conviction that they are in possession of the millions of constantly changing pieces of information that the market processes continually and effortlessly. If we ever let these bureaucrats run free, stores everywhere would run with the smooth Austrian precision of the Department of Motor Vehicles. Naturally, the California legislature's solution to a problem created by the government is: more government! California voters ought to say what the Democratic Party is now gently trying to convey to Bill Clinton—thanks, but you've already done enough. ■

☞ The Democrats' Laboratory: The Host Organism Dies

AUGUST 13, 2003

In June 2002, the liberal *American Prospect* magazine was hailing California as a "laboratory" for Democratic policies. With "its Democratic governor, U.S. senators, state legislature and congressional delegation," author Harold Meyerson gushed, "California is the only one of the nation's 10 largest states that is uniformly under Democratic control." In the Golden State, Meyerson said, "the next New Deal is in tryouts." (Can't you just feel the tension building?)

Just a few years before that, the impresario of this adventure in Democratic governance, Governor Gray Davis, was being touted as presidential material—which wasn't nearly as insulting a thing to say to a politician back then as it is now that we've seen the current crop of Democrats running for president. Analyst Charles Cook said Davis was "a major player in the Democratic Party." Around the time of the 2000 Democratic National Convention in Los Angeles, Davis was forced to announce that he would decline offers to be Al Gore's running mate. Gore advisers cooed that "Gray would certainly be one of those names that would have to be in the mix." Perhaps their campaign slogan could have been "bland and blander." Both were said to be "cautious, moderate 'New Democrats.'" Both were veterans, after a fashion, of Vietnam, which would make a Gore-Davis presidential ticket the only compelling argument yet in favor of friendly fire.

California is, in fact, a perfect petri dish of Democratic policies. This is what happens when you let Democrats govern: You
get a state—or as it's now known, a "job-free zone"—with a
$38 billion deficit, which is larger than the budgets of forty-
eight states. There are reports that Argentina and the Congo are
sending their fiscal policy experts to Sacramento to help stabi-
lize the situation. California's credit rating has been slashed to
junk-bond status, and citizens are advised to stock up for the not-
too-far-off day when cigarettes and Botox become the hard cur-
rency of choice. At this stage, we couldn't give California back to
Mexico.

Democrats governed their petri dish as they always govern.
They buy the votes of government workers with taxpayer-funded
jobs, salaries, and benefits—and then turn around and accuse the
productive class of "greed" for wanting their taxes cut. This has
worked so well nationally that more people in America now work
for the government than work in any sort of manufacturing job.

Strictly adhering to formula in California, as the private sector
was bleeding jobs and money, Governor Davis signed off on comically generous pensions for government workers. Government
employees in the Golden State earn more than the private-sector
workers who pay their salaries—and that's excluding the job security, health benefits, and 90 percent pension plans that come with
"Irish welfare," as government jobs used to be called.

Economists refer to this backward ratio between public and
private-sector salaries as "France." (Inasmuch as they are paid
more and work less than private-sector employees, perhaps we
could ease up on treating public school teachers like Mother
Teresa washing the feet of the poor in Calcutta.) The public-sector
unions repaid Davis with massive contributions to his reelection
campaign. Davis bought himself reelection and is now the most
hated officeholder in America. The people of California are willing to plunge their state into humiliation and chaos just to get rid
of him in a recall election. The fact that Arianna Huffington

hasn't been laughed off a stage yet is a pretty good gauge of the public's frustration with Governor Davis.

And yet Bill and Hillary Clinton and the rest of the Democratic Party think Gray Davis is doing a super job. Democrats have denounced the California recall—a genuine citizens' revolt—as a "circus." According to recent polls, two out of three people in this overwhelmingly Democratic state want Davis out, and still the recall is being called a "Republican power grab." Most touchingly, Democrats claim to be shocked at the exorbitant cost of a recall election. They were not such penny-pinchers when contemplating Enron-style pensions for school crossing guards. Nor did their fiscal conservatism kick in when Davis announced this week that he would sign legislation providing "intolerance and hatred control training" for all California schoolteachers. Yeah, this guy definitely deserves another crack at straightening out the budget.

National Republicans are reluctant to let Davis go. They had been enjoying watching the Democrats' petri dish disintegrate into a parasite's paradise. So there were long faces all around when the Terminator threw his hat into the ring. No longer content to play an evil robot, actor Arnold Schwarzenegger will now be running against one. Far be it from me to tell Republicans to stop enjoying the Democrats' pain, but California is about to fall into the ocean. Either Schwarzenegger will come and dismantle the government employees' Versailles Palace, or California will continue to be a laboratory for failed liberal policies and we won't be able to give it back to Mexico. ■

☞ Nine Out of Ten Caribou Support Drilling

APRIL 18, 2002

Having wearied of opposing the war on terrorism, Democrats are now trying to sabotage the country's energy policy. George Bush has proposed drilling in a tiny, desolate portion of Alaska's Arctic National Wildlife Refuge, or ANWR. A better idea, Democrats think, is to keep sending large amounts of money to countries that nurture homicidal Muslims intent on destroying America.

ABC-NBC-CBS have been accompanying discussions of ANWR with picturesque footage of caribou frolicking in lush, fertile fields—all of which happens to be nowhere near the site of the proposed drilling. ANWR is 19 million acres—larger than Massachusetts, New Jersey, Hawaii, Connecticut, and Delaware combined. If oil is found, less than 2,000 acres would be directly affected. The area targeted for drilling looks a little like the moon, but less inviting.

Consequently, Gale Norton, the secretary of the interior, responded to the campaign of lies by unveiling actual film footage of the area at issue. She sent a true and accurate film of the proposed drilling site to the networks and also posted the footage on the department's website. Representative Ed Markey of Massachusetts (Democrat, needless to say) claims this underhanded dissemination of the truth is illegal. Telling the truth is not merely contrary to the principles of the Democratic Party, now they claim it's against the law. As Markey explains, the law prohibits agencies from promoting any "film presentation designed to support or defeat legislation pending before the Congress." At least we have Markey on the record admitting that a truthful presentation of the proposed drilling site would persuade Congress to support drilling. According to a leading Democratic opponent of the plan, lying is the key to defeating ANWR.

It was bad enough when Democrats just lied a lot themselves, purported not to know what "is" means, and claimed that "everybody" lied, perjured themselves, and suborned the perjury of others. Markey has staked out a more aggressive position by announcing that Republicans who tell the truth are breaking the law.

ANWR exploration is overwhelmingly supported by Alaskans, Eskimos, Teamsters, and caribou. It is opposed by Northeastern liberals who would never set foot anywhere near ANWR and haven't the first idea what it looks like. The word "wildlife" in ANWR's title is somewhat misleading. The coastal plain—where the drilling would occur—is in total darkness half the year and reaches temperatures of 50 below zero. Most of the time it is uninhabited and uninhabitable by wildlife. The only living things in the vicinity of the coastal plain—Eskimos and caribou—enthusiastically support drilling.

When oil exploration began in Alaska's Prudhoe Bay thirty years ago, environmentalists claimed it would yield only a "few months' supply" of oil and would wreck the ecosystem. We started drilling and Prudhoe Bay turned out to be the largest deposit of oil ever found in North America. Not only that, but the caribou of the famous "ecosystem" loved the pipeline. They frolic and play by it, leaping to and fro near the warmth. Apparently, the pipeline makes them frisky, too: In twenty years, the caribou population has skyrocketed, from 3,000 to almost 27,100.

The Teamsters have been huge supporters of drilling in ANWR, but Democrats treat union members the way they treat blacks: Vote for us and we'll give you nothing. Ed "The Truth Is Illegal" Markey responded to Teamster support for ANWR by dismissively sniffing that it was only "one issue." Democrats expect union money and endorsements, but when the prospect of half a million high-paying jobs comes along, the Democrats tell workers it's only "one issue." Luckily, the Democrats have all those other issues dear to the heart of the average blue-collar worker: abortion on demand, gay marriage, and taxpayer-funded crucifixes-submerged-in-urine.

So much for "everyone" sacrificing for the war on terrorism. Little old ladies get strip-searched at airports, but the environmentalists won't budge on an uninhabitable wasteland at the continent's edge. The Democrats' idea of sacrifice after 9/11 is for Senator Teddy Kennedy to stop getting drunk on airplanes and goosing stewardesses.

When not jetting around the country on his private plane, paid for by the deceased husband of his second wife, Senator John Kerry has emerged as a leading opponent of ANWR. Developing new sources of energy, Kerry says, is "old thinking." The Democrats' innovative new thinking is for the little people to wear sweaters and drive smaller cars.

That's a bold stroke: We'll delay starvation by eating a little less each day. The illogic of it confounds reason. Everyone is against waste—except Democrats telling the rest of us to conserve from their Gulfstream private jets. (How about they set an example by conserving our money?) We need more energy. Postponing death is not an energy policy.

Markey has similarly "innovative" ideas. He proposes that we "bring OPEC to its knees" by "our technological superiority." What he means by "technological superiority" is this: "Let's make SUVs get 30 miles a gallon"! How about we make cars and airplanes that run on dirt? Or hot air, and run a pipeline from the Capitol? There is not a thinking man's Democrat in the country. If only caribou voted instead of Democrats, the country would finally have a serious energy policy. ■

☞ All the News We Heard from a Guy at Handgun Control, Inc.

MAY 16, 2002

Having been assured by "Handgun Control, Inc." (aka the Brady Campaign) that the Constitution protects only kiddie porn and says absolutely nothing about guns, the *New York Times* has been viciously denouncing Attorney General John Ashcroft for having the temerity to suggest that the Second Amendment protects the "right of the people to keep and bear arms." This, the *Times* proclaims, is "radical," "ominous," and a "betrayal of [Ashcroft's] public duty." In an eerie coincidence, the Second Amendment actually says, "the right of the people to keep and bear arms shall not be infringed."

In its inimitable Stalinist style, the *Times* claims Ashcroft's position is "contrary to longstanding and bipartisan interpretation of the Second Amendment." This is always how liberals engage in obvious jabberwocky: They smugly announce a "broad consensus" among "respected academics"—meaning one of their interns went to the trouble of calling "Handgun Control, Inc."

First of all, any journalist who is completely unaware that there is debate about the Second Amendment ought to be fired. But more preposterously, though a "bipartisan consensus" has begun to develop, it has gone heavily against the *Times*'s position. For over a decade now, liberal law professors keep setting out to disprove the "pro-gun extremists"—as the *Times* calls people who disagree with the *Times*. Gleefully intending to establish that the Second Amendment refers only to the right of state militias to have guns, the professors invariably conclude, with great lugubriousness, that the gun nuts are right.

By now, the growing roster of law professors who support the "radical," "ominous" Ashcroft position includes Larry Tribe of Harvard, Akhil Amar of Yale, and Sanford Levinson of the University of Texas. (In happier circumstances, these professors are known as "respected" at the *Times*.) Among sitting Supreme Court justices, five have raised the Second Amendment in opinions just since 1990. The Second Amendment even made a cameo appearance in the very opinion that constitutes definition of constitutional law at the *Times: Roe v. Wade*. Every single one of those citations assumes that the right to bear arms belongs to "the people," not only militia members.

Indeed, the one guy the *Times* dredged out of the left-wing toilet willing to provide tepid endorsement to their bunkum was Stanford history professor Jack Rakove. Even Rakove—the only academic still defending Michael Bellesiles's fraudulent antigun book *Arming America*—wouldn't stoop to supporting the *Times*'s preposterous claims. Far from asserting a "bipartisan consensus" for the *Times*'s view, Rakove said it is "no secret" that controversy over the Second Amendment "has escalated in recent years." (Except at the *Times,* where it remains a huge secret.) Moreover, Rakove's big rebuke to Ashcroft consisted of his meek observation that "it is far from clear that the Justice Department's new position would prevail." For taking a position that an antigun zealot says might not prevail, the *Times* says Ashcroft is betraying "his public duty."

But for bald-faced lies, nothing beats the *Times*'s preposterous characterization of Supreme Court precedent. The most recent case directly raising the Second Amendment was *United States v. Miller,* decided in 1939. (Any conservative who demanded deference to a case from 1939 would be accused of trying to lynch blacks and brutalize women.) The *Miller* case simply defined the types of guns protected by the Second Amendment, not who was entitled to have guns. Reviewing the case of two bootleggers charged with failing to pay federal taxes on a sawed-off shotgun, the Court concluded that the "instrument" was not covered by the Second Amendment. Since the *Times* lies about the relevant language, I will quote it in full:

> In the absence of any evidence tending to show that possession or use of a "shotgun having a barrel of less than 18 inches in length" at this time has some reasonable relationship to the preservation or efficiency of a well-regulated militia, we cannot say that the Second Amendment guarantees the right to keep and bear such an instrument. Certainly it is not within judicial notice that this weapon is any part of the ordinary military equipment or that its use could contribute to the common defense.

The vigilant observer will note that the Court did not find that since the defendants were bootleggers—and not members of a militia—they had no Second Amendment rights. Rather, the Court's conclusion turned solely on the fact that a sawed-off shotgun was not "ordinary military equipment." As Professor Levinson (card-carrying member of the ACLU) said of the decision, "Ironically, *Miller* can be read to support some of the most extreme anti–gun control arguments, e.g., that the individual citizen has a right to keep and bear bazookas, rocket launchers and . . . assault weapons."

Now observe how the *Times* mischaracterizes the *Miller* decision. In a ham-handed deception, the *Times* substitutes the word "rights" for "guns," and claims that the Court found that "the Second Amendment protects only those rights that have 'some reasonable relationship to the preservation of efficiency of a well-regulated militia.'" If the *Times* is going to dismiss the views of Harvard and Yale law professors, Supreme Court justices, and constitutional scholars Joseph Story and Thomas Cooley in deference to the press releases of a fanatical antigun lobbying group, they might want to find one with smarter lawyers than Handgun Control, Inc. ■

7

More Liberal Ideas! Sex, Segregation, Gay Marriage, and Banning the G-Word (God!)

———————— ■ ————————

☞ Chicks with D****

JANUARY 2000

(or about one year before *Vanity Fair* noticed *Sex and the City* was about gay men even though everyone yelled at me for saying it in *George* magazine)

It's getting so you can't turn on the TV or open a newspaper without hearing some girl boasting about her latest sexual conquest. From Hollywood starlets embarrassing the adorable Conan O'Brien with their inane prattle about "phallic" symbols, masturbation, and breast augmentation, to every tabloid in the country publishing preposterous female "sex columnists," it seems as if the country has been inhabited by an alien breed of women. The first thing that strikes you about the slutty-girls phenomenon is: This is not how women talk. This is how some men might talk—if women would let them. We have some idea what that sounds like. Some men, oddly enough, aren't willing to curb their instinctive promiscuity and embrace monogamy in order to get a girl. They're known as gay men.

See if you can spot the cultural clues here: In HBO's *Sex and the City*, a classic in the slutty-girl genre, the fictional characters blather endlessly about anal sex, oral sex, casual sex, wrinkled buttocks, spanking, boy toys, sex toys, and the ennui of marriage. This is not girls talking like girls, it's not even girls talking like guys exactly, but girls talking like gay men. (Another hint is that the only appealing male character is a gay man.)

The odd thing is, this campy joke of women playing gay men is apparently lost on everyone outside of Manhattan—at least if you credit the hayseeds who have been eagerly furnishing miss-the-point quotes to various news outlets. Girls living out in America steadfastly insist they find *Sex and the City* totally realistic. "I feel like they really are saying the things we're all thinking," Alana Peters told the *New York Times*. Are sweet Southern belles in Atlanta really all thinking about sex in "coarse euphemisms for body parts"—as the *Times* delicately describes the dialogue on *Sex and the City*? And is Alana's boyfriend having sex with *his* dog? (That was one recent episode.) Please. They're lying. But why?

Curiously, claims about the amazing realism of *Sex and the City* are often accompanied by defensive statements about how cosmopolitan Atlanta or Milwaukee is. "We are a mini–New York here," proclaimed Atlanta resident Lara Preister, explaining her enthusiasm for the show to a *Times* reporter. "It's not like we're Scarlett O'Hara and we get all upset when people swear." Oh dear. These girls seem to imagine *Sex and the City* is real.

In the "Cheese State," Pam Schlesner was quoted in the *Milwaukee Journal Sentinel* saying she, too, sees herself in the fictional characters. Really? The ones encouraging one another to have anal sex? That episode drove a reviewer from the *Village Voice* to remark that the character's "enthusiasm was the tipoff that a man wrote the scene." And yet, Ms. Schlesner praised the dead-on accuracy of *Sex and the City*, saying the show's "writing crew must follow her around for script fodder." More probably, Pam is following the show for life fodder. Pam said she and her friends recently took it upon themselves to spend a weekend "having sex like a man"—a hobby of the *Sex and the City* characters—picking up strangers for sex and then plotting to get the studs out of their homes as early in the morning as possible.

This is taking New York envy to dangerous extremes. A few years ago, I realized that my friends in the Midwest, avid Seinfeld devotees, had no idea that Jerry Seinfeld was Jewish. But that was merely droll: It did not lead them to invite Ted Bundy back to their apartments for sex. Okay Miss Cheese State, we won't call you a backwater hick, but think hard: Do you actually know girls who talk about sex using the d-word and c-word to describe specific body parts? No you don't. You know gay men who do. See, e.g., the *Village Voice*. Indeed, even the show's perky star, Sarah Jessica Parker, reportedly uses language no coarser than "Oh God!" or "geeze Louise" off the set. Girls talking the way they do on *Sex and the City* is about as realistic as George Bush playing a gangsta rapper, talking about "ho's" and "bitches."

Instead of wiping away years of humorless feminist tyranny, this new breed of smutty girls have taken the error of the feminists and raised it. There are differences between boys and girls. One of the big ones is: Girls do not relentlessly pursue casual sex. In one famous study conducted at the University of Hawaii—and one that drives the sexual egalitarians crazy—male and female "researchers" approached single college students of the opposite sex in bars to propose only one of three options: (1) a date, (2) going back to the questioner's apartment, or (3) immediate sex. Fifty percent of men accepted the date; 69 percent agreed to go back to the apartment; and 75 percent agreed to immediate sex. Half the women agreed to a date; 6 percent consented to go to the apartment, and none—zero—agreed to sex.

Not to belabor the obvious, but the only girls who actively seek casual sex seem to be girls in Milwaukee who think *Sex and the City* is how the cool New York City chicks really behave. (Or girls in New York City who think *Sex and the City* is how the cool New York City chicks really behave.)

Meanwhile, gay men totally get it. Hell, a gay man writes it. The TV show *Sex and the City* is the creation of wunderkind Darren Star. Star was also the creator of *Melrose Place* and *Central Park West*, described in the press as "almost cultishly gay faves." The openly gay Star sardonically remarked of his *Sex and the City* creation, "I guess I just have a strong feminine side." Not long after the original *Sex and the City* column debuted in the *New York Observer*, the *New York Times* reported that "'The boys at World Gym' said in a fan letter that they were convinced [the authoress] was a gay man in a woman's body." That's the irony. While being celebrated for being so very outré, even Hollywood is not ready to let gay men out of the closet but has to disguise them in women's bodies. ∎

DECEMBER 5, 2003: Trent Lott Toasts Strom Thurmond
at Thurmond's 100th Birthday Party

☞ Democrats: A Lott of Trouble

DECEMBER 18, 2002

I'm just glad Strom Thurmond isn't around to see this. Statisticians believe Trent Lott is now on track to break Bill Clinton's single-season record for public apologies. During his recent *B.E.T.* appearance, Lott said he supported affirmative action and regretted voting against the Martin Luther King Jr. holiday, and that he'd give *The Bernie Mac Show* another try.

What the Lott incident shows is that Republicans have to be careful about letting Democrats into our party. Back when they supported segregation, Lott and Thurmond were Democrats. This is something the media are intentionally hiding to make it look like the Republican Party is the party of segregation and race discrimination, which it never has been.

In 1948, Thurmond did not run as a "Dixiecan," he ran as a "Dixiecrat"—his party was an offshoot of the Democratic Party. And when he lost, he went right back to being a Democrat. This whole brouhaha is about a former Democrat praising another former Democrat for what was once a Democrat policy.

Republicans made Southern Democrats drop the race nonsense when they entered the Republican Party. Democrats supported race discrimination, then for about three years they didn't, now they do again. They've just changed which race they think should be discriminated against. In the 1920s, the Democratic platforms didn't even call for antilynching legislation as the Republican platforms did.

Thurmond's Dixiecrat Party was not the only extremist spinoff from the Democratic Party in 1948. Henry Wallace, formerly FDR's vice president and agriculture secretary, left the Democratic Party that year to form the Communist-dominated and Soviet-backed "Progressive Party." Much as Thurmond's Dixiecrat Party was expressly prosegregation, Wallace's Progressive Party was expressly pro-Soviet. Indeed, this was the apex of Moscow-directed subversion of U.S. politics. The Progressive Party platform excluded even the mildest criticism of Soviet aggression. It will come as no surprise that many American celebrities supported Wallace. The Progressives received one million votes nationwide, about the same as Thurmond's Dixiecrat Party.

Thurmond went on to reject segregation, become a Republican, and serve his country well as a U.S. senator. By contrast, running a Communist-dominated presidential campaign was Wallace's last hurrah. Yet only an off-the-cuff remark at a birthday party praising Thurmond's presidential campaign is the career-destroyer. Not so fawning references to Wallace's Soviet-backed presidential campaign.

Just two years before Lott's remarks, a hagiographic book on Wallace's life was released, *American Dreamer*. How about a book about a segregationist titled "American Dreamer"? Wallace's version of the American "dream" was Communism every bit as much as Strom Thurmond's dream was segregation. Aren't dreams of murderous dictators, gulags, and death camps at least comparable in evil to segregated lunch counters?

The dust jacket on *American Dreamer* featured a nauseating statement of praise by Senator Edward Kennedy. Kennedy said that the book deserved "to be read by all who care about the American dream." The American dream: Communist totalitarianism. Why wasn't the lecherous liberal asked to retire for his flattering remarks about a proven Soviet fifth-columnist?

In 1999, the Clinton administration dedicated a room at the Agriculture Department to Wallace. At the dedication, former Democratic presidential candidate George McGovern gave a speech explicitly praising Wallace's pro-Soviet positions, such as the idea that the Cold War was "overdone" and that "problems" between the nations "could not be resolved by military means."

McGovern fondly recalled that he himself had voted for Wallace. He chipperly reminded the audience that he had run for president in 1972 "on a similar platform"—with the help of a young Yale law school graduate named Bill Clinton. Inasmuch as Trent Lott was in kindergarten in 1948, he did not vote for Thurmond. He did not run on a "similar" platform to the Dixiecrats. He did not write a jacket-flap endorsement calling a segregationist an "American Dreamer."

The idea that Lott took the occasion of an old-timer's birthday to introduce a new policy initiative to bring back segregation—a

Democrat policy—is ludicrous. Lott is a fine fellow; he just has some sort of liberal-Tourette's syndrome that makes him spout Democrat ideas at random. A few years ago, Lott practically wanted to give the adulterous Air Force pilot Kelly Flinn a silver star for her service. Remember that?

Up until two weeks ago, conservatives were clamoring for Lott's removal precisely because of his annoying habit of saying dumb things. (Showing their inferior intellect, liberals have only recently figured that out.) Republicans should ask Lott to step down as leader, but only for all the nice things he's said about Teddy Kennedy. ■

☞ Ashcroft and the Blowhard Discuss Desegregation

JANUARY 18, 2001

Republican presidents need to start sending at least one Potemkin nominee to the Senate for confirmation hearings. If there were just one cabinet nominee willing to sacrifice his appointment for the opportunity to yell back at that adulterous drunk, Senator Teddy Kennedy might not be so cavalier before launching his premeditated vituperations.

Whatever else the "Stop (fill in name here)! Task Force" can say about John Ashcroft, they cannot say that he drunkenly plunged a woman to a horrifying watery death and then fled the scene of the accident, relying on his family's connections to paper over the woman's drowning. Indeed, Ashcroft has never done anything drunkenly, making him an object of fascination for Mr. Kennedy.

They cannot say that John Ashcroft, like Senator Kennedy, was thrown out of college for cheating on a Spanish test—or that he got into college on the basis of his family pedigree. (Inasmuch as Ashcroft attended an Ivy League college, it was not much help having a father who was a Pentecostal minister, rather than, say, a bootlegger.) And a pants-less, drunken John Ashcroft has never been wandering nearby while his nephew was having sex with a woman whom he had just met and who subsequently accused him of rape at the family compound in Florida on Good Friday. The Ashcroft family doesn't even have a compound in Florida.

Poor John Ashcroft couldn't say any of that when Senator Kennedy erupted in gin-soaked venom at Ashcroft's nomination hearings. He has higher aspirations than talking back to a dissolute slob for laughs. But surely there is someone out there who would go for laughs. Bush should find that guy. Heck, I'll volunteer for this mission myself—if only for the once-in-a-lifetime opportunity to say, on C-SPAN, "We'll drive off the side of that bridge when we come to it, Senator Kennedy."

On the first day of the Ashcroft hearings, Senator Kennedy waxed nostalgic over a court-ordered "voluntary desegregation" plan imposed by an unelected judge on the good people of Kansas City back in the 1980s. Kennedy issued bloodcurdling screams about "the kids": "How costly was this going to be, Senator Ashcroft, before you were going to say that those kids going in lousy schools, that you were going to do something about it?"

You remember what a fabulous success court-ordered "desegregation" plans have been. Few failures have been more spectacular. Illiterate students knifing one another between acts of sodomy in the stairwell is just one of the many eggs that had to be broken to make the Left's omelet of transferring power from cities to the federal courts. In the case of the Kansas City schools, a judge issued an edict doubling the property taxes of the school district's residents. Twelve years and $2 billion later the district is more racially segregated than it was before. Test scores are lower for black students than in the rest of the state. This is the remedy Senator Drunkennedy was so passionately defending.

It's one thing for the federal courts to inform the states and localities that they cannot discriminate on the basis of race—that was duly accomplished back in 1954. It's really quite another for unelected judges to be imposing $2 billion property taxes and ordering school districts to build opulent school campuses replete with Olympic-sized pools, 25-acre wildlife sanctuaries, and a model United Nations with simultaneous translation facilities. The only way this plan could have been more absurd would be if school board members had begun actually, literally throwing bundles of cash at the students. But that's what a federal judge did to Kansas City, under the Olympic-Sized-Pool and Tax-Them-Till-They-Scream clauses of the U.S. Constitution. As a matter of technical constitutional law, the Constitution does not strictly require states to provide public school students with petting farms.

What happened was that over the past several decades, federal judges got it into their heads that black students had to sit next to white students in order to learn. It was all the rage at the elite universities—Harvard in particular. Justice Clarence Thomas responded to the theory by saying, "It never ceases to amaze me that the courts are so willing to assume that anything that is predominantly black must be inferior." The idea was that if the federal courts ordered the states to spend gobs of money building "model schools" with petting farms (and highly paid teachers' unions) in the mostly black city schools, the all-important white students would come. Surrounded by white people, black students' education would improve. The popular appeal of this charming notion gives you some idea why the most frequent modifier to "federal judge" is "unelected." Needless to say, having federal judges and Harvard professors run local school districts on the basis of a preposterous racist theory wrecked school system after school system.

Federal judges managed to wrest control of the school systems in the first place through scam lawsuits between nonadverse parties. It worked like this: A few parents would sue the school board, and the school board would quickly admit guilt. Then the nonadverse adversaries would giddily enter "voluntary" settlements requiring "the school boards" to make lavish improvements, including generous salary increases for school administrators. The court would enter an order confirming the "voluntary" settlement—and the taxpayers would be stuck with the bill. It was nothing but a scam dreamed up by parents and school boards to bilk taxpayers for more money. The educational community refers to this as a "court-ordered remedy." In the real world, such arrangements are known as "organized crime."

These "voluntary" desegregation plans were voluntary in the same way you "volunteer" your wallet to a couple of con men who have just staged a phony confrontation to abet picking your pocket. As Ashcroft explained it to Senator Kopechne, parents and schools would enter into agreements, but "the state was going to have to pay for everything." The plans had as much to do with desegregation as, well, a pickpocket does. It's time for Bush to send in Alan Keyes. He could probably explain all this to the Massachusetts drunk with some trenchancy. ■

☞ Bizarre Political Sect Ousted from Judicial Nomination Process

MARCH 28, 2001

A few years ago I was bitterly disappointed to discover that appellate court judge Pasco Bowman, the otherwise impeccable federal judge I clerked for after law school, had gotten a "Qualified" rating from the ABA. Maybe even—God forbid—"Well Qualified." I don't remember, it was a dark day. For those of you not familiar with the ABA, this would be the equivalent of a would-be ethicist getting a "two thumbs up!" rating from Bill and Hillary. Upon discovering this contretemps I called him to complain. Almost all the cool guys had gotten "Qualified/Not Qualified" ratings. Why not him? Oh, the humiliation!

Among the judicial nominees who won the ABA's coveted "Qualified/Not Qualified" rating is Judge Richard Posner—once described by archliberal Supreme Court Justice William Brennan Jr. as one of the two geniuses he had met in his life. Others were Judges Frank Easterbrook, Stephen Williams, James Buckley, Jerry Smith, and Laurence Silberman. If jurisprudence were an Olympic sport, these guys would be the "dream team." (As would Judge Bowman, but for nagging questions about that ABA endorsement.) Clarence Thomas got an impressive "Qualified/Not Qualified" rating from the ABA—the lowest score ever given to a Supreme Court nominee. Meanwhile, David Souter—that jurisprudential giant, plucked from a state court where he had been deciding pig-trespassing cases—was unanimously voted "Highly Qualified."

Finally and most acclaimed, the ABA ratings committee couldn't decide whether Judge Robert Bork, one of the twentieth century's foremost constitutional and legal authorities, was qualified. Four members voted him "Not Qualified," thus clearly defining "qualified" as "favoring unrestricted abortion on demand." The head of the ABA's selection committee then perjured himself by telling a Senate committee reasonable minds could differ about Bork's qualifications. Oh, okay. How about we compare LSAT scores? There was no possibility the ABA could ever be a nonlaughable organization after that.

Demonstrating its eagle eye for ferreting out unfit judges, the ABA gave "Qualified" or "Well Qualified" ratings to all three federal judges impeached in the last half century. These were Harry E. Claiborne (appointed by Lyndon Johnson), Alcee L. Hastings (appointed by Jimmy Carter), and Walter L. Nixon (appointed by Jimmy Carter). Perhaps this is all a big misunderstanding and what the ABA's rating system really means is "well qualified for future impeachment." This does not include other stellar Carter appointees who served prison terms without ever being impeached, like U.S. District Judge Robert F. Collins of New Orleans. While serving a six-year sentence for taking part of a $100,000 bribe to fix a drug-smuggling case, Collins continued to receive his federal salary from prison—he even got a raise. Only when the House brought impeachment proceedings against him did Collins finally resign. The ABA had ruled Collins "Qualified."

In my judge's defense: (1) Justice Antonin Scalia also got "Qualified"/"Well Qualified" ratings (keep your eye on that guy), and (2) despite the ABA adjudging him "Qualified," Judge Bowman has never been impeached.

Magazines like the *Economist* and *Time* actually cited the impeachments of Democratic-appointed, ABA-approved judges in order to denounce Reagan's judicial nominees for getting low marks from the ABA. The *Economist* mentioned Judge Hastings (ABA rating: QUALIFIED!) and Judge Claiborne (ABA rating: HIGHLY QUALIFIED!) before asserting that criminal indictments of judges were "rare largely because screening of candidates for federal judgeships is so much more rigorous." *Time* magazine repeatedly pondered the irony of the Senate voting on Reagan's nomination of Daniel Manion—whom forty law school deans had opposed—just a month after "Highly Qualified" Claiborne began serving a two-year criminal sentence. (Judge Manion has served with distinction since his appointment in 1986.)

On the basis of the ABA's record, one could certainly understand why Senate Democrats like Chuck Schumer and Patrick Leahy were upset when President George Bush decided to scrap the ABA's review. You wouldn't want to tinker with a fine-tuned system like that. Schumer said eliminating the ABA's role in judicial nominations showed that "instead of quality, they are looking for ideology." Schumer then voted against Bush nominee Miguel Estrada—who had graduated from Harvard Law School magna cum laude, where he had been an editor of the law review; had clerked for the Supreme Court; had been a federal prosecutor; had served for almost five years in the solicitor general's office; had argued more than a dozen cases before the Supreme Court; and was then a partner in one of the most prestigious law firms in the country—because Estrada had not given the Democrats a blood oath that he would uphold abortion on demand. The *New York Times* also attacked Bush for removing the ABA from the process, editorializing that the ABA's ratings were crucial because its "stamp of approval . . . gave people confidence that federal judges were highly regarded members of the profession." If so, only among people who weren't paying attention.

I've been going to ABA annual conventions every few years since my parents took me as a little kid. It used to be that you couldn't get on an elevator at the hotel without stepping on a Supreme Court justice, an appellate court judge, or a U.S. senator. Big important people gave big important speeches. Now it's all nobodies. Every single panel discussion is on women and minorities. Once a convocation of esteemed legal minds, the ABA convention has morphed into a weird sort of twelve-step meeting for the disbarred. That's not entirely fair. The ABA still has marquee speakers, but instead of prominent attorneys, now they're prominent criminals. After he was impeached and held in contempt by a federal court—but before he had his license to practice law suspended and was banned from ever appearing before the U.S. Supreme Court—the ABA invited Bill Clinton to speak. Also joining the list of celebrated felons speaking at the ABA was ex-con Webster Hubbell. Apparently Hubbell was a last-minute stand-in after Mumia Abul-Jamal dropped out because of a scheduling conflict.

Maybe they could get O.J. for one of the minority panels next year. There's no one left to complain—everyone serious has resigned. The first wave of resignations came in 1987, when the ABA couldn't decide on Judge Bork's qualifications. The next major exodus came in 1992, when, on a break from Ya-Ya Sisterhood meetings, the ABA's House of Delegates declared the ABA in favor of abortion on demand. For the next several months, thousands of members exercised their freedom to choose by terminating their ABA memberships. After that, the ABA got loopier and loopier. One distinguished federal judge claims to join every few years just so he can resign in protest. Another said he was compelled to resign because the "impartiality of any judge who continues to belong to the ABA is subject to serious question."

For years now, the ABA has been issuing wild proclamations more appropriate to Janeane Garofalo than a professional association of lawyers. One former ABA president, George Bushnell, called the Republican leadership in Congress "reptilian bastards," paraphrasing the noted constitutional scholar and dictionary buff Julia Roberts. (Why couldn't my judge have gotten that appellation?) The esteemed ABA president also called the Contract with America "an attack on the Constitution comparable to that of the invasion of our shores by foreign forces." You remember the Contract with America? It included pernicious ideas like a balanced-budget amendment and tax incentives for adoption. If I had a nickel for every time I've confused an armed invasion of the U.S. mainland with a balanced-budget amendment, John Kerry would be trying to raise my taxes right now.

Two ABA presidents viciously denounced a proposed flag-burning amendment to the Constitution and—most shockingly—didn't even wait for the results of a study on how flag-burning might contribute to global warming. One former president, Roberta Ramo, said the flag-burning amendment proved Congress had "lost sight of the United States Constitution and Bill of Rights as our nation's lodestar and our soul." Instead of saluting the American flag, the ABA is considering a special seminar on how to burn it. Bushnell said Senator Bob Dole's support for the flag-burning amendment had compromised his "decency as an individual"—proving that it's still okay to vilify a disabled American combat veteran who actually did sustain his injuries on the field of battle.

The decency police at the ABA were offended by Bob Dole, but they didn't have a problem with Bernardine Dohrn, the Charles Manson–admiring former Weatherman and erstwhile member of the FBI's "Ten Most Wanted." The ABA made Dohrn head of their Litigation Task Force on Children. As Bushnell said, "We are tremendously fortunate to have her." That is true in the sense that it is somewhat miraculous that Dohrn didn't blow herself up making pipe bombs as a member of the Weathermen back in the 1970s.

But my judge is "Qualified"? Coming from this gang of leftist-fringe kooks, them's fightin' words. I demand a recount. ∎

☞ Liberals Shocked— Rush Not Jesus Christ

OCTOBER 15, 2003

So liberals have finally found a drug addict they don't like. And unlike the Lackawanna Six—those high-spirited young lads innocently seeking adventure in an al Qaeda training camp in Afghanistan—liberals could find no excuses for Rush Limbaugh.

After years of the mainstream media assuring us that Rush was a has-been, a nobody, yesterday's news, the Rush painkiller story was front-page news last week. (Would anyone care if Howell Raines committed murder?) The airwaves and print media were on red alert with Rush's admission that after an unsuccessful spinal operation a few years ago, he became addicted to powerful prescription painkillers.

Rush Limbaugh's misfortune is apparently a bigger story than his nearly $300 million radio contract signed two years ago. That was the biggest radio contract in broadcasting history. Yet there are only twelve documents on LexisNexis that reported it. The *New York Times* didn't take notice of Rush's $300 million radio contract, but a few weeks later, it put Bill Clinton's comparatively measly $10 million book contract on its front page. Meanwhile, in the past week alone, LexisNexis has accumulated more than fifty documents with the words "Rush Limbaugh and hypocrisy." That should make up for the twelve documents on his $300 million radio contract.

The reason any conservative's failing is always major news is that it allows liberals to engage in their very favorite taunt: Hypocrisy! Hypocrisy is the only sin that really inflames them. Inasmuch as liberals have no morals, they can sit back and criticize other people for failing to meet the standards that liberals simply renounce. It's an intriguing strategy. By openly admitting to being philanderers, draft dodgers, liars, weasels, and cowards, liberals avoid ever being hypocrites.

At least Rush wasn't walking into church carrying a ten-pound Bible before rushing back to the Oval Office for sodomy with Monica Lewinsky. He wasn't enforcing absurd sexual harassment guidelines while dropping his pants in front of a half-dozen subordinates. (Evidently, Clinton wasn't a hypocrite because no one was supposed to take seriously the notion that he respected women or believed in God.)

Rush has hardly been the antidrug crusader liberals suggest. Indeed, Rush hasn't had much to say about drugs at all since that spinal operation. The Rush Limbaugh quote that has been endlessly recited in the last week to prove Rush's rank "hypocrisy" is this, made eight years ago: "Drug use, some might say, is destroying this country. And we have laws against selling drugs, pushing drugs, using drugs, importing drugs. . . . And so if people are violating the law by doing drugs, they ought to be accused and they ought to be convicted and they ought to be sent up."

What precisely are liberals proposing that Rush should have said to avoid their indignant squeals of "hypocrisy"? Announce his support for the wide and legal availability of a prescription painkiller that might have caused him to go deaf and nearly ruined his career and wrecked his life? I believe that would have been both evil and hypocritical.

Or is it simply that Rush should not have become addicted to painkillers in the first place? Well, no, I suppose not. You've caught us: Rush has a flaw. And yet, the wily hypocrite does not support flaws!

When a conservative can be the biggest thing in talk radio, earning $30 million a year and attracting 20 million devoted listeners every week—all while addicted to drugs—I'll admit liberals have reason to believe that conservatives are some sort of superrace, incorruptible by original sin. But the only perfect man hasn't walked the Earth for two thousand years. In liberals' worldview, any conservative who is not Jesus Christ is ipso facto a "hypocrite" for not publicly embracing dissolute behavior the way liberals do.

In fact, Rush's behavior was not all that dissolute. There is a fundamental difference between taking any drug for kicks—legal, illegal, prescription, protected by the Twenty-first Amendment, or banned by Michael Bloomberg—and taking a painkiller for pain.

There is a difference morally and a difference legally. While slamming Rush, Harvard Law professor Alan Dershowitz recently told Wolf Blitzer, "Generally, people who illegally buy prescription drugs are not prosecuted, whereas people who illegally buy cocaine and heroin are prosecuted." What would the point be? Just say no to back surgery?

I haven't checked with any Harvard Law professors, but I'm pretty sure that, generally, adulterous drunks who drive off bridges and kill girls are prosecuted. Ah, but Teddy Kennedy supports adultery and public drunkenness—so at least you can't call him a hypocrite! That must provide great consolation to Mary Jo Kopechne's parents.

I have a rule about not feeling sorry for people worth $300 million, but I'm feeling sentimental. Evan Thomas wrote a cover story on Rush for *Newsweek* this week that was so vicious it read like conservative satire. Thomas called Rush a "schlub," "socially ill at ease," an Elmer Gantry, an actor whose "act has won over, or fooled, a lot of people." He compared Rush to the phony TV evangelist Jim Bakker and recommended that Rush start to "make a virtue out of honesty." (Liberals can lie under oath in legal proceedings and it's a "personal matter." Conservatives must scream their every failing from the rooftops or they are "liars.")

As is standard procedure for profiles of conservatives, *Newsweek* gathered quotes on Rush from liberals, ex-wives, and dumped dates. Covering himself, Thomas ruefully remarked that "it's hard to find many people who really know him." Well, there was me, Evan! But I guess *Newsweek* didn't have room for the quotes I promptly sent back to the *Newsweek* researchers. I could have even corrected *Newsweek*'s absurd account of how Rush met his wife. (It's kind of cute, too: She was a fan who began arguing with him about something he said on air.)

Thomas also made the astute observation that "Rush Limbaugh has always had far more followers than friends." Needless to say, this floored those of us who were shocked to discover that Rush does not have 20 million friends.

So the guy I really feel sorry for is Evan Thomas. How would little Evan fare in any competitive media? Any followers? Any fans? Any readers at all? And he's not even addicted to painkillers! This week, Rush proved his motto: He really can beat liberals with half his brain tied behind his back. ∎

☞ It's the Winter Solstice, Charlie Brown!

SEPTEMBER 24, 2003

David Limbaugh's book *Persecution: How Liberals Are Waging War Against Christianity* will make you cry for your country. (But don't pray for your country if you're anywhere near a public school!) Released this week, Limbaugh's copiously researched book documents how the courts, the universities, the media, Hollywood, and government institutions react to any mention of Christianity like Superman recoiling from kryptonite, Dracula from sunlight, or

Madonna from soap and water. His straight, factual narrative of what is happening in our public schools makes you wonder how much longer America can survive liberalism.

In a public school in St. Louis, a teacher spotted the suspect, fourth-grader Raymond Raines, bowing his head in prayer before lunch. The teacher stormed to Raymond's table, ordered him to stop immediately, and sent him to the principal's office. The principal informed the young malefactor that praying was not allowed in school. When Raymond was again caught praying before meals on three separate occasions, he was segregated from other students, ridiculed in front of his classmates, and finally sentenced to a week's detention.

Before snack time in her kindergarten class in Saratoga Springs, New York, little Kayla Broadus held hands with two of her classmates and recited this prayer: "God is good, God is great, thank you, God, for my food." The alert teacher pounced on Kayla, severely reprimanded her, and reported her to the school administration. In short order, the principal sent a sternly worded letter to Kayla's parents advising them that Kayla was not allowed to pray in school, aloud or with others.

The school board then issued a triumphant press release crowing about its victory over a kindergartner praying before snack time. Thus was creeping theocracy in Saratoga Springs stopped dead in its tracks! Kayla's mother brought a lawsuit, winning Kayla the right to pray out loud. But she was still prohibited from holding hands with others while she prayed. Hearing the G-word in kindergarten might interfere with the school's efforts to teach proper sexual techniques in the first grade.

Thanks to the vigilance of a teacher at Lynn Lucas Middle School outside of Houston, two sisters carrying Bibles were prevented from bringing their vile material into a classroom. The teacher stopped the students at the classroom door and marched them to the principal's office. (Maybe it was just the sight of public school students carrying a book of any kind that set off alarm bells.) The sisters' mother was called and warned that the school intended to report her to Child Protective Services. When the mother arrived, the teacher threw the Bibles in the wastebasket, shouting, "This is garbage!"

In another display of tolerance at Lynn Lucas Middle School, school administrators snatched three students' books with covers displaying the Ten Commandments, ripped the covers off, threw them in the garbage, and told the students that the Ten Commandments constituted "hate speech." (Also, it would be insensitive to expose the Ten Commandments to students who had never been taught to count to ten.)

After the massacre at Columbine High School, students and families were invited to paint tiles above student lockers. The school district had taken all reasonable precautions, immediately deploying an army of secular "grief counselors" with teddy bears to descend on the school after the attack. Nonetheless, some students painted their tiles with "objectionable" messages, such as "4/20/99: Jesus Wept" and "God Is Love." This would not stand: The school removed ninety tiles with offending religious messages. They might have offended the sensibilities of students as they listened to the latest Ludacris or 50 Cent CDs.

A federal court upheld the school's censorship of the religious tiles. Of course, Columbine school officials had earned a measure of deference after having inculcated such a fine sense of morality in their students that two boys could walk into school one day and stage a bloody massacre. You don't argue with a track record like that.

Not all mentions of religion constitute "hate speech." In State College, Pennsylvania, school administrators methodically purged all Christmas carols of any religious content—and then led the children in a chant of "Celebrate Kwanzaa!" At Pattison Elementary School in Katy, Texas, Christmas songs are banned, but students are threatened with grade reductions for refusing to sing songs celebrating other religious faiths.

In New York City, the chancellor of the Department of Education prohibited the display of Nativity scenes in public schools, while expressly allowing the Jewish menorah and the Islamic star and crescent to be displayed. Some would say that was overkill, inasmuch as New York City is already the home of the world's largest public display built in commemoration of Islam: Ground Zero.

Between issuing laws prohibiting discrimination against transgendered individuals and running up a $38 billion deficit, the California legislature mandated a three-week immersion course in Islam for all seventh-graders. A "crash course" in Islam, you might call it, if that weren't so ironic. Students are required to adopt Muslim names, plan a trip to Mecca, play a jihad game, pray to "Allah, the Compassionate," and chant "Praise to Allah! Lord of Creation!" They are encouraged to dress in Muslim garb. Students are discouraged, however, from stoning girls at the school dances, abusing their "Jew" math teachers, or blowing up their classmates.

A popular student textbook, *Across the Centuries,* treats the Inquisition and Salem witch hunts as typical of Christianity, but never gets around to mentioning the Muslims' conquest of Spain, the Battle of Tours, or the execution of Jews in Qurayza. Or 9/11.

There is no surer proof of Christ's divinity than that he is still so hated some two thousand years after his death. Limbaugh's *Persecution* covers it all in staggering, heartbreaking detail. His methodical description of what is happening in our public schools alone will call to mind the hate speech banned in Columbine: "Jesus Wept." ■

☞ Massachusetts Supreme Court Abolishes Capitalism!

NOVEMBER 27, 2003

Last week, the Massachusetts Supreme Judicial Court discovered that the state constitution—written in 1780—requires the state to allow gay marriages. The court gave the legislature six months to rewrite the law to comply with the heretofore unnoticed gay-marriage provision in a 223-year-old constitution, leaving countless gay couples a scant six months to select a silverware pattern. Out of respect for my gay male readers, I'll resist the temptation to characterize this ruling as "shoving gay marriage down our throats."

The Massachusetts Constitution was written by John Adams, who was quite religious. It is the most explicitly Christian document since the New Testament, with lots of references to "the great Legislator of the universe." Adams certainly would have been astonished to discover that the constitution he wrote provided for gay marriage—though one can see how a reference to two men marrying might get lost among the minutiae about the "duty of all men in society, publicly and at stated seasons, to worship the Supreme Being, the great Creator and Preserver of the universe."

The main lesson from the court's discovery of the hidden gay-marriage clause is that these judges are in the wrong job. If they can find a right to gay marriage in the Massachusetts Constitution—never before detected by any human being—we need to get them looking for Osama bin Laden. These guys can find anything!

And if we don't get Massachusetts judges out of the country soon, we could start reading headlines like "Mass. Supreme Court Abolishes Capitalism; Gives Legislature 6 Months to Nationalize All Industry."

The Democratic presidential candidates reacted with glee to the court's gay-marriage ruling, relieved that they could talk about gay marriage instead of their insane ideas on national defense. But then they realized this meant they would have to talk about gay marriage. Except for the nut candidates who always forget to lie about their positions, all the Democratic presidential candidates earnestly insist that they oppose gay marriage. They are for "civil unions" with all the legal rights of marriage. But not marriage! No sir.

As governor of Vermont, Howard Dean actually signed a bill

providing for these magical "civil unions." Having already been forgiven for his remarks about the Confederate flag by both of the black people currently living in Vermont, now Dean wants to be the candidate for guys with Confederate flags in their flower shops. But even Dean emphasized that Vermont's civil-union law does not legalize gay "marriage."

And even in Ben-and-Jerryville, incidentally, it took a court to force the state to recognize civil unions by discovering that right in the Vermont Constitution. (WHERE'S OSAMA?)

The big argument for "civil unions"—but not marriage!—is that gays are denied ordinary civil rights here in the American Taliban. This is where gays usually bring up the argument about all the straight couples living in "sham" marriages, but I see no point in dragging the Clintons into this.

The classic formulation was given by John Kerry in the Democratic debate earlier this week: "What we're talking about is somebody's right to be able to visit a loved one in a hospital, somebody's right to be able to pass on property, somebody's right to live equally under the state laws as other people in the country." You would think there were "Straights Only" water fountains the way Democrats carry on so (as if any gay man would drink nonbottled water).

Apparently, health care in this country is better than we've been led to believe if so few Americans have ever been to a hospital that they think there's a guest list. In case you don't know: Gays already can visit loved ones in hospitals. They can also visit neighbors, random acquaintances, and total strangers in hospitals—just like everyone else.

Gays can also pass on property to whomever they would like, including their cats. Every few years you read about some daft rich widow leaving her entire estate to a cat. It's perfectly legal. You just need to write a will. Liberals have figured out how to get abortions for thirteen-year-old girls without their parents' permission to cross state lines. But we're supposed to believe that they just can't get their heads around how a gay guy could leave property to his partner.

As for "living equally under the state laws as other people in the country," unless Kerry is referring to the precise thing he claims to oppose—gay marriage—gays do live equally under the state laws as other people in the country. There are no special speed-limit laws or trespassing laws for gays. (There is, however, some evidence of gay profiling with regard to the enforcement of fashion "don'ts.")

What gays can't do is get married—something all Democrats swear up and down to oppose. Instead, the Democrats demand "civil unions" and then throw out a series of red herrings to explain why. In fact, the only difference between what the Democrats claim to support (civil unions) and what they claim to oppose (gay marriage) is the word "marriage." As John Kerry explained, "I think the term 'marriage' gets in the way of what is really being talked about here."

Republicans ought to try that: We don't support "guns"—the term "gun" gets in the way of what is really being talked about here—we want choice in personal security devices. We don't want a "ban" on partial-birth abortions; we just don't want there to be any of them. We don't support "tax cuts"; we support a "union" between people and 70 percent of their money. We don't support "war" with Iraq; we are talking about somebody's right to be able to visit a loved one in a hospital. (Huh?)

Except the difference is: All those positions are popular with voters, so Republicans don't have to lie. The Democrats' purported opposition to gay marriage is like all their other phony policy statements that are the opposite of what they really believe.

When they're running for office, all Democrats claim to support tax cuts (for the middle class), to support gun rights (for hunters), and to "personally oppose" abortion. And then they get into office and vote to raise taxes, ban guns, and allow abortions if a girl can't fit into her prom dress.

The common wisdom holds that "both parties" have to appeal to the extremes during the primary and then move to the center for the general election. To the contrary, both parties run for office as conservatives. Once they have fooled the voters and are safely in office, Republicans sometimes double-cross the voters. Democrats always do. ∎

☞ The Passion of the Liberal

MARCH 3, 2004

In the dozens and dozens of panic-stricken articles the *New York Times* has run on Mel Gibson's movie *The Passion of the Christ*, the unavoidable conclusion is that liberals haven't the vaguest idea what Christianity is. The *Times* may have loopy ideas about a lot of things, but at least when they write about gay bathhouses and abortion clinics, you get the sense they know what they're talking about.

But Christianity just doesn't ring a bell. The religion that has transformed Western civilization for two millennia is a blank slate for liberals. Their closest reference point is "conservative Christians," meaning people you're not supposed to hire. And these are the people who carp about George Bush's alleged lack of "intellectual curiosity."

The most amazing complaint, championed by the *Times* and repeated by all the know-nothing secularists on television, is that Gibson insisted on "rubbing our faces in the grisly reality of Jesus' death." The *Times* was irked that Gibson "relentlessly focused on the savagery of Jesus' final hours"—at the expense of showing us the Happy Jesus. Yes, Gibson's movie is crying out for a car chase, a sex scene, or maybe a wisecracking orangutan.

The *Times* ought to send one of its crack investigative reporters to St. Patrick's Cathedral at 3 P.M. on Good Friday before leaping to the conclusion that *The Passion* is Gibson's idiosyncratic take on

Christianity. In a standard Sunday ritual, Christians routinely eat the flesh and drink the blood of Jesus Christ, aka "the Lamb of God." The really serious Catholics do that blood- and flesh-eating thing every day, the sickos. The *Times* has just discovered the tip of a 2,000-year-old iceberg.

But the loony left is testy with Gibson for spending so much time on Jesus' suffering and death while giving "short shrift to Jesus' ministry and ideas"—as another *Times* reviewer put it. According to liberals, the message of Jesus, which somehow Gibson missed, is something along the lines of "be nice to people" (which to them means "raise taxes on the productive").

You don't need a religion like Christianity, which is a rather large and complex endeavor, in order to flag that message. All you need is a moron driving around in a Volvo with a bumper sticker that says "be nice to people." Being nice to people is, in fact, one of the incidental tenets of Christianity (as opposed to other religions whose tenets are more along the lines of "kill everyone who doesn't smell bad or answer to the name Mohammed"). But to call it the "message" of Jesus requires . . . well, the brain of Maureen Dowd.

In fact, Jesus' distinctive message was: People are sinful and need to be redeemed, and this is your lucky day because I'm here to redeem you even though you don't deserve it, and I have to get the crap kicked out of me to do it. That is the reason He is called "Christ the Redeemer" rather than "Christ the Moron Driving Around in a Volvo With a 'Be Nice to People' Bumper Sticker on It."

The other complaint from the know-nothing crowd is that *The Passion* will inspire anti-Semitic violence. If nothing else comes out of this movie, at least we finally have liberals on record opposing anti-Semitic violence. Perhaps they should broach that topic with their Muslim friends.

One *Times* review of *The Passion* said, "To be a Christian is to face the responsibility for one's own most treasured sacred texts being used to justify the deaths of innocents." At best, this is like blaming Jodie Foster for the shooting of Ronald Reagan. But the reviewer somberly warned that a Christian should "not take the risk that one's life or work might contribute to the continuation of a horror." So the only thing Christians can do is shut up about their religion. (And no more Jodie Foster movies!)

By contrast, in the weeks after 9/11, the *Times* was rushing to assure its readers that "prominent Islamic scholars and theologians in the West say unequivocally that nothing in Islam countenances the Sept. 11 actions." (That's if you set aside Muhammad's many specific instructions to kill nonbelievers whenever possible.) *Times* columnists repeatedly extolled "the great majority of peaceful Muslims." Only a religion with millions of practitioners trying to kill Americans and Jews is axiomatically described as "peaceful" by liberals.

As I understand it, the dangerous religion is the one whose messiah instructs, "If one strikes thee on thy right cheek, turn to him the other also" and "Love your enemies . . . do good to them that hate you, and pray for them that persecute and calumniate you." By contrast, the peaceful religion instructs, "Slay the enemy where you find him" (Surah 9:92).

Imitating the ostrich-like posture of certain German Jews who ignored the growing danger during Hitler's rise to power, today's liberals are deliberately blind to the real threats of violence that surround us. Their narcissistic self-image requires absolute solicitude toward angry savages plotting acts of terrorism. The only people who scare them are the ones who worship a Jew. ∎

☞ W.W.J.K.?: Who Would Jesus Kill?

MARCH 10, 2004

The *New York Times*'s Frank Rich described Mel Gibson's movie *The Passion of the Christ* thus: "With its laborious build-up to its orgasmic spurtings of blood and other bodily fluids, Mr. Gibson's film is constructed like nothing so much as a porn movie, replete with slo-mo climaxes and pounding music for the money shots." (I'll leave it to your imagination as to how the *Times*'s film and theater critic knows gay porn well enough to be tossing industry lingo around.) Yes, Christ's followers take pleasure at the thought of his torture. The people sobbing throughout *The Passion* all around the country were clearly having the time of their lives.

Six months ago, Rich was predicting that *The Passion* would be a box office disaster. In the August 3, 2003, *New York Times,* he wrote, "Indeed, it's hard to imagine the movie being anything other than a flop in America." Now that *The Passion* is breaking box office records, Rich sneers that Gibson was just in it for the money. On *Hardball* last week, he condescended to Tony Blankley, "I hate to break it to you, Tony, but this was a movie made to make money." So Rich is obviously someone whose opinion is to be respected.

I guess calling Gibson a fag is all liberals have left now that the pogroms have failed to materialize. The fact that Frank Rich is still alive would seem to be proof positive that Americans are incapable of being roused to anti-Semitic violence.

But William Safire wasn't so sure. Safire, the *New York Times*'s in-house "conservative"—who endorsed Bill Clinton in 1992, like so many conservatives—was sure Mel Gibson's movie *The Passion of the Christ* would incite anti-Semitic violence. With all the subtlety of a Mack truck, Safire called Gibson's movie a version of "the medieval 'passion play,' preserved in pre-Hitler Germany at Oberammergau, a source of the hatred of all Jews as 'Christ killers.'" (Certainly every Aryan Nation skinhead murderer I've ever met was also a devoted theater buff and "passion play" aficionado.)

The "passion play" has been put on in Germany since at least 1633. I guess 1633 would be "pre-Hitler." In addition, Moses walked the Earth "pre-Hitler." The wheel was invented "pre-Hitler." People ate soup "pre-Hitler." Referring to the passion play as "pre-Hitler" is a slightly fancier version of every adolescent's favorite argument: You're like Hitler!

Despite repeated suggestions from liberals—including the in-house "conservative" and Clinton-supporter at the *Times*—Hitler is not what happens when you gin up Christians. Like Timothy McVeigh, the Columbine killers, and the editorial board of the *New York Times*, Hitler detested Christians. Indeed, Hitler denounced Christianity as an "invention of the Jew" and vowed that the "organized lie [of Christianity] must be smashed" so that the state would "remain the absolute master." Interestingly, this was the approach of all the great mass murderers of the last century—all of whom were atheists: Hitler, Stalin, Mao, and Pol Pot.

In the United States, more than 30 million babies have been killed by abortion since *Roe v. Wade,* versus seven abortion providers killed. Yeah—keep your eye on those Christians!

But according to liberals, it's Christianity that causes murder. (And don't get them started on Zionism.) Like their Muslim friends still harping about the Crusades, liberals won't "move on" from the Spanish Inquisition. In the entire 350 years of the Spanish Inquisition, about 30,000 people were killed. That's an average of less than 100 a year. Stalin knocked off that many kulaks before breakfast.

But Safire argues that viewers of *The Passion* will see the Jewish mob and think, "Who was responsible for this cruel humiliation? What villain deserves to be punished?" Let's see: It was a Roman who ordered Christ's execution, and Romans who did all the flaying, taunting, and crucifying. Perhaps Safire is indulging in his own negative stereotyping about Jews by assuming they simply viewed Romans as "the help."

But again I ask: Does anyone at the *Times* have the vaguest notion what Christianity is? (Besides people who go around putting up Nativity scenes that have to be taken down by court order?) The religion that toppled the Roman Empire—anyone?

Jesus' suffering and death is not a Hatfields-and-McCoys story demanding retaliation. The gist of the religion that transformed the world is: God's only son came to Earth to take the punishment we deserved. If the Jews had somehow managed to block Jesus' crucifixion and He had died in old age of natural causes, there would be no salvation through Christ and no Christianity. Whatever possible responses there may be to that story, this is not one of them: Damn those Jews for being a part of God's plan to save my eternal soul!

Gibson didn't insert Jews into the story for some Machiavellian, racist reason. Christ was a Jew crucified by Romans at the request of other Jews in Jerusalem. I suppose if Gibson had moved the story to suburban Cleveland and portrayed Republican logging executives crucifying Christ, the Left would calm down. But it simply didn't happen that way.

Of course, the original text is no excuse in Hollywood. The villains of Tom Clancy's book *The Sum of All Fears* were recently transformed from Muslim terrorists to neo-Nazis for the movie version. You wouldn't want to upset the little darlings. They might do something crazy. The only religion that can be constantly defamed and insulted is the one liberals pretend to be terrified of. ∎

JUNE 5, 2004: President Ronald Reagan passes away
at the age of ninety-three.

☛ Let's Rewrite One for the Gipper!
JUNE 16, 2004

I read the *New York Times* last week and apparently a fellow named "Iran-Contra" died recently. But that's all I'll say about the people who have consistently been on the wrong side of history and whose publisher is a little weenie who can't read because he has "dyslexia." The three key ingredients to Ronald Reagan's sunny personality were: (1) his unalterable faith in God; (2) for nearly thirty years, he didn't fly; and (3) he read *Human Events* religiously but never read the *New York Times*.

Even in his death, liberals are still trying to turn our champion into a moderate Republican—unlike the religious-right nut currently occupying the White House! The world's living testament to the limits of genetics, Ron Jr., put it this way at Reagan's funeral: "Dad was also a deeply, unabashedly religious man. But he never made the fatal mistake of so many politicians of wearing his faith on his sleeve to gain political advantage."

Wow. He's probably up in heaven—something Ron Jr. doesn't believe in—having a chuckle about that right now. To hear liberals tell it, you'd think Reagan talked about God the way Democrats do, in the stilted, uncomfortable manner of people pretending to believe something they manifestly do not. (In a recent *Time* magazine poll, only 7 percent of respondents say they believe Kerry is a man of "strong" religious faith, compared to 46 percent who believe Bush is.) Or, for that matter, the way Democrats talk about free-market capitalism.

The chattering classes weren't so copacetic about Reagan's religious beliefs when he was in office. In 1984, *Newsweek* breathlessly reported that "Reagan is known to have read and discussed with fundamentalist friends like [Jerry] Falwell and singer Pat Boone such pulp versions of biblical prophecies as Hal Lindsey's best-selling *The Late Great Planet Earth,* which strongly hints of a nuclear Armageddon." One hundred Christian and Jewish "leaders" signed a letter warning that Reagan's nuclear policy had been unduly influenced by a "theology of nuclear Armageddon." In the second presidential debate that year, President Reagan was actually asked to clarify his position on "nuclear Armageddon."

Most confusing to Democrats, at the time Reagan was doing all of this Bible reading and consorting with preachers, he hadn't even been accused of cheating on his wife. *What kind of angle is he playing?* liberals asked themselves.

Meanwhile, President Bush says he appeals to "a higher father" and liberals act like they've never heard such crazy talk from a president.

Newsweek's Eleanor Clift says Bush is unlike Reagan because Reagan "reached out, and he was always seeking converts." That's true, actually. I think Reagan would have favored converting Third World people to Christianity. (Now why does that idea ring a bell?) Clift continued: "That is the big difference between Ronald Reagan and the president we have today. The president today would like to consign his political opponents to oblivion."

Here is how Reagan "reached out" to Democrats:

Reagan on abortion: "We cannot survive as a free nation when some men decide that others are not fit to live and should be abandoned to abortion or infanticide."

Reagan on gay rights: "Society has always regarded marital love as a sacred expression of the bond between a man and a woman. It is the means by which families are created and society itself is extended into the future. In the Judeo-Christian tradition it is the means by which husband and wife participate with God in the creation of a new human life. It is for these reasons, among others, that our society has always sought to protect this unique relationship. In part the erosion of these values has given way to a celebration of forms of expression most reject. We will resist the efforts of some to obtain government endorsement of homosexuality."

Reagan on government programs to feed the "hungry": "We were told four years ago that 17 million people went to bed hungry each night. Well, that was probably true. They were all on a diet."

Would that more Republicans would "reach out" to Democrats the way Reagan did!

Most peculiar, the passing of America's most pro-life president is supposed to be a clarion call for conservatives to support the disemboweling of human embryos—in contrast to that heartless brute President Bush always prattling on about the value of human life. Someone persuaded poor, dear Nancy Reagan that research on human embryos might have saved her Ronnie from Alzheimer's. Now the rest of us are supposed to shut up because the wife of America's greatest president (oh, save your breath, girls!) supports stem-cell research.

Ironically, the always market-oriented Ronald Reagan would probably have asked his wife, "Honey, if embryonic stem-cell therapy is such a treasure trove of medical advances, why isn't private research and development funding flocking to it?"

President Bush has never said that fetal stem cells cannot be used for research. He said "federal money" cannot be used to fund such research. If leading scientists believed fetal stem-cell research would prove to be so fruitful in curing Alzheimer's, why is the private money not pouring in hand over fist? Do you realize how many billions a cure for Alzheimer's would be worth, let alone all the other cures some are claiming fetal stem-cell research would lead to? Forget Alzheimer's—do you know how much middle-aged men would pay for a *genuine* baldness cure? Then again, if we ever cured baldness Porsche sales would probably fall off quite a bit.

But you can't blame Nancy. As everyone saw once again last week, she's still madly in love with the guy. She'd probably support harvesting full-grown, living humans if it would bring back Ronnie. Of course, I thought it was cute and not creepy that she consulted an astrologer about Reagan's schedule after he was shot. That didn't make astrology a hard science. But liberals who once lambasted Nancy for having too much influence on Reagan's schedule now want to anoint her Seer of Technology.

The lesson to draw from what liberals said about Reagan then and what they are forced to say about him now is that the electable Republican is always the one liberals are calling an extremist, Armageddon-believing religious zealot. That certainly bodes well for President George W. Bush this November, thank—you should pardon the expression—God. ■

8

The Battle Flag

■

During the Democratic primaries for the 2004 presidential election, Howard Dean set off a tsunami of indignation when he said he wanted to be "the candidate for guys with Confederate flags in their pickup trucks" (just like Bill Clinton was the candidate for the guy with the Astro-turf in the bed of his pickup truck). Like clockwork, every presidential election year the Confederate flag becomes a major campaign issue. This always thrills the Democrats, because it finally gives them an issue to run on: Their support for the Union side in the Civil War.

After Dean's contretemps, Al Sharpton denounced the Confederate flag as an "American swastika," saying, "Imagine if I said that I wanted to be the candidate of people with helmets and swastikas." After briefly considering a personal-injury lawsuit, Senator John Edwards lectured Dean, saying, "Let me tell you, the last thing we need in the South is somebody like you coming down and telling us what we need to do." John Kerry said he wanted to be "the candidate of the guy whose limo driver keeps a Confederate flag in the back window of his Towne Car" and Dennis Kucinich said he wanted to be "the candidate for the guys in the low-emission hybrid vehicles with the Confederate flags in them."

At first, Dean refused to apologize, prolonging the Democrats' joyous self-righteousness. Dean defended himself saying, "I think the Confederate flag is a racist symbol"—apparently under the impression that it would help matters to explain that, yes, in fact, he did want to be the candidate of racists. But eventually Dean buckled and said it was Republicans' fault: "I think there are a lot of poor people who fly that flag because the Republicans have been dividing us by race since 1968 with their Southern race strategy." Carol Moseley Braun backed him up, saying the Democrats needed to "get past that racist strategy that the Republicans have foisted upon this country." Okay, so just for the record, this was Carol Moseley Braun urging someone *not* to play a race card.

In fact and needless to say, it is the Democrats who have turned the Confederate flag into a federal issue, because they relish nothing more than being morally indignant. Not about abortion, adultery, illegitimacy, the divorce rate, or a president molesting an intern and lying to federal investigators. Indeed, not about anything of any practical consequence. Democrats stake out a clear moral position only on the issue of slavery. Of course, when it mattered, they were on the wrong side of that issue, too.

In addition to expressing outrage over a nonissue, Democrats take sadistic pleasure in telling blacks that everyone hates them. Demonstrating their famous appreciation of "nuance," liberals believe the Confederate flag is pure evil and anyone who flies the flag is pure evil—and George Bush is a moron who sees the world in simplistic black-and-white terms of good and evil. I guess that's what liberals mean by "nuance."

Despite recent revisionist history written by liberal know-nothings—the "nuance" devotees—the Civil War did not pit pure-of-heart Yankees against a mob of vicious racist Southerners. If it had, the North might not have fought so hard to keep Southerners as their fellow countrymen. President Lincoln—the Great Emancipator himself—wrote to the editor of the *New York Tribune* in August 1862, "If I could save the Union without freeing any slave, I would do it; if I could save it by freeing all the slaves, I would do it; and if I could save it by freeing some and leaving others alone, I would also do that." Indeed, Lincoln did not even issue the Emancipation Proclamation until well into the Civil War, and then largely as a war tactic. Yes, the South had slaves. Martin Luther King was an adulterer. Life is messy.

In his second inaugural address, Lincoln said the Civil War was God's retribution to both the North and the South for the institution of slavery. By allowing slavery to continue past God's appointed time, Lincoln said, all of us had sinned: God "gives to both North and South this terrible war as the woe due to those by whom the offense came." *Jerry Falwell, please pick up the white courtesy phone. Jerry Falwell* . . . If only Falwell had said the 9/11 terrorist attack was God's retribution for abortion, sodomy, and *slavery,* maybe liberals wouldn't have been so snippy. Six hundred thousand white men died to end the offense to God of slavery. Never have so many died to prove what "all men are created equal" means. God have mercy on us when the country is called to account for abortion.

What is commonly known as the "Confederate flag"—by Vermonters, for example—is the Southern Cross, the battle flag Confederate troops carried into the field. It was not the official flag of the Confederacy and never flew over any Confederate buildings. It was the flag of the Confederate army.

The great Confederate general Robert E. Lee opposed slavery and freed his slaves. Lee fought on the Confederate side because Virginia was his home and he thought Virginia had the right to be wrong. Lee was an honorable man as well as a great general. His men followed him, many of them hungry and barefoot, because of his personal qualities and because they lived in the South—not because they held a brief for slavery. Shelby Foote describes perplexed Union soldiers asking a captured Confederate, poor and shoeless, why he was fighting when he clearly didn't own any slaves. The soldier answered, "Because you're down here." Indeed, a small number of blacks served in the Confederate army, presumably for reasons other than their vigorous support of slavery. At an abstract level, of course, the war was about slavery, but that's not why the soldiers fought. They didn't own slaves—their honor is really inviolate.

And they were good soldiers. The Confederate battle flag is a symbol of military valor, a separation from the "Do as I say, not as I do" North. It symbolizes what F. Scott Fitzgerald called a romantic lost cause fought by charming people. Ask any male who ever played Civil War games as a boy if there was a marked preference for one side or the other. Invariably, little boys fight bitterly over who gets to play the Confederates. This obviously has nothing whatsoever to do with slavery: The preference for the South is based purely on the military criteria of little boys. Soldiers in the Confederate army were simply cooler than those in the Union army. They had better uniforms, better songs, and better generals. And they had the rebel yell. Who would you rather be—J.E.B. Stuart in the dashing gray uniform and a plume in his hat or some clodhopper from Maine?

The Civil War was hideous as only civil wars can be. But the victors allowed the vanquished to go home knowing they had done their duty with unsurpassed courage and devotion. Because the South was treated with honor and respect, the war did not degenerate into an unending guerrilla war, as has happened with other nations' civil wars. Confederate soldiers became a romantic army of legend, not sullen losers.

When Confederate soldiers surrendered their arms, the Union general accepting the surrender, Joshua Chamberlain, ordered his men to salute the defeated army. In response, Confederate general John Gordon reared his horse and—as Chamberlain described it—"horse and rider made one motion, the horse's head swung down with a graceful bow and General Gordon dropped his sword point to his toe in salutation." General Ulysses S. Grant drew up generous surrender papers for Lee to sign, precluding trials for treason. After Lee had signed, General Grant ordered Union troops to turn over a portion of their food rations to hungry Confederate troops. Years later, Lee would allow his students to say no unkind words about Grant, calling him a great man who had honored the dignity of the South. When the news came to Washington that Robert E. Lee had surrendered, President Lincoln came out on the White House lawn to announce the South's defeat. He asked the band to play "Dixie." This was an unbelievable way to end a war—and ensured that it really did end. Winston Churchill described the Civil War as the "last war fought between gentlemen." (Perhaps F. Scott Fitzgerald and Churchill should be banned along with the Confederate flag.)

It is the proud military heritage of the South that the Confederate flag represents—a heritage that belongs to all Southerners, both black and white. The whole country's military history is shot through with Southerners. Obviously boys from all over fought in this country's wars, and fought bravely, but it is simply a fact that Southerners are overrepresented in this country's heroic annals.

These are just some of the sons of the South:

- Sergeant Alvin York, who received the Medal of Honor in World War I for leading seven men to capture 128 Germans, including four officers, was from Tennessee.
- The most decorated soldier of World War II, Audie Murphy, was from Texas.
- The first Marine awarded the Medal of Honor in World War II, Hank Elrod, was from Georgia.
- General Lucius Clay, commander of the Berlin Airlift, was from Georgia.
- General Dwight Eisenhower was born in Texas.
- Admiral Chester W. Nimitz, the Pacific commander in chief of the Navy during World War II, was from Texas.
- General Douglas MacArthur, who commanded Allied forces in World War II in the Southwest Pacific, was from Arkansas.

- General William Westmoreland, commander of U.S. troops in Vietnam, was from South Carolina.
- Lieutenant General Lewis Burwell "Chesty" Puller, considered by many to be the greatest Marine ever and the only Marine to be awarded the Navy Cross five times for heroism and gallantry in combat, was from Virginia.
- Tommy Franks, the army general who led the attack on the Taliban in Afghanistan after the attack of 9/11, grew up in Texas.
- Famous draft-dodger Bill Clinton was from Arkansas— showing once again that the exception proves the rule.

Phil Caputo, author of the anti-Vietnam book *Rumor of War,* was one of the first Marines in Vietnam. He says all his best soldiers were Southerners: They could walk for hours and hit anything—as he puts it—just like their Confederate grandfathers.

In his book about World War II, *Citizen Soldiers,* Stephen Ambrose tells of the amazing feats of Lieutenant Waverly Wray from Batesville, Mississippi: "A Baptist, each month he sent half his pay home to help build a new church. He never swore. . . . He didn't drink, smoke, or chase girls. Some troopers called him 'The Deacon,' but in an admiring rather than critical way." With his "Deep South religious convictions," Wray's worst curse was to exclaim "John Brown!"—referring to the abolitionist whose actions helped spark the Civil War. Wray single-handedly killed eight German officers by sneaking up on them "like the deer stalker he was," Ambrose writes. "You don't get more than one Wray to a division, or even to an army." There was only one like him in World War I, Ambrose reports—"also a Southern boy."

The love of home that motivated Confederate soldiers would be transmuted generations later into a virulent patriotism in the South. James Webb, former secretary of the navy, describes Southern soldiers in his military novels whispering "and for the South" under their breath when saying their duty to their country (as if

Southerners need to be reminded not to commit treason). They die at war not for Old Glory, "but for this vestige of lost hope called the South." When General George Pickett rallied his men before their history-making charge at Gettysburg, all he had to say was "Don't forget today that you are from old Virginia."

The majority of military bases in the continental United States are named after Confederate officers—Fort Bragg, Fort Benning, Fort Hood, Fort Polk, Fort Rucker. Are you beginning to see the pattern? Or consider this: When was the last time you heard a GI being interviewed on TV who didn't have a Southern accent? These are the guys who are in the military when there isn't even a war. It is career military people—largely Southerners—who are left with the job of drafting fresh-faced kids from civilian life and whipping them into shape when it's time to go to war. Southerners are truly America's warrior class.

This is a shared cultural ethic among all Southerners, not just the "Sons of the Confederacy." And there are, incidentally, black members of "Sons of the Confederacy." In February 2003, just a few months before the Democrats were working themselves into a lather over Dean's remark about the Confederate flag, a Confederate funeral was held for Richard Quarls, whose unmarked grave had recently been unearthed. The memorial service was organized by the Sons of Confederate Veterans and the United Daughters of the Confederacy. Though Quarls had died in 1925, the service was packed with about 150 people, including Quarls's descendants, community leaders, Civil War reenactors, and Confederate daughters. They sang "Dixie." Quarls's great-granddaughter told the newspapers, "He was a proud man and would have been honored to see this." The honored man was a former slave who had fought for the Confederacy.

The disproportionate number of blacks in the military is a reflection of the disproportionate number of Southerners in the military. Five black Marines were posthumously awarded the Medal of Honor for their service in Vietnam. In mind-boggling acts of heroism, they actually dove on exploding enemy grenades to protect their comrades. This is what they were trained to do. Three of the five were from the South.

In 2001, about 30 percent of blacks in Mississippi voted to keep the 1894 state flag, which displays the Confederate flag in the upper left corner. As Larry Elder has noted, would 30 percent of Jews vote to keep a swastika on a state flag? After touring the South, General Colin Powell concluded that there was no impediment to a black being elected president in America, noting that he received his strongest support from white Southerners.

Slavery is among the ugliest chapters in this nation's history— the ugliest after abortion, which Democrats will get around to opposing in the year 3093. But it was not unique to this country and it was not unique to the South. The American flag could more plausibly be said to symbolize slavery than can the Confederate flag. Slavery was legal under the Stars and Stripes for more than seventy years—far longer than any Confederate flag ever flew. The Ku Klux Klan did not begin using the Confederate flag until the fifties. Before that, they flew the Stars and Stripes. White-supremacist nuts living in their mothers' basements don't have a copyright to the Confederate battle flag any more than they own the copyright for the Chevy pickup truck or the Christian cross— another symbol appropriated by the Klan.

And why does native African kinte cloth get a free pass? It is a historical fact that American slaves were purchased from their slave masters in Africa, where slavery exists in some parts to this day. Indeed, slavery is the only African institution America has ever adopted. But while some Americans express pride in their slave-trading ancestors by calling themselves "African-Americans" and donning African garb, pride in Confederate ancestors is deemed a hate crime. Perhaps, in a bid for the Catholic vote, Democrats could demand that those Masonic symbols be removed from the Great Seal of the United States. And how about the

American eagle? The eagle is a bird of prey and hence offensive to rodents, a key Democrat constituency.

It is a vicious slander against the South to claim the Confederate battle flag represents admiration for slavery. It is pride in the South—having nothing to do with race—and its honorable military history that the Confederate battle flag represents, values that exist independently of the institution of slavery. Anyone who has ever met a Texan has an inkling of what Southern pride is about. Ever heard of a bar fight starting because somebody said something derogatory about the North? The battle flag symbolizes an ethic and honor that belongs to all the sons of the South.

Liberals love to cluck their tongues at such admiration for militaristic values. (The only time liberals pretend to like the military is when they claim to love soldiers so much they don't want them to get hurt fighting a war.) We do well to remember that it was disproportionately Southerners—some wearing Confederate battle flags under their uniforms—who formed the backbone of the military that threw back tyrants from Adolf Hitler to Saddam Hussein. Somebody had to engage in all those insane, mind-boggling acts of heroism, and it wasn't going to be graduates of Horace Mann High School (Anthony Lewis's alma mater). It was graduates of places like the Citadel and the Virginia Military Institute.

Every year after the war was over, Civil War veterans used to return to Gettysburg to reenact the famous battle. On the 50th anniversary, as the Confederate veterans began reenacting Pickett's charge, the Northerners burst into tears and ran down the hill to embrace the Rebels, overcome with emotion at how insanely brave Pickett's charge had been. That's how much Union soldiers respected Confederate soldiers. Man for man, the Confederate army was the greatest army the world had ever seen. It is outrageous for Northern liberals and race demagogues to try to turn the Confederate battle flag into a badge of shame, in the process spitting on America's gallant warrior class. ▪

9

Give Us Twenty-two
Minutes, We'll Give Up
the Country

———■———

*"[People should not] believe everything they read in
the newspapers."*
—JAYSON BLAIR, former *New York Times* reporter
extraordinaire

Four days after the *New York Times* factually identified
the Drudge Report as "notoriously unreliable," the
Times misidentified Republican Senate candidate Pete
Coors in a photo as a Ku Klux Klan member who mur-
dered a black sharecropper. (Coors spokeswoman Cina-
mon Watson remarked of the notoriously unreliable
Times's screw-up, "It could have been worse, she joked.
Pete could have been identified as John Kerry.")

Less than a decade ago, more people would have read
the *Times*'s unsubstantiated assertion that the Drudge Report was "notoriously unreliable" than would ever have
read how actually unreliable the *New York Times* is. In December 1995, only 14 percent of Americans were on the

Internet. By December 2003, two-thirds of Americans were on the Internet, 66 million on a typical day. While the old, notoriously unreliable media still act as if they are the commissars of truth for the now-dead Soviet Union, imagine what they were like when only 14 percent of Americans could get the truth online.

In 1996, *Nightline* ran a vicious smear on Pat Buchanan, then running for president, accusing him of being a racist, an anti-Semite, and generally a very bad man. Apart from vague accusations from anonymous Buchanan-haters and Pat's professional rivals, *Nightline*'s only evidence, such as it was, connecting Buchanan to anything anti-Semitic was the claim that his father listened to an anti-Semitic radio broadcaster from the thirties. In Ted Koppel's words, Buchanan's father "listened to the bigoted and isolationist radio orator Father Coughlin, who stirred populist passions and controversy on the eve of World War II." So if your dad is accused of being anti-Semitic, that automatically makes you anti-Semitic, too. (Gee, I hope this doesn't cause Mel Gibson any problems.)

Koppel then ran quotes from Father Coughlin as if Coughlin were Buchanan's campaign manager: "Now we risk our Americanism and our Christianity, therefore, for the blood profits to be gained by the internationalists." Internationalists, Koppel explained, meant "Jews." Here's Ted's line of reasoning: The patriarch Buchanan listened to a Jew-hating priest on the radio almost seventy years ago, so Pat must hate Jews today. If only the prosecution's burden of proof had been that easy in the O.J. Simpson case.

Except the problem was, Buchanan's father had never even heard of Father Coughlin, much less listened to him. *Nightline* just made it up. In fact, the closest any member of the Buchanan family has ever come to listening to an anti-Semitic radio broadcast was the time Pat accidentally tuned into NPR. Responding to a series of calumnies in the *Nightline* broadcast in a press conference six days later, Bay

Buchanan, Pat's sister, said, "Neither Pat nor I have ever heard my father refer to the late Father Charles Coughlin, the so-called radio priest of the 1930s," and the first time Pat "ever heard of this fellow was when he went to New York City to do graduate work and studied about him at that time." She continued: "Somebody tells me that my father spoke about things in my home, and no one called to ask one of us if it's ever been done in our home, and puts it on his television as fact."

Even other members of the press—who know how mendacious they are—were stunned that no one from *Nightline* had even called to ask about the Father Coughlin story.

> QUESTION: You're saying that no one from *Nightline* ever contacted you or anyone in your family prior to that airing?
> BAY BUCHANAN: Nobody. No one. No one. That is correct.

When told *Nightline* was "standing by" its report, Bay said, "Go ahead and stand by it, but somebody maybe should have some ethics here, some standards, some journalistic standards. Don't they exist anymore for Ted Koppel? He could just put anything he wants on television without even making a phone call?"

This was evidently the first time Bay had ever seen *Nightline*. No one's been so unjustifiably shocked by a lie since the last time Jimmy Carter dealt with the Soviets. In a related story, the phrase "journalistic standards" recently set a new record for "world's biggest oxymoron."

Despite all the gobbledygook about the "profession" of journalism and the absurd conceit that "journalism" is a well-honed craft one has to master over time, the only standard journalists respect is: Will this story promote the left-wing agenda? Like all good propagandists, the major media mix truth with lies and then make a big show of correcting trivial errors while doggedly refusing to issue corrections for the real whoppers. They stare into a camera and claim that they are "professional enough to keep their reporting evenhanded" and then hide behind startled laughter when anyone calls them on it.

After the *New York Times* star reporter Jayson Blair was exposed as making up facts for his articles, the paper conducted an internal investigation to figure out how inaccurate reporting could have ended up in the august pages of the *Times*. (During his first job interview at the *Times* Blair said, "I still believe in a place called Hope," which should have been a huge red flag for somebody.) Apart from the catchall "a failure of communication" and a reminder that the black kid was sneaky, the *Times*'s main excuse for Blair's reporting was their claim that there had been "few complaints from the subjects" of Blair's articles. By "few complaints," apparently what the *Times* means is "There were lots of complaints about facially implausible facts reported in Blair's articles, but the editors decided not to issue any corrections."

In one of the *Times*'s major front-page articles on the Virginia/D.C. sniper investigation in October 2002, Blair reported that sniper John Muhammad had been on the verge of confessing to local officials—when the U.S. Attorney's office broke off the interrogation. It was a stunning revelation, showing an appalling disregard for justice by overeager officials in the Bush administration. Curiously, no other news organization had anything on this major story. The Associated Press and others picked up the *Times*'s story and soon the botched "confession" was being repeated in news outlets across the country, based solely on the fact that it had appeared in the pages of the *New York Times*. *Slate* magazine referred to the "Abbott-and-Costello competition" between state and federal law enforcement, stating, "Already, investigators have complained that [the U.S. Attorney's] rush to file federal charges against

Muhammad and Malvo cost them a possible confession." The *Rocky Mountain News* proclaimed, "Let the States Prosecute the Sniper," saying, "The overly eager actions of a U.S. attorney might have cost investigators a chance of obtaining a confession from John Muhammad."

Meanwhile, the subject of the story, U.S. Attorney Thomas M. DiBiagio, was screaming from the rooftops that the story was patent nonsense. He issued a statement saying, "The allegations in the *New York Times* article today are false." Muhammad had not been about to confess, and in fact, DiBiagio said, there was "no indication throughout the day that either of the individuals were yielding any useful information." FBI Agent Gary Bald denied the *Times*'s claim that federal officials were acting on orders from the White House and the Department of Justice. Numerous other unnamed government officials also contradicted the *Times*'s account.

Not only were the subjects of the article publicly denying Blair's article, legal commentators were remarking on the sheer implausibility of the *Times*'s account. On CNN, Joe DiGenova called the *Times*'s story "hokum," saying that "if there had been a confession about to occur, they never would have moved that suspect." Roy Black said, "I also don't believe anybody would interrupt in a confession going on."

So here was a case where there were lots of public complaints from the subject of Blair's article, scores of on- and off-the-record denials, in addition to widespread skepticism from legal commentators. In response, the *Times* concluded . . . Blair's account was accurate. A correction to the story of how federal officials botched sniper John Muhammad's confession would not run until May 2003— more than six months after the story had run and only when the *Times* was engulfed in the Jayson Blair scandal. Even then, the *Times* issued a halfhearted correction, claiming that Blair's story was "plainly accurate in its central point." Evidently, the "central point" was not the point considered "central" at the time and which was repeated in newspapers across the country, to wit: that federal officials had broken off John Muhammad's interrogation as he was about to confess. The "central point," according to the *Times*'s correction, was simply that "local and federal authorities were feuding over custody of the sniper suspects." That is not a story that, under ordinary circumstances, would make the front page.

The *Times* is caught lying, so they lie to explain why they were lying: There were "few complaints from the subjects" of Blair's articles. This is like recommending a surgeon by saying, "Why, he hasn't killed anyone in almost a week!" But even that wasn't true. It wasn't even plausible. The *Times* routinely ignores all complaints. The only reason Blair was exposed is that another member of the Fourth Estate, the *San Antonio Express-News,* caught Blair plagiarizing its stories. (On May 1, Jayson Blair submitted his letter of resignation, which began with the words "To be, or not to be" and ended with the words "You won't have Jayson Blair to kick around anymore.") Indeed, just a few months after the Jayson Blair scandal broke, the *Times* was again ignoring angry denials from the people quoted in articles. They're like cockroaches, these liberals. You stomp on them, they lie still for a few minutes, and then they start moving again.

A *Times* article by Charlie LeDuff quoted Lieutenant Commander Mike Beidler as he headed off to Iraq commenting on the antiwar protests: "It's war, Commander Beidler said, and the nation is fat. 'No one is screaming for battery-powered cars,' he added." The *Times* reporter then quoted Beidler's wife "as she patted down [her husband's] collar" saying, "'I'm just numb, I'll cry myself to sleep, I'm sure.'" Amazingly, LeDuff had gotten the perfect quote for an article titled "As an American Armada Leaves San Diego, Tears Are the Rule of the Day." This is what's known among purveyors of the craft of journalism as a "big whopper."

When Beidler saw the article—like U.S. Attorney DiBiagio—he immediately wrote to the *Times* strenuously denying virtually every aspect of LeDuff's account. His alleged comments about national fatness and battery-powered cars, he said, "were completely fabricated by Mr. LeDuff." According to Beidler, he simply said, "Protesters have a right to protest, and our job is to defend those rights. But in protesting, they shouldn't protest blindly; instead, they should provide reasonable solutions to the problem"—all of which sounds suspiciously unlike "the nation is fat." Beidler denied that his wife had said she would cry herself to sleep and even pointed out that his wife did not "pat down my collar either, which was impossible for her to accomplish with my civilian shirt hidden under my jacket and a duffel bag hanging on my shoulder closest to her."

After "thoroughly" looking into Beidler's complaint, senior editor Bill Borders wrote back to Beidler, saying Mr. LeDuff "thinks that he accurately represented his interview with you and your wife, and therefore so do I." Thus, a man in New York who had never met the Beidlers described for them a conversation they recently had with a reporter in San Diego. Borders then returned to his primary task of polishing up the new *Times* slogan, "All the News That's Fit to Print, and Then Some!" No correction ever ran. If not for the Internet, no one would know the *Times* simply invented the Beidlers' quotes.

The principal goal of *Times* reporters is to prevent an articulate opposition statement to escape into the world. As long as you can't get them to admit they're lying, they say you can't prove they're lying. They respond with such mystification to corrections of their lies, it is legitimate to ask: How intelligent are the people reporting the news, these constitutionally protected guardians of the truth?

☞ Great Gray Lady in Spat with Saloon Hussy

NOVEMBER 20, 2002

I did not realize how devastating the midterm elections were to liberals until seeing the Great Gray Lady reduced to starting a cat-fight with Fox News Channel. It has come to this. The *New York Times* was in high dudgeon this week upon discovering that Fox News chairman Roger Ailes sent a letter to the Bush White House nine days after September 11. As the corpses of thousands of his fellow Americans lay in smoldering heaps, Ailes evidently recommended getting rough with the terrorists. One imagines Karl Rove running down the hallway to the president's office waving Ailes's letter and shouting "Mr. President! Mr. President! I have the memo! We've got to fight back!"

I assume it's superfluous to mention that there is nothing illegal about Ailes giving advice to the president—though admittedly, I have not consulted the "living Constitution" in the past twenty-four hours to see if a new penumbra specifically about Fox News has sprouted. But the *Times* was a monument of self-righteous indignation, because hard-news men are supposed to stay neutral between America and terrorists.

Of course, the *Times* hasn't been reticent in giving the president advice on the war. (Surrender now!) Other great moments in journalistic neutrality include NPR's Nina Totenberg leaking information about Anita Hill that she got from Senator Howard Metzenbaum's staff, and the *Washington Post*'s Ben Bradlee yukking it up on the phone with President Kennedy and later cheering when President Nixon resigned. So it's interesting that the *Times* viewed Ailes's letter as an affront to objective journalism.

But this was more than the media's usual insane point that they—the least impartial industry in America—must maintain absolute neutrality between George Bush and the terrorists. The

Times went further to imply that by supporting his own country in the war on terrorism, Ailes had unmistakably marked himself as a "partisan conservative."

If Ailes had written a letter recommending a tax hike, a new hate-crimes law, or going easy on the terrorists, I assume the *Times* would not have accused Ailes of showing a conservative bias. Instead, he had recommended the harshest measures possible against the terrorists. As far as the *Times* was concerned, this was the smoking gun of partisanship. The paper railed that Ailes purports to be an "unbiased journalist, not a conservative spokesman." Fox News is "the self-proclaimed fair and balanced news channel." But now the *Times* had caught him red-handed, pursuing "an undisguised ideological agenda." Ailes is secretly rooting for America!

At least we finally have it from the horse's own mouth. The *Times* openly admits that the "conservative" position—but not the liberal position—is to take America's side against the terrorists. Why do they get so snippy when I say that? The *Times* was a whirligig of pointless insinuations—"secretly gave advice to," "back-channel message," "shocking," "confirmed yesterday," and "revelations." (Eager *Times* readers will have to wait another day for any "revelations" about Pinch Sulzberger's SAT scores.) Belittling Fox News is so pleasurable for the *Times* that it didn't occur to them that they had given up the ghost on their faux patriotism. It is simply taken for granted that liberals root against their own country. As the *Times* said of Ailes's letter, it "was less shocking than it was liberating—a little like the moment in 1985 when an ailing Rock Hudson finally explained that he had AIDS." Same back at you! We always knew you were traitors, and now you've admitted it.

Fox News should agree to admit it is conservative if all other media outlets will admit they are liberal. Fox is manifestly closer to the center than the others. Referring here to the *Times*'s definition of "conservative" (harsh with the terrorists) and "liberal" (soft on the terrorists), I believe the public is with Fox News. We took a pretty conclusive poll on that a couple of weeks ago. The people, in their infinite wisdom, have spoken. ∎

☞ How a White Male from Alabama Learned the Craft of Journalism from a Young Reporter Named Jayson Blair

MAY 14, 2003

The *New York Times* is to be commended for ferreting out Jayson Blair, the reporter recently discovered to be making up facts, plagiarizing other news organizations, and lying about nonexistent trips and interviews. A newspaper that employs Maureen Dowd can't have had an easy time settling on Blair as the scapegoat. Blair's record of inaccuracies, lies, and distortions made him a candidate for either immediate dismissal or his own regular column on the op-ed page.

The editors have set up a special e-mail address for readers to report falsehoods they discover in Jayson Blair articles. Okay, but how about setting up one for Paul Krugman? The *Times* ought to seize the moment and claim all those front-page articles predicting a "quagmire" in Iraq were also written by Blair.

The *Times* has now willingly abandoned its mantle as the "newspaper of record." It was already up against the Internet and LexisNexis as a research tool. But with Jayson Blair it has managed to leapfrog beyond mere technological obsolescence. All the *Times* had left was its reputation for accuracy. As this episode shows, the *Times* is not even attempting to preserve a reliable record of events. Instead of being a record of history, the *Times* is merely a record of what liberals would like history to be: *The Pentagon in Crisis! A Quagmire in Iraq! Global Warming Is Melting the North Pole! Protests Roil the Augusta National Golf Club!* Publisher Arthur "Pinch" Sulzberger has turned the paper into a sort of bulletin board for Manhattan liberals.

In the Soviet-style reporting preferred at the *Times*, its self-investigation of the Blair scandal included copious denials that race had anything to do with it:

- "Mr. Boyd [managing editor] said last week that the decision to advance Mr. Blair had not been based on race."
- "Mr. Blair's *Times* supervisors . . . emphasize that he earned an internship at *The Times* because of glowing recommendations and a remarkable work history, not because he is black."

Did Jayson Blair write the article on the investigation of Jayson Blair?

The very next sentence notes that the *Times* offered Blair "a slot in an internship program that was then being used in large part to help the paper diversify its newsroom." If the *Times* "diversity" program did not consider Blair's race, then it wasn't much of a diversity program, now was it? This is like job advertisements that proclaim, "Equal Opportunity, Affirmative Action Employer." Well, which is it?

In one of several feverish editorials supporting the University of Michigan's race-based admissions program, the *Times* denounced the Bush administration for imagining "that diversity can be achieved without explicitly taking race into account." Any diversity program that failed to do so, the *Times* lectured, was "necessarily flawed." But then it gets caught publishing Jayson Blair and the *Times* demurely insists that its own affirmative-action program scrupulously ignored race. Oh, okay.

The *Times* not only expressly took race into account but also put Blair's race above everything—accuracy, credibility, and the paper's reputation. It hired a kid barely out of college. In fact, it turns out Blair was not yet out of college. He had no professional journalistic experience, except at the *Times*. He screwed up over and over again, and the paper had to print over fifty corrections to articles he'd written.

Despite all this, Blair was repeatedly published on the front page, promoted, and sent love notes from the editor in chief, Howell Raines. Ignoring the warnings of a few intrepid whistle-blowers, top management kept assigning Blair to bigger stories in new departments without alerting the editors to Blair's history, because— as Raines said—it would "stigmatize" him. (Speaking of stigmas, after this scandal, does the demand for black heart surgeons go up or down?) Raines jettisoned the *Times*'s famous slogan, preferring the slogan "The *New York Times*: Now With Even More Black People!"

Publisher Sulzberger summed up the episode with these words: "The person who did this is Jayson Blair. Let's not begin to demonize our executives." To put that in plain English: Even though we hired him, we promoted him, and we covered up for him, and even though it's our name on the masthead, we assume absolutely no responsibility for any of this whatsoever. If mismanagement at Enron had been this clear-cut, the *Times* would be demanding the death penalty for Ken Lay. Indeed, taking a page from all corporate chieftans caught in scandals, the *Times* insists that the organization is fine; it was just one bad apple. As I recall, the *Times* editorial page did not accept that explanation when Merrill Lynch said it about Henry Blodget.

Raines's behavior is far worse than the corporate chieftains'. He clearly bears the most responsibility for this fiasco, but when disaster strikes . . . he blames the black kid! So far, Raines's response has been basically to say, "You try to help these people . . ." (Raines's other great contribution to race relations was his unintentionally comical magazine piece about his black maid, "Grady's Gift.") It is absolutely Clintonian. Just as Clinton blamed "THAT WOMAN" and said anyone who blamed him was probably a Christian fundamentalist and a menace to a woman's right to choose, Raines is setting up the defense that his detractors must be bigots opposed to affirmative action. You posture, posture, champion this righteous cause and that righteous cause, abuse your responsibil-

ity—and when you get in trouble, you blame "THAT WOMAN."
("The b—— set me up.")

Put aside whether race should be used as a hiring criterion.
Even people who support affirmative action don't have to support
Raines's approach of refusing to hold blacks responsible for anything, ever—including fake reporting. What Raines did to Blair
was cruel. Think of it in a nonracial context: Suppose the owner of
a big company sends his kid to learn the business and tells low-
level managers to treat him just as they would treat anyone else.
The managers try to curry favor with the boss by reporting that his
son is doing great and is a natural genius for this business. So the
kid keeps getting praised and promoted, until one day he is actually put in charge of something he has no ability to run. That is
cruel. And it's the story of Pinch Sulzberger, isn't it? ■

☞ The Weather's Great, Wish I Were Here

MAY 21, 2003

RIO DE JANEIRO—Actually I'm in Brooklyn right now, but I'm
counting on my employer to follow the strict fact-checking methods in operation at the *New York Times*. Under the *Times*'s scrupu-
lous reporting procedures, reporter Jayson Blair kept turning in
reports with datelines from places like West Virginia and Maryland—while submitting expense receipts for the same time period
from Joe's Bar in Brooklyn. You can't really blame him. He could-
n't very well turn in articles with the dateline "My Mom's House."

In the current *Newsweek* magazine, Seth Mnookin reports that
Blair was forced to resign from the student newspaper at the University of Maryland, the *Diamondback,* for precisely the same misconduct he engaged in at the *Times*—phony reporting, plagiarism,
irresponsibility, and fantastic lies. Once known as "the Newspaper
of Record," the *Times* is now trying out the motto "Almost as Accurate as the Maryland *Diamondback*."

Editor Howell Raines ignored Blair's repeated, brazen mendacity. He ignored his editors' urgent demands that Blair be fired. He ignored press conferences in which public officials remarked that Blair's stories were full of lies. Raines ignored it all—until finally one day, another newspaper caught Blair plagiarizing one of its stories and blew the whistle on the *Times*. And then Raines claimed to be shocked to discover that Blair was engaging in "a pathological pattern of misrepresentation, fabricating and deceiving." After all, the *Times* had issued Blair a series of warnings. (One sternly worded memo urged Blair to be "more black.")

This episode is considered a low point in the paper's 152-year history. Not as low as when it endorsed Jimmy Carter, but still pretty low. As has now been widely reported, publisher Arthur Pinch Sulzberger responded to the meltdown at the *Times* by bringing a stuffed toy moose to an internal meeting with reporters to discuss the burgeoning scandal last week.

Also at the meeting, Raines finally admitted the blindingly obvious fact that he engaged in egregious mismanagement because Blair was black. Raines said, "Does that mean I personally favored Jayson? Not consciously, but you have a right to ask if I as a white man from Alabama with those convictions gave him one chance too many by not stopping his appointment to the sniper team. When I look into my heart for the truth of that, the answer is yes." So for being a warmhearted white liberal, he wants a pat on the head (much as his black maid, Grady, used to give him).

Raines said he would not resign, and Pinch said he would not accept Raines's resignation if offered. Which brings us to Pinch.

While we are having a debate about diversity and race-based policies, can't we all agree that no one should be defending nepotism? In one of 4 billion columns attacking President Bush this year, *Times* columnist Maureen Dowd accused him of getting into Yale only because he was a legacy. She sneered at the argument of White House aides that Bush also earned a degree from Harvard Business School, despite there being no Bush relatives who went to

Harvard. Dowd responded, "They seemed genuinely surprised when told that Harvard would certainly have recognized the surname and wagered on the future success of the person with it."

I believe Sulzberger is a pretty well-known name, too. The Sulzberger-Ochs dynasty has controlled the most powerful newspaper in the world for the last century. A college admissions committee would not have to wager on young Pinch's future success. It was his birthright to run the *New York Times* someday. No messy elections could stand in his way. And yet it appears that Harvard managed to turn him down. He was a legacy at Columbia University, but they didn't want him either. Maureen might want to stay mum on the subject of dumb rich kids, at least as long as her boss is Pinch Sulzberger.

Like Raines, Pinch blithely washed his hands of the stunning mismanagement at the *Times*. Commenting through his spokesman, a small stuffed moose, Pinch made the Churchillian pronouncement "We didn't do this right. We regret that deeply. We feel it deeply. It sucks." Uday Hussein had more right to be in charge of Iraq's Olympic committee than Pinch Sulzberger does to be running a newspaper.

Under the race-based admissions at the University of Michigan, applicants are given four points for being a legacy and twenty points for being black. Does anyone think Pinch got only four points to be publisher of the *Times*? Couldn't the Sulzberger family just buy him a boat? ◼

☞ Here's a Traitor!

During my recent book tour, I resisted the persistent, illiterate request that I name traitors. With a great deal of charity—and suspension of disbelief—I was willing to concede that many liberals were merely fatuous idiots. (In addition, I was loath to name

names for fear that liberals would start jumping out of windows.)
But after the *Times*'s despicable editorial on the two-year anniversary of the 9/11 terrorist attack, I am prepared—just this once—to
name a traitor: Pinch Sulzberger, publisher of the *New York Times*.

To be sure, if any liberal could legitimately use the stupid defense, it is the one Sulzberger who apparently couldn't get into Columbia University. At a minimum, Columbia has four hundred
faculty members who start each day by thinking about how to get
their kooky ideas onto the *Times*'s op-ed page. For an heir to the
Times not to attend Columbia, those must have been some low
SAT scores.

But the clincher was an editorial on the two-year anniversary
of the September 11 attack in which the *Times* endorsed the principle of moral equivalence between the United States and the 9/11
terrorists. In the *Times*'s meandering, mind-numbing prose, it explained that the terrorists might have slaughtered thousands of
Americans in a bloody attack on U.S. soil—but the United States
has had imperialistic depredations of its own!

By not opposing a military coup by the great Augusto Pinochet
against a Chilean Marxist, Salvador Allende, the *Times* implied,
the United States was party to a terrorist act similar to the 9/11 attack on America. This is how the *Times* describes Pinochet's 1973
coup: "A building—a symbol of the nation—collapsed in flames in
an act of terror that would lead to the deaths of 3,000 people. It
was Sept. 11."

Allende was an avowed Marxist, who, like Clinton, got into office on a plurality vote. He instantly hosted a months-long visit
from Castro, allowing Castro to distribute arms to Chilean leftists.
He began destroying Chile's economy at a pace that makes California governor Gray Davis look like a piker. No less an authority
than Chou En-lai warned Allende that he was pursuing a program
that was too extreme for his region. When General Pinochet
staged his coup against a Marxist strongman, the United States
did not stop him—as if Latin American generals were incapable of

doing coups on their own. And—I quote—"It was Sept. 11."
Parsed to its essentials, the *Times*'s position is: We deserved it.

This from a paper that has become America's leading spokesman for the deposed Baathist regime in Iraq. Interestingly, we
started to lose this war only after the embedded reporters pulled
out. Back when we got the news directly from Iraq, it was all victory and optimism. Now that the news is filtered through the
mainstream media here in America, all we hear is death and destruction and quagmire. See if you can detect a pattern in two
weeks of news at the *Treason Times:*

- "Since the beginning of the Iraq war, 292 soldiers have been
  killed in Iraq and Kuwait, including 152 SINCE PRESIDENT
  BUSH DECLARED ON MAY 1 THAT MAJOR AMERICAN COMBAT
  OPERATIONS HAD ENDED." (September 13, 2003)
- "So far, 290 American troops have died in Iraq or Kuwait
  since the beginning of the Iraq war, including 150 SINCE
  PRESIDENT BUSH DECLARED ON MAY 1 THAT MAJOR AMERI-
  CAN COMBAT OPERATIONS HAD ENDED." (September 12,
  2003)
- "It was impossible to watch Mr. Bush's somber speech
  without remembering that FOUR MONTHS AGO, WHEN THE
  PRESIDENT MADE HIS 'TOP GUN' LANDING ON AN AIRCRAFT
  CARRIER AND DECLARED AN END TO 'MAJOR COMBAT
  OPERATIONS,' the White House was worried about giving
  the world the impression that Americans were gloating."
  (September 8, 2003)
- "The speech was Mr. Bush's first extended address about
  Iraq SINCE HE DECLARED AN END TO MAJOR COMBAT
  OPERATIONS in a May 1 speech." (September 8, 2003)
- "When President Bush DECLARED AN OFFICIAL END TO
  MAJOR HOSTILITIES IN IRAQ in May, Reuters moved Dana
  to Baghdad to give him a safer assignment." (September 7,
  2003)

- "SINCE PRESIDENT BUSH DECLARED THE END OF MAJOR COMBAT OPERATIONS IN IRAQ, hundreds of violent and disruptive attacks have been waged by an array of forces." (September 7, 2003)
- "The address will come . . . four months after Mr. Bush's last nationally televised prime-time speech on Iraq, from the deck of the carrier *Abraham Lincoln*, WHERE HE DECLARED THAT 'MAJOR COMBAT OPERATIONS' HAD ENDED." (September 6, 2003)
- "Eleven British soldiers have been killed SINCE PRESIDENT BUSH DECLARED AN END TO MAJOR COMBAT ON MAY 1." (September 5, 2003)
- "Not long AFTER PRESIDENT BUSH DECLARED AN END TO THE MAJOR FIGHTING IN IRAQ, Jessica Porter hatched an ambitious plan: She would make a quilt for every family of an American soldier who had died in the war." (September 3, 2003)
- "At least 64 American troops have now died from hostile attacks SINCE PRESIDENT BUSH DECLARED THE END TO MAJOR COMBAT OPERATIONS IN IRAQ ON MAY 1." (August 28, 2003)
- "More American troops have now died SINCE PRESIDENT BUSH DECLARED AN END TO MAJOR COMBAT ON MAY 1 THAN WERE KILLED FIGHTING THE WAR IN IRAQ." (August 27, 2003)

Hey—does anyone know when Bush declared major combat operations had ended? Because I think there may have been one article in the sports section of the *Times* last week that didn't mention it. The *Times* is even taking shots at the war in the Arts section, stating authoritatively in a recent movie review, "And with the war in Iraq threatening to turn into a Vietnam-like quagmire . . ." (How about getting some decent, impartial reporters embedded at the *Times*?)

Apparently, the *Times*'s stylebook now requires all reports of violence anywhere within a thousand miles of Iraq to be dated from Bush's speech declaring an end to "major combat" operations. How about dating everything from the day Pinch Sulzberger got his SAT scores back and realized he wasn't going to Columbia University?

I gather the *Times* is trying to convey something by the infernal references to Bush's speech declaring an end to major combat in Iraq—but what? That we haven't turned a savage fascist dictatorship into a peace-loving democracy overnight? Iraq is considerably better off than Chile was under Salvador Allende—the *Times*'s second-favorite world leader after Saddam Hussein. ∎

☞ CBS Could Show Augusta How to Really Discriminate

DECEMBER 11, 2002

The *New York Times* is in such a lather about the Augusta National Golf Club's ban on women members, it has briefly interrupted news coverage of *The Sopranos* to write about it. The outrage over Augusta is not a naturally occurring phenomenon that is simply being reported by the media. It's a synthetic scandal cooked up in the *New York Times*'s PC laboratory. One of the best female golfers in the world, Nancy Lopez of the World Golf Hall of Fame, has said she has no problem with Augusta's policy. But scribblers at the *Times* have flogged Augusta so relentlessly, it almost seems as if the nation is about to go to war over a golf club's "no girls" policy.

Anyone who compares the plight of women to the plight of blacks is a racist. Only the bizarre antisexual psychology of liberals could fail to grasp the insanity of treating gender like race. Men and women are ineluctably bound to one another. They are also utterly different. Phyllis Schlafly's point that no one wants to end the tradition of separate bathrooms for men and women is so fundamentally true that there is nothing else to be said. (Except in France, where the practice is common.)

But it is really more than the public should have to bear to listen to the last bulwark of legal discrimination in America harping about the membership policies of a private club. The media openly discriminate against half of America: Republicans. There is not a single person in any half-important job in the mainstream media who might have voted for Ronald Reagan. That can't be easy. There aren't that many people in the country who didn't vote for Reagan. In 1984, he won the largest electoral landslide in history.

Fittingly, the only member to resign in protest from Augusta so far is Thomas Wyman, the former chairman of CBS News—specializing in intolerance for half a century. Wyman was never disturbed by the blatant discrimination at CBS. He proudly presided over a club where membership ran the gamut from Walter Cronkite to Dan Rather. Indeed, CBS was so discriminatory and hateful toward Republicans there's even a book about it: *Bias*, by former CBS star reporter Bernard Goldberg.

While privileged enforcers of the ideological Jim Crow system like Wyman received million-dollar bonuses, talented young journalists were excluded from Wyman's elite media club. Aspiring newsmen who happened to be Republicans had to find work elsewhere or get used to peanut butter for dinner and fourth-floor walk-ups. Dreams were dashed and careers ended. Hearing Wyman complain about discrimination at a golf club would be like hearing Hugh Hefner complain about bawdy language on TV sitcoms.

Inasmuch as he hails from the most discriminatory industry in the nation, if Wyman hadn't resigned in a self-righteous snit, he probably could have taught Augusta a few tricks of the trade. Frankly, Augusta has been going about this in entirely the wrong way.

Point One: Simply deny that Augusta excludes women. Try something like: "Augusta is not exclusive. It's humanitarian." This is how CBS's Walter Cronkite explained the employment of only liberals in the mainstream media: It's not "liberal, it's humanitarian." Or how about "I have always believed that if you get women out of the way, then decent, reasonable golfers would figure out a way to run a golf club." Don Hewitt, executive producer of CBS's *60 Minutes* said, " I have always believed that if you get the NRA out of the way, decent, reasonable Americans would figure out a way to respect the Second Amendment."

Point Two: Claim that *both* men and women feel they are excluded from Augusta. Cite ludicrous "studies" proving it. As Lesley Stahl said of the liberal media, "Everybody complains about us, right wing, left wing, Democrats, Republicans. They all pound on us. They all think we're unfair to them." She said "this big huge study" had concluded that "the mainline media is sucked in by the right-wing conspiratorialists."

Point Three: While openly excluding women, make a big ruckus about any discrimination based on minor, inconsequential differences among men. Commission studies to determine if tall men are getting as much tee time as short men. The glossy magazines won't allow a single Republican to write for them. But they are consumed with grief that not enough models of color have appeared on their covers.

Point Four: Patronizingly instruct women to stop whining and go start their own golf club. Then if they do, attack it. This is what media elites told conservatives for years. We finally got Fox News, and now they savagely denounce it.

This is how an entire industry serving the public interest explains its own continuous and ongoing discrimination against half the country. Poor little Augusta just wants to exclude girls from a golf club. ■

☞ Give Us Twenty-two Minutes, We'll Give Up the Country

FEBRUARY 19, 2003

Rich liberals are planning to fund a talk-radio network because they believe—as the *New York Times* put it—they have been "overshadowed in the political propaganda wars by conservative radio and television personalities." If liberals think they are losing elections because of conservative bias in the media, they might as well give up right now. Their first problem is going to be finding liberals who can work on their little project, since they're all already employed at the networks.

But liberals insist they need a radio network "to counterbalance the conservative tenor of radio programs like *The Rush Limbaugh Show*." Rush has been driving them crazy for years. In 1994, CNN dedicated an entire program to figuring out how the "mainstream media" could combat Rush Limbaugh, asking the question "Does Rush Limbaugh deserve all this attention, and what should the mainstream media be doing about it?" In 1996, the Democratic National Committee went so far as to establish a speakers' bureau/talk-radio initiative to strike back at conservative talk radio by monitoring talk radio and teaching liberals "radio skills."

Among the "alternatives to Rush" that liberals have tried over the years are: former New York governor Mario Cuomo, Harvard law professor Alan Dershowitz, former Connecticut governor Lowell Weicker, former California governor Jerry Brown, former U.S. senator (and *Monkey Business* skipper) Gary Hart, and former Virginia governor Doug Wilder. Liberals keep serving up their own dreary radio hosts, and the public keeps turning the dial back to Rush Limbaugh.

To be sure, conservative radio talk-show hosts have a built-in audience unavailable to liberals: people driving cars to some sort of job. But it should not be surprising that when given a choice, people don't want liberal hectoring being piped into their homes and cars. It would be like being Winston Smith in George Orwell's *1984,* forced to listen to Big Brother twenty-four hours a day. Indeed, it's difficult to imagine a world in which people voluntarily choose to listen to liberals. There is no evidence that it has ever happened.

For years, liberals would pass off mediocrities as broadcasting geniuses for surviving the brutal competition of . . . a monopoly. In the precable era, Phil Donahue was promiscuously called a "legend," a "star," the "daytime guru," "daytime television's biggest star"—even a "major star." In 1993, Donahue was inducted into the Academy of Television Arts & Sciences' Hall of Fame. His millions of viewers were touted as proof of his massive talent.

Of course, back when there were only three TV stations, it was a little difficult to tell whether "major stars" like Donahue had any talent to attract viewers. Did people actually enjoy watching a man with the IQ of a bright chimpanzee who passed himself off as Bertrand Russell, or did they just want to watch something on TV?

Now we have the answer!

In a controlled scientific experiment, Donahue was given his own TV show on MSNBC in the new competitive environment of cable TV. *That Boy's* ratings were the lowest in prime-time TV for any news program. In fact, his ratings were so low, Nielsen could barely detect them. If only MSNBC could go back and give shows to all the other pompous liberal blowhards once forced on the public, like Edward R. Murrow and Walter Cronkite, we could see how they would have fared with a little competition. My hunch is Nielsen would not have been able to *See It Now.*

Liberal speakers lose in all competitive environments; they win only by cheating or by force. One of many failed "alternatives" to Rush, Jim Hightower recommended that liberals make "stronger efforts to insist that their voices be heard." Conservatives, he said, "do this all the time." They "hammer the networks and the owners to be heard." And that's how we ousted Katie Couric and Dan Rather from the airwaves and ended up with a solid lineup of authentic Americans on ABC, NBC, and CBS. Oh, no wait. That didn't happen.

One thing about liberals is they're pesky devils. They'll never quit. And now they are back again looking for the next "liberal alternative" to Rush. They have the money, the business consultants, the radio talent. Now all they need are ideas! Ah, there's the rub.

The paradox of liberal talk radio is that if liberals cared about ideas or knew any facts, they would cease being liberals. Liberalism thrives on ignorance. Even the audience for the Left's government-supported radio network, National Public Radio, has more conservative listeners than liberal listeners. (As Mickey Kaus said, "No wonder conservatives are so pissed off.") According to a Pew Research Center study released in the summer of 2002, conservatives consume far more news than liberals—including listening to NPR and watching PBS more than liberals. Liberals get their news from Lifetime: TV for Women, NBC's *The West Wing*, and 4 billion *Law & Order* episodes in which the perp turns out to be a white, Christian male who recites the Second Amendment before disemboweling a poor minority child.

Liberal persuasion consists of the highbrow sneer from self-satisfied snobs ladled out for people with a 40 IQ. This is not an ideology that can withstand several hours a day of caller scrutiny where their goofball notions can be shot down by any truck driver with a cell phone. ∎

☞ Journalism: Where Even the Men Are Women

JANUARY 2, 2003

I generally avoid mentioning even widely published lies about me, or I'd never have time to do the things that provoke liberals to lie about me. But inasmuch as one of the media's favorite pastimes is to invent inane quotes and attribute them to conservatives—and then refuse to run corrections—I thought we could use a few real-life examples to examine the ethics of the scribbling profession.

One apocryphal quote that has long perplexed me was the one falsely attributed to me in Salon.com by Christina Valhouli, renowned expert on "fat farms" and "squishy tummies." (See www.curve-film.com: "You don't need to be a size 2 to be a perfect 10.") What I never said, but fat-farm expert Valhouli thinks I *should* have said, is this: "Women like Pamela Harriman and Patricia Duff are basically Anna Nicole Smith from the waist down. Let's just call it for what it is. They're whores."

I don't even understand what that sentence means. Aren't all women basically the same "from the waist down"? (No wonder liberals are so insistent on sex education classes.) That quote has now been attributed to me in the *Washington Monthly,* the *Washington Post,* and hundreds of websites—all citing Salon.com. I have racked my brain to understand why a fat-farm expert and "plus size" historian would do me such a bad turn. Readers? Anyone?

One of my favorite fabricated statements was the one created for me by Andrew Grossman of the *Hollywood Reporter.* He was reporting an exchange on the *Today* show about my 9/11 column in which I said of the terrorists and their sympathizers, "We should invade their countries, kill their leaders, and convert them to Christianity." *Today* host Katie Couric asked me if I thought that was the best way to battle terrorism.

Here is my precise answer: "Well, point one and point two, by the end of the week, had become official government policy. As for converting them to Christianity, I think it might be a good idea to get them on some sort of hobby other than slaughtering infidels. I mean, perhaps that's the Peace Corps, perhaps it's working for Planned Parenthood, but I've never seen the transforming effect of anything like Christianity."

Grossman's full account of this exchange in the *Hollywood Re-*

porter was: "'Do you still believe that's the best way to fight terror-ism?' Couric demanded. That quote was taken out of context, Coulter insisted." My parents are still waiting for the day that I formulate an argument as succinct and elegant as "That was taken out of context. Now I'll go back to eating my turkey." Even my worst enemies would not believe I was a nonparticipant in an ar-gument about me. This is the form of stupidity I admire the most: *How should I know how to work LexisNexis?* Apart from being a college professor, there is no job in the universe easier than being a journalist. For 99.999 percent of writers, there is no heavy lifting, no physical danger, no honest day's work. Andrew Grossman has found a way to make it even easier. No research!

At the other end of the spectrum are energetic journalists who think all words spoken by Ann Coulter are one long ticker tape that can be cut up and strung together at random to produce any imaginable quote. On December 8, 1998, the topic on *Rivera Live* was how long an impeachment trial would take. Alan Dershowitz said it would take up to ten months. Geraldo Rivera said three months. Lawyer Roy Black offered the important and persuasive point that "people with a brain" wanted me to stop talking.

This is the relevant exchange about the length of the impeach-ment trial—which, I note, took about one week:

MS. COULTER: The idea that a Senate trial would go on and on and on is absurd. It would take about a week. . . .

PROF. DERSHOWITZ: Can you make a tape of that? Yeah, Geraldo, make a tape of that and replay that over and over again as we get into the sixth week, the tenth week, the twentieth week, the thirtieth week, the fortieth week. We'll have Ann Coulter say-ing, "It will take a week. It will take a week."

MS. COULTER: Well, I don't know. So far, I could be quoted back to myself many times, like on the Secret Service privilege, the attorney-client privilege, the dead man's privilege. Really, my track record is pretty good on predictions.

On another TV show the following March, about the time Hillary Clinton was first thinking about running for the Senate and her presumed opponent was Rudolph Giuliani, I said I thought Whitewater would prevent Hillary from challenging Giuliani. Giuliani got prostate cancer and decided not to run, so now we'll never know. The *Washington Monthly* reported my quotes as "I think [Whitewater]'s going to prevent the first lady from running for Senate. . . . My track record is pretty good on predictions."

They get an A for effort on that one. Little Andrew Grossman wouldn't even look up the show he was writing about. These people search the record for two different quotes, in two different places, on two different TV shows, on two different topics, months apart, reverse the order, and patch them together to try to make a monkey out of me.

I've also said "yes." How about stringing these sentences together to make me look brilliant:

Q: Will Jimmy Carter win the Nobel Peace Prize, Madonna make a movie that bombs, and North Korea develop nuclear weapons?

ANN COULTER: Yes.

I think I'm owed that.

Most journalists are so stupid, catty, lazy, and vengeful that the fact that they are also humorless is often overlooked. For an example of journalists' fine-tuned sense of humor, consider CBS-News.com's response to the first sentence of my column about the gnashing of teeth over Trent Lott's toast to Strom Thurmond on his hundredth birthday. I wrote, "I'm just glad Strom Thurmond isn't around to see this." CBSNews.com earnestly corrected me: "At last check by CBS News, the world's most famous 100-year-old was doing fine."

A *People* magazine reporter writing a profile on me in 2001 asked me if I had a boyfriend. My precise answer—typed out in an e-mail no less—was: "No. When I feel a need for intimacy, I go to an airport security checkpoint." As quoted by *People,* my answer was "No. I go to an airport security checkpoint."

But the winner of "best in show" for journalists' great sense of humor, sadly, does not involve one of my own quotes. Amid liberal squawking about William Safire's calling Hillary Clinton a "congenital liar" in his *New York Times* column, Safire claimed it was a typo and that he meant to say she was a "congenital *lawyer.*" That hotbed of liberal wit, the *Nation* magazine, indignantly responded, "Sure, Bill, we believe you. Say, that steno's name wasn't Rosemary Woods, was it?"

From their commitment to exactitude to their terrific sense of humor, all of the feminists' very best qualities now dominate the profession of journalism. Poor Jayson Blair just happened to be the one who got caught. ■

☛ I Guess You're Right: There Is No Liberal Media Bias

OCTOBER 8, 2003

Response to interview questions of Edward Nawotka of *Publishers Weekly:*

QUESTION: [Al] Franken claims that there are numerous falsehoods in your book, especially buried in the footnotes.... Who is ultimately responsible for the errors, you, the publisher, or both?

COULTER: I see we're off to a good start! In your interview with Al Franken, after suggesting that some readers may want Franken to run for president, you ask him hardball questions like:

- "It's got to be a little grating to see your book on the same *New York Times* best-seller list as the Ann Coulter book."
- "You fact-checked Ann Coulter's book and found a lot of

inconsistencies, outright lies, and quotes that are taken out of context. Who is responsible for those kinds of errors, the author or the editors?"

- "How should booksellers deal with this?"

You ask me questions like these:

- "Who is ultimately responsible for the errors [in your book], you, the publisher, or both?"
- "What gives—was this an honest mistake or malfeasance as he suggests?"
- "Why all the name-calling?"

Apparently, Ed, it never occurred to you that Franken's allegations of errors in my book—or "outright lies" as you put it—are false.

It's interesting that the most devastating examples of my alleged "lies" keep changing. As soon as one is disproved, I'm asked to respond to another. This is behavior normally associated with tinfoil-hat conspiracy theorists. One crackpot argument after another is shot down—but the conspiracy theorists just move on to the next crackpot argument without pause or reconsideration. Certainly without apology.

So before responding to the two alleged "lies" you cite from Franken, the source of all wisdom, I shall run through a few of the alleged "lies" from Franken's book that I have already been asked to respond to—and which have now been dropped by the Coulter hysterics as they barrel ahead to the next inane charge.

Franken's very first charge against me is that I told a reporter from the Observer *that I was "friendly" with Franken, when in fact, we are not "friendly."*

Needless to say, I never claimed to be friendly with Al Franken. Inasmuch as I barely know Franken, a normal person might have looked at that and realized the reporter misunderstood me. But apparently Franken thinks he has a pretty cool name to drop—the oddest case of reverse name-dropping I've ever heard of.

I don't hear about this "lie" so much anymore.

Franken hysterically accuses me of "lying" for calling my endnotes "footnotes" in interviews on my book.

Yes, notes at the end of a book are technically "endnotes," not "footnotes." Franken will have to take his case up with the *New York Times,* the *Los Angeles Times,* and the *Washington Post* and the rest of the universe—all of which referred to my 780 endnotes as "FOOTNOTES." Also God, for inventing the concept of "colloquial speech."

I don't hear so much about this "lie" anymore.

Franken claims I complain that conservatives don't get on TV enough.

Inasmuch as I am on TV a lot, this would be a hilarious point. Too bad I never said it. My book *Slander*—which Franken seems to have gone over with a fine-tooth comb—would have been a good place to make that point if I wanted to make it. *Slander* contains an entire chapter on the media, and yet I never claim that conservatives are not on TV enough. What I say is: "Democrats in the media are editors, national correspondents, news anchors, and reporters. Republicans are 'from the right' polemicists grudgingly tolerated within the liberal behemoth."

By the way, I also say, "The distinction between opinion journalism and objective news coverage is seemingly impossible for liberals to grasp." Franken's absurd description of my point proves it.

I haven't heard so much about this "lie" anymore.

I claim Evan Thomas's father was the socialist party presidential candidate, Norman Thomas.

Franken drones on and on for a page and a half about how Norman Thomas was not Evan Thomas's father—without saying that he was Evan's grandfather. This was one of about five inconsequential errors quickly corrected in *Slander*—and cited one million times by liberals as a "LIE." Confusing "father" with "grandfather" is a mistake. Franken's deliberate implication that there was no relationship whatsoever between Norman and Evan Thomas is intentional dishonesty.

I haven't heard so much about this "lie" anymore.

I incorrectly claimed Dale Earnhardt's death was not mentioned on the front page of the New York Times *the day after his death.*

In my three best-selling books—making the case for a president's impeachment, accusing liberals of systematic lying and propagandizing, arguing that Joe McCarthy was a great American patriot, and detailing fifty years of treachery by the Democratic Party—this is the only vaguely substantive error the Ann Coulter hysterics have been able to produce, corrected soon after publication.

CONGRATULATIONS, LIBERALS!!!

The *Columbia Journalism Review* was crowing about this great victory over Ann Coulter a year ago. A search of "coulter" and "earnhardt" on Google turns up over a thousand hits. Now Franken dedicates another two pages in his book to it. I believe this triumph of theirs has been sufficiently revisited by now. At least I didn't miss the Ukrainian famine. See Pulitzer Prize–winning *New York Times* reporter Walter Duranty.

I don't heard so much about this "lie" anymore.

Frazier Moore, a fantasist for the Associated Press, wrote an article accusing me of using "routinely sloppy"

research and "contrived" facts. Like you, the AP
fantasist treats Franken as the source of all wisdom,
citing one killer example from Franken:

"Here's one: On pages 265–266, Coulter blasts *New York Times* writer Thomas Friedman for opposing racial profiling in a December 2001 column. She quotes (and credits) several passages that seem to back up her complaint. But it turns out that Coulter misappropriated Friedman's words in a way that has nothing to do with racial profiling or anything else addressed in his column, as anyone who reads it will discover. His column actually drew the less-than-startling conclusion that a new age of terrorism threatens our personal safety and our free society."

This is what is known as "bicycle accident reporting." I defy anyone to explain what head-injury boy is trying to convey in his crucial, accusatory sentence: "Coulter misappropriated Friedman's words in a way that has nothing to do with racial profiling or anything else addressed in his column." Huh? The AP could throw a deck of cards out the window and wait to see who picks up the four of clubs to find someone who writes better than Frazier Moore.

But as long as I'm already breaking my rule about not responding to meritless, overwrought attacks, I'll go for broke and break my rule about not responding to gibberish. Apparently, head-injury boy here is very upset about how I characterize a Friedman column and it has something or other to do with racial profiling.

In the column at issue, titled "Fly Naked," Friedman spends six of ten paragraphs discussing airport security after 9/11 and concludes that flying naked is the only solution, because, inter alia, "It's much more civilized than racial profiling." I wrote, "*New York Times* columnist Thomas Friedman sniffed that racial profiling was not 'civilized.'" I'm really trying to grasp the lie in that statement, but I don't see it.

Incidentally, contrary to head-injury boy's characterization, only four paragraphs at the end of the Friedman column discuss "personal safety and our free society"—as anyone who reads it will discover. I salute the AP's unorthodox affirmative-action program, but they might want to assign reporters who are not developmentally disabled to write the articles accusing me of "sloppy" research and "contrived" facts.

I haven't heard much about this "lie" since the AP article came out and normal people took the trouble to look up Friedman's column and post it on the Internet.

Now you spring two all-new alleged "outright lies" on me. I shall respond to these two, and then I'm through. Henceforth, I shall rely on sensible people to see that I have answered the liberal hate groups' first seventeen rounds of indignant charges against me. If they had a better example out there, we would have heard it before the eighteenth round.

First, you say, "At one point [Franken] accuses you of having taken a quote from a book review quoting a book [page 14 of Franken's book] to argue your point. Do you feel this is an accurate representation of what you wrote? An accurate use of a quote? If not, then why? If yes, then who is ultimately responsible for the errors, you, the publisher, or both?"

I'm not sure I grasp the accusation here and I'm sure you do not. I wrote, "For decades, the *New York Times* had allowed loose associations between Nazis and Christians to be made in its pages." Among the quotes I cited, one came from a *New York Times* book review. The quote made a loose association between Nazis and Christians. *New York Times* book reviews are printed in the pages of the *New York Times*. The *Times* allowed that quote to run in its pages. How else, exactly, are you suggesting I should have phrased this, Ed?

Second, you say, "Likewise, [Franken] accuses you of sloppy research, in so far as you appear to have missed a number of *New York Times* articles citing such things as speeches by Jesse

Jackson. What gives—was this an honest mistake or malfeasance as he suggests?"

It was neither, but thanks for asking. I wrote, "In an upbeat message delivered on British TV on Christmas Day, 1994, Jesse Jackson compared conservatives in the U.S. and Great Britain to Nazis: 'In South Africa, the status quo was called racism. We rebelled against it. In Germany, it was called fascism. Now in Britain and the U.S. it is called conservatism.' The *New York Times* did not report the speech."

The *New York Times* did not, in fact, report the speech. Franken does not say otherwise. My guess is—and this is just a stab in the dark—Franken doesn't say otherwise because he can't say otherwise, inasmuch as . . . THE *NEW YORK TIMES* DID NOT REPORT THE SPEECH. What Franken says is that my search method was faulty—though, somehow, it still managed to produce the truth! (To wit: The *New York Times* did not report the speech.)

Among my searches, I searched the *New York Times* database for all of December 1994 and January 1995 for "Jesse Jackson and Germany and fascism and South Africa." (In my footnotes, I often give my readers clear descriptions of some of the LexisNexis searches I run—something, as far as I know, no other writer does.)

Franken does not mention the lines I had just quoted from Jackson's speech—you know, the one that was *not* reported in the *New York Times*—but refers to it only as a "controversial speech." He then acts incredulous that I would run a search for "Jesse Jackson and Germany and fascism and South Africa," as if I tossed in the terms "Germany" "fascism," and "South Africa" for no reason whatsoever. To my observation that this search turned up no documents, he says sarcastically, "Well, yeah."

To borrow a line from a trained journalist: What gives, Ed? Was this an honest mistake or malfeasance? ∎

10

Say, Does Anyone Know If Max Cleland Lost His Limbs in Combat?

———————■———————

☞ Cleland Drops a Political Grenade

FEBRUARY 11, 2004

Former Senator Max Cleland is the Democrats' designated hysteric about George Bush's National Guard service. A triple amputee and Vietnam veteran, Cleland is making the rounds on talk TV, basking in the affection of liberals who have suddenly become jock-sniffers for war veterans, and working himself into a lather about President Bush's military service. Citing such renowned military experts as Molly Ivins, Cleland indignantly demands further investigation into Bush's service with the Texas Air National Guard.

Bush's National Guard service is the most thoroughly investigated event since the Kennedy assassination. But the Democrats will accept only two possible conclusions to their baseless accusations: (1) Bush was "AWOL," or (2) the matter needs further investigation.

Thirty years ago, Bush was granted an honorable discharge from the National Guard—which would seem to put the matter to rest. But liberals want proof that Bush actually deserved his honorable discharge. (Since when did the party of Bill Clinton, Ted Kennedy, and Robert Byrd get so obsessed with honor?)

On *Hardball* Monday night, Cleland demanded to see Bush's pay stubs for the disputed period of time, May 1972 to May 1973. "If he was getting paid for his weekend warrior work," Cleland said, "he should have some pay stubs to show it."

The next day, the White House produced the pay stubs. This confirmed what has been confirmed a million times before: After taking the summer off, Bush reported for duty nine times between November 29, 1972, and May 24, 1973—more than enough times to fulfill his Guard duties. (And nine times more than Bill Clinton, Barney Frank, or Chuck Schumer did during the same period.)

All this has been reported—with documentation—many times by many news organizations. *George* magazine had Bush's National Guard records three and a half years ago. All available evidence keeps confirming Bush's honorable service with the Guard, which leads liberals to conclude . . . further investigation is needed! No evidence will ever be enough evidence. That Bush skipped out on his National Guard service is one of liberals' many nondisprovable beliefs, like global warming.

Cleland also expressed outrage that Bush left the National Guard nine months early in 1973 to go to Harvard Business School. On *Hardball,* Cleland testily remarked, "I just know a whole lot of veterans who would have loved to have worked things out with the military and adjusted their tour of duty." (Cleland already knows one who did—Al Gore!)

When Bush left the National Guard in 1973 to go to business school, the war was over. It might as well have been 1986. Presidents Kennedy and Johnson had already lost the war, and President Nixon had ended it with the Paris Peace Accords in January.

If Bush had demanded active combat, there would have been no war to send him to.

To put this in perspective, by 1973 John Kerry had already accused American soldiers of committing war crimes in Vietnam, thrown someone else's medals to the ground in an antiwar demonstration, and married his first heiress. Bill Clinton had just finished three years of law school and was about to embark upon a political career—which would include campaign events with Max Cleland.

Moreover, if we're going to start delving into exactly who did what back then, maybe Max Cleland should stop allowing Democrats to portray him as a war hero who lost his limbs taking enemy fire on the battlefields of Vietnam.

Cleland lost three limbs in an accident during a routine noncombat mission where he was about to drink beer with friends. He saw a grenade on the ground and picked it up. He could have done that at Fort Dix. In fact, Cleland could have dropped a grenade on his foot as a National Guardsman—as one of what Cleland sneeringly calls "weekend warriors." Luckily for Cleland's political career and current pomposity about Bush, he happened to do it while in Vietnam.

There is more than a whiff of dishonesty in how Cleland is presented to the American people. Terry McAuliffe goes around saying, "Max Cleland, a triple amputee who left three limbs on the battlefield of Vietnam," was thrown out of office because Republicans "had the audacity to call Max Cleland unpatriotic." Mr. Cleland, a word of advice: When a slimy weasel like Terry McAuliffe is vouching for your combat record, it's time to sound "retreat" on that subject.

Needless to say, no one ever challenged Cleland's "patriotism." His performance in the Senate was the issue, which should not have come as a bolt out of the blue, inasmuch as he was running for reelection . . . to the Senate! Senator Cleland had refused to vote for the Homeland Security Bill unless it was chock-full of pro-union perks that would have jeopardized national security. ("OH MY GOD! A HIJACKED PLANE IS HEADED FOR THE WHITE HOUSE!" "Sorry, I'm on my break. Please call back in two hours.")

The good people of Georgia—who do not need lectures on admiring military service—gave Cleland one pass for being a Vietnam veteran. He didn't get a lifetime pass.

Indeed, if Cleland had dropped a grenade on himself at Fort Dix rather than in Vietnam, he would never have been a U.S. senator in the first place. Maybe he'd be the best pharmacist in Atlanta, but not a U.S. senator. He got into office on the basis of serving in Vietnam and was thrown out for his performance as a senator.

Cleland wore the uniform, he was in Vietnam, and he has shown courage by going on to lead a productive life. But he didn't "give his limbs for his country" or leave them "on the battlefield." There was no bravery involved in dropping a grenade on himself with no enemy troops in sight. That could have happened in the Texas National Guard—which Cleland denigrates while demanding his own sanctification. ∎

☞ My Readers Respond!

Dear Ms. Coulter:
I referenced your comment about Max Cleland losing his limbs in a noncombat accident to a local talk-show host. He told me I was wrong. I told him he was wrong because you said it in your column. He said you distort the truth regularly. Would you please tell me where to find your source for how Max lost his limbs?

Dan, Kansas City

A right-wing hit lady named Ann Coulter charged that Max Cleland, who won a Silver Star in Vietnam and is a prominent Kerry supporter, lost his three limbs while getting ready to drink beer with pals. She said it just as easily could have occurred in the Texas Air National Guard. That's irrelevant, that's vicious, and that's a lie. Captain Cleland lost his legs and an arm on a reconnaissance mission in Vietnam. They don't usually carry live grenades and M-16s in the Texas Air National Guard. This despicable venom was carried on the Heritage Foundation website.

Al Hunt, CNN's The Capital Gang, *February 14, 2004*

The reason why Democrats are doing this [being hysterical about Bush's National Guard service]—let me give you an example. Today in her column, Ann Coulter attacked Max Cleland, the Vietnam war hero. She said Cleland lost three limbs "in an accident during a routine noncombat mission, where he was about to drink beer with friends. He saw a grenade on the ground and picked it up. He could have done that at Fort Dix as a National Guardsman." Now, that's the sort of thing—I also have here—I also have here Cleland's citation for his Silver Star that he received four days before that at Khe Sanh in Vietnam in 1968.

Joe Klein, CNN's Paula Zahn Now, *February 12, 2004*

It doesn't take much imagination to guess how far into the gutter the presidential race will dip before it's all over [such as] the continuing, shameful treatment of former Georgia Senator Max Cleland by the likes of Ann Coulter, who in a recent Townhall.com column derided his loss of three limbs in Vietnam. . . .

Joy-Ann Reid, Miami Herald, *February 16, 2004*

Friday, it was the Democrats' turn for outrage. . . . The villain in this case is conservative pundit Ann Coulter, whose column on the Heritage Foundation website said that Cleland, who lost three limbs in a grenade accident in Vietnam during the war, "didn't 'give his limbs for his country.'"

Dana Milbank, Washington Post, *February 15, 2004*

But for sheer, vicious nastiness, no one can compete with Ann Coulter, whose latest error-riddled effusion is an attack on former

Georgia Senator Max Cleland, who has been critical of the Bush administration. Apparently in an effort to make George W.'s incomplete in the National Guard look better, Coulter wrote a column distributed by the Heritage Foundation saying Cleland, a triple amputee, had showed "no bravery" in Vietnam, "didn't give his limbs for his country," is not a war hero. My favorite sentence is, "Luckily for Cleland . . . he happened [to lose his limbs] while in Vietnam," her point being that if he had been injured at Fort Dix, he wouldn't be a hero.

Molly Ivins, February 17, 2004 ∎

☞ File Under: "Omission Accomplished"

FEBRUARY 19, 2004

Liberals are hopping mad about last week's column. Amid angry insinuations that I "lied" about Senator Max Cleland, I was attacked on the Senate floor by Senator Jack Reed, Molly Ivins called my column "error-ridden," and Al Hunt called it a "lie." Joe Klein said I was the reason liberals were being hysterical about George Bush's National Guard service. (No wonder liberals can't win politically if little scrawny me gets them so upset.)

I would have left it at one column, but apparently Democrats want to go another round. With their Clintonesque formulations, my detractors make it a little difficult to know what "lie" I'm supposed to be contesting, but they are clearly implying—without stating—that Cleland lost his limbs in combat.

It is simply a fact that Max Cleland was not injured by enemy fire in Vietnam. He was not in combat, he was not—as Al Hunt claimed—on a reconnaissance mission, and he was not in the battle of Khe Sanh, as many others have implied. He picked up an American grenade on a routine noncombat mission and the grenade exploded. In Cleland's own words: "I didn't see any heroism in all that. It wasn't an act of heroism. I didn't know the grenade was live. It was an act of fate." That is why Cleland didn't win a Purple Heart, which is given to those wounded in combat. Liberals aren't angry because I "lied"; they're angry because I told the truth.

I wouldn't press the point except that Democrats have deliberately "sexed up" the circumstances of Cleland's accident in the service of slandering the people of Georgia, the National Guard, and George Bush. Cleland has questioned Bush's fitness for office because he served in the National Guard and was not sent to Vietnam. And yet the poignant truth of Cleland's own accident demonstrates the commitment and bravery of all members of the military who come into contact with ordnance. Cleland's injury was of the routine variety that occurs whenever young men and weapons are put in close proximity—including in the National Guard.

But it is a vastly more glorious story to claim that Cleland was injured by enemy fire rather than in a freak accident. So after Saxby Chambliss beat Cleland in the 2002 Georgia Senate race, liberals set to work developing a carefully crafted myth about Cleland's accident. Among many other examples, last November, Eric Boehlert wrote in *Salon:* "During the siege of Khe Sanh, Cleland lost both his legs and his right hand to a Viet Cong grenade."

Sadly for them, dozens and dozens of newspapers had already printed the truth. Liberals simply can't grasp the problem Lexis-Nexis poses to their incessant lying. They ought to stick to their specialty—hysterical overreaction. The truth is not their forte.

One of the most detailed accounts of Cleland's life was written by Jill Zuckman in a long piece for the *Boston Globe Magazine* on August 3, 1997:

"Finally, the battle at Khe Sanh was over. Cleland, 25 years old, and two members of his team were now ordered to set up a radio relay station at the division assembly area, 15 miles away. The three gathered antennas, radios and a generator and made the 15-minute helicopter trip east. After unloading the equipment, Cleland climbed back into the helicopter for the ride back. But at the last minute, he decided to stay and have a beer with some friends. As the helicopter was lifting off, he shouted to the pilot that he was staying behind and jumped several feet to the ground.

"Cleland hunched over to avoid the whirring blades and ran. Turning to face the helicopter, he caught sight of a grenade on the ground where the chopper had perched. It must be mine, he thought, moving toward it. He reached for it with his right arm just as it exploded, slamming him back and irreparably altering his plans for a bright, shining future."

Interestingly, all news accounts told the exact same story for thirty years—including that Cleland had stopped to have beer with friends when the accident occurred (a fact that particularly irked Al Hunt).

"He told the pilot he was going to stay awhile. Maybe have a few beers with friends. . . . Then Cleland looked down and saw a grenade. Where'd that come from? He walked toward it, bent down, and crossed the line between before and after" (*Milwaukee Journal Sentinel,* December 5, 1999).

"[Cleland] didn't step on a land mine. He wasn't wounded in a firefight. He couldn't blame the Viet Cong or friendly fire. The Silver Star and Bronze Star medals he received only embarrassed him. He was no hero. He blew himself up" (*Baltimore Sun,* October 24, 1999).

"Cleland was no war hero, but his sacrifice was great. . . . Democratic Senate candidate Max Cleland is a victim of war, not a casualty of combat. He lost three limbs on a long-forgotten hill near Khe Sanh because of some American's mistake" (*Atlanta Journal-Constitution,* September 29, 1996).

The story started to change only last year when the Democrats began citing Cleland's lost Senate seat as proof that Republicans hate war heroes. Indeed, until the myth of Republicans attacking Cleland for his lack of "patriotism" became central to the Democrats' narrative against George Bush, Cleland spoke only honorably and humbly about his accident. "How did I become a war hero?" he said to the *Boston Globe* reporter in 1997. "Simple. The grenade went off."

Cleland even admitted that but for his accident, he would have "probably been some frustrated history teacher, teaching American government at some junior college." (Okay, I got that wrong: in my column I said he'd probably be a pharmacist.)

Cleland's true heroism came after the war, when he went on to build a productive life for himself. That is a story of inspiration and courage. He shouldn't let the Democrats tarnish an admirable life by "sexing up" his record in order to better attack George Bush. ∎

☞ My Readers Respond! (Part II)

E-MAIL EXCHANGE WITH *TIME* MAGAZINE

Friday, February 20, 2004
Ann:
I'm a correspondent in *Time*'s Washington bureau.
I'm interested in the back-and-forth over the military service of President Bush and former Sen.
Max Cleland.
—Eric Roston, *Time* magazine

QUESTION: *1. Why write a second column about Cleland?*
ANSWER: Liberals were lying—which isn't new—but the facts were indisputable, and it's always fun pointing out when liberals are lying.

QUESTION: *2. What role could the veteran vote play in November?*
ANSWER: I am sublimely confident that most military types will vote for Bush.

QUESTION: *3. Traditionally, the Republicans have been popularly thought to be the party for veterans, not Democrats. If Sen. Kerry becomes the Democratic nominee, could that confuse these traditional categories?*

ANSWER: No.

QUESTION: *4. What is a good definition of "combat mission" and "battlefield"? Is it useful to draw a distinction between "combat" and "combat zone"? Four days before then–Capt. Cleland's accident, four soldiers were killed near that spot by enemy mortar. Would you characterize it then as occurring in a "combat zone"?*

ANSWER: The Purple Heart committee seems to have figured it out, you may take up your quarrel with them.

QUESTION: *5. The validity of your arguments appear to hinge on how you define these words. How do you explain the discrepancy of what appears to be very technical usages of "combat" and "battlefield" and what appear to be nontechnical uses of words such as "treason" and "slander"?*

ANSWER: a) Again, you may pursue your argument with the people who award Purple Hearts, but whatever else it means, I believe the technical definition of "combat" would include: "a time and place when you are not about to have beer with your friends."

b) I do use treason and slander "technically," I simply apply the terms to liberals as a group, not a single individual.

QUESTION: *6. You write: "Cleland could have dropped a grenade on his foot as a National Guardsman." The grenade was said to be dropped by the soldier behind Cleland. The problem, according to people on the scene, was that this soldier had been straightening the pins in his grenades, for easier access during enemy fire. Since that would not likely have been the case at Ft. Dix, do you still stand by that notion?*

ANSWER: Look up the meaning of "ordnance." As I said in my column, whenever young men and ordnance are put together, there are a staggering number of casualties, which is why military training and discipline are so important. I would hazard a guess that more pilots are killed in National Guard flight training than servicemen are killed by negligently picking up grenades. Perhaps you could put one of your crack investigators on this.

QUESTION: *7. People familiar with Cleland's experience say that he requested to be moved from a desk job in Saigon, to a place closer to the action. Then from there, he requested to become active in Khe Sanh. Do you believe this to be accurate? If so, does it affect your argument?*

ANSWER: It has absolutely nothing to do with my argument. I hear he's also nice to his mother. If I ever write about how Cleland treats his mother or write a review of his entire military career I'll be sure to mention both. I simply accused snivelers like you, who in the blink of an eye have gone from being Army-haters to jock-sniffers for war veterans, of sexing up Cleland's accident.

QUESTION: *8. Approximately one-third of US casualties in Vietnam were caused by some sort of "friendly fire" or accident. Following your logic, does that mean that none of these soldiers died or were wounded for their country?*

ANSWER: No, to the contrary, they all died for their country, but they did not die in combat. Dishonest reporters like you apparently think that's not good enough and have insisted on suggesting that Cleland lost his limbs in combat.

QUESTION: *9. You appear to belittle then-Capt. Cleland for being willing to drink a beer under noncombat conditions. Given an opportunity to drink a beer over a hill from the battle of Khe Sanh, would you do so?*

ANSWER: a) I'm not belittling it at all—but I'm glad you're finally willing to concede it was "noncombat."

b) It is so breathtakingly stupid to claim I was "belittling" Cleland for "being willing to drink a beer under noncombat conditions" that I question your ability to comprehend
anything you read.

c) Yes, I might, but if I then stepped on a grenade, I
would not accept canonization from the likes of you or believe that it entitled me to a job for life in the US Senate.

Tuesday, February 24, 2004
Ann:
Thanks for your help last week. The story was
held for space. Will advise. ER
—Eric Roston, *Time* magazine ■

NEW YORK TIMES

THE 2004 CAMPAIGN: THE FORMER SENATOR:
For Ex-Senator, Kerry Race Is Chance
to Rejoin the Battle
February 26, 2004
BY SHERYL GAY STOLBERG
[Last big scoop: "Many Americans believe marriage
is between a man and a woman."—Reporter Sheryl
Gay Stolberg in her July 2, 2003, article, "White
House Avoids Stands on Gay Marriage Measure,"
www.timeswatch.org]

Excerpt:

One exception is Ann Coulter, the conservative columnist,
who has recently taken Mr. Cleland to task for "allowing
Democrats to portray him as a war hero" when his injuries
were the result of an accident, rather than enemy fire.

The accident occurred on April 8, 1968. Mr. Cleland, then

a twenty-five-year-old army captain and communications officer, had taken a helicopter to a hill near Khe Sanh, to set up a
radio relay site for battle. He unloaded his equipment and
boarded the copter for the return trip, only to change his mind
at the last minute, deciding to stay on the hill to finish the job
and drink a beer with friends.

As he ducked under the helicopter blades, he spotted a
grenade on the ground. Thinking it was his own—and that the
pin was intact—he picked it up, and it exploded. "He could
have done that at Fort Dix," Ms. Coulter wrote.

————

E-mail to *New York Times* ombudsman and letter to the editor, which the *Times* did not print:

> *Friday, February 27, 2004*
> To the editor:
> Sheryl Gay Stolberg lied about what I wrote. ("For
> Ex-Senator, Kerry Race Is Chance to Rejoin the
> Battle," February 26, 2004).
>
> I simply pointed out that the same people who
> are demanding George Bush's dental records from
> his Alabama National Guard service are routinely
> "sexing up" Max Cleland's record in order to smear
> Bush's service and the National Guard. Liberals
> falsely claim Cleland lost his limbs in combat
> rather than in an accident. Fantastically enough,
> Stolberg actually quotes an academic in her ar-
> ticle—Merle Black of Emory—who repeats the
> standard lie, claiming Cleland lost his limbs in
> "battle." My point was that the truth of Cleland's
> own accident demonstrates the bravery of all
> members of the military who routinely come into
> contact with ordnance.
> —Ann Coulter

Friday, February 27, 2004
Dear Ms. Coulter,
Bill Borders, the senior editor in charge of following up on corrections, has asked me to have you clarify your complaint.

Where did Sheryl Stolberg lie about what you wrote in her article?

Ann Coulter's reply:

Friday, February 27, 2004
"One exception is Ann Coulter, the conservative columnist, who has recently taken Mr. Cleland to task for 'allowing Democrats to portray him as a war hero' when his injuries were the result of an accident, rather than enemy fire."

It is a lie to say I complained that Cleland was being portrayed as a "war hero." My complaint was that liberals were portraying Cleland as having LOST HIS LIMBS IN COMBAT. Stolberg intentionally edited out the rest of that sentence in order to give a completely different meaning to what I said. I wrote: "Cleland should stop allowing Democrats to portray him as a war hero WHO LOST HIS LIMBS TAKING ENEMY FIRE ON THE BATTLEFIELDS OF VIETNAM." The point was how Cleland lost his limbs—on the battlefield or in an accident—NOT whether he was a "war hero."

"As he ducked under the helicopter blades, he spotted a grenade on the ground. Thinking it was his own—and that the pin was intact—he picked it up, and it exploded. 'He could have done that at Fort Dix,' Ms. Coulter wrote."

I did not lightly dismiss Cleland's injuries, which is precisely what this sentence suggests. The point of my saying Cleland could have had an accident with ordnance at Fort Dix was to defend the National Guard by pointing out that all military training is dangerous, even far away from enemy fire. By quoting nothing but my saying "that could have happened at Fort Dix," Stolberg falsely suggests I was dismissing Cleland's accident as not such a big deal. You may read both columns at www.anncoulter.com.

Monday, March 1, 2004
Dear Ms. Coulter,
Thank you for your message.

I include below a response from Bill Borders, senior editor in charge of following up on corrections.

I have studied Ann Coulter's letter about Stolberg, and so have responsible editors in the Washington bureau and on the national desk. We all agree that no correction is needed. Here are Ms. Coulter's two points:

On the "war hero" quote: Stolberg did indeed quote only part of what Coulter wrote. But the rest of Stolberg's sentence renders the rest of Coulter's thought accurately. Stolberg's paraphrase following the words "war hero" precisely defines the "war hero" concept in exactly the way Coulter did, making the point that there was nothing heroic about the way Cleland was wounded. Neither of them is addressing whether he might have been a "war hero" in some other way at some other time. In other words, Stolberg represents what Coulter said exactly right.

On the Fort Dix quote: Coulter says that the Stolberg quote "suggests" that Coulter made light of Cleland's injuries with the Fort Dix quote. But there is really no way that such an interpretation can be read into the Stolberg sentence. Stolberg's use of the Fort Dix quote precisely reflects Coulter's point—that it was in no way a battlefield injury. But nothing in the Stolberg piece says that Coulter or anyone else thinks that Cleland's injuries were not extremely serious. (I mean, how could they? That would be ridiculous.) There is simply no way that Stolberg's representation of what Coulter wrote could be interpreted as meaning that Coulter thinks his accident was "not such a big deal."

Sincerely,

Arthur Bovino

Office of the Public Editor

The *New York Times*

———

POSTSCRIPT: My column: Cleland didn't lose his limbs in combat.

New York Times version: Cleland isn't a war hero.

New York Times ombudsman: those are the same thing.

Once known as "the newspaper of record," the *Times* is now referred to as "one way of looking at things." ∎

11

The Only Cop the *New York Times* Likes Is the One in the Village People

———■———

🖙 They Weren't Overzealous This Time

JUNE 19, 2000

Topping off the National Puerto Rican Day Parade in New York City last Sunday—making their strongest case yet for statehood—hordes of marauding Puerto Rican men entered Central Park and began stripping women and groping their breasts and buttocks. Some women were stripped naked. The attacks occurred in broad daylight in a well-traveled area near Central Park South.

Chanting, "Soak her! Soak her!," the mob sprayed water on a honeymooning French tourist, pulled off her skirt and underpants, and yanked two gold chains from her neck. The woman's husband clawed his way through the crowd and threw himself on top of her until the men moved to their next target. The couple ran from the park and reported the attack to law-enforcement officers, who called for reinforcements.

In another attack, the men besieged a kickboxing instructor on in-line skates, knocking her to the ground and trying to rip off her shorts. The kickboxing instructor later said, "I never felt in my entire life that I couldn't protect myself until then." At last count, there were thirty-seven victims of the sexual assaults. Police have arrested eight men in the attacks.

Naturally, the victims are suing the city for failing to protect them, and the *New York Times* is raising dark accusations that the police were negligent. Yes, you heard me right: The *New York Times* thinks the police weren't aggressive enough. And that's not just the malt liquor talking. Since reading that, I've been lost in a reverie imagining what the *Times*'s news story would be if the police had reacted with somewhat greater vigor.

I think it would go like this:

HEADLINE:
Police Shoot Unarmed Man in Central Park Melee

BODY: An unarmed Bronx man with no criminal record was killed late yesterday by a New York City police officer who fired four shots at him at close range in Central Park, the police said.

It was unclear yesterday why the police officer had opened fire on the man at 6:35 p.m. in the southeast section of the park near Central Park South and the Avenue of the Americas. The man, Jose Rivera, 23, of the Bronx, who had attended the Puerto Rican Day parade earlier in the day, died at the scene, the police said. Relatives and friends described Mr. Rivera as a hardworking entrepreneur with a ready smile.

In another public relations disaster for the crisis-wracked Giuliani administration, the shooting grew out of a violent confrontation between police officers and members of New York's Hispanic community. The melee began when five baton-wielding police officers entered the park and set upon a group of parade revelers.

Police officials said officers patrolling the area near Central Park South were approached at 6:15 p.m. by a French couple on their honeymoon. The 28-year-old woman told the officers—Continued on Page B14—she had been accosted moments earlier by a group of men in the park.

Mayor Rudolph W. Giuliani urged people to withhold judgment on the case and defended the police. "These courageous police officers were attempting to subdue a mob of hoodlums who had attacked a woman in Central Park," he said.

But it was not clear yesterday whether the French couple had been attacked by the men or had merely misunderstood the revelers' intentions. Some witnesses to the incident suggested that the woman's husband attacked her, and blamed the fracas on the police. "This was another overreaction by Giuliani's racist Gestapo," one woman said.

Jane Doe, a kickboxing instructor, who had been skating in the park at the time of the fray, said the police acted without provocation. "It was broad daylight in Central Park. I felt perfectly safe," Doe said. "To be a Hispanic man and go into Manhattan, you're walking around with a target on your back."

Ms. Doe said she planned to attend a rally organized by Rev. Jesse Jackson outside police headquarters at 1 p.m. on Tuesday.

In unusually harsh language, Hillary Rodham Clinton, who is running for the U.S. Senate, accused Mayor Giuliani last night of intentionally polarizing New York City by leading "a rush to judgment" over the disputed circumstances of Sunday's fatal police shooting of an unarmed Hispanic man. "Unfortunately," she said, "the mayor is willing to try, convict and execute a man simply for enjoying our great park after a parade."

The U.S. Attorney in Manhattan, Mary Jo White, said her office would open an inquiry into the shooting. The Rev. Al Sharpton, lawyers for Mr. Rivera's family, and Bruce Springsteen have requested a meeting with Deputy Attorney General Eric Holder, the Justice Department's second-ranking official. The officer involved in the shooting has been put on administrative leave.

All eight revelers attending the Puerto Rican Day Parade appear to have been Hispanic. An investigation into racial profiling charges is pending. The French couple avoided being charged with inciting a riot by agreeing to attend racial sensitivity training classes. ■

☞ Murdering the Bell Curve

JUNE 27, 2002

Despite their hysteria a few years ago over Charles Murray and Richard Hernstein's book, *The Bell Curve*, liberals have finally embraced the concept of IQ—provided it is used only to spring vicious killers from death row. In 1996, Eric Nesbitt, a U.S. airman at Langley Air Force Base, was brutally murdered by Daryl Renard Atkins, a repeat violent criminal. It was a heinous and pointless murder: Atkins already had Nesbitt's money and car when he unloaded his gun into the defenseless airman. According to a cellmate, Atkins later laughed about the murder. After hearing the overwhelming evidence against him, a jury sentenced Atkins to death.

Last week, the Supreme Court overturned Atkins's death sentence. The Court ruled that Atkins cannot be executed if he can prove he is "retarded." In other words, Atkins avoids his capital sentence if he is at least smart enough to know how to fail an IQ test. The only silver lining is, at least we can start using the word "retarded" again.

Consider what "retarded" means in this context. It does not mean that Atkins could not understand the difference between right and wrong. The law already accounts for that possibility with the concept of legal insanity. It does not mean he could not assist in his own defense. The law already accounts for that possibility with the concept of legal incompetence. Nor, incidentally, does it mean that Atkins was so retarded that he could not plan a crime, murder a man, and then hide the gun. (The police never retrieved the murder weapon.) This may be why the jury heard the evidence that Atkins was retarded but still decided to impose the death penalty.

Atkins is just dumb—not an uncommon trait among violent criminals. As far back as 1914, criminologist H. H. Goddard concluded that "25 percent to 50 percent of the people in our prisons are mentally defective and incapable of managing their affairs with ordinary prudence." Crimes of violence in particular—murder, rape, and assault—are all correlated with low IQs. Thus, the Supreme Court has now prohibited the death penalty for precisely those people who are most likely to commit death-penalty-level crimes, which is a bit like excluding women from a program of maternity benefits.

As noted in the excellent new book *Slander: Liberal Lies About the American Right,* liberals acknowledge the concept of IQ only when attacking Republican presidents or trying to spring a criminal from death row. According to the Supreme Court, using an IQ test to hire employees is a civil-rights violation (*Griggs v. Duke Power Co.*), but now we have to give IQ tests before executing killers.

Back when *The Bell Curve* was released, liberals denounced the idea of intelligence as a sadistic, racist ploy. Yale University psychologist Robert Sternberg was widely quoted as saying that IQ accounts for less than 10 percent of the variation in human behavior—including the tendency to commit crimes. "Would you want to make your entire national policy around something that has less than a 10 percent effect?" No, it turns out—not unless we are talking about a national policy banning the death penalty.

The publication of *The Bell Curve* unleashed a frenzied campaign to discredit the idea of a standardized measure of intelligence, including the infamous "emotional intelligence" movement, which holds that intellectual capacity is really a measure of one's emotional well-being. Yes, being emotionally "centered" really comes in handy when solving quadratic equations.

The *New York Times* made the sophisticated argument that one of the authors of *The Bell Curve*—Murray—was "a political ideologue." (Is it ironic that the notion of measurable intelligence is attacked with such a stupid argument—or is that just funny?) While admitting that *The Bell Curve* had created "an aura of scientific certitude," the *Times* warned that other scholars would soon "subject its findings to withering criticism." Not yet—but soon! The *Times* was especially irritated that the book had "ignored the huge gaps in understanding the precise nature of intelligence" and implied that low test scores proved only "biased testing." (Those must have been some low SAT scores publisher Pinch Sulzberger had. I say Dan Quayle outscored Pinch on the SATs and I'll contribute to Emily's List if I'm wrong.)

But now liberals are overjoyed that such a biased test—of a human trait that we don't even vaguely understand—is going to be used to empty the nation's death rows. In an editorial titled "The Court Gets It Right," the *Times* gushed that "there are scores, perhaps even hundreds, of inmates whose low IQs will now qualify them for a sentence reduction to life in prison." Great, now we're even dumbing down murder and rape.

Now that the topic of *The Bell Curve* is a matter of constitutional law, rather than "pseudo-scientific racism," "indecent, philosophically shabby and politically ugly," "disingenuous," and "creepy"—all quotes from the liberal *New Republic* describing *The Bell Curve*—let's turn to the guys who were experts in the field before liberals admitted it was a field. According to *The Bell Curve*, the truly retarded are far underrepresented in the criminal population because those with very low IQs "have trouble mustering the competence to commit most crimes." As Justice Scalia put it in his dissent, the Court's portrayal of the retarded as "willfully cruel" does not comport with experience. To the contrary, he said, "being childlike generally suggests innocence rather than brutality."

But we've got liberals on the record: The *New York Times* claims that people with low IQs have "little understanding of their moral culpability"—a notion that would also account for much of the content of the *Times*'s editorial page. If IQ is such a precise gauge of self-awareness, will liberals finally agree to consider it as a basis for admission to University of Michigan Law School? ∎

☞ The *New York Times* Goes Wilding on the Central Park Jogger

OCTOBER 16, 2002

Probably feeling "humiliated," in 1989, a mob of feral beasts descended on Central Park to attack joggers and bicyclists. They brutalized a female jogger while incomprehensibly chanting "Wild Thing" in their ghetto patois. The jogger, a 110-pound, white female investment banker, was beaten so badly she was declared "dead on arrival" at the hospital. Her skull was crushed and she had lost two-thirds of her blood. Her attackers spent the night in jail joking about the attack, singing a rap song, and whistling at policewomen. In his written confession, Yusef Salaam said, "It was fun."

At the onset of the first Central Park rape trial, the *New American*, a black newspaper in New York City, ran a front-page headline about the jogger titled "The Truth About the Whore." (Or as the *New York Times* described the headline, it employed "a sexual epithet.") The article spun out the "theory" that her boyfriend had attacked her. The editor "acknowledged that the article was not based on any specific evidence. 'That's why it was called a theory,' he said. 'A theory means no evidence.'" Recently the media have been spinning out their own theories about the attack, using the precise same definition of "theory."

The newsflash being billboarded across every New York news outlet right now is that prison inmate Matias Reyes has confessed to being the jogger's sole attacker. Breathless news accounts claim that the police were shocked to discover that new DNA testing has now proved Reyes alone attacked the jogger and that the others did not.

This is a lie. Liberals so long to claim that every criminal is innocent, they forget that the Central Park rape case received a lot of media attention when it happened, so they can't lie and scream about another phony DNA "exoneration" this time. The facts are easily accessible on LexisNexis. In fact, it was undisputed that the semen found on the jogger did not match any of the defendants. Headlines at the time proclaimed, "Semen Tested in Jogger Case Was Not That of Defendants" (*New York Times*); "Semen, Suspects No Match, Says DNA Expert in Jog Case" (*Newsday*); "DNA Expert: No Semen Links to Defendants" (Associated Press); and "Expert Says Semen on Jogger Is Not Teens'" (*The Record*). Whatever evidence convinced two juries to convict the five animals, it was not DNA evidence. As usual, the media simply waited a decade, and then rushed to print with the same arguments used by the defense at the time claiming it was "new evidence." This is standard operating procedure in "exonerating" convicted criminals.

In a stunningly dishonest article, the *New York Times* states that "results from a battery of new DNA tests, which show that Mr. Reyes raped the jogger, have all been consistent with his version of events." The new DNA tests are consistent with precisely one part of Reyes's story: Matias Reyes raped the Central Park jogger. This is not new information. It was always known that a sixth rapist was out there; the police just didn't know who he was. In her summation to the jury, prosecutor Elizabeth Lederer told the jurors, "Others who were not caught raped her and got away."

Consequently, the new DNA tests are also consistent with the version of events presented in court, subjected to attack by defense counsel, and believed unanimously by two multiracial juries. The five primitives on trial were described as among those who attacked the jogger. No new evidence contradicts those five guilty verdicts. Knowing that a sixth rapist had gotten away, the jury still convicted the five who were caught.

The evidence that convinced two juries to convict the savages was primarily their videotaped confessions. There was other evidence—such as one defendant's undershorts full of semen, dirt, grass, and other debris. (According to accounts of their deliberations, one juror held up the undershorts and said, "How do you think they got this way?" What was the kid doing, fertilizing the lawn?) The ten videotaped statements were made in the presence of the suspects' parents, provided graphic details about the attack, were tested in court, and were believed by unanimous juries. Antron McCray's videotaped confession included this: "We charged her. We got her on the ground. Everybody started hitting her and stuff. She was on the ground, everybody stomping and everything. . . . I grabbed one arm, some other kid grabbed one arm and we grabbed her legs and stuff. Then we all took turns getting on top of her." Now these confessions are supposed to be trumped by the untested, unchallenged jailhouse confession of a murderer and serial rapist who claims he acted alone.

At trial, the defense was that the boys had lied in their confessions. The defendants' lawyers vigorously attacked the confessions, leaping in to highlight any inconsistencies or exculpatory facts now being treated as "new evidence" by the *New York Times*. Antron's father told the jury that he had instructed his son to lie to the police and tell them he raped the girl, so the police would let him go. This is often what happens when you tell the police in graphic and gruesome detail how you gang-raped a woman: The police let you go. With arguments like that, Antron's father could soon be giving legal commentary on *On the Record with Greta Van Susteren*.

The jurors evaluated the credibility of the stories and the witnesses. They observed the demeanor of the defendants, the police, and other witnesses. After carefully weighing all the evidence, the jurors decided the defendants were guilty. The public got a glimpse of what the jurors saw when Yusef Salaam was interviewed by Mike Wallace on *60 Minutes* in 1992. Salaam said he suspected the jogger—the one declared DOA at the hospital—was "faking." He also said that even though he lied in his confession, people should believe he was telling the truth about the confession being a lie because he was a Muslim. "That's all a Muslim has," he said—explaining why he lied—"his word." That may be good enough for the *New York Times*, but apparently it wasn't good enough for the jury.

Providentially, our criminal justice system presupposes that juries are better positioned to evaluate the truth than *New York Times* reporters looking for the next Scottsboro Boys case. Two juries already heard all the arguments now being reported as shocking "new evidence"—and unanimously disbelieved the defendants. This isn't the latest Scottsboro Boys case. It's the latest Tawana Brawley case. ∎

☞ DNA Evidence Exonerates Hitler!

OCTOBER 23, 2002

The anti–death penalty lobby never sleeps. Unable to convince the public that savage murderers should be given radio shows rather than lethal injections, anti–death penalty zealots lie about murderers being "exonerated." None of their rabid emotionalism on behalf of rapists and murderers ever had the slightest effect on public opinion. Support for the death penalty only started to decline when people were told that convicted felons were constantly being "proved innocent." The phony DNA "exoneration" project was the first attack on the death penalty that ever worked.

What the public doesn't realize is that years after juries have rendered their guilty verdicts and the police, prosecutors, and victims have all died, moved on, gotten new jobs, left the state—criminal defense lawyers are still hard at work. With no one to argue back, procriminal zealots are free to hatch new theories of innocence and dredge up synthetic "new" evidence. The defense bar can spin its lies to gullible reporters without contradiction. Evidently, it has never occurred to any journalist that criminal defense lawyers might be giving them only one side of the story. Sensational cases in which the defendants were manifestly guilty are particularly vulnerable to these one-sided attacks. Nothing undermines the public's faith in the criminal justice system so completely.

The current baby seals of the "exoneration" racket are the feral beasts who raped, brutalized, and nearly murdered a female jogger in Central Park. It was only a matter of time before the criminal defense lobby would turn to the widely publicized 1989 wilding attack. Strictly adhering to formula, the defense bar has produced a shocking confession from a criminal who—coincidentally—can no longer be prosecuted for the attack. Matias Reyes now claims he alone raped the jogger.

This barbaric crime is a good target for the phony "exoneration" project. The savages have served their time, the victim remembers nothing, and no one cares as much as the anti–death penalty fanatics. In fact, the Manhattan district attorney himself adamantly opposes the death penalty. With zero political cost, he can guarantee himself a favorable obituary in the *New York Times* by overturning the jury verdicts.

In addition to the media's lies about the DNA evidence covered in last week's column, credulous reporters are also retailing these lies about Reyes:

—Reyes's claim to have acted alone is supported by the fact that he does not know the five males already convicted of the crime.

This is preposterous. It is undisputed that about thirty savages were rampaging through Central Park the night of April 19, 1989, engaging in wolfpack attacks on joggers and bicyclists. The thirty savages didn't know one another any more than the mob of hoodlums molesting women after the 2000 Puerto Rican Day Parade knew one another. Two defendants, Antron McCray and Raymond Santana, had never met their codefendant, Yusef Salaam, until the night of the attack and did not know his name. This did not cause the jury any consternation before voting to convict all three.

—Reyes is thirty-one, much older than the defendants, "all of whom were sixteen or younger at the time," as the Associated Press reported.

This is the sort of fallacy of construction that makes you wonder if reporters are as dumb as you suspect or if they just think their readers are that dumb. Reyes is thirty-one *now*. Thirteen years ago—when the gang-rape occurred—he was a teenager, too.

—In the words of the criminal defense bar's sock puppets at the *New York Times* (reporters Jim Dwyer and William K. Rashbaum), Reyes had committed a "nearly identical crime" nearby days earlier.

"Nearly identical" evidently refers to the fact that both crimes were: (1) rapes, (2) in Central Park. That's where the similarity ends. In the first rape, Reyes casually approached a woman doing tai chi in Central Park in broad daylight and began chatting her up. When she moved away from him, he pounced, beating her about the head and raping her. Her screams attracted a man, who broke off the attack.

The gang rape of the jogger two days later was an ambush in the dark of night. The victim was dragged 200 yards, rendered unconscious, and left in a coma. The crimes are so dissimilar that, under the rules of evidence, one rape could not have been admitted into evidence in a trial on the other rape—but the *New York Times* deems it sufficient to overturn two jury verdicts.

—Reyes's claim to have committed the rape by himself is supported by the fact that acting alone "was typical of [Reyes's] other crimes"—as the *New York Times* put it.

In addition to convictions for robbery and burglary, Reyes's "other crimes" include:

- raping and butchering a pregnant woman in the presence of her three children
- a sexual attack on his mother
- rape at night
- rape in broad daylight
- rape in a park
- rape in a home
- rape on a street
- rape of a woman doing tai chi

I believe the only "typical" characteristic of Reyes's crimes is their utter bestiality. But according to the *Times,* Reyes's "typical" crime is absolutely inconsistent with a gang rape.

—As the criminal lobby's sock puppet at the *Times* also excitedly reported, the rapes of the woman doing tai chi and the jogger "were the second and third of the year in the Central Park precinct."

The idea that rape is such a rare occurrence in New York that only one rapist could possibly be responsible for both rapes is insane. There were 3,254 reported rapes in New York in 1989. Prolific though he was, Reyes had some help from other rapists.

Every criminal "exoneration" you have ever read about was concocted by anti–death penalty zealots and pawned off on jour-

nalists who are either extraordinarily stupid or extraordinarily du-
plicitous. The only difference this time is that the truth about the
original case is available on LexisNexis. ■

☞ Media Support Citizenship Awards
for Central Park Rapists

DECEMBER 4, 2002

Hoping for a different result, journalists are relitigating the Central Park rape case in their pages, skipping the fuss and bother of
trial. The *New York Times* recently announced that "so far," there is
"almost nothing to back the original findings of guilt." That's if
you don't count ten videotaped confessions and five guilty verdicts
rendered by two duly constituted juries. But don't fall for the cheap
substitute of a trial by jury when there are one-sided accounts
available in the pages of the *Times*! (Remember the good old days
when being "tried by media" resulted in a guilty verdict?)

As part of the media's continuing series on how every criminal
is innocent (except asbestos manufacturers and abortion clinic
protesters), the *Los Angeles Times* said of the Central Park rapists,
"Jurors were swayed by physical evidence during the trial, such as a
blond hair apparently from the victim found on one teenager's
clothes. New forensic testing has shown that the hair did not come
from the jogger."

If reporters bothered to do research rather than accepting
whatever the "Innocence Project" tells them, they would know
that the lone hair evidence used against defendant Kevin Richardson could not possibly have "swayed" the jurors.

According to AP reports at the time, the most powerful testimony about the hairs found on Richardson's clothes came from a
detective who boldly proclaimed that the hairs "could have" come
from the jogger. On cross-examination, he admitted "he could not
determine that a hair definitely came from a specific individual."

He also said "that hair could end up on someone's clothing by casual contact or from being airborne."

On the other hand, evidence tending to implicate Richardson included this:

- He led prosecutors to the scene of the crime.
- There were grass stains and dirt in the crotch of his undershorts.
- He confessed on videotape to being at the scene of the attack.
- He gave a detailed description of the attack.
- He admitted that the deep scratch wound on his cheek was inflicted by the jogger.

So it's not quite accurate to say a single stray hair was the sole fact in favor of convicting him.

But wait! The "Innocence Project" has produced an eleventh-hour confession from a sixth rapist, Matias Reyes. Stunning no one but idiot reporters, Reyes claims he acted alone. As is always the case with surprise confessions allegedly exonerating convicted criminals, Reyes faces no penalty for this confession. The statute of limitations has run out on the rape and Reyes is already serving life in prison. To the contrary, Reyes is surely the toast of his cell block—where, by happenstance, he is serving time with one of the convicted Central Park rapists, Kharey Wise. (The only convicted criminal the *New York Times* has ever doubted was Pedro Hernandez, imprisoned with Reyes, who claimed Reyes had admitted to him that he raped the jogger along with the five other animals. You won't read much about Hernandez in the Criminal Defense broadsheets.)

Compare Reyes's new confession to the videotaped confessions of the five animals back in 1989. Their confessions were "statements against interest" in the strongest sense of the phrase. Knowing they would go to prison if they confessed, all five still confessed. Their confessions were tested in court, attacked by defense counsel, and believed by two unanimous juries.

But liberals treat these confessions as laughable frauds. Only Reyes's literally inconsequential confession is treated like Holy Scripture.

The odds of an innocent man being found guilty by a unanimous jury are close to nil. When the media assert a convict was "exonerated," what they mean is: "his conviction was thrown out on a legal technicality." Up and down the criminal justice system, guilty criminals are constantly being set free. Evidence of guilt is excluded at the drop of a hat. Not so, evidence of innocence. The criminal justice system is a one-way, prodefendant ratchet. So is the media, the only difference being that in court, evidence of guilt is not actually prohibited.

Consider only the odds of a false confession leading to a conviction. If the judge believes a confession is not an expression of free will, the confession will be thrown out. If the jury believes a confession is not an expression of free will, the confession will be thrown out. If an appeals court finds the confession was not voluntary, the confession will be thrown out. If the police fail to read the suspect his Miranda rights, the confession will be thrown out. If the defendant lyingly claims he was not read his Miranda rights and gets some appeals court to believe him, the confession will be thrown out. If the police question a juvenile outside the presence of his parents, the confession will be thrown out.

The videotaped confessions of the animals convicted in the Central Park attack were not thrown out. They were admitted into evidence and believed by two multiracial juries. In ten videotaped statements, members of the wolf pack implicated one another as well as themselves. They corroborated aspects of one another's stories.

The idea that the police randomly chose five black men to frame for the attack and then forced them to confess is absurd. Recall that when the savages confessed, it was still possible that the jogger would emerge from her coma, remember everything, and scream out "my boyfriend did it!" (Of course, if she had identified her attackers with eyewitness testimony we would now be reading copious articles in the *New York Times* about how head injuries can easily distort memory and render eyewitness testimony unreliable.) The police had obtained statements from dozens of teenagers who were in the park the night of the attack. In the end, only five of those who gave statements were prosecuted for the attack on the jogger.

It is more likely that the Central Park jogger was raped by space aliens than that Matias Reyes acted alone. But through their loudmouthed lobbying in the media, criminal defense lawyers are determined to turn these beasts into Rosa Parks.

———

POSTSCRIPT: The Manhattan district attorney, Robert M. Morgenthau, called for the convictions to be overturned, assuring himself a nice obituary in the *New York Times* someday. Justice Charles J. Tejada of State Supreme Court in Manhattan, who overturned the convictions, was quickly rewarded in the *Times* with an article that said he was "known as a fair, thorough judge" with a "reputation for understanding the problems of poor people" and had a "very good reputation for being thorough and patient and scholarly."

Three of the five animals later sued the city for $50 million apiece.

Michael Warren, the criminal defense attorney who produced Reyes's implausible "I acted alone!" confession—and who also represented charmers like Sheik Omar Abdel Rahman—was later involved in a major witness-intimidation scandal. Three eyewitnesses to a murder had picked his client out of a lineup as the murderer, but the witnesses later conveniently retracted their identifications on tape in Warren's office. Curiously, they had been brought to Warren's office by a member of the Bloods gang, who stayed in the room to hear the witnesses' retractions—something Warren neglected to mention on the tape. When a fourth witness who had refused to retract his statement was murdered, the first three renounced their retractions, saying the Bloods gang member who had escorted them to Warren's office had told them, "Lie or die."

The criminal lobby now has a bloody shirt to wave every time a guilty criminal confesses. In an April 4, 2004, article, the *New York Times* argued for the innocence of a man who had confessed to—and been convicted of—killing his parents, saying, "The concept of false confession was little known then, though modern DNA evidence has since proved it can happen, as in the Central Park jogger case" (Bruce Lambert, "Questions About a Son's Guilt, and a Cop's Methods"). ∎

12

What the Clintons' Ghostwriters Should Have Written

———■———

☞ At Least with Monica He Only
Bit His Own Lip

MARCH 6, 1999

Well, we got another "first" last week. In the Barbara Walters interview, Monica Lewinsky affirmed—happily, giddily—that Clinton did things "that made [her] feel, as a woman, happy and contented." Now, I can't remember back to the Nixon era, but I'm pretty sure Clinton just became the first president to have his capacity to induce orgasm described on national TV. He can add this to his growing list of firsts, including "first president accused of rape within two weeks after being acquitted in an impeachment trial."

Monica admitted that she was an emotional wreck over her affair with the president, whining to anyone who would listen, and throwing fits at the White House West Gate. She said she does not have the "self-worth a woman should have." During her ten-month banishment from the White House, she consoled herself with a sexual relationship with a man at the Pentagon, a certain "Thomas," which led to a pregnancy and an abortion. (I wondered how Thomas was enjoying the interview.) She described the thong-flashing incident as a "subtle flirtation." She admitted that she's had affairs with other married men before, that she was in therapy, that she's contemplated suicide, and that she was currently on antidepressants. Barbara Walters should have taken Monica's deposition for the Senate trial, especially if the lusty little tart promised to load up on the Prozac again.

At least Monica seems to have overcome that self-worth problem. Instead of wanting to crawl into a hole the way a normal person might, Monica seemed to think she was Gwynnie Paltrow promoting a new blockbuster movie.

Though Clinton didn't know Monica's name until the third time she showed up to earn her presidential kneepads—apparently having to swat away half the national press corps to get there—Monica earnestly told her interlocutor she thought Clinton "loved" her. He never actually *said* he loved her, though he did tell her, "You look skinny." In response to her profession of love he said, "That means a lot to me." Many people would have taken that as a hint. But Monica thought he loved her by "the way he looked at me."

What really sold Monica on the idea that Bill "These Allegations Are False" Clinton loved her was the now-famous gift: Walt Whitman's *Leaves of Grass*. That, she told Walters, is the "sort of gift that you wouldn't give someone that you didn't hold in a certain place in your heart." Except Clinton apparently had a closet full of them. The *Leaves of Grass* gift was reputedly the detail that finally sent Hillary over the edge: It was the first gift he gave her, too. There are probably a lot copies floating around out there.

The very first time Monica earned her presidential kneepads, Clinton was (1) on the telephone, and (2) didn't know her name.

They had their first substantive discussion—defined loosely—after their sixth sexual encounter. Porno movies have more intriguing plotlines and a lot more dialogue than what she terms her "relationship" with the president. But Monica assured viewers that Clinton did not see her as his "sex object." Why? Because Bill "These Allegations Are False" / "Monica, You Look Skinny Today" / "I Was Never Alone in a Hotel with Paula Jones" / "I Promise a Middle-Class Tax Cut" / "I Will Pull American Troops Out of Bosnia in One Year" Clinton said so. He even "started to tear up" when the astute young Monica complained of feeling like his sex object. Monica began her description of the crying episode by saying, "You'll probably find it hard to believe." Not that hard, actually. At least with Monica, he only bit his own lip.

Everyone makes fun of Linda Tripp for saying "I am you," but far more disconcerting was Monica's smug assumption of what a sympathetic figure she cut. Whenever I hear about Monica's fabulous wit, intelligence, and personality, I wonder—who's *not* witty, intelligent, charming? I just want to know for purposes of comparison. Consider that Monica's answer to the question of whether she thought the president was genuinely remorseful or just sorry he got caught was a real cliff-hanger. (She did get it right.)

I'm not sure what I would have done if I had been in Linda Tripp's untenable position, though I think I would have airdropped the tapes across America. The only person whose reaction was without precedent in the animal kingdom was Monica's father, Dr. Bernard Lewinsky. Upon discovering the married president had been using his halfwit daughter for sex games, Dr. Lewinsky decided to earn his own presidential kneepads.

Monica explained her father's psychotic reaction by saying it was hard for him to express his anger when the guy who "hurt [his] baby" is thepresident of the United States. Yes, Dr. Lewinsky did have a little trouble expressing that thought. Some might say he sent a mixed message when he gushed to Katie Couric on the *Today* show: "I respect President Clinton," and remarked that he and the president had something in common—"two young daughters that are intelligent." By contrast, Dr. Lewinsky venomously attacked Independent Counsel Ken Starr—who only asked Monica questions—for "persecuting my daughter with McCarthyism tactics, grip-torture technique." As Monica snippily said of Linda Tripp, "I pity her. I wouldn't want to be her." ∎

☞ Hillary: Pro-Dung

OCTOBER 5, 1999

Hillary's presumed Senate campaign is off to a smashing start. She has now established herself four-square *pro*-dung. Dung on the Virgin Mary. Dung and graphic pornographic pictures on the Virgin Mary. Mayor Rudy Giuliani must have thought he'd died and gone to heaven when this feminist cornpone decided to throw her hat into the ring.

It took Giuliani about thirty seconds to flush out Hillary on the dung issue. About a week ago, New York Mayor Rudy Giuliani proposed that the Brooklyn Museum of Art stop using taxpayer money to fund attacks on religion. As he put it, "Hard-earned public tax dollars should not be used for what I consider to be, and I think many people in the city, a desecration of religion and then, also, some other very, very sick things. The animals. The pedophiles. So don't use public tax dollars." The exhibit, titled "Sensation," includes, among other works, animals submerged in formaldehyde, maggots eating an ox's head, and—most notoriously—a picture of the Virgin Mary with elephant dung and pornographic pictures affixed thereto.

Hillary attacked the mayor, saying, "Our feelings of being offended should not lead to the penalizing and shutting down of an entire museum." Well, for one thing, she's not all that offended. Liberals are only offended by religious symbols that are displayed respectfully, caterwauling about the nonexistent "separation of church and state" they claim is in the Constitution. But publicly funded *attacks* on religion, they like. You can't "tolerate" the things you like. As Joe Sobran has remarked, this is like saying the Pope "tolerates" Catholics. Free speech that liberals don't like is labeled "hate speech" and banned.

But moreover, the mayor was not trying to "shut down" any museum. On Hillary's theory, the government is guilty of "censoring" anything it doesn't subsidize. Based on this conception of free speech, I feel the cruel lash of government censorship when the government doesn't pay me to write this column. As Giuliani said, "Just use your own money."

One only has to read the press's straight-faced descriptions of the exhibit to see what a political home run the pro-dung stance was for Hillary. On Friday, October 1, the *New York Times* ran a front-page photo of one of the exhibits, dryly reporting, "A shark in a tank of formaldehyde drew positive responses, but some thought a cut-up cow did not work as well."

The Associated Press reported that at a chichi private showing of the exhibit several attendees "said they enjoyed the show, particularly a controversial dung-decorated Madonna." Commenting on *The Holy Virgin Mary,* a painting of a black Madonna with elephant dung on one breast and cutouts of genitalia from pornographic magazines in the background, one art lover explained, "Dung is considered a respectful symbol."

Museum director Arnold Lehman—no stranger to dung himself—said of the dung-covered Madonna and other charming exhibits, "What they tell us is not a statement of blasphemy, but of reverence, but in a language that may be foreign to many of us. . . . If people do not make the effort to understand, if people do not exercise tolerance and mutual respect, then we all suffer." That statement itself is a work of art.

I paid a little field trip to the Brooklyn Museum to see "Sensation" and this is what it made me think. I'd say the Elephant Man's oeuvre is a piece of s***, but that would be a really bad pun. I wouldn't have even noticed it if I hadn't been guided by the audio tour—which, by the way, was the single most creative part of the exhibit. Until going to the "Sensation" exhibit, I did not know it was possible to use the words "ironic" and "whimsical" five thousand times in thirty minutes. I just couldn't figure out why the audio tour guide sounded like a very pompous Michael Caine. I was in *Brooklyn*. Why not Brooklyn accents? That would have been much more appropriate, to say nothing of ironic and whimsical.

The famous Madonna is barely recognizable as a depiction of a woman. If the Elephant Man hadn't managed to get the nose between the eyes, I wouldn't have known it was a human. The female genitalia pasted on the picture were, however, very true to life, which is not surprising inasmuch as they were actual cutouts from pornographic magazines. Very deep—even "ironic" and "whimsical," I would say. The artist has said that his use of elephant dung, which he gets from the zoo, is intended to reflect African culture. Haven't the poor people of Africa suffered enough without some phony artiste using elephant dung to symbolize Africa? One collector defended the Elephant Man's use of dung, saying it took "some work" to air out the rancid odor, but it was worth it because the artist was simply trying "to make you think."

The exhibit did not provoke "shock, vomiting, confusion, panic, euphoria, and anxiety" as the much ballyhooed signs at the exhibit entry had warned. Or let's just say, not nearly as much as the subway ride to the exhibit did. There was a lot of gross pornographic stuff, centering mainly on the pedophilic. If *Hustler* magazine editor–cum–Clinton aide Larry Flynt could make a buck appealing to the prurient interests of pedophiles, this would be the official *Hustler* museum. One artist, or combination of artists, had the "ironic" and "whimsical" idea of taking department store dummies of little girls and redesigning them (this is where the artistic talent comes in) so that some of their noses were penises, mouths were anuses or vaginas, and their little bodies were fused together in various bizarre Siamese twin fashions. In one of several such exhibits, the little girls' bodies were fused in ways that looked as though they were engaged in various forms of non-Euclidian sex. It was a statement about society.

I'll grant them that it did make me think. I kept thinking, What commonplace couldn't be touted as a "statement about our society"? I am chewing gummy bears. In masticating the diminutive and brightly colored creature constructs—imagine Michael Caine saying this on the audio—and transforming them into new paradigms, resembling wads of chewed-up gum, I am making a statement about the kind of society that would eat cute little bears.

The pretentious audio tour described a refrigerated bust made out of the artist's own blood—which was not even sculpted, just poured into a cast—as a statement about life itself. When the blood is inside us, you see, we think of it as part of us, but when the blood is outside our bodies, it's something outside of us. Just like toenail clippings. I didn't take notes, but I swear that is an accurate rendering of the meaning of the blood bust. (Except the toenail clippings point, which was my own artistic addition.)

Also "ironic" and "whimsical" is the fact that if the refrigeration is turned off, the blood bust would melt to liquid. This shows the transitory nature of our essential beings. Or that solids can melt to liquid if you turn off the refrigerator. I think it may have also said something about society. Or maybe it was life. Or death. Or sex.

On a few occasions, the audio tour indicated that such-and-such an artist had been rejected from various art schools before having the grand vision to put a bunch of poor dumb animals in formaldehyde. The audio guide seemed unaware that this sort of datum is interesting only if the art school reject turns out to be a brilliant artist. But it wasn't really that ironic here. I think the art schools were on to something. The director of the Metropolitan Museum of Art, Philippe de Montebello, no slouch in these matters, wrote an op-ed for the *New York Times* about the "Sensation" exhibit, remarking that these artists "deserve to remain obscure or be forgotten."

The only actual art in the exhibit consisted of four large paintings of horses. Oddly enough, they were identifiable as horses, which is so unlike modern art. After having come up with words to describe a 6-by-6-foot painting that was entirely red (titled *Raspberry*), the audio tour guide was absolutely garrulous in describing paintings that actually looked like something. But the horse paintings would have felt neglected if the guide didn't say something idiotic about them, too. The horses, it seems, belonged to the artist, who lives in England . . . and in England there is a lot of racism and sexism. The taped tour really did say that.

Back in New York City, where there's a lot of asinine-ism, the media are in high dudgeon about Mayor Giuliani's decision not to bilk the taxpayers for this preposterous exhibit. In a phony poll taken by the New York *Daily News*, respondents were asked this completely ridiculous question:

"The Brooklyn Museum of Art is planning a show that includes a controversial portrait of the Virgin Mary *that Mayor Giuliani finds offensive.* The mayor wants to withdraw city funding for the museum if it goes through with the show. The museum says withdrawing city funds would violate the museum's First Amendment right to exhibit works of art it finds appropriate. Whose position do you agree with more?"

Needless to say, only 30 percent agreed that the mayor ought to be able to distribute public funds on the basis of his personal reaction to an art exhibit. Sixty percent agreed "more with" the museum. Not to belabor the obvious, but the issue is not whether Mayor Giuliani personally finds the art offensive—it's that the taxpayers are being forced to subsidize alleged art that consists of, for example, the Holy Virgin Mary covered in vaginas and cow dung.

But in Manhattan's elite salons, it is received wisdom that Giuliani's decision to cut the Brooklyn Museum's public funds is going to kill him politically. Indeed, when Giuliani showed up for opening night at the Metropolitan Opera House recently, he was greeted with a round of boos from the society crowd.

At least when I'm out of touch with the average American, I know it. Not to put too fine a point on it, but opera fans aren't numerous enough to sustain the opera. They're not going to make or break a Senate campaign. Indeed, opera buffs are so expendable that they are regularly dismissed with derision by populist politicians in debates over government-sponsored art. (In case you were wondering, Congress got into the business of sheering taxpayers for "art" pursuant to the "provide-funds-for-chocolate-covered-women" provision of Article 1 section 8 of the Constitution.)

During a Senate hearing on the National Endowment of the Arts back when I was working in the Senate, one of the Republican senators actually began denouncing the NEA for subsidizing "opera tickets for the rich"—rather than bringing art to the poor and disadvantaged, or some such cant. (When did our guys start getting weepy about the poor? Republicans should go back to being crusty old men complaining about *high* taxes.) For a brief fleeting moment, I supported the NEA. I figured at least the rich are getting some of their tax money back. But my reverie is unimportant. The point is: No politician has ever been hurt by ticking off opera lovers.

Still, the *New York Times* quoted a couple of experts confidently asserting that Giuliani's battle with the Museum would hurt him with voters. Mitchell L. Moss, director of the Taub Urban Research Center at New York University, said, Giuliani is "going to lose some of the Democrats who otherwise might have voted for him." Lee M. Miringoff, director of the Marist College Institute for Public Opinion, concurred, saying that Giuliani's position "is going to turn off the people who were neutral on Rudy, who were kind of the moderate types."

Admittedly, New York is a liberal state: It is not an accident that of all the states Hillary has never lived in, she chose New York as the place to run for public office. But there is one profession in which a capacity to accurately discern voter sentiment is a job requirement—unlike university professorships, one need hardly add. However talentless they are at everything else, the one hundred members of the United States Senate know what sells politically. About the time experts were claiming Giuliani had shot himself in the foot and opera fans were booing him, the United States Senate voted unanimously—unanimously—in favor of a resolution supporting the withholding of federal funds from the Brooklyn Museum unless the Museum canceled the "Sensation" exhibit. Giuliani is anti-dung. Hillary is pro-dung. And I am now taking bets on the New York Senate race. I'm not gambling, I'm making an ironic and whimsical statement about society. ◼

☞ We're Number Two!

NOVEMBER 19, 1999

We almost won the title. In the *New York Post* poll of the "Top 25 Most Evil People of the Millennium," only Hitler edged out our own Bill Clinton, by 39 votes. The president's impressive second-place showing handily beat Joseph Stalin ("One death is a tragedy but a million is only a statistic"), who came in at number 3. Our boy also beat Pol Pot and Dr. Joseph Mengele—numbers 4 and 5, respectively. Hillary took a respectable 6th place, ahead of Saddam Hussein, Adolf Eichmann, and Charles Manson.

Moreover, when their scores are combined, Bill and Hillary slaughtered Hitler. Together, the Power Couple—"Buy one, get one free"—got 2,390 votes. That's 726 more than Hitler's paltry 1,664. Of course, Bill and Hillary were severely handicapped *by not appearing on the ballot*. The president and his lovely wife, Hillary, were the only entries on the entire "Most Evil" list who made it on write-in votes alone. Hillary was the only woman on the list. Finally: A poll I can believe. The poll was conducted over the entire month of October on the *New York Post*'s Internet site and received over 19,000 responses. Where were all those Americans who opposed impeachment of the lovable rogue and allegedly despise Linda Tripp? Don't they know how to use the Internet?

One of the most interesting aspects of the poll is that 16 of the 25 "Most Evil" made their mark working for the government. This is not surprising. In his book *Death by Government* political scientist R. J. Rummel estimates that in the twentieth century alone governments have killed almost 170 million people. As Rummel notes, "governments—particularly nondemocratic governments—clearly should come with a warning label: 'This power may be a danger to your life and limb.'" So keep voting to send more power to Washington.

Of all the grisly government bureaucrats on the list, from Vlad the Impaler to Muammar Qaddafi, only two were from America: Bill and Hillary! On write-in votes! The six other American winners were all murderers—Charles Manson, Jeffrey Dahmer, Ted Bundy, John Wayne Gacy, Jim Jones, and Timothy McVeigh. Their combined score was lower than the First Couple (2,169 votes for six of America's worst multiple murderers, and 2,390 votes for Mr. and Mrs. Clinton). The only nongovernment workers on the list were the American mass murderers, plus the Marquis de Sade (number 23) and Jack the Ripper (number 25).

Fascists took places number 1, 5, 8, 13, and 17 for a combined total of 3,779 votes (Adolf Hitler, Dr. Joseph Mengele, Adolf Eichmann, Benito Mussolini, and Ivan the Terrible). Excluding the Clintons, Communists took numbers 3, 4, and 18 for a combined total of 2,486 votes (Joseph Stalin, Pol Pot, and Fidel Castro). This is odd when you consider that the Nazis killed a mere 12 million people, while the Soviet regime slaughtered almost 62 million. Chairman Mao ("A revolution is not a dinner party") didn't even make the list and he murdered about 35 million people in the "Great Leap Forward" alone. (It is believed that Mao may have lost points in the "Most Evil" poll for killing so many intellectuals.)

But this is no time for nitpicking. Back to number 2. Bill Clinton scored higher than Charles Manson, Jeffrey Dahmer, Ted Bundy, and John Wayne Gacy together (1,625 to 1,615). He did better than the combined score of Joseph Stalin and Ivan the Terrible (1,625 to 1,589). Our number 2 received almost 6 times the number of votes as Timothy McVeigh and more than 7 times the number of votes as the Marquis de Sade. Clinton got almost 1,000 more votes than Saddam Hussein. Apparently, Saddam's score took a hit when he became SCUD missile target practice for some lunatic trying to distract from his personal problems last December. So, for now, Bill Clinton will have to settle for being second. This is probably good because, like Avis, being number 2 will only make him try harder. ■

☞ These Charges Are False— Reel No. 857

JULY 18, 2000

At least you could print what John Rocker said. The latest in a long list of "false" (subject to later revision) stories circulated about the Clintons comes from Jerry Oppenheimer's page-turner *State of a Union*, in which he reports that Hillary called one of the people working for Bill Clinton a "f–ing Jew bastard." The Clinton era was once again charting new ground in television standards!

The World's Smartest Woman did *not* respond to the charges by saying, *I might well have said that, but those obviously aren't my feelings, people sometimes use ugly words when they're angry, I'm sorry if I used those, but please judge me by my record and not some childish tantrum I threw twenty-six years ago.*

No, what Hillary said was that it was a lie put out by her political opponents:

"You know, there's a history of these kinds of charges coming from the people in question [author's note: the other charges were all eventually proved true, even if it took a full federal investigation], and they've been false in the past [author's note: only the denials, the excuses, and the defamatory charges against the Clintons' accusers have turned out to be "false"]. They're false now [author's note: that's what she said the last time]. And I don't know what the reason behind it is, but it didn't happen."

For the record, I personally did not go ballistic over some baseball player's (printable) remarks to *Sports Illustrated*. I personally thought that O.J. cutting off Nicole Brown Simpson's head was worse than Mark Fuhrman using the N-word. But even stipulating that the charges aren't career-ending—Hillary is the one who has now put the veracity of the charge at issue. Did she say it or didn't she?

The most persuasive evidence that Hillary said it, of course, is that she denies having said it. And if that's not enough for you, America's most famous perjurer, President William Jefferson Clinton, denies it too.

The *New York Times* ran a lead editorial on Hillary's "current complication"—as the paper called her anti-Semitic slur—titling it "Mrs. Clinton's Credible Response." The *Times*'s evidence that Hillary was telling the truth is that she opposed the Vietnam War and tried to get President Nixon impeached. This is normal *New York Times* logic. But even weirder, the editorial sportingly stressed that Ms. Vast Right-Wing Conspiracy gave "a passionate, almost teary response to the allegation of anti-Semitic language." Huh? A Clinton denial is supposed to mean something now?

When did we make the transition from treating a Clinton denial—subsequently discredited or retracted—as just so much necessary political filler because "anyone would have lied in those circumstances" to suddenly treating it as truth because the Clintons said it? Wouldn't anyone have lied about using the phrase "f—ing Jew bastard," too—particularly if that anyone was running for a Senate seat from New York? Why do we have to keep considering each successive denial by the Clintons as if it occurred in a vacuum? It's as if we're living in an eerie *Twilight Zone* episode in which no one can remember what happened yesterday.

It's not as if Tipper Gore stands accused of saying "f—ing Jew bastard." We're talking about Hillary. Hillary the lamp-throwing harpie whose warm Southern charm was widely credited with costing her husband his second race for the Arkansas governorship and whose concern for the little guy resulted in the Travel Office bloodbath. Curiously, neither Hillary nor her husband disputed that she had used the phrase "f—ing bastard." But they insist Hillary would not have alluded to the religion of the f—ing bastard. Even when cursing like a sailor, she's ethnically sensitive.

And just by the way, there are three witnesses to this particular charming utterance of Hillary's: Paul Fray, the campaign manager of Clinton's failed 1974 congressional bid and target of the slur; Fray's wife, Mary Lee, who was in the room at the time; and a third campaign worker, Neil McDonald, who was standing outside the room. Fray's wife said Hillary shouted so loud "it rattled the walls."

Other witnesses, from Dick Morris to the Arkansas state troopers, corroborate similar statements from the Dragon Lady. Their track records on truth-telling are somewhat more impressive than those of America's Most Famous Perjurer and his wife. By now, the troopers have been completely vindicated on even their most bizarre charges against the Clintons. Trooper Larry Patterson has said he heard Hillary use the phrases "Jew bastard" or "Jew boy" or "Jew MF" on numerous occasions—"four, five, six times." Instead of a War Room to put out "bimbo eruptions," Hillary may need a War Room to put out Hebraic-slur eruptions.

Conforming to pattern, Hillary's accusers came under a swift attack. Clinton flacks Lanny Davis and Gail Collins showed up for work with long research packets on Hillary's accusers. This was especially striking in Collins's case, since, generally, she avoids including facts in her columns. But even Collins was bursting with information about the little-known Frays. As with the Clintonian denials themselves, we're supposed to pretend this is the first time we've seen a rapid-response team smear witnesses against the Clintons. The rapid-response team's denunciations of the Frays are starting to blend with earlier denunciations of Gennifer Flowers, Paula Jones, Monica Lewinsky, Linda Tripp, Kathleen Willey, Juanita Broaddrick, the Travel Office employees, and Elián's "Miami relatives." All witnesses against the Clintons are: trashy people looking for publicity, have a minor criminal offense in their past (such as drunk driving or shoplifting), once sent nice letters to the Clintons, have a bitter relative somewhere who doesn't much care for them and will say so on the record, and are part of a right-wing conspiracy to bring false charges against the long-suffering, completely innocent Clintons.

I must say, I've been looking forward to this moment for years. You may have forgotten this, but back in the pre-Clinton era, sexual harassment was bad. It was bad even if it was just smutty remarks and there was only a single spurned woman who claimed it had happened. But then Clinton was caught doing it, and it turned out sexual harassment really isn't such a big deal. Women lie about these things all the time, everybody does it, and a real woman would have slapped the lovable rogue and walked away. Groping your female employees also used to be bad. But then Clinton did it, and Gloria Steinem announced on the *New York Times* op-ed page that the new standard is: The boss gets one free grope. Rape also used to be bad. But then Clinton was accused of rape by a credible woman with four corroborating witnesses. Clinton didn't deny it, and only 18 percent of Americans polled said they thought the accusation was probably not true. But no one cared, the country wanted to "move on," so I guess rape isn't such a bad thing now either.

The single accusation that remained a career-killer was to be accused of using an ethnic slur. Even cutting off a white woman's head wasn't so bad if the cop who found the evidence against you was accused of having used the N-word almost ten years earlier.

That's why I've been waiting and waiting for one of the Clintons to be caught using an ethnic slur. Now there's nothing you can't do.

———

POSTSCRIPT: In 2004, Hillary Clinton had to apologize for joking that Mahatma Gandhi once worked as a gas station attendant in St. Louis. Mrs. Clinton later admitted that the gas station owner in question was probably not from India, since he once tried to "Jew her down" on a set of new tires. ■

☞ Liberals Shocked: Impeached Felon Took Ottoman

FEBRUARY 11, 2001

I always thought it would be thrilling to be a liberal. Because I'm a cranky conservative, the world simply reinforces my prejudices on a daily basis. But for liberals, everything is always an exciting surprise. They seem to live in a state of perpetual shock. I used to keep a file of *New York Times* headlines expressing breathless astonishment at the achingly obvious. There would be bold proclamations along the lines of: "Parole Officers Shocked Child-Murderer Kills Again"; "Experts Baffled: Crime Rates Decline While Prison Populations Surge"; "Mental Illness Surprisingly High Among Homeless"; and "New Study: Rent Control Reduces Available Housing."

Most recently, liberals have made this exciting new discovery: Bill Clinton is a crook! I hate to sound indifferent to this development, but it wasn't too long ago that liberals were defending this guy on charges of perjury and obstruction of justice. They had no problem with the president killing foreigners to distract from his personal problems. They were willing to overlook credible charges of rape against a sitting president. They didn't mind that the president chatted with congressmen about going to war while Monica was earning her "presidential kneepads." (Speaking of which, they didn't mind that Clinton introduced the phrase "presidential kneepads" into the national dialogue.) But the Clintons take an ottoman when they leave the White House and the entire liberal establishment goes apoplectic.

I guess you find out who your real friends are when you lose the ability to save *Roe v. Wade*. It's nice that the whole country is finally on the same page about Bill Clinton, but frankly the Vast Right-Wing Conspiracy is getting a little bit bored with the Born-Again Clinton-haters. Back when Clinton could choose Supreme Court justices, the *New York Times* sneered about those yahoo Republicans thinking perjury, obstruction of justice, and numerous other felonies committed by the president constituted impeachable conduct. Now that he's out of office, the *Times* has finally developed the capacity for outrage. How is it, the *Times* recently demanded to know, that "a departing president and his wife come to put sofas and flatware ahead of the acute sense of propriety that ought to go with high office"? Bill Clinton—a lack of propriety? Wait a minute. Are we talking about the same Bill Clinton? Chubby fellow? Used to be president?

The *Washington Post* has run two editorials denouncing Clinton's most recent felonies. The first, titled "Count the Spoons," said the Clintons' decision to create a gift registry for people who wanted to give the First Couple farewell gifts "demonstrates again the Clintons' defining characteristic: They have no capacity for embarrassment." The editorial continued, "Words like 'shabby' and 'tawdry'... don't begin to do it justice." How about this for a word that does Bill Clinton justice: "Impeached"! (And no thanks to you and your petulant editorials opposing impeachment, *Washington Post*!) In a follow-up editorial titled "And Count the Couches," the *Post* called the Clintons' sticky fingers with the White House furniture "ultimately the Clintons' worst offense." If this is the worst, I'm just wondering where the *Post* ranks rape. How about that thing with the cigar? How about bombing an aspirin factory in Sudan on the day Monica Lewinsky returned to the Grand Jury?

Two years ago, the *Economist* magazine denounced Clinton's impeachment as a "partisan witch-hunt." Recently, the *Economist* ran an item titled "Beyond Shame," informing its readers that with Clinton, "the sleaze keeps coming in." Yeah, see, that was the thinking of the partisan witch hunters, which is why we wanted to get him out of office a long time ago. The *Economist*'s groundbreaking news was that a guy who perjured himself repeatedly in front of a federal judge and grand jury, bought off witnesses, bombed innocent foreigners to distract from a sex scandal, and sodomized an intern hours after a Bible-toting stroll from church on Easter Sunday *also* did this: "On February 5th the *Washington Post* revealed that the 'personal' gifts that the Clintons carted off with them included $28,000 worth of furnishings that were given not to the Clintons but to the National Parks Service."

At this very moment, you could knock me over with a feather.

Former Clinton Kool-Aid drinker Margaret Carlson dedicated her entire *Time* magazine column to the Clintons' "tacky" farewell-gift registry. It "just smells bad," Carlson was compelled to say. Oral sex from a White House intern was evidently a more ambiguous case. Carlson said the Clintons' friends "insisted Hillary simply wouldn't do" such a thing, but now—now!—"we have proof they would"! Wondering why the Clintons would "troll for freebies they can surely afford," Carlson sadly concluded, "only Freud could sort it out."

Not to brag, but that's what the Vast Right-Wing Conspiracy has been trying to tell you. But do we get thanks, maybe even a little apology, or at least a polite nod in our direction for having grasped the obvious years before Carlson? Oh no. To the contrary, Carlson takes a shot at the "vast right-wing conspiracy," incoherently claiming that since only conservatives complained about the felonies, but now liberals are upset about the ottoman, the Clintons had better take note. "The Clintons have long dismissed the criticism of those in the vast right-wing conspiracy whom they don't respect," Carlson says. "But how do you dismiss the views of those you do respect—who insist you would never sink so low, until they are silenced by proof of your grasping?" I'm not sure I grasp Carlson's point here, but I think she's trying to appeal to the consciences of felons by citing the opinions of idiots.

Another loony-left columnist, Mary McGrory, spent the seventies demanding President Nixon's impeachment and spent the eighties demanding President Reagan's impeachment, and then when the nineties finally produced an actual presidential impeachment, McGrory was grumpy about it. "The Republicans are beyond reason," she screeched a few years ago, and Clinton's impeachment "will disgrace them as much as Bill Clinton has disgraced himself." But that was before the Clintons had sunk so low as to take the ottoman. Recently, McGrory wrote of the Clintons' classy departure, "If the Bushes had called in an exorcist it would not have been excessive." Gee. We just wanted to impeach him.

And all this liberal hysteria was just about the furniture. I haven't even mentioned the pardons. The heretofore unshockable Left was truly shocked—shocked—about Clinton selling a presidential pardon to fugitive financier Marc Rich.

Representative Major Owens (Democrat of New York), member of the Clinton-loving Black Caucus, said of the impeachment of a known felon and probable rapist, "Our posterity will spit upon us for allowing this madness to reach this level. This is a political crucifixion." But this past week, referring to the Marc Rich pardon, Owens said of his constituents, "They think, 'I may have done one-millionth of what they did, but I'm sitting in jail.'" (His constituents must have been thrilled with that description.) I wonder what happens to Owens's "constituents" when they tamper with just one witness? What happens to them when they get caught telling just a few lies under oath? How many employees are they able to grope and flash before losing their jobs?

Senator Patrick Leahy of Vermont, who had criticized the

Clinton impeachment as the result of "extreme partisanship and prosecutorial zealotry," sputtered that the Rich pardon was "inexcusable . . . outrageous." It was also made possible by the decision of senators such as Leahy not to remove Clinton from office when they had the chance. Senator Paul Wellstone (Democrat of Minnesota) voted to acquit Clinton, saying anyone with "a sense of fairness and proportionality" knows that "the House overreached" when it voted to impeach the felon. But the Rich pardon, Wellstone said, raised "all the questions about values and ethics in relation to the Clinton administration." What were those questions again? Clinton lied to the country, lied to his staff, lied to his wife, lied to his party, lied in private, lied in public, and lied under oath. The Senate Democrats voted to keep him in office anyway. But now they profess shock that the man can't be trusted.

Barney Frank called Clinton's impeachment an "extraordinary triumph of ideology." If it's the Republicans who elevate ideology over reality, how come it's always the Democrats who are being floored by reality? These days Frank can be found wandering around wailing about "a real betrayal by Bill Clinton of all who had been strongly supportive of him." Senator Joseph Biden (Democrat of Delaware) accused Clinton of being "brain-dead" when he granted the Rich pardon. Yeah, what kind of idiot would have failed to anticipate that the same Democrats who warmly embraced perjury, obstruction of justice, and sexual perversion would draw the line at a presidential pardon?

Senator Arlen "Not-Impeachable-Under-Scottish-Law" Specter responded indignantly to the pardon, saying, "President Clinton technically could still be impeached." Maybe under Scottish law, but not under the U.S. Constitution. In his passion for truth, Specter once again stopped short of reading the Constitution. Representative Christopher "Rape-Isn't-Impeachable" Shays (Republican of Connecticut) has announced that Clinton's pardon of Rich is "sleazy." A rapist sleazy? Who woulda thunk? When you're sending half your bank account to the IRS this April, remember it's because the government thinks geniuses like Chris Shays can spend your money better than you can.

During the impeachment proceedings, *Washington Post* columnist David Broder described the evidence against Clinton on obstruction of justice as "very shaky." The evidence included: testimony from Clinton's secretary that Clinton coached her to lie in her testimony; Monica Lewinsky's testimony that Clinton told her how to hide the gifts he had given her from Paula Jones's lawyers; and Vernon Jordan's testimony that, at Clinton's behest, he had frantically called corporate magnates to line up a job for Monica, a crucial witness against the president. That, according to Broder, was a shaky case. But now Broder has written that of all the scandals, felonies, lies, and general slime to come out of the Clinton White House, "nothing came close to matching Clinton's exercise of the pardon authority." The Rich pardon finally demonstrated Clinton's "sheer arrogance of power." These people are literally insane.

Most beautifully, the *New York Times*—the same *New York Times* that haughtily instructed the Senate on its "duty to restrain the zealous House prosecutors" from removing Clinton from office—is now demanding that both the House and Senate investigate the Rich pardon. "A thorough investigation and a reconstruction of the events leading to the pardon are required. . . . It may be appropriate for the Justice Department and the Federal Bureau of Investigation to examine whether any laws were violated."

Well, well, well. Kind of a Johnny-come-lately on the need for an investigation, aren't we? In a breaking development, Ken Starr already performed an investigation. And surprisingly enough, it turned out laws *were* broken by the president. Lots of 'em, too. But for all his diligence and hard work, the *New York Times* got snippy with Ken Starr. So why exactly do we need another investigation now? If the idea is to find out whether Clinton sold presidential pardons, I think I can save the country the trouble of an investigation. The answer is: Yes, Virginia, Clinton did sell presidential pardons. In case you missed the Clinton presidency, he also sold the Lincoln bedroom, plots in Arlington Cemetery, government jobs, access to the president, a naval facility in Long Beach, California, and anything else the Park Service couldn't physically nail down.

Without embarrassment, the *Times* lauded Republican Dan Burton for investigating the pardons, reminding its readers that "this page has had scant praise" for Burton. Yeah, I remember that. "This page" was really annoyed with Burton for trying to point out that Clinton was a crook. Now the *Times* is hopping mad at having just discovered that Clinton is a crook. Who's been hiding that from the *Times*? Either the entire liberal establishment has been guzzling truth serum or they don't need Clinton to save *Roe v. Wade* anymore. ■

☞ Tell Him There's a Stopover in Bangkok
APRIL 10, 2001

On April 1, Chinese pilots harassing our surveillance planes over international waters got too close and caused a crash and both planes went down. The Chinese pilot died and the Chinese government seized our crew, refusing to release them until President Jiang Zemin received a fulsome apology from the United States for not preventing a Chinese plane from ramming an American plane. President Bush was in a pickle. On one hand, it is totally humiliating for an American president to have to apologize to a three-foot-tall dictator for his plane crashing into our plane. But on the other hand, short of all-out thermonuclear war, there was no other choice if we can't bear the idea of Americans being treated the way the Chinese government treats its own people.

So this was my idea: Have President Clinton apologize. He'd get all weepy, bite his lower lip, ramble on and on and on—the full

Jimmy Swaggart routine. But at the same time, everyone would know he didn't mean it. We could even have two separate tape reels, one short action shot for Jiang's "constituencies" and one with the outtakes for American viewers. Remember the footage of Clinton at Ron Brown's funeral? The full tape showed Clinton happily strolling along, smiling and laughing—until he catches sight of a camera. Then he quickly hangs his head and pretends to wipe away a tear. It's a beautiful moment.

And now his country needs him. No other human so thoroughly lacks a capacity for embarrassment. (He's probably headed in China's direction right now on that Thai sex tour anyway.) Actually, we don't even need Clinton. Darrell Hammond from *Saturday Night Live* could do it. Americans can barely tell the difference; the Chinese surely can't.

In lieu of the Jimmy Swaggart solution, I have Backup Auxiliary Plan Number 2. This one I call the "win-win solution." But it requires some background information. In the last election, Bush won: the election, two recounts in Florida permitted by law, a third recount not permitted by law, and a count of all Florida absentee ballots—before the U.S. Supreme Court finally said enough. (It seems like I'm getting off-topic, but bear with me.) Now it turns out Bush also won every conceivable method of counting the Florida ballots concocted by the *Miami Herald* (which endorsed Gore) and *USA Today* (which did not endorse a presidential candidate)— but one. Pursuant to this one single counting method—which was not among the seventeen methods requested by Al Gore or ordered by the Democratic Florida Supreme Court—Gore might be three votes ahead of Bush. Literally, five months after the election, they think they've finally found a method of counting ballots that puts Gore three votes ahead. Commenting on the media recounts that produced the exact same result as all the official tabulations, the *New York Times* said the postelection vote counts "provide stark evidence of how imprecise our voting system is."

More important background information: In a classic Tax-

Cuts-for-the-Rich exposé, the *New York Times* began a story last week, "Carrie Villa of Helena, Mont. has a dream—a house of her own on a nearby mountain." She thought she might achieve her dream when President Bush came through Montana recently, promoting his tax cut. She'd "heard the president talk about a 'typical family' making $40,000 a year" and that "the Bush plan would return $1,600 to that family." Excitedly, she rushed home, "took out a calculator and a tax form and did some numbers." Sadly, Villa's hopes were dashed. After working with the calculator for a while, "Ms. Villa discovered that the president's tax cut would not put a single extra dime in her pocket"—no doubt because the *entire tax cut* was going to Halliburton. All that information was on the front page, above the fold. You had to persevere to page A-18 to find out that Ms. Villa *doesn't pay any federal income tax.* What the hell was she doing with the calculator? *Hmmm, I pay zero dollars in federal income tax now, so if my entire tax burden were reduced to zero under the Bush plan, I'd be up . . . zero dollars! Let's run those numbers again.*

So this is my plan. Don't we have journalists in China? Next time let's make a trade. They give us the Americans and we'll let them keep any *New York Times* reporters. ∎

☞ True Grit

JUNE 11, 2003

I could hardly breathe. Gulping for air, I started crying and yelling, "What do you mean? What are you saying? Why are the Clintons back again?"

Interviewing Hillary Clinton last Sunday night about her book *Living History,* ABC's Barbara Walters began with such hardball questions as:

- "Are you a saint?"
- "[Is it] tougher than being first lady, being a senator?"

- "You know, you have been working on so many bills with Republicans. . . . How do you turn old enemies into allies? . . . I mean, no hard feelings?"
- "How do you get on with this?"
- "There were the accusations that [your husband] was a womanizer." (I believe a DNA test revealed that they were more than accusations.) "How'd you deal with it?"

Hillary dealt with it. Hillary is a survivor. As Walters said, Hillary's book *Living History* is a "wife's deeply personal account of being betrayed in front of the entire world." In fact, it was so deeply personal, it took several ghostwriters to get it right.

Walters brazenly probed the question on everyone's mind: How could Hillary be so brave, so strong, so downright wonderful? As Walters recounted, once our plucky heroine even lived in Arkansas! Summarizing Hillary's sacrifice, Walters said, "You were young. You were smart. You had a future in Washington. But you gave it up to be with Bill Clinton, to move to Arkansas. . . . Why on earth would you throw away your future?" Admittedly, even Bill Clinton couldn't wait to get out of Arkansas. Manhattanites cannot conceive of a greater hardship.

Walters also astutely observed that "in addition to being first lady, you're a mother." Will Hillary's mind-boggling feats never end?

Describing interviews like these, *New York Times* television reviewer Alessandra Stanley said Hillary was finally able to show her "grit, an outsize will and discipline that has nothing to do with gender." This, Ms. Stanley said, was a welcome change from Hillary's more recognized role as "an emblem of the modern female condition." So on one hand, Hillary has grit and determination. But on the other hand, she is a living, breathing icon. It's good to see the *New York Times* really going the extra mile to give both sides these days.

In "her" book, Hillary explains that the story of how Nelson

Mandela forgave his jailers inspired her to forgive Bill for his infidelity. Okay, but they locked up Mandela only once. Revealingly, Ms. Stanley claims that "millions of women have forgiven far worse of philandering husbands." Far worse? Really? No wonder liberal women hate men so much.

If you credit news reports, the public can't get enough of Hillary. The crush of ordinary people buying Hillary's book seems baffling in light of recent polls. According to an ABC poll, 48 percent of Americans have an unfavorable impression of Hillary, 53 percent of Americans don't want Hillary to ever run for president, and 7 percent of Americans have been date-raped by Bill Clinton.

First in line for Hillary's book at Barnes & Noble at Lincoln Center on Sunday night was Charles Greinsky, who told the New York *Daily News* he rushed out at midnight to get one of the first books because he supported Hillary's health-care plan. A few years ago, the Associated Press identified Greinsky more fully. It turns out he is "a longtime Clinton campaigner" from Staten Island, who has been the Clintons' guest several times both at the White House and at their home in Chappaqua, New York. Lining up at midnight to buy Hillary's book is street theater for liberals. I suppose shelling out $30 to support the concept of Hillary is less dangerous than the pernicious nonsense liberals usually fund. Hillary has already gotten a record $8 million advance from Simon & Schuster for the book—reportedly the most anyone has ever received for rewriting history.

Another average individual eager to get Hillary's book was Greg Packer, who was the centerpiece of the *New York Times*'s "man on the street" interview about Hillary-mania. After being first in line for an autographed book at the Fifth Avenue Barnes & Noble, Packer gushed to the *Times*, "I'm a big fan of Hillary and Bill's. I want to change her mind about running for president. I want to be part of her campaign."

It was easy for the *Times* to spell Packer's name right because he is apparently the entire media's designated "man on the street" for all articles ever written. He has appeared in news stories more than a hundred times as a random member of the public. Packer was quoted on his reaction to military strikes against Iraq; he was quoted at the St. Patrick's Day Parade, the Thanksgiving Day Parade, and the Veterans' Day Parade. He was quoted at not one—but two—New Year's Eve celebrations in New York's Times Square. He was quoted at the opening of a new "Star Wars" movie, at the opening of an H&M clothing store on Fifth Avenue, and at the opening of the viewing stand at Ground Zero. He has been quoted at Yankees games, Mets games, Jets games—even getting tickets for the Brooklyn Cyclones. He was quoted at a Clinton fundraiser at Alec Baldwin's house in the Hamptons and the pope's visit to Giants Stadium.

Are all reporters writing their stories from Jayson Blair's house? Whether or not it will help her presidential ambitions, it occurs to me, *Living History* definitely positions Hillary nicely for a job as a reporter. ■

☞ Moby's Dick

JUNE 23, 2004

According to the front page of the *New York Times*—so it must be true!—the release of Bill Clinton's latest round of lies, *My Life,* has "many of his old antagonists . . . gearing up again." Among many others, MSNBC's Bill Press said the book was "bringing all the Clinton haters out from under their rocks. I mean, they're salivating because they get another chance to get into all of these issues."

We're not salivating with anticipation—that's drool as we fall into a coma.

Since Clinton was impeached, liberals have been trapped in a time warp. They just can't seem to "move on." Books retelling Clinton's side of impeachment—only since the decadent buffoon left office—include: Joe Conason's and Gene Lyons's *The Hunting of the President: The Ten-Year Campaign to Destroy Bill and Hillary Clinton* (endorsed by America's most famous liar!), David Brock's *Blinded by the Right: The Conscience of an Ex-Conservative,* Sidney Blumenthal's *The Clinton Wars,* Joe Eszterhas's *American Rhapsody,* Joe Klein's *The Natural: The Misunderstood Presidency of Bill Clinton,* Hillary Rodham Clinton's *Living History,* and now, the master himself weighs in with *My Life.*

As far as I know, conservatives have produced one book touching on Bill Clinton's impeachment in this time: In 2003, *National Review's* Rich Lowry decided it was finally safe to attack Clinton and thereupon produced the only Regnery book with Bill Clinton's mug on the cover that did *not* make the *New York Times's* best-seller list. That's how obsessed the Clinton-haters are.

Now there's even a documentary version of liberals' Vast Right-Wing Conspiracy fantasy *The Hunting of the President.* If we're so obsessed with it, why do they keep bringing it up? O.J. had more dignity.

Okay, uncle. You win, Mr. President. If I buy a copy of your book, will you just shut up once and for all, go away, and never come back? It will cost me $35, but, judging strictly by weight, that isn't a bad price for so much cow manure. At 957 pages, this is the first book ever published that contains a twenty-minute intermission. Readers are advised to put it down and read a passage from Clinton's 1988 DNC speech nominating Dukakis just to stay awake. This thing is so long, he almost called it *War and Peace.* Or, I suppose, more properly, *War and a Piece.*

Considering how obsessed liberals are with turning their version of Clinton's impeachment into the historical record, it's interesting how these books spend very little time talking about Clinton's impeachment. In lieu of discussing the facts of his impeachment, Clinton simply makes analogies to grand historical events—events notable for bearing not the remotest relationship to his own sordid story.

Clinton claims, for example, that conservatives decided to target him in lieu of the Soviet Union after the Cold War ended and conservatives needed a new villain. In other words, Clinton is equating himself, in scale and importance, to the Soviet Union, the global Communist conspiracy, and the Marxist-Leninist Revolution. Nope, no ego problem there. (*My Life* was Clinton's second-choice title, after the publisher balked at naming the book *I Am God, and You Are All My Subjects.*)

Alternatively, Clinton claims conservatives hated him because he represented "the '60s." As is now well known, four lawyers, toiling away after-hours and on weekends, worked quietly behind the scenes to propel the Paula Jones case to the Supreme Court and bring Monica Lewinsky to the attention of the independent counsel. All four of us were five to eight years old when Bill Clinton graduated from Georgetown in 1968.

So I'm pretty sure it wasn't our anger about "the '60s" that inspired feelings of contempt for Bill Clinton. (Actually, it was the seventies that I really hated, but that's another column for another day.) It must have been something else—some ineffable quality. Let's see, what was it again? Ah yes! I remember now! It was that Clinton is a pathological liar and sociopath.

If Clinton wasn't the Soviet Empire or "the '60s," then he was Rosa Parks! Clinton actually compares his battle against impeachment to civil rights struggles in the South. Haven't blacks been insulted enough by the constant comparison between gay marriage and black civil rights without this horny hick comparing his impeachment to Selma?

And that's when Clinton is even talking about his presidency. From what I've heard, roughly half of Clinton's memoir—hundreds and hundreds of pages—is about every picayune detail of his life before becoming president. Through sheer force of will I shall resist the urge to refer to this book as a "blow-by-blow" account of Clinton's entire miserable existence.

Most presidential memoirs start right away with the president part, on the assumption that people would not be interested in, for example, Harry Truman's deal-making as Jackson County executive or Jimmy Carter's initiatives as a state senator in Georgia—let alone who they took to their junior high school proms. When Ulysses S. Grant wrote his memoirs, he skipped his presidency altogether and just wrote about what would be most interesting to people—his service as a Civil War commander.

But Clinton thinks people are dying to read nine hundred pages about his very ordinary life. He views being president as just one more episode in a life that is fascinating in all its stages because he is just so fascinating as a person—at least to himself. In a perverse way, it's utterly appropriate. What actually happened during the Clinton presidency? No one can remember anything about it except the bimbos, the lies, and the felonies. Fittingly, in the final analysis, Clinton will not be remembered for what he did as president, but for who he did. ∎

13

Elián González: The Only Immigrant Liberals Ever Wanted to Deport

———— ■ ————

"I think that it is important for everyone now to move on."
—JANET RENO, the day after ordering a SWAT team raid on
Elián González's residence in Florida

I'm not quite ready to move on. After all the nonsense that was reported about the Elián González case, the truth is breathtaking. When it came to Elián, liberals abandoned every seditious cause they had once held dear—dysfunctional families, judicial activism, illegal immigrants, their opposition to the use of military force, their fear and hatred of "assault-type weapons," the Constitution as a living document, Fourth Amendment rights, and a weak executive branch. As with abortion, the rules kept changing in order to achieve liberals' driving objective—in this case, sending a small boy back to Cuba.

Now that the nation is embroiled in the war on terrorism, liberals are enraged about the dangerous new powers given to the attorney general by the Patriot Act. But look at all Janet Reno managed to accomplish in Miami—and Waco—without a Patriot

Act. Would that liberals directed a little of that venomous anger they had for a Cuban immigrant toward foreign enemies on U.S. soil.

I wasn't paying much attention to the Elián González story for the first seventeen weeks of nonstop, front-page coverage in the *New York Times*, beginning in the fall of 1999. Cuba is a lousy country, if you go for things like freedom, but so are a lot of countries. I figured Reagan won the Cold War, and Fidel Castro was going to have to get around to dying someday. Living in a nice free country, I didn't have to bother myself about what to do with little Elián. But I did have to bother myself about little Elián because I occasionally picked up a newspaper or turned on the TV, and it was "All Elián! All the Time!" Liberals were obsessed with Elián González from the moment he arrived on our shores. They forced me into paying attention and, as usual, it turned out liberals were up to no good. As far as liberals were concerned, the Cold War was very definitely not over. Sending Elián back to Cuba had become a cause célèbre bigger than defending Alger Hiss. Liberals lost 300 million people when their beloved Soviet Union was defeated by Ronald Reagan, but Elián gave them a chance to grab one back! The Elián González case became the Left's last stand for Communism.

Until Elián arrived, liberals were constantly wailing about the senseless cruelty of deporting illegal immigrants, criminal aliens, and immigrants with AIDS. If only Elián had knocked over a liquor store and maybe pistol-whipped an old lady in the process, we could have kept him, by golly! At the Oscars in 1993, Tim Robbins and Susan Sarandon used their presentation of an award to make a plea for the hundreds of AIDS-infected Haitians who had been captured trying to enter America illegally. Alas, Elián was not infected with a dread disease, or perhaps they would have spoken up for him, too.

After Congress passed a law requiring the deportation of aliens convicted of committing felonies in this country, *New York Times* columnist Anthony Lewis wailed about the "human realities" of deporting a "person who made a mistake long ago." But when Elián's Miami relatives fought to keep him from being returned to a totalitarian dictatorship, Lewis compared the relatives to "howling mobs confronting federal marshals" trying to enforce school desegregation in Little Rock, Arkansas. "Are we going to be governed in this country by law or by mob?" Let an AIDS-infected drug dealer dash across the border and liberals get teary-eyed about the American dream. But if the immigrant is a little boy who lands on our shores only because his mother wanted him to grow up in freedom so badly that she was willing to risk her life bringing him here, liberals can't get him deported fast enough. At least liberals are consistent with regard to the rights of the innocent and the guilty: They also believe it's perfectly acceptable to kill an innocent unborn baby, but morally unthinkable to execute a serial rapist/murderer.

More jarring than liberals' sudden urge to deport an illegal alien was their newfound respect for "family values." At the outset of the Elián ordeal, liberals mentioned Elián's father only as an afterthought. The main point was: Cuba was a glorious socialist paradise and Elián was goddamn lucky to live there! As *Newsweek*'s Eleanor Clift said, "To be a poor child in Cuba may, in many instances, be better than being a poor child in Miami." Without laughter or even skepticism, CBS news ran a clip of a Cuban citizen in December 1999 saying, "I think that the children in the U.S. cannot have a life similar to the one they have in Cuba, because we have been seeing on television, for example, that there have been many shootings in the schools even. So I think that the education here in Cuba is good." On another episode of *CBS News*, Dan Rather said, "There is no question that Castro feels a very deep and abiding connection to those Cubans who are still in Cuba. And, I recognize this might be controversial, but there's little doubt in my mind that Fidel Castro was sincere when he said, 'listen, we really want this child back here.'"

But most liberals realized it wasn't helping to say such things out loud, so they concentrated on the biological father's right to take his son into his custody. Liberals had never been particularly enamored of the family unit before this. Hillary Clinton, for example, famously compared the family to slavery (prompting Pat Buchanan to remark, even more famously, "Speak for yourself, Hillary"). Inasmuch as liberals deny what Hillary said, I shall quote her in full. In the 1973 *Harvard Education Review*, Hillary wrote:

"The basic rationale for depriving people of their rights in a dependency relationship, is that certain individuals are incapable of or undeserving of the right to take care of themselves and consequently need social institutions specifically designed to safeguard their position. . . . Along with the family, past and present examples of such arrangements include marriage, slavery and the Indian reservation system." (Quick reminder: This woman wants to be your president someday.)

Hillary was not alone. Liberals have long directed a bewildering barrage of abuse at television shows like *Father Knows Best* and *Leave It to Beaver*—apparently for failing to portray the family as the den of incest and dysfunction they believe it to be. The Clinton administration wasted little time in signing the completely preposterous United Nations Convention on the Rights of the Child, which had been repeatedly rejected by Presidents Ronald Reagan and George Bush. The Rights of the Child treaty would have bound the United States to a panoply of children's "rights" against their parents. (Fortunately, the treaty went straight from the White House to Senator Jesse Helm's in-box, where it sat gathering dust for the next several years.) Liberals think parents shouldn't be allowed to force their children to wash the dishes but should be allowed to force them to live in a Communist dictatorship.

If liberals take a dim view of the family, fathers they deem positively malignant. The National Organization for Women has worked tirelessly to defeat fathers'-rights laws in legislatures across the country. They despise anything paternal—except the state. Parents are not important enough to deserve notification of their minor daughter's abortions, and fathers are so irrelevant under the law that they have no say about whether their own children will be aborted. Dan Quayle was savaged for criticizing the glamorization of single motherhood on the TV show *Murphy Brown*. Elián González was the only child liberals ever believed needed a father. Liberals believe that Elián's mother should have been able to abort Elián without input from the father but that she could not give him freedom without the father's consent.

At least the Elián case finally gave liberals a cause they were willing to go to war for. On April 22, 2000, at 5:10 in the morning, Attorney General Janet Reno ordered about two dozen INS agents to stage a commando raid on the home of Elián González's Miami relatives in a preemptive attack without approval from France or Germany. Masked, machine-gun-toting federal agents doused protesters outside the house with pepper spray and tear gas before smashing through the gate, bursting into the house, and seizing the terrified little boy, who was hiding in a closet. As the SWAT team carried Elián away, he cried out in Spanish, "What's happening? What's happening? Help me! Help me!" If only he had been a Muslim terrorist, we might have heard from Amnesty International. (At least the INS agents did not demand a list of books Elián had checked out of the local library!)

According to Janet Reno's Press Office at CNN, a member of the Miami SWAT team later said he had "never encountered this much resistance." If a seven-year-old boy in the home of law-abiding, unarmed citizens presented the most resistance a border patrol officer has ever encountered, I suppose we shouldn't be shocked that Mohammed Atta slipped through their net a few years later.

Before Reno was aware that there was a photo clearly showing a federal agent pointing a machine gun at Elián's head, she informed reporters, "The gun was pointed to the side." (The gun wasn't pointed at Elián; the gun was pointed *with* Elián.) If not for that photograph, Reno would have announced that the agents' guns were never out of their holsters. You always need documentary proof with these Democrats—photos, DNA-stained dresses, roll-call Senate votes. Naturally, the media spent more time chastising themselves for showing the photo than actually showing it.

The *New York Times* reported that "some officials had urged Ms. Reno to allow the agents to take steps to prevent photographs from being taken. But Ms. Reno had rejected the idea, along with a proposal to park a large vehicle in front of the house to block television crews from filming the event." Reno's much-heralded rejection of the idea was apparently not communicated to the SWAT team. "We got Maced, we got kicked, we got roughed up," said Tony Zumbado, the NBC cameraman on duty to provide the pool coverage shared by all the networks and cable channels. When Zumbado got inside the door of the house, he was kicked in the stomach by a federal agent and knocked to the floor. Mr. Zumbado's only weapon was a camera.

Shortly after the raid, Reno said, "one of the beauties of television" is that it can show "exactly what the facts are." That's interesting. Then why did the SWAT team incapacitate the only television cameraman at the house? What possible law-enforcement objective could this serve? And what law-enforcement objective was served by the federal commandos wearing ski masks? Reno gamely noted that the photo proved that the agent pointing a machine gun at Elián did not have his finger on the trigger. As any halfwit knows, the only time your finger is on the trigger is when you are about to shoot. The fact that the federal agent did not have his finger on the trigger proves nothing more than that he didn't actually shoot Elián. Good for him!

Relying on the media's complete, abject ignorance of firearms, the administration and its lackeys insisted on calling the MP-5 submachine guns carried by the Delta Force Gang "automatic rifles." That sounds so much more gentle than "machine gun"— which is what an "automatic rifle" is. (By contrast, those "assault weapons" liberals are so terrified of are semi-automatic rifles, considerably less lethal than the gun pointed at Elián's head.) The ACLU was "troubled" by the government instituting a SWAT team raid to seize a child, the only legal justification for which was an invalid warrant, but believe the Patriot Act is going to "turn our country into a police state"—in the words of Howard Simon, executive director of the Florida ACLU.

We were repeatedly told that Reno was merely enforcing "the law." But upon examination it turned out—just as with impeachment—everything liberals said about "the law" was a lie. One "law" those wily Cuban-American scofflaws were allegedly violating was the legal presumption that a father be given custody of his son. The *Economist,* for example, authoritatively stated, "American and international law are both clear—the boy should go back to his father." This was in an item that used such legally precise phrases as "frenzied Castro-hater[s]" and "the bloody-mindedness of Miami's Cuban-Americans."

As long as we're going to be sticklers about "the law," the laws that grant a father custodial rights to his children refer only to legitimate children. Though the media tried to hide it, a close reading of their bilge revealed that Elián was Juan Miguel González's illegitimate son. González was not married to Elián's mother when Elián was born. He wasn't even married to Elián's mother when Elián was conceived. According to the *New York Times*, Elián's parents were divorced in May 1991; Elián was born on December 6, 1993. I know Cuba is in the advanced stages of HillaryCare, but I don't think even Cuban health care could screw up the length of a pregnancy. Nor did Juan Miguel ever rectify Elián's bastardy. Elián's true father was his stepfather who drowned at sea along with Elián's mother trying to bring him to America. By contrast, the woman with whom Elián was forcibly "reunited" was not—as the media called her—his "stepmother." She was the woman married to the man who knocked up his mother.

At common law, biological fathers had absolutely no rights to their illegitimate children. This quaint legal notion preceded the Magna Carta by a considerable stretch. Indeed, that was the law roughly from the beginning of history until the early seventies. Of course, we've come a long way since marriage was considered a consequential institution. But even in swinging, post–sexual revolution America, a father's legal right to an illegitimate child is highly contentious—and prodigiously litigated. The U.S. Supreme Court last weighed in on the legal rights of unwed fathers in 1989, when it cut off all of the biological father's rights to his child, including visitation rights. Visitation!

Florida law takes an especially dim view of the legal prerogatives of fathers toward their illegitimate children. In the early nineties, white-trash sperm donors kept appearing out of nowhere to demand that their biological children be ripped from the arms of loving, adoptive parents. In the wake of the "Baby Jessica" and "Baby Richard" cases, Florida, like many other states, enacted a "pre-birth abandonment" law. The law provides that, in the absence of a marriage contract, the biological father's rights to a child hinge on whether he had provided "emotional support" to the mother during her pregnancy. In a 1995 case, *In re: The Adoption of Baby E.A.W.*, the Florida supreme court found that the father had "abandoned" his illegitimate child during gestation and therefore had no legal right to object to an adoption, relying on such evidence as the mother's testimony that the father was an "ice cube" during a visit to the doctor. In 1999, a Florida appellate court described the rights of an unwed father to his biological child as "a mere inchoate right to establish legal fatherhood." In other words, if Elián's biological father had lived in Ohio rather than Cuba, he would probably have been denied custody of Elián. Unfortunately for Elián, his father lived in Cuba, a place liberals admire, in contradistinction to a tacky state like Ohio.

But forget that Juan Miguel was not married to Elián's mother when Elián was born (or anytime thereafter). Let's assume Cuba's own José Buttafuoco had made Elián's mother an honest woman.

Child custody laws always make an exception for parents who are deemed "unfit." This is obviously a high hurdle, but Juan Miguel didn't become Castro's toady for lack of effort. Before allowing Juan Miguel to leave Cuba in April 2000, Castro gave a speech about Elián. In splendid dictatorial style, he claimed to be reading from a letter written by Juan Miguel. Oddly enough, Juan Miguel's demands were identical to Castro's! (Another clue that Castro might have helped draft Juan Miguel's letter: It took over eight hours to read it out loud.) In the alleged letter, Juan Miguel demanded that U.S. officials allow him to "travel from the airport to wherever I am told the child is"—the "child" being his son—"pick him up, return to the airport, and return, immediately, to Cuba." What with thousands of Americans hopping on rickety rafts every year to escape this hellhole and flee to Cuba, this was only a necessary precaution. In another extremely realistic touch, just four months earlier, Juan Miguel told *Nightline* that he could tell Elián was "being made to do things against his will because if he were able to say or to defend Fidel, he would do it." If there's one thing six-year-old boys really go for, it's murderous Stalinist dictators who look like Bigfoot in fatigues. The burden of being a dictator is that no one will dare tell you that it is completely preposterous to imagine that six-year-old boys are constantly bubbling over with fulsome praise regarding your leadership qualities.

But let's leave aside the fact that Juan Miguel was a Communist tool—a bounder, a bum. What is absolutely uncontested is this: Instead of going to Miami to retrieve Elián himself, Juan Miguel allowed a federal SWAT team armed with submachine guns to stage a military-style assault on his son in Miami. The *New York Times* reported that even Janet Reno—who had no trouble gassing all those kids at Waco—was reluctant to use force to retrieve Elián. But Elián's father insisted on it. To be fair, according to *Newsweek*, the horror experienced by the last pro-Castro relatives to visit Elián's Miami home was that they were "rudely rebuffed." So one can certainly understand why Elián's father would order a machine-gun raid on his son to avoid that sort of unpleasantness.

Whatever else "unfit" means, I believe it would include: someone who demands that his son be subjected to a machine-gun, predawn raid in order to gain custody. What kind of father would knowingly put his son in harm's way simply to avoid a minor inconvenience to himself? The kind, evidently, that Janet Reno gave custody to. (One wonders what might have happened if Reno, in her Solomonic wisdom, had decreed that Elián be cut in two so one half could be returned to Cuba and the other half remain here.)

Ah, but, we were told, Reno was just enforcing "the law" and the Miami relatives kept "moving the goalposts." One would think, the way we kept hearing paeans to the "rule of law," that every court to have looked at Elián's case had ruled that he had to go back to Cuba, pronto. In point of fact, the courts largely ruled in favor of keeping Elián here in the United States. But the Clinton administration kept changing its mind about which tribunal it would listen to—depending on the results. When liberals first discovered that one of Castro's subjects had escaped, they were adamant that Florida state courts decide Elián's fate as a simple custody dispute. Liberals assumed that if the case was treated as a child custody matter, the Florida courts would order Elián sent back to Cuba to be with his biological father. This way, Elián could be sent back to Cuba without the Clinton administration expressly ordering it.

Under the headline, "Courts, Not Feds, to Decide Custody," one typical news story dated November 30, 1999, reported, "U.S. government officials said yesterday they will not intervene in deciding whether 5-year-old Elián González . . . should rejoin his father in Cuba or remain with relatives in Florida—a question they said can be answered only in state courts. . . . State Department and immigration officials concluded in a late-afternoon meeting that they simply have no legal say in the matter. 'It is our understanding this is an issue for the courts,' said a State Department official."

In early December, the *New York Times* reported that Elián's case "was referred to the Florida state courts because they take precedence in custody disputes." The *Times* explained that "American officials said a Florida state court should decide whether Elián should be raised in the United States or returned to his father and grandparents in Cuba." NBC reported, "Tonight the U.S. State Department and the Department of Justice once again reiterated that they do not believe this is an issue for them to deal with. They say this belongs in family court in Florida's court system."

But then, to liberals' shock and dismay, the Florida courts ruled that Elián should stay in the United States. In what the *Washington Post* called "a surprising legal victory" for Elián's relatives, a Florida state court ruled on January 11, 2000, that Elián was to stay with his uncle. Returning Elián to Cuba, the court found, could cause him "imminent harm."

In an act some might compare to "moving the goalposts," the administration promptly denounced the Florida state court, saying it had no jurisdiction in the matter. Janet Reno fired off a letter to the Miami relatives' lawyer the next day, announcing that any ruling from a Florida state court "has no force or effect" on the administration's decision to return Elián to Cuba. The question of what to do with Elián, Reno said, "is a matter of federal immigration law." Forget moving the goalposts—this was more like tearing them down altogether. And yet, suddenly, "legal analysts" consulted by the *New York Times* said Reno was right: federal immigration law takes precedence over a child custody ruling by a Florida court. This left unexplained why the INS didn't just deport Elián to begin with, instead of allowing the Florida state courts to spend weeks deciding the matter, amid the administration's loud proclamations that Elián's fate would be decided in the Florida courts.

Liberals were a little vague about what other "laws" the Miami relatives might be violating, but there were a lot of nasty insinuations. On March 28, Peter Jennings opened ABC's *World News Tonight* saying, "In Miami today, immigration officials met with the Miami relatives of Elián González again and once again the government has failed to get the kind of cooperation from the relatives that might allow the case of this young boy to end in a civilized manner that is best for him." In fact, Elián's Miami relatives consistently abided by the law even insofar as "the law" consisted of Janet Reno's personal feelings. From the moment the very first court ruled, there was never a time when the Miami relatives did not have either a state or federal court ruling in their favor.

The crucial point to understand is that when the administration talked about "the law," they were referring to Janet Reno's feelings—no court order, no official ruling, no agency proceeding. As an illegal alien, Elián was always technically in the "custody" of the INS, over which the attorney general presides. Fortunately, even the Clinton administration didn't think it was a good idea to send small children to live with Janet Reno. Consequently, after Elián's rescue, the INS paroled him to the care of his great-uncle, Lázaro González, in Miami. Under "the law," the attorney general could theoretically revoke an illegal alien's parole at any time, without a court order, and reparole the alien to anyone else—Jeffrey Dahmer, a guest on the *Jerry Springer Show*, or his Commie stooge father. But the INS did not revoke Elián's parole to his great-uncle until April 12, 2000. So lo those many months we kept hearing about the Miami relatives defying the law—"moving the goalposts," blah blah blah—they were doing no such thing. The INS itself had granted Uncle Lázaro legal custody of Elián.

Most important, even after the INS finally did revoke Elián's parole on April 12, the uncle was still not violating any law. He had no legal responsibility to do anything but wait for the INS to come get Elián. Though Janet Reno acted as if she had the powers of a Communist dictator, she was not technically authorized to order Uncle Lázaro to travel to Washington, D.C. The INS's revocation of Elián's parole did not mean the uncle had to bring Elián anywhere. It meant only that the uncle would have to hand Elián over if the INS showed up and asked for him. This the INS never did.

Indeed, though there were plenty of recriminations from Elián's Miami relatives about Reno's plan to send Elián back to Cuba, their lawyers consistently said they would release Elián if the INS ever came to get him. On April 1, for example, Manny Diaz, attorney for the Miami relatives, said, "If INS says, 'The father is here, and we hereby revoke the parole, and we're coming to pick up Elián because we're sending him to his father tomorrow morning,' the family would not interfere." A few days later on ABC's *This Week,* Sam Donaldson asked Diaz point-blank if the relatives would release the child to federal officials. "Yes," he said. "If the INS shows up tomorrow morning to their house and says, 'We are here, we have revoked the parole, we are here to take Elián with us,' they will of course comply with that mandate."

In a *Washington Post* op-ed piece dated April 9, 2000, two former INS general counsels eager to return Elián to a Communist dictatorship said that the INS's unwillingness to revoke the relatives' custody and go pick Elián up could only be based on "the fear that the family might not comply." In other words, when a Muslim who has trained in al Qaeda training camps is loose in the United States, government officials aren't allowed to act until he actually blows something up. But when the government anticipates that law-abiding Cuban-Americans might not comply with them, it's appropriate for the government to act both "preemptively" and "unilaterally" by sending in a federal SWAT team. Even the former INS lawyers had to admit, "To date the relatives have obeyed every order of the federal government, and they have repeatedly stated that they will continue to do so." They were right, of course—the Miami relatives did continue to obey the law.

By contrast, the Department of Justice did not. In applying for a search warrant from a federal judge, INS Senior Special Agent Mary Rodriguez signed an affidavit stating that Lázaro González had "concealed" Elián. Concealed? The entire time Elián was at his uncle's home, Elián was the only person in the entire universe whose whereabouts could be established twenty-four hours a day by the simple expedient of turning on the television. The only way Elián could have gotten any more media coverage would be if he had been living at the Neverland Ranch. Rodriguez also said Elián was being, I quote, "unlawfully restrained"—perhaps by a child car seat. On behalf of U.S. Attorney Thomas E. Scott, Assistant U.S. Attorney Dexter A. Lee signed an application for the search warrant, reiterating the absurdity that Elián was being "unlawfully restrained" by his great-uncle. The application cited the government's need "to protect the life and well-being of the kidnap victim"—making Elián the first kidnap victim in history to be delivered into the hands of his abductors by his own mother.

The claim that Uncle Lázaro was unlawfully restraining Elián—much less that the boy was a "kidnap victim"—was an outrageous lie. Elián was at Uncle Lázaro's home only because no one from the INS ever showed up and asked for him. And yet the allegation that Uncle Lázaro was "unlawfully restraining" Elián was the judge's sole basis for issuing the search warrant justifying the SWAT team's raid. You don't need to believe in a "living Constitution" to grasp that the Fourth Amendment prohibits federal agents from storming a private home on the basis of an invalid warrant. But liberals want us to believe that John Ashcroft is a menace to our constitutional rights. Unfortunately, even a legal finding that the search warrant for Uncle Lázaro's home was obtained by deceit—as it manifestly was—would not prevent Elián from being returned to liberals' favorite Communist paradise after North Korea. The government always had the right to do what it could have done in the first place: Knock on Uncle Lázaro's door and say, "Hi! We're here for Elián" and then send him back to Cuba.

To summarize: The Miami relatives were never, not once, in

violation of any law. In June, long after Elián had been snatched from his Miami relatives, a federal court of appeals pointedly said, "It has been suggested that the precise policy adopted by the INS in this case was required by 'law.' That characterization of this case, however, is inaccurate." The only time the relatives had any legal obligation to do anything other than care for Elián in their home came on April 12, 2000, when the INS revoked Elián's parole. At that point, they had the additional legal obligation of not interfering if someone from the INS—on a break from sending out green cards to terrorists—came to retrieve Elián. The predawn, machine-gun raid was an outrageous, unfathomable violation of law-abiding citizens' constitutional right to be secure in their homes. (But apart from these few details, Reno's handling of the Elián González case was beyond reproach.)

A few weeks after the raid, Elián and his father spent a Saturday night at a dinner party at the Georgetown home of Smith and Elizabeth Bagley, major Democratic fundraisers. Must have been a barrel of laughs for a six-year-old. (It is unclear whether father and son were free to mingle during the party or were kept in a glass cage in the center of the dining room for the amusement of the other guests.) This was an important engagement: Time was running out on reacclimating Elián to life under a Communist dictator, and a Georgetown dinner party with a bunch of Democrats was just the place to start! Soon there were leaks from Reno's reeducation camp, claiming Elián had expressed a desire to go back to Cuba. It's possible. At least he'd be safe from Janet Reno there.

We were told so repeatedly that the administration was merely enforcing "the law" by sending Elián back to Cuba, it started to ring true, albeit irrelevant. It was "the law," after all, that the slave Dred Scott be returned to his master in Missouri. The Supreme Court's refusal to look beyond "the law" to a higher moral authority in *Dred Scott* has not gone down in history as one of the Court's nobler moments. Under scrutiny, however, it turned out that resort to higher law was not even necessary in Elián's case. This time, the law was on the slave's side. The Clinton administration was simply hell-bent on returning Elián to Cuba. When the Florida courts didn't order Elián back to Cuba, administration officials invoked immigration law and denied Elián asylum.

The law on asylum states that "any alien . . . irrespective of such alien's status, may apply for asylum." The Clinton administration first rejected Elián's application, claiming that the words "any alien" excludes six-year-olds. A federal appeals court rejected this absurd interpretation, saying, "The I.N.S. has not pointed to (nor have we found) statutory, regulatory or guideline provisions which place an age-based restriction on an alien's ability to apply for asylum. And we have found no pre-existing requirement that a minor, in submitting an asylum application, must act through the representative selected by the I.N.S." Inasmuch as Elián was an "alien," he came within the meaning of "any alien." (The law isn't as complicated as liberals would like you to believe.)

But a grant of asylum also requires a finding that the alien would face political persecution from his home government. That is a question committed to the discretion of the executive branch—which was then occupied by one William Jefferson Clinton. Cuba has no freedom of speech and no freedom of the press and it jails journalists and homosexuals—but that's not persecution. "Persecution" is John Ashcroft detaining Muslim illegal immigrants after 9/11. Clinton concluded that Elián would not face persecution in Cuba. No court could overrule him.

In June 2000, the Eleventh Circuit Court of Appeals upheld the Clinton administration's decision to deny Elián González asylum, explaining that a federal court had no authority to overrule the president's foreign policy. You can't build a restaurant in this country without fifteen years of litigation. But the courts were very efficient when clearing the way for the government to send Elián back. While noting that many people "might regard things like involuntary and forcible 're-education' as persecution," the court said that was not for the judiciary to decide—apparently unlike abortion, contraception, gay marriage, and the religious content of high school convocations. A judicial decree stating that a person would face persecution in his home country "would have significant consequences for the President's conduct of our Nation's international affairs," the court said, because such a rule concerned "the qualities of the government." And in "no context," the court said, "is the executive branch entitled to more deference than in the context of foreign affairs." Why is it that whenever the federal courts see the merits of judicial restraint, it's in a case where we could really use a little judicial activism, like whether to send a little six-year-old boy back to a Communist dictatorship?

Essentially, the court ruled that it was not for the courts to overturn the president's Commie-loving foreign policy. The determination that a Communist country is a fine place to live was President Clinton's call alone. Naturally, therefore, Elián was sent back to Cuba. Elián was always going to be sent back to Cuba. Liberals like Cuba more than they like the U.S.A.—which admittedly isn't saying much. But they really like Cuba. *Newsweek* reporters Brook Larmer and John Leland sentimentally described Elián's transition from America to Cuba, saying, "The boy will nestle again in a more peaceable society that treasures its children." They even threw in the old chestnut about Cuba's "education and health-care systems" being "among the best in the Americas." Yes, and apparently the concentration camps where Cuban AIDS patients are kept against their will are particularly nice. On the April 3, 2000, *Today* show, NBC's Katie Couric said, "Some suggested it's wrong to expect Elián González to live in a place that tolerates no dissent or freedom of political expression. They were talking about Miami." You'd be arrested for committing a "hate crime" if you talked about Muslim Americans the way liberals talk about Cuban-Americans.

The lesson of Elián González is: If you put a Democrat in the White House, be prepared to live with his foreign policy, which in the Democrats' case consists of warm admiration for Fidel Castro.

Unfortunately, Democrats can't grasp that the reverse is also true: A Republican president gets to effect his foreign policy, too. When the Bush administration announced plans for military tribunals in the war on terrorism, Democratic senator Patrick Leahy accused the Bush administration of thinking it had a "monopoly on authority." In fact, when it comes to waging war, the man the Constitution calls the "Commander in Chief" actually does have a "monopoly on authority." But the Democrats were testy with Bush for not treating the Senate as his "partner" in being commander in chief. The *New York Times* editorialized that Bush's plan for military tribunals was "an insult to the exquisite balancing of executive, legislative and judicial powers that the framers incorporated into the Constitution." The *Times* thinks the president's foreign affairs powers are absolute only when being used to send a child back to a Communist dictatorship. Perhaps we could get liberal support for detaining terrorists if instead of placing them in military tribunals, we sent them to North Korea.

Elián González was sent back to Cuba not because of any law but simply because President Clinton was partial to Communist dictatorships. This is among the many reasons that Democrats should be kept away from foreign policy. I know what you're thinking, but, nope, not even to keep them away from domestic policy.

Fortunately, Cuban-Americans in Florida figured that out just in the nick of time. After giving nearly 40 percent of their vote to Clinton in 1996, they turned out in force in 2000, giving an estimated 77 percent of their votes to George Bush.

Elián's arrival in America had always seemed like a miracle. There were thirteen people in Elián's escape party, including Elián's mother. All of them but Elián drowned at sea. Alone in the world, this little six-year-old boy held on to his inner tube for two days, tossed and turned by the sea under a hot tropical sun. On Thanksgiving Day, 1999, fishermen found him a few miles off of Fort Lauderdale. Some Cuban-Americans compared Elián to

Moses and some compared him to Jesus. In April 2000, Maria Elena Quesada told the *Washington Post*, "Elián is a sign from God saying to the exile community: 'I haven't forgotten you.'" Whatever happened next, she said, was "in the hands of God."

The presidential election that year was decided by less than 500 votes in Florida. If Elián González had never landed in America, Al Gore would have been in the White House on September 11, 2001. Thank you, Elián González, for doing more for freedom in this country than Chuck Schumer, Nancy Pelosi, Tom Daschle, and the rest of that party combined has ever done. ■

14

The Democrats' New Symbol: Two Sets of Standards

———— ■ ————

Whenever you hear that "both Republicans and Democrats" are guilty of something, it's a lie. That's the sound of Republicans surrendering. Democrats savagely attack Republicans, and then Republicans think they've scored a magnificent comeback if they can persuade people that "both Republicans and Democrats" are at fault. (The Republican negotiating motto should be "I'll meet you nine-tenths of the way.") It's never true. Democrats are always worse.

Trent Lott's allegedly racially insensitive toast to Strom Thurmond in late 2002 was nothing compared with Senator Chris Dodd's ostentatiously racially offensive tribute to Senator Robert Byrd less than a year and a half later. Lott's remark was an impromptu toast at an old-timer's hundredth birthday party; Dodd's remark was made before C-SPAN cameras in a speech on the Senate floor. The subject of Lott's toast, Strom Thurmond, had once been a segregationist presidential candidate; the subject of Dodd's tribute, Byrd, had once been a member of the Ku Klux Klan. And not just a member—Byrd had been a recruiter for the Klan, known as a "Kleagle," signing up Klan members for $10 a head.

Most important, Lott didn't mention anything about race at all; Dodd did. In his toast, Lott said if Thurmond had been elected president, "we wouldn't have had all these problems over all these years." That could have been a reference to anything from Jimmy Carter's Iran policy to Bill Clinton's intern policy to *Hee-Haw* reruns. But liberals rushed to fill in the blanks, claiming Lott obviously meant "blacks" when he said "all these problems." By contrast, Dodd left nothing to the imagination in his speech on the Senate floor, saying loud and clear that former Klanner Byrd "would have been right during the great conflict of Civil War in this Nation." A former Kleagle would have been "right" during the *Civil War*?

The difference was so stark it was as if Dodd were taunting Republicans: *Now let me show you what Democrats can get away with*. For months after Lott made his toast, it was headline news across the country. The *New York Times* alone mentioned Lott's toast in 99 articles over a six-month period, including 18 major, front-page stories, totaling about 30,000 words. Indeed, the *Times* did everything short of renaming him Trent "Segregation Defender" Lott. Eventually Lott was forced to step down as Senate majority leader.

But a little over a year later, when a Democratic senator said a former Ku Klux Klan Kleagle "would have been right" during the Civil War, the *Times* ran only one small item on page B-6, titled "Dodd Says He Regrets 'Poor Choice of Words.'" Even that article again flogged Lott's toast—and misidentified Thurmond as a "Republican" during his prosegregation period. Someone at the *Times* might have noticed that the official name of the segregationist party was "The States' Rights *Democratic* Party." Someday, the *Times* will be identifying Byrd's organization, the Ku Klux Klan—an organization that was originally formed to engage in terrorism against Republicans—as "the Republican Party."

Even Democrats complained about a double standard—but they meant against the Democrats. When Lott made his toast to Thurmond, Dodd had gone on CNN's *Late Edition* and said, "If Tom Daschle or another Democratic leader were to have made similar statements, the reaction would have been very swift. I don't think several hours would have gone by without there being an almost unanimous call for the leader to step aside." But about a year later, when Dodd said something indisputably worse, no senator—Republican or Democrat—called for any sanction against Dodd, and the media largely ignored his gaffe.

Moreover, Tom Daschle *did* make a similar statement. The Democratic Senate leader expressly reiterated Dodd's racist point, agreeing that Senator "Kleagle" Byrd "would have been a great senator at any moment," apparently including—as Dodd said—during the Civil War. Democrats seem to have decided blacks are safely on the plantation and Democrats can say or do anything. Not one Republican senator—not even Lott—commented on the Democrats' unseemly tributes to a former recruiter for the KKK. Daschle had the audacity to say Lott's comment was worse than Dodd's. Conservative pundits said the comments were either equally bad or equally innocent—despite the fact that on every score Dodd's comment was worse. Like America's approach to al Qaeda before 9/11, the Democrats have declared war on Republicans and Republicans aren't even aware there's a war going on.

Democrats repeatedly start World War III over Republican Supreme Court nominations, and conservatives respond by saying—as Peter Berkowitz wrote in National Review Online in April 2002—that "both parties must bear responsibility" for the "crude politicization" of judicial nominations. Let's look at that.

After Senate hearings on Clarence Thomas's nomination to the Supreme Court had concluded uneventfully, with even the abortion-on-demand crowd admitting that Thomas's nomination seemed viable and his confirmation all but certain, Democrats suddenly produced a woman who claimed she had been sexually harassed by Thomas years earlier. The harassment was so severe that his accuser, Anita Hill, continued working for Thomas for years, followed him to other jobs, exchanged friendly correspondence with him, and kept the story of her brutal victimization a secret for the next, oh, decade or so. Thomas passionately denied the accusations, as did a dozen witnesses who had worked with both Thomas and Hill. Indeed, every single person who knew both Thomas and Hill believed Thomas. In polls after the hearings, two-thirds of Americans said they believed Thomas. Democratic senator Joe Biden believed Thomas. Even Senator Arlen Specter believed Thomas. Not surprisingly, Republicans believed Thomas, too. Not only that, but they had the audacity to defend him from the Democrats' scurrilous eleventh-hour attack.

On ABC's October 15, 1991, *Nightline,* after Thomas had been confirmed, Ted Koppel described the entire imbroglio as "a battle in which both Republicans and Democrats found themselves covered, not with glory, but with mud." Indeed, Koppel suggested that Thomas had been confirmed because victory had gone "to the side that was better at gutter politics"—a point subtly alluded to in the title of the program: "Did Gutter Politics Get Thomas Confirmed?" You mean like checking the video stores in Thomas's neighborhood to see if he had rented any porno tapes? That kind of gutter politics, Ted? Just think: The same Democratic Party hacks and leg-breakers who looked up Thomas's video rental records from the 1970s are now complaining about the Patriot Act being too intrusive.

Democrats attack, and if Republicans do not immediately acquiesce they are being vicious brutes. It is conservatives' obligation to surrender whenever liberals bully them. Otherwise liberal lips quiver and they start crying and claim you've injured them cruelly. How about: Democrats stop lying about Republicans and then Republicans won't have to defend themselves thereby hurting Democrats' feelings? Why does the armistice begin only after they've taken the first punch?

The confirmation hearings on Democratic nominees to the Supreme Court go somewhat more smoothly. This is because Republicans would apparently confirm a doorknob. During Ruth Bader Ginsburg's confirmation hearings, the nominee said laws against abortion violated the Equal Protection Clause because only women can get pregnant. It's quite a challenge, but this is a legal premise even nuttier than the "penumbra" rationale actually used by the Court in *Roe v. Wade*. On Ginsburg's theory, topless beaches are mandated under the Equal Protection Clause of the Constitution, at least if men are allowed to go topless at a beach. (But the Equal Protection Clause says absolutely nothing about "recounting" some ballots in Florida three times more than other votes.) Some ninety minutes later, when most of the Judiciary Committee members had stopped giggling, Ginsburg said the death penalty for rape was unconstitutional because rape laws were intended to avenge a man's property right: "If [a woman] was raped before marriage, she was damaged goods. It was a theft of something that belonged first to the father, and then to the husband"—whereupon the Judiciary Committee declared a fifteen-minute recess so that Ginsburg's Thorazine could kick in.

Despite the fact that Ginsburg was obviously crazier than a bedbug, Republicans didn't even oppose her on the merits. They certainly did not produce some long-ago coworker to level outrageous sexual harassment charges against her. Then–Senate Republican leader Bob Dole of Kansas said of Ginsburg's nomination to the highest court

in the land, "It looks like a good choice." Republican Senator Charles Grassley said, "She's a Democrat nominee that
even conservatives can like and respect." Former Grassley
aide Samuel Gerdano said the Senate hearing on Ginsburg
was like "Barney the dinosaur for adults: 'I love you. You
love me.'"

In other words, *both Republicans and Democrats* engage
in mud-throwing, gutter politics over Supreme Court nominations.

It is also not true that both Republicans and Democrats
failed to do enough to prevent the 9/11 terrorist attack.
We wouldn't have mentioned it if Democrats hadn't
started blaming the Bush administration for failing to stop
9/11, but gee, I kind of remembered it was the Democrats
who imposed absurd restrictions on law enforcement and
spent the last three decades trying to bulldoze the CIA and
FBI. But I must be wrong. Otherwise how could Democrats have the effrontery to complain about the FBI and
CIA not having done enough to stop 9/11?

In the early 1970s, when Democrats had dominant majorities in both houses of Congress, the Church Committee—so named for its chairman, Democratic senator Frank
Church—went after the CIA like it was going after the
Nazis. The agency was gutted, hampered, and hamstrung
with endless bureaucratic regulations. In 1980, Congressman Ron Dellums (California Democrat)—who believed
that Fidel Castro "would have been right" during the great
conflict known as the Cold War—vowed to "totally dismantle every intelligence agency in this country, piece by
piece, nail by nail, brick by brick." In 1993, the Democratic
caucus voted Dellums chairman of the House Armed
Services Committee in a 198–10 vote. The *New York
Times* took the occasion to shower Dellums with praise.
Throughout the 1990s, Senator John Kerry repeatedly
voted to cut billions of dollars from intelligence services,
so money spent fighting terrorism could be spent on some-

thing more important, like reducing class size. In a 1997 speech on the Senate floor, Kerry bleated, "Why is it that our vast intelligence apparatus continues to grow even as government resources for new and essential priorities fall far short of what is necessary?" There were half a dozen terrorist attacks on Clinton's watch; all of them went unanswered. Ronald Reagan responded more forcefully to Islamic terrorism when he was busy toppling a fifty-year-old Evil Empire. Clinton was in office for eight years preceding the 9/11 attack; Bush had been in office for less than eight months. Most enragingly, everything liberals complain Bush was not doing before the 9/11 attack is what they are furious at him for doing *after* the 9/11 attack.

So let's review: Which party was constantly trying to strip intelligence agencies of money? Which party made it impossible for the CIA and the FBI to talk to each other? Which party demands proof that crime was committed before allowing law enforcement to look for evidence? Which party was responsible for preventing the government from opening Moussaoui's laptop? I think we're talking about the Democrats and their pals. Rules that Republicans disagreed with were put in place over their objections, which prevented them from doing a better job in ferreting out a terrorist plot before it was executed on 9/11—and then the Democrats have the chutzpah to blame Republicans for not breaking the laws Democrats wrote. In response to this, Republicans think it's a great comeback to say "both parties" were equally responsible for the flaws in law enforcement that failed to prevent 9/11.

Finally, it is not true that George Bush would have behaved like Al Gore after the 2000 election had the situation been reversed. This is patently absurd, but it is an absurdity that has gained credibility with the Left's usual mind-numbing repetition. As luck would have it, I know how conservatives would have responded if Bush had lost the election while winning the popular vote. The day before the 2000 election, I was at the editorial meeting of *Human Events*—Ronald Reagan's favorite newspaper, and the most influential conservative publication in America. Editor Terry Jeffrey began the meeting by raising the prospect of Gore's winning the electoral college and losing the popular vote. (Everyone forgot this later, but before the election, that was considered the more likely prospect. No one seems to have ever imagined that the reverse would occur.) Jeffrey said if Gore won the electoral college and lost the popular vote, *Human Events* would run a front-page article vehemently defending the electoral college. No one at the meeting disagreed.

Of course, you don't have to take my word for it. The entire world knows how a Republican presidential candidate would react to winning the popular vote, but losing the electoral college because . . . that's exactly what happened in 1960. Despite the myth of John F. Kennedy's popular vote victory in 1960, more popular votes were cast for Richard Nixon that year. As Pulitzer Prize–winning historian Walter A. McDougall explained in an op-ed in the *New York Times,* in the 1960 election Kennedy did not win all the Democratic ballots in Alabama. Five Democratic independent electors cast their votes for Senator Harry Byrd's segregationist States' Rights Democratic Party that year. Thus, McDougall notes, "at least 173,620 Alabama Democrats were not voting for Kennedy on Election Day." Democrat voters and States' Rights Democratic Party voters together won the national popular vote in 1960 by only 113,000 votes, so that means Kennedy actually lost the popular vote by about 60,000 votes—and this isn't including the massive vote fraud in Illinois and Texas. The myth of Kennedy's popular vote victory in 1960, McDougall says, was started by "Kennedy admirers in journalism and the academy" who at some point began counting the popular votes for Byrd in Alabama as popular votes for Kennedy. Nixon's response to losing the electoral college while winning the popular vote was to concede the election. Al Gore showed the world how a Democrat responds. (So which man goes down in history as "shredding the Constitution"?)

After the 2000 election the media simply assumed that conservatives would have thrown a tantrum had the shoe been on the other foot. One much trumpeted article by *Daily News* reporter Michael Kramer had quoted an anonymous "Bush aide" before the election saying Bush planned to stage a major assault on the election if he lost the electoral college but won the popular vote. Adding credibility to Kramer's account, the anonymous "Bush aide" predicted that if Bush challenged the election . . . the media would back him! Yep, Republicans can often be found whiling away the days boasting about how pro-Republican the media is. (And if all else fails, we can always count on NPR!) But according to Kramer, Mr. Anonymous said, "I think you can count on the media to fuel the thing bigtime. Even papers that supported Gore might turn against him because the will of the people will have been thwarted." Mr. Anonymous also confided to Kramer, "You think 'Democrats for Democracy' would be a catchy term for them?" (In fairness, it sure beats "The People, Not the Powerful.") I gather by "Bush aide," Kramer meant "some guy I met on a bus." Inasmuch as the chairman of the Democratic National Committee has gone on CBS's *Face the Nation* and called me—an opinion columnist with no connection whatsoever to the Republican Party or George Bush—"a top Republican operative," what liberals mean by terms like "Republican operative" and "Republican aide" is rather broad, including "anyone to the right of Barbra Streisand."

While *Human Events* was prepared to back Gore if he was the electoral college winner, liberals' affection for the electoral college seems to depend on how the election comes out, revealing the essence of being a liberal: the absolute conviction that there is one set of rules for you, and another, completely different set of rules for everyone else. Before the election—when Gore was the one who was supposed to win the electoral college but lose the popular vote—University of Southern California law professor Erwin Chemerinsky stated categorically, "The Constitution says that it is the electoral college that determines who is the president. It leaves no doubt." But after Gore lost the electoral college, Chemerinsky found room for doubt! This apparently follows from Chemerinsky's notion that the Constitution is a "living document"—as in Dr. Frankenstein screeching, "It's alive! It's alive!" In the *Los Angeles Times,* Chemerinsky demanded that Florida's 25 electoral votes be split evenly between Bush and Gore in order "to effectuate the will of the people." Florida voters had divided their votes evenly, giving about 3 million votes apiece to Bush and Gore; thus, Chemerinsky said, their "will" was to split their electoral college votes. But that's not how the electoral college works. It was the "will" of 42 percent of California voters that Bush get their electoral college votes, and yet every single one of California's 54 electoral votes went to Gore. Chemerinsky was not so troubled about ignoring the will of 4.6 million Bush voters in California.

As we know from the media consortium that examined Florida ballots after Gore finally conceded, Bush would have won under every recount requested by any party or ordered by any court. But it took the media consortium eleven months of playing "Carnac" with Florida ballots to tell us that. Had the Democrats gotten their way, Florida election officials still would have been holding ballots to the light by the fairly important date of September 11, 2001. ■

NOVEMBER 7, 2000: The networks incorrectly call a Gore victory in Florida while the polls are still open in the Florida Panhandle, suppressing the vote for Bush, who still wins. The networks switch their call to Bush. Gore concedes the election and then retracts his concession, beginning our long election nightmare.

☞ Elections in Clintonville

NOVEMBER 10, 2000

I have a sick, sinking feeling: It's impeachment all over again. But this time it's about the results of a presidential election. Like his mentor Bill Clinton, Al Gore is willing to precipitate a constitutional crisis in order to hold on to power. Democrats are going to turn the world's most successful method of transferring power into another O.J. slow-speed car chase. I no longer care about taxes, abortion, affirmative action—I just want to be rid of these people.

Gore's endgame is to delay confirmation of the Florida vote for as long as possible—just the way his role model of a boss would in these circumstances. (Maybe Hillary can find some extra Gore votes in the White House living quarters where she found those missing Whitewater files that had been under subpoena for two years.) Under the Twelfth Amendment, the president is to be chosen by "a majority of the whole number of Electors appointed." If Gore can prevent Florida from appointing its electors by December 18, when the electors meet, Florida's electors will be excluded. Gore will win with 260 electoral votes. In football this is known as "running out the clock." In politics it's called "cheating."

Gore has a number of stratagems for throwing roadblocks in the way of Florida's appointing electors, mostly featuring time-consuming legal challenges. Nostalgic Stalinists from Brooklyn, now transplanted to Florida in their dotage, have already trotted out lawsuits demanding a second chance to vote because they were confused by the ballot. I've been to law school and I've still never heard of the "Stupidity Clause." It doesn't matter that Gore's legal machinations are precisely as meritorious as President Clinton's "Secret Service privilege" claim. If enough lawsuits are filed, maybe Gore will win the lottery. But in any event, pointless litigation buys him more time.

The law schools are chock-full of droning professors who will attest to the legitimacy of the Democrats' phony legal claims. Having rested up from impeachment and the O.J. trial, they're ready to tackle a presidential election. Liberals have even dusted off the old impeachment catchphrases, condescendingly instructing the public not to make a "rush to judgment" and to "take a deep breath."

As with impeachment, the spin is having its effect: We've gone from a Bush win—subject to a single state's recount—to "the next president, whoever that may be." We've gone from *this will be resolved by 5 P.M. tomorrow* to *this could take weeks.* We've gone from rolling our eyes at hapless old people claiming they slipped and voted for the wrong guy to Morton Kondracke saying of the ballot, "Well, yeah, sure, *now* it looks easy." We've gone from stark horror at the idea of a hostile takeover determining the next leader of the free world to *New York Times* lawyer Floyd Abrams saying that lawsuits are "part of the process." Perhaps strangest of all, the networks have taken the Chinese curse "may you live in interesting times" and begun referring to it as merely a "saying," a "proverb"— even a "blessing"!

We are being inured to the proposition that Bush has not won. Inured to the idea that any states and districts that Gore lost should be subject to a do-over. Inured to the idea that meaningless expressions of popular approval should prevail over constitutional mechanisms for selecting the president. Inured to the notion that the presidential election is not decided on election day, or even the next day, but can sometimes be a months-long process. Once we were shocked by the suggestion that the president could be shown to have committed felonies and still continue in office. But after a while, we got used to that, too.

This isn't a two-out-of-three match. If it were, Bush would have won already. If Gore loses the third recount (which may have been mercifully curtailed by the time we go to press), there will be a fourth. Even if we pretend there is no such thing as a "deadline," it is simply not the case that each recount increases the accuracy of the vote count. Each recount increases the number of scores we have—it does not increase their accuracy. As statisticians quoted in the *New York Times* have said, "Every time you count [large numbers], you're going to get a different answer." Democrats will not accept a recount as true and accurate until they finally concoct one that makes Gore the winner.

When and if that happens, righteous prigs in the Republican Party will somberly call on Bush to concede, to show how honorable "we" are—forgetting the little detail about Bush having already won. Even when they've won, Republicans instinctively lunge toward defeat. In response to the insanely partisan recount of three Democratic districts in Florida, many Republican flacks simply demanded that Republican counties be included in the hand recount, too. How about this for a Republican bargaining position: Bush won. Let's move on (as they used to say about a certain felon in the White House).

John O'Sullivan, editor-at-large of *National Review*, has counseled losing, saying a Gore presidency could be a "blessing in disguise" in light of the fact that the economy is likely to tank during the next president's term. That certainly is a good disguise—it bears not the slightest resemblance to a "blessing." Republicans have gotten good at losing and they want to stick with what they're good at. I'm not convinced you ever really hit pay dirt by losing, but I am positive it's not a good idea right now. It's bad enough for Americans to have witnessed a known lawbreaker sitting in the Oval Office. Criminal methods—perjury, obstruction of justice, witness tampering, using the instruments of federal government to intimidate witnesses—all these have been shown to work. On the heels of a Clinton presidency, it cannot be good for the country to watch a presidential election being openly stolen by the horny hick's vice president. To put it in liberal terms, letting Gore steal this election might "send the wrong signal."

On Day 2 of America Held Hostage, former president George Bush—father of President-elect Bush—was on television commending his son for the dignity he had shown during this national emergency. Yes, we're all very proud. Al Gore, the rube, has demanded a recount in Florida, while Bush has decorously refrained from requesting recounts in Iowa, Wisconsin, and New Mexico—not to mention Missouri, where anti-Bush vote fraud was credibly charged. Bush's brother, the Florida governor, graciously removed himself from involvement in the Florida recount, but Florida's attorney general—who happens to be Al Gore's campaign chairman in that state—boorishly did not. Al Gore goes around loutishly declaring himself the popular-vote champion, while Bush genteelly refrains from any such boasts. The symbol for the Democratic Party shouldn't be a donkey, it should be two sets of standards.

This is no time for Republicans to be putting their good breeding on display. The Democrats have declared war. Jesse Jackson is presiding over rioting in the streets. There is a movement afoot to call in Janet Reno. (Maybe she could send federal troopers to Midland, Texas, to gas George Bush.) All we need now are chickens in the street and beggars with leprosy to complete the picture. This is no time for dignity. President Bush had dignity. Senator Bob Dole had dignity. They lost. In particular, they lost to the two blackguards in the White House now dragging the country into yet another constitutional crisis. It will never end until these people are gone. It's time for Bush to stop acting like a lockjaw Connecticut WASP and start acting like a Texan. ■

NOVEMBER 11, 2000: Bush files suit in federal district court, arguing that the selective recounts violate the Constitution's Equal Protection Clause.

NOVEMBER 13, 2000: U.S. District Court Judge Donald M. Middlebrooks, appointed by Clinton, finds that the selective recounts do not violate the Constitution and orders the partial hand recount to continue.

☞ New Equal Protection Clause: One Man, Several Votes

NOVEMBER 13, 2000

As Soviet dictator Joseph Stalin said, "It doesn't matter who votes. It only matters who counts the ballots." That's just what Al Gore is betting on as he demands his third recount in Florida, this one conducted exclusively in Democratic bastions such as Palm Beach County. A selective hand recount is calculated to ensure that Gore's margin will increase, even if an equal number of Bush votes were missed by voting machines statewide. Any hand recount will increase the total number of votes cast by resuscitating formerly invalid ballots—even ballots that would never be accepted by any voting machine—and the revived ballots will tend to reflect the voting preferences of the district. So hand recounts conducted only in counties Gore won will undoubtedly swell his votes. This is like having mothers judge their own babies in a beauty contest. No one even remotely familiar with the principles of free and fair elections would allow such a procedure to take place, which may explain why we haven't heard from Jimmy Carter.

The media have been portraying the Bush legal team's argument as a general attack on all hand recounts. That's part of it certainly, which should not come as a surprise to anyone who has seen the nudnicks counting ballots on TV—holding punch cards to the light, interpreting smudge marks on the ballots, and consulting tarot cards to divine the voters' elusive intent. This could be the first time in U.S. history the results of a presidential election are determined by TV psychic Miss Cleo. The room for error, manipulation, and general mayhem is gargantuan. Punch card ballots are not like wine; they do not improve with age. Not only do different counties have different rules about how to read the animal entrails, but whenever humans are introduced into any process, there will be errors. Ask NASA about that Mars landing.

But Bush has a separate equal-protection argument that does not indict hand counts across the board but only hand counts conducted exclusively in three lucky Florida Democratic counties. Voters in only certain select counties get to have their ballots given an extra visual inspection, while voters in other counties are denied the right to a visual inspection of their ballots. Allowing the voters of only certain Democratic counties two chances to have their ballots read (first by machine, then by hand) while allowing voters in the rest of the state only one chance to have their ballots read (by machine only) is as unconstitutional as a state's giving Democratic counties two days to vote and Republican counties only one day. Only an insane, rogue judge would allow such a selective recount to take place. (Let's just hope this doesn't end up in the Florida Supreme Court!)

It is true—as Gore's combatants never tire of pointing out—that the scam they've pulled off is permitted under Florida law, which allows candidates to request hand recounts in particular counties within a specified time period after an election. But we have a tradition in this country of striking down state laws that violate the U.S. Constitution. It is hardly "ironic"—the Democrats' attack du jour—for *Republicans* to argue that the Florida law is unconstitutional. Respecting states' rights does not mean respecting a state's right to enforce unconstitutional laws. Even assuming Bush was ambushed and it's his own fault for not demanding a hand recount in Republican-leaning districts, neither Bush nor any candidate has the right to waive someone else's constitutional rights. If Florida citizens have an equal-protection right to have their votes count as much as those of citizens who live in other parts of the state, this is not a right that can be taken away by state law—or the happenstance of one candidate not asking for a recount because he already won the election.

There isn't a lot of relevant precedent—it's not often someone tries to steal a presidential election—but in a case called *O'Brien v. Skinner*, 414 U.S. 524 (1974), the Supreme Court struck down a New York election law less insane than the three-county hand count in Florida. The law at issue in *O'Brien* permitted pretrial detainees to obtain absentee ballots only if they were jailed in a county other than the county of their residence, while inhabitants of jails in the counties of their residence were denied absentee ballots. Because the law distinguished voting rights on the basis of one's residence, the court held, it placed "an unconstitutionally onerous burden on the . . . exercise of the franchise."

But now a federal judge appointed by Clinton found that a state's decision to give the ballots of only some lucky (Democratic) counties an extra visual inspection—based solely on the county of their residence—doesn't violate the Equal Protection Clause. (How odd that a Bill Clinton appointee could have so little regard for the Constitution.) If nothing else, at least it can now be said: The U.S. Supreme Court is more solicitous of the voting rights of the criminally accused than a Clinton-appointed judge is solicitous of the voting rights of Republicans. ■

☞ The Liar Next Time

NOVEMBER 14, 2000

In a fast-breaking story like the Democrats' attempt to steal a presidential election, it can be hard to keep up with the barrage of lies. Before today's lies become "old news," I thought it would be useful to begin a running tabulation. A recount shall be ordered in Democratic counties only.

Lie No. 1: We don't know who won the election yet.

Yes we do. George W. Bush won, albeit extremely narrowly in one state, with a total of 271 electoral votes. Al Gore demanded a recount in one of the states he lost narrowly. After the Gore Loser got his recount, it turned out the winner was . . . Bush again! (Subject only to a final count of the overseas ballots, which have historically gone Republican in Florida and elsewhere.)

Consequently, Gore insisted upon yet a third count, this time with a highly manipulable and probably unconstitutional hand recount in Democratic counties only. By his fourth try Gore will be insisting on counting only the ballots of Gore campaign staff.

Lie No. 2: Gore has nothing to do with the Florida recount, which is mandated by law.

This is false. Gore is completely responsible for dragging the country through this nightmare. The recount is not like some unstoppable Star Chamber death warrant. Gore set the recount in motion when he retracted his concession to Bush on election night. The "shall order a recount" language means only that the loser doesn't have to pay for a recount in close elections. This is not an insignificant point: Recounts are extremely expensive. But it does not mean that in a national election to determine the next leader of the free world the loser is absolutely required to drag the country though seventeen recounts and endless litigation before finally conceding. The Florida recount provision explicitly states, "A recount need not be ordered with respect to the returns for any office, however, if the candidate or candidates defeated . . . request in writing that a recount not be made."

The current crisis is all Gore's fault. He could put an end to this madness at any time by conceding like a man. Bush can't stop it, because he's not the loser. Gore is.

Lie No. 3: The butterfly ballot is illegal under Florida law.

In the November 10 *Washington Post*, Philip Heymann, former Harvard Law School professor and Clinton deputy attorney general, claimed that the now infamous butterfly ballot was "a plain violation of the law." (What a pity that so many Florida precinct chiefs, almost all of them Democrats, approved of the butterfly ballot before the election.) Heymann said the law requires voters to "vote for a candidate whose name is printed on the ballot—place a cross [x] mark in the blank space at the right of the name of the candidate" (Section 101.151). The "critical point" he said, is that the butterfly ballot sometimes required voters to "mark on the right, as the law required, and sometimes on the left."

It might have struck a lot of readers that in addition to stating that the mark must be on the right, the law requires a "cross [x] mark" to be put on the ballot. The butterfly ballot does not permit cross marks anyplace. Stay with me here because this can get pretty confusing if you've never completed the "think and do" section in a *Highlights* magazine. Apparently what voters are required to do with a butterfly ballot is: Find the name of their preferred candidate, follow the arrow from his name to a circle, and punch a hole in the circle. It's all quite baffling, and thank heaven we have fancy, high-priced lawyers to explain complicated legal issues like this.

The reason the circles were not "at the right" of candidate names on the butterfly ballot is that the "at the right" requirement has nothing to do with butterfly ballots. That phrase comes from a chapter tellingly titled "Voting by paper ballot"—you know, the kind of ballot on which it is possible to "place a cross [x] mark in the blank space"—not to be confused with a butterfly ballot. If you read down just a little bit, down past the section on "paper ballots," there is a completely different chapter titled "Voting machine ballots"—which would include butterfly ballots. This section clearly states that the location of the "push knob, key, lever, or other device" must simply "indicate to the elector" which candidate the "push knob, key, lever, or other device" refers to. Remember this episode the next time you hear a Harvard Law professor rambling on about what "the law" requires.

Lie No. 4: Pat Buchanan could not *possibly* have received three thousand-odd votes in Palm Beach County.

Just four years ago Pat Buchanan received three times that many votes in a primary in Palm Beach. A primary! So we know there are at least 9,000 potential Buchanan voters in Palm Beach— and they're the kind of dedicated voters who come out for primaries. This year, the Reform Party candidate for the House of Representatives received over seven thousand votes from Palm Beach.

Lie No. 5: I believe President Clinton.

Whoops! That's "old news." ■

☞ This Is What the Electoral College Is Supposed to Prevent

NOVEMBER 16, 2000

Like many of you, I've been on tenterhooks waiting for New York's junior senator to weigh in on the electoral college. Just days after her election, Hillary finally ended the suspense. She vowed to combat the electoral college so that "the popular vote, the will of the people" will reign triumphant. Where was all this concern for the will of the people when she was trying to shove HillaryCare down our throats?

It should come as no surprise that Hillary opposes the electoral college. Alexander Hamilton explained that the whole point of the electoral college was to interpose "every practicable obstacle" to "cabal, intrigue, and corruption," which, interestingly enough, are the three virtues embossed on the Clinton family coat of arms. The Constitution's roundabout method of choosing a president was intended to frustrate "the adversaries of republican government" and prevent them from gaining "an improper ascendant in our councils."

The framers opposed a pure popular vote for president, believing it would reward oily candidates practiced, as Hamilton put it in *Federalist* No. 68, at the "little arts of popularity"—such as feeling our pain. Instead of relying upon "existing bodies of men who might be tampered with beforehand to prostitute their votes," the people would vote for electors, and the electors would have the "temporary and sole purpose" of choosing the president. The system obviously isn't foolproof: Bill Clinton slipped through the net. But the electoral college has largely been free of the corrupting influences that worried the framers. Electors have occasionally wandered off the reservation, as in 1988 when a lone Dukakis elector cast his vote for Lloyd Bentsen, but as a group they've been pretty incorruptible.

No elector has ever been convicted of taking bribes—as judges and members of Congress have been. The profoundly senile are generally not chosen to be electors, but they can and often do attempt to vote in Palm Beach County. The *New York Times* has never run an op-ed piece proposing that electors trade their votes—as it did recently with regard to Nader and Gore voters trading popular votes across state lines. Electors have never been stolen outright by a Chicago mayor or Texas precinct captain—as popular votes have been. If you try to dump ten thousand electors into Lake Michigan, somebody's bound to notice.

The electoral college is supposed to be enigmatic and complex—the better to foil "foreign powers," "cabals," and other "enemies of republican government," as Hamilton put it. It remains to be seen if the electoral college can frustrate the Clintonized Democratic Party. The current crisis foisted on the nation by Al Gore illustrates with some clarity the sort of mischief the electoral college is intended to prevent. By tallying presidential votes state by state, the electoral college isolates the effect of voter fraud in any one state. If the national total were up for grabs, the whole country would quickly be initiated into the Chicago vote-stealing customs now taking place in Florida. Mysterious ballot boxes would be turning up in every black church in America. Hapless old people nationwide would be taking to the airwaves to claim they were really trying to order a Whopper but somehow ended up voting for Pat Buchanan. Homeless people in Milwaukee would be bribed with cartons of cigarettes to vote for Al Gore—wait, that one actually happened.

Even assuming Gore's popular vote advantage holds (and Bush's numbers would surely be higher if the media hadn't incorrectly projected a Gore win in Florida before the polls closed), the candidates' nationwide tallies are separated by a sneeze. At some point you have to cut off debate or there will be chaos and warfare. People can't live like liberals, endlessly jawboning hypothetical possibilities and refusing to submit to rules. This is America, not the UN. If a lawyer is one day late filing the complaint, Granny loses her slip-and-fall case. That's how rules work. There have to be institutional boundaries to curtail endless navel-gazing. Legitimate claims—which Gore's is not—are sometimes devalued for a stable social order. More horrifying than the curious prospect of a popular-vote "winner" losing the electoral vote is the fact that Hillary "Cattle Futures" Clinton is going to be a United States senator, but those are the rules, and we've learned to live with that.

The electoral college establishes a set of rules and those rules make Bush the winner. Bush has already won more popular votes than Bill Clinton got in either of his elections. You remember Clinton—he was the guy liberals said we couldn't impeach because that would overturn "the results of an election." ■

☞ The Law, Not the Court, Has the Last Word

NOVEMBER 20, 2000—

the day before Florida's Kangaroo Court issued its
first opinion on Gore's tantrum

It ought to be apparent from the way the media have been carrying on about the "highly respected" Florida Supreme Court that the court is on the verge of openly violating the law. By the time this early Thanksgiving issue arrives in your mailbox, the court's willful disregard of the law will probably have attained the status of hard fact.

The portion of Florida election law the court intends to violate is this, Section 102.111: "If the county returns are not received by the Department of State by 5 P.M. of the seventh day following an election, all missing counties *shall be ignored*, and the results shown by the returns on file shall be certified" (part to be flagrantly violated by the Florida Supreme Court in italics). Note that the law, duly enacted by the other two branches of Florida government, does *not* say that results submitted past the deadline "may be ignored." It says "shall be ignored." Note that it also does not say "shall be ignored, unless the Florida Supreme Court disagrees because Al Gore needs more time to steal votes." There's also no reference here to confused, elderly Jews.

That's not the only provision in Florida law that makes the seven-day deadline for submitting election returns mandatory. Section 102.112 (helpfully titled "Deadline for submission of county returns to the Department of State; penalties") states— again unequivocally—"Returns *must be* filed by 5 P.M. on the seventh day following the . . . general election" (part to be flagrantly violated by the Florida Supreme Court in italics).

Under the law, the only person who has discretion to waive the mandatory seven-day deadline is Florida's secretary of state: "If the returns are not received by the Department [of State] by the time specified, such returns *may* be ignored and the results on file at that time may be certified by the department" (part to be flagrantly violated by the Florida Supreme Court in italics).

Whether or not the secretary of state—in her discretion—accepts any late-filed election returns, she is commanded to fine "each board member" of the country election board "$200 for each day such returns are late, the fine to be paid only from the board member's personal funds."

So the seven-day deadline imposed by law is pretty unambiguous. Two sections of Florida law make the deadline mandatory ("shall be ignored" and "must be filed"); another gives the secretary of state discretion to ignore any late-filed returns ("may be ignored")—in which case, the delinquent board members are to be fined personally. There are a lot of murky, complex issues in the law. This isn't one of them.

Naturally, therefore, the Democrats argue that the seven-day deadline imposed by Florida law is optional—just a suggestion, nonbinding thoughts tossed out by the legislature, something akin to Democrats' view of the Commandments against lying and adultery: you're free to take it or leave it. The *New York Times* has referred to "the Republicans' contention that state law allowed no leeway in the deadline." Unambiguous statements of the law are now called mere "contentions" of Republicans.

Al Gore lost the election, lost the recount, and also lost the third manual recount to the point permitted by law. Now he wants a bunch of corrupt judges to change the law two weeks after the election has taken place, to give him yet a *fourth* opportunity to steal enough votes to win.

And the "highly respected" Florida Supreme Court will probably let him. Leave it to Democrats to turn a presidential election into the sequel to "The Night the Lights Went Out in Georgia."

Not to worry, though. The Florida Supreme Court justices may think they have the powers of Pol Pot, but there are other branches of government capable of following the law, despite the rulings of this Kangaroo Court.

One surmises that Secretary of State Katherine Harris will have some crucial role to play. The giveaway is that Harris hasn't done anything yet, but she is already being viciously attacked by the Democrats' Election-Stealing Task Force. Harris has been called a "crook" by O.J.-and-Clinton defender Alan Dershowitz. She has been called a "hack" and "Soviet commissar" by Gore spokesman Chris Lehane. (Liberals take a principled stand against the death penalty in all circumstances except in cases of killing the messenger.)

The *Washington Post* devoted an entire article to sneering about Harris's makeup: "they were the [eye] lashes of Tammy Faye . . . cartoon lashes," "she looked as if she were wearing a mask," "to be honest, [she] seems to have applied her makeup with a trowel." Would that the evil Katherine Harris were a ravishing sexpot like Janet Reno or Ruth Bader Ginsburg! This is the same crowd that will tell you with a straight face that Bill Clinton is "handsome"— exhibit A of people being literally blinded by their ideology. Harris is getting the Linda Tripp treatment from liberals because she seems like the sort of person inclined to follow the law. Democrats hate that. The Florida Supreme Court they can work with; obsessive rule-followers are the bane of Democrats' existence.

Suppose the Florida Supreme Court directs the secretary of state to violate the law—as they surely will—by ordering Harris not to ignore election returns submitted after the mandatory statutory deadline she is required by law to follow. Should Harris obey the written law, enacted by the legislature and signed by the governor prior to knowing whom the law would benefit? Or should Harris follow the results-oriented, lawless ruling of seven judges— all appointed during Democratic administrations—intended to

give a Democratic presidential candidate yet a fourth shot at stealing an election he's already lost? Hmmm . . . that's a tough one.
The rule of law, or a partisan scam—which should prevail? Either
way, Harris will be violating some official decree.

Harris ought to follow the real law. That's not going to be easy.
The *Washington Post*'s attacks on Harris's mascara are just a sample
of what is to come if Harris fails to obey a dishonest ruling from
the Kangaroo Court. The *Washington Post* has a rapid-response
team fully assembling even now, prepared to attack Harris's hair,
her wardrobe, even her accessorizing if it will help Al Gore. If
Harris follows the written law, the Florida attorney general, Bob
Butterworth—also known as "Gore's Florida Campaign Chairman"—may well try to prosecute Harris for violating a court order.

In the end, it might dawn on the members of the Florida
Supreme Court that other government officials will be reviewing
their handiwork. The U.S. Supreme Court might do loopy things
from time to time, but it's hard to imagine that the justices could
miss the unmistakable language of Florida's seven-day deadline on
election returns. It's also hard to imagine that they would overlook
the rank corruption inherent in a court altering the rules for judging a presidential election after the election has already been held.
If the Florida Supreme Court judges are not as stupid as they are
partisan, the court might well follow the law to avoid being overruled by the U.S. Supreme Court and shut down this nightmare
once and for all. But I wouldn't count on it. The "most ethical administration in history" can't seem to leave without giving the
country one last kick in the pants. ∎

NOVEMBER 21, 2000: The Florida Supreme Court orders manual recounts to continue until November 26, or early November 27.

☞ Certify the Electors, Then the Judges

NOVEMBER 22, 2000

After having denounced the Florida Supreme Court as a corrupt and dishonest Kangaroo Court long before its lawless ruling earlier this week, I'm kind of relieved that they didn't prove me wrong. Still, it's breathtaking how totally detached from any sort of legal reasoning the court's decision is. While taking a sledgehammer to the law, this Warren Court with a thyroid condition insisted it was engaging in a delicate and serious balancing analysis, affording due concern to competing interests. Except the problem is: That's not their job. The Florida legislature had already engaged in a balancing of competing interests. And it came to a different conclusion.

Taking into account many and various factors—finality, accuracy, sore losers demanding interminable recounts, and so on—the Florida legislature decided that counties would be permitted to indulge in all the recounting they desired, but then they had to turn in their election returns seven days after the election. The decision of where to strike the balance has already been made and enacted in law—written by the legislature, signed by the governor, put on the Florida statute books. But Al Gore lost the election, lost the recount, lost the absentee ballot returns, and lost all the manual recounts that could be completed within seven days. So he asked the Florida Supreme Court to give him more time to keep recounting, relying on Bill Daley's genetic vote-counting skills to eventually make him the winner.

The problem was that pesky seven-day deadline (aka "the law"). The Florida Supreme Court was not interpreting an ambiguous statute, resolving a conflict, or filling in a blank space in the law. What Gore requested, and what the Kangaroo Court granted, was a judicial coup overturning the unambiguous seven-day deadline put on the books by the other two branches of government and replacing it with a nineteen-day deadline.

The court papered over its lawless ruling with this inane sophistry: If the law permits recounts, it must permit recounts to go on and on and on, until the loser can finally steal enough votes to win or the whole country dies of exhaustion. It is true that manual recounts are permitted by Florida law. But that doesn't mean there's no deadline. Gore may as well have argued that because there's Christmas shopping, there's no such thing as Christmas. You can shop and shop and shop—but Christmas imposes a deadline. Florida counties can indulge in recounts to their hearts' desire, but seven days after the election is the deadline. If Florida election law had a motto, it would be "When it absolutely, positively has to be filed within seven days."

To put the law in terms understandable to Democrats: You can give homeless people cigarettes in exchange for votes, you can register felons and illegal immigrants, you can count "dimpled chads," animal entrails, ballots pulled out of disappearing Vote-o-Matics. But you have to steal all the votes you're going to steal by 5 P.M. seven days after the election. If Gore still hasn't won, you have to stop bothering everyone and go home.

But Gore's idiotic demand found a receptive audience with the Florida Supreme Court. It appears that the justices' mental acuity has been impaired from the fumes of all those ambulances they spent their careers chasing. (The chief justice of that court gave $500 to Clinton-Gore in 1992, but did not recuse himself from a case in which Gore is a party—which at least reversed the usual flow of funds one expects in such a court.) The justices claimed to be stumped by blindingly clear statements of the law. It's as if the justices of the Florida Supreme Court read Oliver Wendell Holmes's stirring words about judges having "jurisdiction only to declare the law" and not "authority to make it"—and said, "Huh?

Does anybody know what that means?" Now the whole country isn't sure whether to wait out the process or call 911.

The Florida court's ruling is even more insane than the typical judicial imperialism. Usually, when judges are hankering to legislate, they choose territory where there is no written law at all. Where the law is silent, they concoct "penumbras" and "emanations" and discover hitherto unnoticed, invisible provisions. At least with *Roe v. Wade,* the U.S. Supreme Court invented clauses where the Constitution was silent. The Florida decision is even more lawless than *Roe.* Florida law isn't silent on the question of when the election is over. In no uncertain terms, the law imposes a mandatory seven-day deadline on the submission of election returns. The Kangaroo Court simply took the seven-day statutory deadline and replaced it with a nineteen-day deadline.

Poor Secretary of State Katherine Harris is subject to directly opposed legal commands. She is, of course, required to follow Florida law, as are all Florida residents (except, evidently, judges). And Florida law explicitly directs her to "ignore" any election returns submitted after the seven-day deadline and to certify the electors. This is, quite literally, the job she swore an oath before God she would faithfully execute. But at the same time, the order of the Florida Supreme Court commands Harris to defy the law— the one duly enacted by proper legislative channels long before anyone knew precisely how much time Al Gore would need to steal votes (which is apparently nineteen days). In order to follow the real law, she will have to violate the court's lunatic order.

It's as if state law set a 60-mile-an-hour speed limit and the Florida Supreme Court came along and ordered Katherine Harris to drive her car at 120 miles per hour and to disregard traffic signals (provided George W. Bush were in front of her car). Sane state officials in Florida still have to do their jobs. As Ken Starr can attest, Democrats make it extremely difficult for people to do their jobs when that consists of enforcing the law. But it's Katherine Harris's job to certify the electors as provided in the real law (seven-day deadline) and not the Junta's manifesto (nineteen-day deadline—until we sober up long enough to start issuing more orders).

The legislature has a responsibility to protect its authority to write laws and have them given effect. It should act promptly to confirm the electoral slate certified by Harris. And Governor Jeb Bush has a duty to enforce the law. We're sorry he's the president-elect's brother, but it was the networks that created this fiasco in Florida—rather than in a state where the president's brother is not the governor—by incorrectly calling the election for Gore while the polls were still open in Florida. Instead of being a gentleman to thieving Democrats, it's time for Jeb to exhibit a little of that famous Bush gallantry toward a beleaguered state official trying to obey the law. ■

NOVEMBER 22, 2000: Gore says both he and Bush should start planning their White House transitions.

NOVEMBER 24, 2000: After legal experts have assured us that the U.S. Supreme Court won't hear Bush's appeal of the Florida Supreme Court's decision, the Court agrees to hear the case.

NOVEMBER 26, 2000: Florida Secretary of State Katherine Harris certifies the election results on the date set by the Florida Supreme Court. Bush wins a 537-vote victory over Gore.

☞ Things Only a Democrat Will Say with a Straight Face
NOVEMBER 29, 2000

If you have any doubt that Al Gore's selfless pleas for "democracy" are part of his scheme to steal the election, consider this: In one of

Gore's many pending lawsuits against the Florida election results, he asked the court to declare him the winner on the grounds that there are still thousands of votes to be counted. That's funny. If the ballots haven't been "counted" yet, how does he know he's the winner? In order to make sense of this, you have to presume that Gore won the election (as Gore clearly has done) and work backwards from there.

In the category of "Things Only a Democrat Would Say with a Straight Face," Florida State Representative Debra Danburg told Chris Matthews on CNBC's *Hardball* that some voters meant to vote but didn't actually punch the ballot (for Gore, no doubt) be-cause—I quote—they were "afraid to hurt the machine."

Unpunched ballots are a gold mine for Democrats. As we know from the chads littering the floors of the "counting" areas, these late-breaking votes are not being "counted" three weeks after the election—they are being cast. Through pure brazenness Democrats are turning uncast votes into votes for Gore. We've en-tered the *Alice in Wonderland* realm of polls, spin, and counting earwax on punch card ballots. This is the liberals' playing field. Truth doesn't matter, honor doesn't matter, fairness doesn't matter. Once Democrats are freed from the tyranny of objectivity, they are liberated to lie and cheat and steal.

Liberals always prefer spin to hard facts. They promote the concept of a "living" Constitution unbounded by the objective and determinant words in the document. They want phony polls to de-termine constitutional questions like impeachment. They want the census to be determined by "sampling" rather than an "actual enu-meration," as the Constitution specifies. They want criminals pun-ished not merely for the act of, say, committing murder, but also on the basis of a subjective determination of whether the murder was committed out of "hate"—in contradistinction to all those crimes being committed out of love. They want SAT scores dropped as a criterion for college admissions, preferring purely subjective evalu-ations of the applicant's "diversity." It's probably just a matter of

time before someone in the Gore camp declares the recounts irrelevant because "people have different ways of voting."

After suffering through months and months of polls purporting
to demonstrate that 20 million "swing voters" were wildly rushing
back and forth each week from Bush to Gore, Gore to Bush, and
on and on, finally—finally!—we took the only poll that counts.
A focus group of 100 million Americans chose a president by cast-
ing secret ballots. Gore lost but refused to concede . . . and now
we're right back to hearing who the polls say should be president.

Gore's lawyer David Boies—fast becoming the William Ginsberg of the 2000 election—argued that the unambiguous seven-
day deadline for election returns imposed by Florida law is
optional. In short order the media took up the cudgel—*Who's to
say? There are arguments on both sides. Democrats and Republicans are
both just playing politics. . . .* And giving the final patina of legitimacy to a crackpot argument, the Florida Kangaroo Court "interpreted" "seven days," as written in the law, to mean "nineteen
days." That really happened.

Only a Democrat could come up with such brazenly illogical
arguments. Gore insists on manual recounts. But he wants manual
recounts in only three heavily Democratic counties in a single
state—so that "every vote" will count! Democrats denounce the
"butterfly" ballot as racist and borderline sadistic. But the ballot
was designed by, and its use approved of by, Democrats. Democrats claim a manual recount will remedy the dastardly "butterfly"
ballot which caused confused old people to vote for someone other
than Gore by mistake. But they have not explained how a manual
recount is going to help people who claim they voted for the
wrong candidate. Democrats claim Gore voters were intimidated
from approaching the polls—which I suppose is possible if Gore
voters follow traffic laws as well as they follow voting laws. But
they have not explained how a manual recount will rectify alleged
voter intimidation. It is all utterly incoherent, but coherence is ir-

relevant. Only spin matters. Al Gore and the Democrats will say anything, do anything to win. ▪

NOVEMBER 30, 2000: A Florida legislative committee rec-ommends a special session to name the state's 25 represen-tatives to the electoral college.

DECEMBER 1, 2000: The U.S. Supreme Court hears ar-guments on the Florida Supreme Court's extension of the election deadline.

DECEMBER 4, 2000: The U.S. Supreme Court vacates the Florida Supreme Court's decision and remands to the court with instructions to please read the Constitution and federal law next time.

☞ *National Lampoon*'s Florida Supreme Court Vacation

DECEMBER 6, 2000

Despite morale-boosting claims in the mainstream media that the U.S. Supreme Court's unanimous ruling didn't really do any-thing—or as Al Gore put it (*Twilight Zone* theme music here), was "neutral," perhaps even "favorable"—the U.S. Supreme Court's opinion just knocked the air out of the Supreme Court of Florida (SCOFLA).

For openers, the Supreme Court vacated SCOFLA's silly rul-ing. It didn't have to do that. The Court could have remanded with instructions without vacating the decision. The Court could have declined to review the decision altogether—as scores of legal "ex-perts" swore up and down it would. Not least of all, the Court could have affirmed the opinion as a proper exercise of SCOFLA's judicial powers. As Florida's learned state senator Debbie Wasserman explained on CNN's *Crossfire*, "There is something called the separation of powers, and the system of checks and balances. And the judicial branch—unfortunately, Governor Bush doesn't realize this—but the judicial branch interprets the laws." Apparently, the United States Supreme Court didn't "realize" it either. After getting a gander at how SCOFLA exercised the "separation of powers," a unanimous U.S. Supreme Court said: VACATED. The Court referred SCOFLA to the Constitution and federal law as helpful little guideposts the Florida court might want to consult before issuing any more opinions. (The Court also ordered state senator Wasserman to retake ninth-grade U.S. history.)

The Supreme Court repeatedly invoked the deference normally accorded state courts, but said there are exceptions. After one such tribute to the nobility of state courts, the Supreme Court said, "But in the case of a law enacted by a state legislature applicable not only to elections to state offices, but also to the selection of presidential electors, the legislature is not acting solely under the authority given it by the people of the state, but by virtue of a direct grant of authority made under Article II, Section 1, Clause 2 of the United States Constitution."

State courts may deserve deference, but if a state court orders federal troops to attack Canada, for example, the order is going to be reversed. And if a state court "interprets" a seven-day deadline in the state's law on presidential elections to mean a nineteen-day deadline, the court's decision will be reversed. The real Supreme Court reminded SCOFLA that a presidential election is a federal issue, a matter committed to the state *legislatures* by the U.S. Constitution—and if you try to usurp the role of the legislature, the real Supreme Court is ready to reverse you.

It's going to be an adjustment for SCOFLA. Back during the halcyon days when SCOFLA thought it was immune from review, the court's hearings resembled nothing so much as a Soviet show trial. During oral argument, one Florida justice impertinently demanded of Bush's attorney, "What are the laws in Texas, Mr. Carvin?" What does one say to something like that? The justice may as well have asked him if he didn't think "nineteen" was a prettier word than "seven." For the benefit of the justices on the Florida Supreme Court, as well as anyone else without a working knowledge of the law, the election laws of other states have no bearing on the election laws of Florida. None whatsoever. The election laws of Uganda have as much binding authority in Florida as the laws of Texas. Raising the election laws of Texas is the sort of glib political jab the six viewers of CNN's *Crossfire* expect to hear from Paul Begala right before he cuts to a commercial. It is astonishing that a judge would make it.

While claiming total befuddlement at SCOFLA's decision, the Supreme Court said it sure hoped the court hadn't ignored the Constitution and federal law! This is how parents discipline small children: *I sure hope no one's reading under her covers after bedtime!* The Court's face-saving directive was clear to all but the willfully blind. Of course, SCOFLA found the meaning of the word "seven" to be an impenetrable mystery, so there's no assurance that subtlety will work with these guys. But there is one entity for whom we can be pretty sure the Supreme Court's ruling will not be a devilish puzzle—the Florida legislature. As the Supreme Court reminded the world, the Constitution provides that states shall appoint presidential electors "in such manner as the legislature thereof may direct." So knock yourself out, Seminole County! Exclude military ballots! Exclude ballots from all registered Republicans! The Florida legislature has the last word. ∎

DECEMBER 8, 2000: The Florida Supreme Court orders manual recounts for 43,000 ballots that registered no vote. The court adds 383 votes to Gore's total.

DECEMBER 9, 2000: The U.S. Supreme Court orders the manual recounts stopped.

DECEMBER 11, 2000: The U.S. Supreme Court hears oral arguments on the Florida Supreme Court's decision.

DECEMBER 12, 2000: The Florida House of Representatives votes to certify a slate of electors for George W. Bush.

DECEMBER 12, 2000: The U.S. Supreme Court finds that the half-assed recount ordered by the Florida Supreme Court is unconstitutional. Seven justices find it violates the Equal Protection Clause; three of the seven find it also violates Article II of the Constitution, which grants state legislatures authority to determine the manner of choosing presidential electors (the correct grounds). Only two justices, Ruth Bader Ginsburg and John Paul Stevens, find that a partial recount of only some ballots in some Florida counties does not violate the Equal Protection Clause. According to Justice Ginsburg, the Equal Protection Clause refers only to abortion, it has nothing to do with voting rights.

☞ My Court Is Bigger Than Your Court

DECEMBER 12, 2000

Apparently, there are few better methods of becoming a trusted TV legal "expert" than being consistently wrong in your legal analysis. Smugness while issuing idiotic opinions is especially valued. There was a lot of both the week before the real Supreme Court vacated the Florida Kangaroo Court's crackpot interpretation of "seven days" in Florida election law to mean "nineteen days." Now that the U.S. Supreme Court has overruled everything the Florida Supreme Court did and ordered the recounts to stop, let's look at how the professors fared in their predictions over the last few weeks.

On CNBC's *Rivera Live,* Harvard Law professor Alan Dershowitz, finally emerging from his shell, explained the Supreme Court's original decision to hear the case this way: "Let me give you a theory of why I think the Supreme Court took the case. I think the Supreme Court took the case because of Jim Baker. The Supreme Court saw Jim Baker trashing a state Supreme Court, saying, in effect, that it's okay to defy the law of the highest court of the state, and I think there's some justices who said, 'We have to protect the judiciary here.'"

"Reversed!"

On Fox News's *O'Reilly Factor,* another Harvard Law professor, Martha Field, predicted that the "main principle" of the Supreme Court's ruling would be that "the U.S. Supreme Court will not interpret the meaning of state law." The learned professor sniffed, "I don't think the U.S. Supreme Court has a lot to say about this."

So there you have it. Except—oops—"Reversed!"

Professor Field was not only completely wrong, but irritated that Florida legislators had the audacity to disagree with her uniformly incorrect statements of the law. She scoffed at the little people in the Florida legislature for "suggesting that their decision would trump a decision of the Florida Supreme Court." If they believed that, Professor Field said, "they're pretty far out of line."

In fact, what the U.S. Supreme Court found "pretty far out of line" was the Florida Supreme Court's delusion (shared by Professor Field) that it could trump the Florida legislature in determining the manner in which presidential electors are appointed. So out of line that it reversed SCOFLA's ruling, explaining that "the State legislature's power to select the manner for appointing electors is plenary; it may, if it so chooses, select the electors itself." Students at Harvard Law School intent on learning the law, as opposed to learning to be arrogant while incorrectly stating the law, would be well advised to take some sort of legal correspondence course.

And not just Harvard students are in trouble. Nat Stern, a law professor at Florida State University, was quoted in the *St. Petersburg Times* saying that the election case was "a fairly ordinary matter" of a state court doing its job and that of course Bush would lose. Constitutional law professor Martin Redish of Northwestern University said, "I'd be flabbergasted if the Supreme Court actually accepted the Bush argument." (This was in contradistinction to the watertight argument of the Florida Supreme Court, which is: "It depends on what the meaning of 'seven' is.") In an article for *American Lawyer Media,* Vikram David Amar, constitutional law professor at Hastings College, referred to the "creative—and dare I say extraordinary"—argument of the Bush lawyers that the Florida Supreme Court ruling was invalid because it extended election deadlines that were set before the election.

A unanimous U.S. Supreme Court didn't find the Bush argument so "extraordinary." To the contrary, the Court agreed with Bush's lawyers, saying, "A legislative wish to take advantage of the 'safe harbor' [by enacting a seven-day deadline for election returns] would counsel against any construction of the Election Code that Congress might deem to be a change in the law." Seven justices agreed that what the Florida Supreme Court had done violated the Constitution's Equal Protection Clause. Five justices found that the only remedy was to stop the recount and allow the legislature to certify the electors.

Blowhard liberal law professors can never stick to just being wrong. They are compelled by some invisible force to be both wrong and supercilious. Law professor Lis Wiehl of the University of Washington repeated the Dershowitz theory that the Supreme Court had agreed to hear the case in order to express its deep and profound respect for SCOFLA. On CNBC's *Rivera Live,* Professor Wiehl said, "And I think that's why the Supreme Court decided to take this, not because they thought there was something wrong with the decision, but that they're going to uphold the [Florida] Supreme Court decision."

Professor Wiehl got testy with fellow *Rivera Live* panelist Joe DiGenova for questioning the great and inscrutable wisdom of the SCOFLA: "When he—when he talked about the Florida courts' actions being questionable, I'm so tired of that." The tired Professor Wiehl continued, "If you look at the Florida Supreme Court opinion, what you'll see is that they took two conflicting statutes and they did what courts all over the country do every day. They interpreted two statutes, and they chose to go with the statute that was the more recent statute and the one that is more particularized. That is just common, everyday judicial interpretation."

And now it's also: "Reversed!" ■

15

Hello, Room Service?
Send Up a Bottle,
a Blonde, and a Gun

———■———

☞ Ruger Is a Girl's Best Friend

JULY 1999

About a year ago a mugger just waltzed right up to me on a bridge here in Washington, D.C. It was early evening and I was a stone's throw from my apartment in what is considered a nice neighborhood, as neighborhoods go in "Murder Capital"—the richly deserved nickname for the nation's capital. I won't belabor my cunning and completely fortuitous escape, except to say that for the few minutes I was standing there waiting to be mugged, I was fuming. I knew he knew I didn't have a gun.

It's illegal here in Murder Capital. Not merely illegal, but a felony carrying up to a five-year prison sentence. Just as I could look at my prospective mugger and see that he was not the kind of fellow who would be a fanatic about property rights, he could see from fifty yards that I was not the type to be casually committing felonies.

I wanted a gun, but more than that, I wanted him to think I might possibly have a gun. I wanted him to at least accord me the respect I get from criminals in other cities, where they have to exercise a little creativity, lying in wait, sneaking up from behind, hiding in bushes and dark alleyways, that sort of thing. No, in Washington, they just walk right up to you on a brightly lit street. As an apparently law-abiding citizen, I am ostentatiously defenseless.

But let's forget about completely defenseless little me on the bridge for a moment.

The framers' primary reason for including the right to bear arms in the Bill of Rights was so that the people could defend their liberties against a tyrannical government, just as they do by virtue of the vastly overrated First Amendment. As Alexander Hamilton observed in *Federalist*, No. 29, if the government were to "form an army of any magnitude, that army can never be formidable to the liberties of the people while there is a large body of citizens, little if at all inferior to them in discipline and the use of arms, who stand ready to defend their rights and those of their fellow citizens." Some may be willing to rely on withering editorials in the *New York Times* to preserve their liberty. I'd prefer a tasteful Sigsauer.

If the courts ever interpreted the Second Amendment the way they interpret the First Amendment, we'd have a right to bear nuclear arms by now. Interestingly, the Supreme Court is constantly having to remind Americans of their First Amendment rights, issuing over a hundred decisions in the past half century alone. The Court has only ruled on the Second Amendment in a handful of cases ever—the last time in 1939. But still, about half the citizenry deeply, passionately believe that they have a right to bear arms. Give the First Amendment no support from the courts for over half a century and see if anyone remembers why we're supposed to let Nazis march in Skokie.

But the half of the country that intuitively assumes a right to bear arms don't live in my neighborhood. That's why I'm getting exasperated with the constitutional argument. Too few people—

girl people in particular—appreciate the central point: Guns are our friends.

When it comes to the First Amendment, everyone gets warm patriotic feelings, tearing up over John Stuart Mill's "marketplace of ideas." They think immediately of our right to engage in political speech, scientific research, and avant-garde art and to burn politicians in effigy (or maybe that's just me). Speech on the fringe, like Aryan Nation propaganda or *Screw* magazine, is understood to be an unpleasant if inevitable by-product of a freedom we cherish.

But with the Second Amendment, all we hear about is the downside. It's all *Screw* magazine. No upside, just school shootings and the apocryphal danger of "gun accidents." In 1945, for every million Americans, there were 350,000 firearms and 18 fatal gun accidents. By 1995 the supply of guns had more than doubled to 850,000 per million, but fatal gun accidents had plummeted by two-thirds to only 6 per million.

Guns are our friends because in a world without guns, I'm what's known as "prey." All females are. Any male—the most sickly 98-pound weakling—could overpower me in a contest of brute force against brute force. For some reason, I'm always asked: Wouldn't I prefer a world without guns? No. I'd prefer a world in which everyone is armed, even the criminals who mean to cause me harm. Then I'd at least have a fighting chance.

What the arms-control faithful really want is a world without violence—not a world without weapons. These are the ideological descendants of the authors of the Kellogg-Briand Pact, which purported to outlaw war. But we can't have a world without violence, because the world is half male and testosterone causes homicide. A world with violence—that is to say, with men—but without weapons is the worst of all possible worlds for women. As the saying goes, God made man and woman; Colonel Colt made them equal.

Prey like me use guns against predators about a million times a year. Fifteen different studies (including studies sponsored by gun-control groups) estimate that guns are used to stop a crime several hundred thousand times per year at the low end and several million times at the high end.

I especially want criminals to have to worry that I might be armed. In numerous surveys, criminals have confirmed the blindingly obvious point that they are disinclined to attack a victim who might be armed. Countries with those fabulously low crime rates and fabulously fascistic gun-control laws—like Canada, the Netherlands, and Britain—have more burglaries of occupied homes than we do in the armed-to-the-teeth United States. Canada's burglary rate of occupied homes is over three times that of the United States. Although murder is lower in Britain, rape, robbery, burglary, and assault are all substantially higher than in the United States.

It must be said, the framers were not unaware of the crime-prevention qualities of firearms. Standing armies in this country and in France had become nothing more than roving bands of criminals. The Second Amendment was, in part, a response to these earliest cases of police brutality. (Why is it that the same people who have the least confidence in the police and military are the most willing to allow only the police and the military to have guns?)

Democratic darling Thomas Jefferson, for example, wrote, "Laws that forbid the carrying of arms . . . disarm only those who are neither inclined nor determined to commit crimes. . . . Such laws make things worse for the assaulted and better for the assailants; they serve rather to encourage than to prevent homicides, for an unarmed man may be attacked with greater confidence than an armed man."

That night in Washington, by the way, I was rescued by a man. I'm all for men, I like to have them around all the time. But they can't be. Sometimes they have to go buy things for us. More pertinently, sometimes they're ex-husbands coming after us with machetes. We live in a world in which men are supposed to freeze when we say "no," our bodily integrity is sacrosanct, we are autonomous beings, I am woman hear me roar, but we're not allowed to defend ourselves from a physical attack with the only effective means possible. Just stand waiting on the bridge, and hope for a nice man to come along. ∎

☞ I'd Burn My Neighbor's House Down
SEPTEMBER 15, 2000

I did everything I could and it's not my fault. As a legal resident of the noble 4th District of Connecticut—once represented by glamorous, brilliant, smart-aleck Clare Boothe Luce, and currently represented by a hand-wringing pantywaist—I tried to take out the pantywaist.

For those of you who don't have Irish Alzheimer's (we forget everything but our grudges), Representative Chris Shays was one of only five Republicans to vote against the impeachment of a lying, felonious, contemptible president; one of only two Republicans to go on a whirlwind, grandstanding campaign against the impeachment of the lying, felonious, contemptible president; and the only Republican called on by Representative John Conyers (Democrat of Michigan) on the day of the vote to argue against impeachment of a lying, felonious, contemptible president.

I didn't run in the primary against Shays, because, as a writer, I'd have to give up my livelihood to do so. If I were a dentist, I could continue to remove molars while campaigning against Shays. As a writer, I'd have to abandon my career the moment I announce. I'll give up a month or two for a grudge match, but not six, seven, or eight.

Moreover, an excellent Connecticut Republican, Jim Campbell, did step to the plate to primary the pantywaist, offering Nutmeggers the enticing prospect of voting for someone who not only would represent Republicans but also would represent the district, rather than representing the *New York Times*. No one had ever heard of Campbell. He emerged out of nowhere, and the principleless Connecticut Republican Party establishment was dead-set against him. (If Joseph Stalin called himself a Republican and was an incumbent in Connecticut, he'd have the full backing of the state party apparatchiks.) Still, Campbell took about 40 percent of the vote from Shays.

Though I wasn't willing to sacrifice my profession (and life) for the absolute minimum six months it would have required to run in a primary, I was willing to forsake my profession (and life) for about six weeks simply to achieve the greater glory of causing Shays to lose. My idea was that I'd run a total sham, media-intensive, third-party, Jesse Ventura campaign for one month before the election, and hope for enough votes to cause the (official) Democrat to win.

I just needed to find a third party that would have me. Since I hate the government, and the Libertarians hate the government, I figured: That's my party. Except the thing is, the local Libertarians' opposition to government is totally focused on one small aspect of government: the drug laws. Until going through several weeks of negotiations with the Connecticut Libertarian Party over their pro–drug legalization stance, my position on drugs was to refuse to discuss drug legalization until I don't have to pay for the food, housing, transportation, and medical care of people who want to shoot up heroin all day.

It's not like we live in the perfect Libertarian state of nature with the tiny exception of those pesky drug laws. We live in a Nanny State that takes care of us from cradle to grave and steals half our income. I kept suggesting to the local Libertarians that we might want to keep our eye on the ball. (One of the Libertarians' other big issues is privatizing Yosemite. Seriously.)

In theory, our areas of agreement should have included, among other things: eliminating the Department of Health and Human Services; eliminating the Department of Education; eliminating the Department of Commerce; eliminating the National Endowment for the Arts; eliminating the National Endowment for the Humanities; eliminating the Department of Agriculture; eliminating the Department of Housing and Urban Development; eliminating the Department of Transportation; and eliminating the progressive income tax and instituting a flat tax.

Our sole area of disagreement was whether to abolish the drug laws before or after completing the above tasks. But that wasn't good enough for them. I was deemed not a "true Libertarian" by the CT-LP because my idea was to defer the drug-legalization issue until we had made a little more headway in dismantling the Nanny State.

(The National Office of the Libertarian Party grasped this point, and was only concerned about what I would say about their presidential candidate. I believe we could have worked something out, but that was at least a practical problem. While I'm sure someone who loathes the government would make a splendid president, I couldn't credibly pretend I thought either that Harry Browne had a real shot at winning or that a Gore presidency wouldn't wreck the country.)

The other "evidence" these Sherlocks found contradicting my claim that I do too hate the government was that in a computer search of my name plus "conservative," versus my name plus "libertarian," there were only 400 hits with "libertarian" and over a thousand with "conservative."

But, of course, unless I throw a tantrum and demand a particular designation, I have no control over how I am identified on television or anywhere else. For example, TV producers have an annoying predilection of calling anyone who is not a socialist a "GOP adviser." I finally blew up at this uninvited designation, saying I only wished the "GOP" would take my @#%&* advice. That ended the "GOP adviser" title.

Once I was on a program with Angela Davis, who has run for president on the Communist Party ticket several times. I worked for a Republican senator one time for two years and that's the extent of my involvement in partisan politics. Davis was identified as a "community activist" and I was called a "Republican lawyer." To be completely accurate, I don't call myself anything. As far as I'm concerned, I'm a middle-of-the road moderate and the rest of you are crazy.

The final nail in my coffin was that I hadn't been attending the CT-LP's meetings, which seemed rather incongruous to the concept of libertarianism. These people oppose organized government, but demand an organized CT-Libertarian Party that will enforce party discipline like a Soviet commissar. In any event, I've changed my position on the drug-legalization issue after conferring (interminably) with the Libertarians on the matter. There's a joke about a Frenchman, an Englishman, and a Russian who are told they have only one day until the end of the world. The Frenchman says he will spend his last day with a bottle of Bordeaux and a beautiful woman. The Englishman says he will take his favorite sheepdog for a walk across the moors. The Russian says he will burn his neighbor's house down. I'm with the Russian.

Consequently, since the CT-LP has denied me my sole remaining goal of defeating Chris Shays, I have moved from being completely uninterested in drug legalization to being virulently, passionately opposed to it. See this space next week for why drug legalization is an incredibly dumb idea—the second in my new Irish Alzheimer's series. ■

☞ Drug Shills

SEPTEMBER 14, 2000

Like everyone else in America, I had never really listened to the arguments of the drug-legalization crowd since: It's not going to happen. These are like people whose area of expertise is pottery in ancient Tibet. Their ideas could be completely spurious, but no one cares enough to bother arguing with them.

Stupid Argument No. 1: The first argument one always hears about drug legalization is: Alcohol and cigarettes are at least as bad and probably worse than marijuana.

Gary Johnson, governor of New Mexico, only the most recent Republican to discover that the path to fawning media coverage is to adopt liberal positions, is quoted in just such a fawning article in the *New York Times*, saying, "Last year 450,000 people died from smoking cigarettes. Alcohol killed 150,000, and another 100,000 died from legal prescription drugs. How many people died last year from the use of marijuana? Few, if any. From cocaine and heroin? Five thousand."

I'll accept all the drug legalizers' lying statistics and demonstrate that their arguments are still stupid, but you have to say, someone who lies in formulating an argument is not to be trusted. And that figure on cigarette deaths is a bald-faced lie.

The 450,000 figure refers to all "smoking-related" deaths. A "smoking-related" death is any death that, theoretically, could be connected to smoking—even if the person who died never came within a mile of a lit cigarette. "Smoking-related deaths" include emphysema, any respiratory disease, heart attacks, and a plethora of cancers. If an obese ninety-nine-year-old man dies of a heart attack while shoveling snow, his death would be listed as a "smoking-related" death.

Under the methodology used by the American Cancer Society to come up with the statistics on "smoking-related" deaths, 504,000 people die each year from insufficient exercise, and 649,000 die from improper diets. Indeed, the books are so cooked on the "smoking-related deaths" that a 1993 article in the *American Journal of Epidemiology* was able to show that by using the exact same methodology, smoking *saves* 277,621 lives each year.

There are no serious studies of the long-term effects of daily marijuana use, but we know marijuana smoke is much worse for the respiratory system than cigarette smoke. The only reason you never hear about people dying from marijuana is that—well, for one, like the old-timer shoveling snow, a pot smoker who dies of emphysema is listed as a "smoking-related" death. But also people don't smoke pot the way they smoke cigarettes. One reason for that is: Marijuana is illegal. If people smoked pot as much as they drink and smoke, we undoubtedly would have a much better sense of the health consequences of sustained marijuana use, but by then it would be too late. Once people have spent a few decades smoking pot at restaurants, family gatherings, and football games, it's going to be hard to create a taboo around marijuana use. See, for example, Prohibition.

But even stipulating to the drug legalizers' phony statistics, let's assume alcohol and cigarettes induce dependency; ruin lives; cause disease, depression, countless traffic injuries, and fatalities; and increase the incidence of homicide and suicide. This is supposed to be an argument for legalizing another drug like them?

Stupid Argument No. 2: Prohibition failed.

No it didn't. Prohibition resulted in startling reductions in alcohol consumption (over 50 percent), cirrhosis of the liver (63 percent), admissions to mental health institutions for alcohol psychosis (60 percent), and arrests for drunk and disorderly conduct (50 percent).

That doesn't mean Prohibition was a good thing. Christ's first miracle wasn't turning wine into water. But Prohibition is one of the strongest arguments *against* legalizing marijuana. The reason Prohibition failed was that alcohol had become a respectable libation, it was part of the social fabric in high society and low. Once the genie is out of the bottle (so to speak), it's hard to put it back.

Stupid Argument No. 3: One of the leading Libertarian arguments made for legalization is that drug use would decrease if drugs were legal, because, I quote, the government just "messes everything up." While it's hard to argue with that premise, one thing governments are really good at is criminalizing stuff. People like me hate the government because of the things it prohibits— earning money, flushing toilets, owning and developing property, and engaging in political speech—not because the government isn't good at it. The idea that making an activity legal would reduce its incidence is preposterous. This is exactly like the Clintonian statement about wanting to make abortion "safe, legal and rare." The most effective way to make something "rare" is to make it illegal.

It ought to stop you in your tracks that politicians like Gary Johnson want to legalize drugs so the government can tax drugs. Whenever politicians say they want to restrict something by taxing it, you know they're lying: The very fact that they are taxing it means they need people to keep doing it. Otherwise they'd run out of revenue. Just as they are doing with gambling, the government is trying to horn in on a criminal enterprise. It never occurs to politicians to make government more like Microsoft. Successful capitalist enterprises they want to destroy. It's the Crips and Bloods they see as a useful organizational model.

Stupid Argument No. 4: We've "lost" the drug war.

We've "lost" the murder war too—if winning is defined as total abolition. People persist in taking drugs because they want to. We don't have laws prohibiting what no one wants to do. Laws against drugs have surely reduced drug use, just as laws against murder and robbery reduce the incidence of murder and robbery.

Stupid Argument No. 5: As aspiring pothead Governor Johnson puts it, "Half of what we spend on law enforcement, half of what we spend on the courts and half of what we spend on the prisons is drug related. Our current policies on drugs are perhaps the biggest problem that this country has."

I won't dispute the governor's presumably apocryphal facts. We spend a lot of money enforcing murder and robbery laws, too. So what? It's supposed to be a disaster for the country that the drug laws keep a lot of people gainfully employed working for law enforcement and prisons? That doesn't mean we should randomly criminalize things to create jobs for prosecutors and prison guards, but the horrifying consequence of providing people with good jobs at good wages is not a strong argument for repealing drug laws. As an added benefit, the drug laws help rid the streets of people who are, by definition, the sort of people who are willing to break laws.

Stupid Argument No. 6: The quintessential Libertarian argument for drug legalization is that people should be allowed to do what they want with their own bodies even if it ruins their lives. But that's not true. Back on earth, we live in a country that will not allow people to live with their own stupid decisions. Ann has to pay for their stupid decisions.

We have to "invest" in our future by supporting people who freely choose to inject drugs in their own bodies and then become incapable of holding jobs, obtaining housing, and taking care of their children. So it's not really quite accurate to say drugs hurt no one but the user, at least until we've repealed the welfare state. And don't give me the now-we'll-have-to-regulate-fatty-foods slippery-slope argument. Precisely because you can see a difference in eating a hamburger and smoking crack means there is a difference between the top of the slope and the bottom. That, in a nutshell, is why pure slippery-slope arguments are always fatuous.

Even John Stuart Mill said there were some things people could not be permitted to choose to do with their own bodies in a free society: "The principle of freedom cannot require that he should be free not to be free. It is not freedom to be allowed to alienate his freedom." Drugs enslave people. Maybe cigarettes and alcohol do too, but that just brings us back to Stupid Argument No. 1. ■

☞ Capitol Punishment

APRIL 1999

The really, totally appropriate setting for writing an article about dating in the nation's capital would be in my D.C. apartment home, alone on a Saturday night. By chance, however, I'll be in New York this weekend. By chance, I've been in New York every weekend for approximately the previous 147 weeks, give or take a few shuttle mishaps.

But since all my stuff is in D.C., I do have to drop in occasionally. Consequently, I've become a minor authority on dating in Washington. Maybe not dating exactly but one crucial element of any date: "the Ask." Boys in Washington don't know how to ask for a date. What they do is try to trick you into asking them for a date. They say, "I know you're really busy, so call me when you'd like to go out to dinner" or "Call me when you're back in Washington" or, my favorite, "Are we ever going to get together?"

What are you supposed to say to completely insane things like that? I've never figured that out, which is why these conversations tend to end in hostile silences. "Call me when you'd like to go out to dinner" isn't asking for a date; it's asking me to ask you for a date.

For my male readers in Washington, asking for a date entails these indispensable components: an express request for a female's company on a particular date for a specific activity. Oh yes, and the request has to be made to the female herself. Roughly once every two weeks, I get a female on my answering machine asking me if I'd like to go out with some dumbass male friend of hers who's too afraid to call me himself. (For those outside Washington, I'm not kidding.)

This isn't a screeching, hate-filled, anti-male screed. It is a screeching, hate-filled anti-D.C. screed. There's no large sociological point about relations between the sexes here. It's Washington.

I know this, because while D.C. males are on my answering machine with vague announcements that they've called, I still get messages from boys in New York saying, for example, "I have tickets for the opera next Friday. Would you like to go?" (If you're having trouble following the plotlines here, I never actually answer my phone; I sit at my computer listening to people leave messages and respond, if necessary, by typing out an e-mail.)

Males in every other city know how to ask for dates. So it's not me, it's not feminism, it's not the millennium.

I've begun aggressively inquiring of every female I come across,

"Pardon, but have you noticed that boys in Washington don't know how to ask for dates?" The consistent response has been a raft of stinging denunciations too numerous to catalogue here. If I were asking something preposterous, like "Say, have you noticed all the alligator carcasses in the street lately?," I wouldn't be getting such emphatic affirmations every time.

Recently, I asked a female on Capitol Hill about the phenomenon and she said right off, as if I were a psychic, "We were just talking about that on Saturday night!" She had been talking about it in a mixed crowd and reported that the boys began hectoring the girls—*C'mon, this is the twentieth century. You're modern women, you can ask for dates.*

I asked her if waiting for women to ask them for dates had worked for these guys. No, they just sit around with friends, year after year, waiting for their theory to play out. This is also how government programs are conceived and tested, so it makes perfect sense that only in Washington are males still waiting for action on the no-ask dating plan.

In fact, the incapacity of the D.C. male to ask for a date is the perfect synecdoche for this whole pathetic city. First, there is a total absence of normal civilized conventions in Washington. The customer is always wrong, the cabs don't have meters, and complete strangers ask for the sports section of your paper on the subway. In every real job I've ever had, it was standard for the boss to give a Christmas gift to the people who work for him. In Washington, minimum-wage staffers take up a collection to buy Christmas gifts for the senator and chief of staff.

There's a reason boys asking for dates is a convention of civilized society. Someone's going to have to face rejection. It may as well be the aggressive, testosterone-pumping, hunter male. Speaking for myself, I'll take 69 cents on the dollar (or whatever the current feminist myth is) never to have to ask for a date. But the whole point of this convention is to reduce, if not eliminate, the need for rejection anyway.

The entire dating system runs on implicit understandings. If the hunter male doesn't like a girl, he doesn't call. That's the end of it. If the hunted female doesn't like the boy, she's unavailable without a good excuse three times in a row. No explanations, no hurt feelings. When you start fiddling with a centuries-old system like this, you're just asking for trouble. If you can't operate by covert signals, you're going to get horrifying, misery-inducing explanations. (And if you ask a stranger for her sports section on the subway, you're going to get Maced.)

Second, no one makes any money in D.C. From this, I deduce that it's important for young men to make loads of money. There may be grating aspects to twenty- and thirty-somethings earning kazillion-dollar bonuses, but at least it gives them the self-confidence to ask for a date.

Third, TV is reality in Washington. Restaurants close at 8 P.M. There are a few really, really late-night places that stay open until nine or ten, but even these sometimes close unexpectedly at eight. (In addition to being always wrong, the customer is an impediment to the serious business of Washington, which is watching TV.) So everyone is home watching TV all the time.

Like most New Yorkers, I never had a TV, but I got one when I moved to Washington. The peculiar thing about watching TV after a long lapse is that you are actually aware of TV changing your perception of reality. I've started subconsciously associating men of the cloth with murderous, Nazi conspiracies, for example. I've got a million more television-induced perception shifts, but the relevant one here is that females are invariably the sexual aggressors on TV. The typical romantic overture on the small screen is: Boy meets girl, girl drops dress.

TV hasn't ruined me yet, though. My romantic fantasy is still this: Girl meets moving-company guy, girl moves back to New York. ∎

☞ A Republican Tribute to John

JULY 22, 1999

If you grew up when the most prominent living Kennedy was Teddy, a lot of the Camelot imagery is probably lost on you. So it was a little disconcerting, for this Republican at least, to be bombarded with the usual Camelot cant in connection with the death of John F. Kennedy Jr. John was no run-of-the-mill Kennedy. The media's Kennedy fever demonstrates nothing but journalists' own insularity and narrow-minded parochialisms. I knew John F. Kennedy Jr. I worked with John F. Kennedy Jr. John F. Kennedy Jr. was a friend of mine. And you, Senator Kennedy, are no John F. Kennedy Jr.

So before the public memory of John is overtaken by the deluge of nauseating news coverage reminiscent of the bulimic princess Lady Di, I'd like to pay a Republican tribute to John. You don't have to believe in abortion on demand to see that John Kennedy Jr. actually did have the looks, charm, intelligence, humility, kindness, and class the mainstream media mysteriously discern in all Kennedys.

The first time I met John was at a *George* magazine luncheon at Le Cirque a few years ago to honor the magazine's "Twenty Most Intriguing Women in Politics." First of all, consider that I was named one of them. I've been reading those women's magazines' special power-woman editions for years and have yet to see a right-winger in the lineup. Gloria Steinem and Patricia Schroeder—yes. Phyllis Schlafly and Bay Buchanan—not a chance. But the magazine founded and edited by the scion of the country's most famous Democratic family was truly a political magazine, not a Democratic magazine (as *Vogue, Cosmopolitan, GQ, Esquire, Time,* and *Newsweek* are).

After the lunch, John asked me what the reaction had been at MSNBC to a blurb *George* magazine had run on some unflattering remarks I had made on air about Pamela Harriman earlier in the year. It was nothing worse than what the *New York Times* had said about Harriman in its formal obituary, and considerably less harsh than what Maureen Dowd had written about Harriman's funeral, but unflattering nonetheless. I told John MSNBC had fired me for it—but rushed to assure him, not to worry, they fired me a lot and had always hired me back. I still felt kind of bad about all the firings. The network had hired me because I was a conservative and then would fire me every time they discovered I was a conservative. But I might as well have told John I had won the Nobel Peace Prize. He perked right up, his face brightened, and he asked me what other comments I had been fired for.

Now, my Democrat friends in Washington had seen the tapes and they thought MSNBC was nuts, but this was the first time anyone had treated the firings as if they were a notch in my belt. And not just anyone, but Über-Democrat, definition-of-cool John Kennedy Jr. He thought it was tremendous that MSNBC kept firing me—he told me I was like Howard Stern—and a few months later *George* ran a bemused item on my repeated firings. That was the first time I stopped feeling lousy about my tenuous work relationship with MSNBC. (And the first time I stopped feeling lousy about John's death was when someone sent me an e-mail saying only "maybe he's waving at you." I keep waving out my window back at him now.)

About a year and a half after the luncheon, John hired me as a regular *George* columnist. Wow! This really was a new kind of Democrat. John wasn't a part of the older generation of Stalinist liberals who try to censor differing viewpoints and engage in the "politics of personal destruction" to harm those who disagree with them. As his magazine's motto says, this was "not just politics as usual." The importance of what John was doing to political discourse in this country cannot be overstated. If you've ever been on the receiving end of the "politics of personal destruction," it's not always fun being called a racist, sexist, homophobe, etc. etc. One can see why a lot of people might decide to opt out of the whole political enterprise altogether. Through his magazine, and his very being, John had begun to take the bitter acrimony out of political dialogue. While political neophytes out of Hollywood yammer about getting the younger generation involved in politics, John actually did it.

Precisely because he was a both Democrat and a celebrity, John was able to begin altering the political dialogue in a way that no one else ever could. Not only was he making politics fun and interesting, but he was fair and kind to his presumed political opponents. This, truly, was "not just politics as usual." That is why it is so painful to hear the media talk of John in terms of the Kennedy mystique of liberal mythology or to hear him compared to a dysfunctional, air-head princess. Despite the liberal media's praise, John was a great man. Perhaps more important, he was a good man.

I was often asked—and not just by Republicans—if John was a mere figurehead at *George* and an intellectual lightweight. Neither could be farther from the truth. John would call me directly to propose article ideas. When I accepted and then tried to reject his idea that I write a column about dating in Washington, he refused to let me change my mind. He was right: For a while, that piece was my most-read column. He read all my columns during editing, and would sometimes call to comment on them full of the sort of enthusiastic praise that makes a writer want to write an even better one next time. And let me mention again: I'm a *Republican.* My most recent article for *George* was a paean to the virtues of guns. John was particularly fond of a piece I wrote for *George* attacking a certain congressman (representing the fourth district of Connecticut)—for being a rotten liberal. In one of our last conversations, he made fun of one of the magazine's liberal columnists for being a predictable bore.

Despite the massive publicity John had received for flunking the New York bar examination, he was quite bright—contrary to all my preconceptions about a Kennedy. During my book tour for

High Crimes and Misdemeanors, I spoke at a *George* magazine breakfast about my book. John came to the meeting, and after my presentation he was the first to start asking questions. He had clearly read the book—unlike so many interviewers—and his questions, though from an opposing view, were good ones. In fact, John's questions raised some of the exact same points renowned intellectual William F. Buckley would be raising with me on *Firing Line* a few weeks later. I was so surprised by what clever questions John was asking that I realized even I had been subconsciously assuming that someone so good-looking could not possibly be intelligent, too.

It's not particularly meaningful that he failed the bar exam, if you think about it. I've taken the New York bar exam, and I can tell you it's not an IQ test. It's an exam about facts you have to learn. I would imagine that a celebrity stud living in New York City in his twenties might well be tempted away from the grindstone.

That is part of what was so impressive about John. Though on some level it sounds preposterous, it probably isn't a day at the beach to be remarkably wealthy, famous, and good-looking. Why bother getting up in the morning? Why not go the way of Howard Hughes or Elvis? It has always impressed me about Steve Forbes, for example, that he was born fabulously rich and still manages to be productive and civic-minded and have a normal, happy family life. John, too, could have become a degenerate rich kid. But he didn't. Rather, he was making it safe to talk about politics again. For that, this Republican is deeply grateful and mourns his loss. ■

16

What You Could Have Read If You Lived in a Free Country

———— ■ ————

Take heart, young right-wingers. Just a few short years ago, I was nearly living in a box under the Brooklyn Bridge. For more than a decade, virtually no one would publish me. Even after actively soliciting articles from me, magazine editors always decided they were more interested in publishing conservatives in the abstract than in reality. (Maybe a sensible conservative like David Gergen, who worked for Clinton, but not that nut Ann Coulter.) I was the polar opposite of Maureen Dowd, who has apparently never written anything that was rejected. For the first few years my literary agent had me as a client, all she did was negotiate "kill fees," which magazines pay writers for articles they've commissioned but don't publish, like a consolation prize. It's like a parting gift that a game show loser gets after they say, "Thanks for playing our game!" and hustle you off the set. Turning lemons into lemonade, conservative writer George Gilder has managed to get kill fees from magazine after magazine for the exact same article.

Interestingly, other than scholarly journals, the only

two magazines that would publish me were Ronald Reagan's favorite publication, *Human Events*—even though it had to break a half-century "no girls" rule to hire me—and John Kennedy Jr.'s *George* magazine. Even after I wrote my first *New York Times* best-seller, *High Crimes and Misdemeanors*, no newspaper in America big enough to be on LexisNexis would carry my syndicated column. In fact, so few papers carried it, I only earned a few hundred dollars a month from that column (for tax mavens, that works out to about $6 after taxes). I would have made more money by delivering newspapers than by writing for them.

Even my books got killed. After my second book, *Slander*, was killed by the publisher, I went months and months without a possibility of publication, even as prepublication orders were pouring in. I not only had no publisher, I had to pay back the book advance I had originally gotten from HarperCollins (owned by right-wing media magnate Rupert Murdoch, pretty much proving Al Franken's theory of a *conservative media bias*—italics added to indicate sarcasm, Al!). In other words, I had a somewhat different experience from that of Jayson Blair, who was writing front-page articles for the *New York Times* before he had, in the strict sense, graduated from college.

But then Crown Publishers came along and published *Slander* and it was another hit. And then they published *Treason* and it was my third hit. Now everything has changed. I live in a nice house. It is still the case, however, that, except for *Human Events*, no national publication will print my columns. And it is still true that no newspaper in America big enough to be on LexisNexis will carry my syndicated column. Apparently the only people who want to read me are actual Americans. Liberals defend every manner of pornography and filth on the grounds that it's "what the people want." Editors, we are constantly lectured, only "want to sell newspapers." The only material too prurient to let the public read is anything written by a conservative.

And I'm a conservative success story! If editors believe the general public has no interest whatsoever in hearing from a conservative whose three books were best-sellers, how many right-wing writers out there have we never heard from at all? How many never had a Crown Publishers come along and publish them after a decade of rejection? How many switched careers—or switched their politics? How many boxes can fit under the Brooklyn Bridge? Alas, we will never be among *Cosmopolitan* magazine's "fun fearless females" like Kate Harrington (February 2000) "because as costume designer for last summer's smash hit *The Thomas Crown Affair,* she made the fearless move to dress Rene Russo in Celine and Halston." With no rich liberals to give us MacArthur Foundation "genius" grants or to buy up radio stations for us (after throwing minorities off the air in Los Angeles, New York, Chicago, and San Francisco), conservative writers merely face starvation. On second thought, young right-wingers, abandon hope of ever being a writer. Become an editor.

The few conservative publications that exist aren't much help. Among the stupidest theories liberals have about conservatives is the idea that we are a well-oiled political machine. Hillary Clinton somberly warns of a Vast Right-Wing Conspiracy. The *New York Times* has actually published a flowchart of the "neoconservative" cabal. Conservatives couldn't put together a three-car funeral without producing six books denouncing one another. It is doubtful that two neoconservatives could agree on where to have lunch—which is going to complicate their secret plans to trick the nation into perpetual war. Even apart from the pathetic efforts of craven conservatives to win admiring glances from editors of the *New York Times* by attacking fellow conservatives, right-wingers get into death-match struggles about who said what at a dinner party ten years ago when no one is watching. And those are the good times. With precious few column inches to fight over in conservative publications, conservative writers typically detest one another.

By contrast, liberals are good Leninists: They care only about power. Teddy Kennedy crawls out of Boston Harbor with a quart of Scotch in one pocket and a pair of pantyhose in the other, and Democrats hail him as their party's spiritual leader. President John F. Kennedy would actually edit news articles written about him by his flunkies in the press. Consequently, only recently have we discovered that for the last eight years of his life, JFK was a stupefied drug addict basically being carried around on a gurney with a needle hanging out of his arm. (The *New York Times* noted that "even a partial list" of Kennedy's medications as president is "a daunting one, including hydrocortisone, testosterone, codeine, methadone, Ritalin, antihistamines, antianxiety drugs, barbiturates to help him sleep, and regular injections of Procaine to ease his back.") Ah, the charm and athleticism of "Camelot." Al Franken is fawned over in a *New York Times Magazine* cover story written by Russell Shorto, who is fawned over in a *New York Times* book review written by Kevin Baker, who is fawned over in a *New York Times* "New and Noteworthy" list. But leave the reservation and the liberal admiration ends. Myrna Blyth, who was editor of *Ladies' Home Journal* for two decades, wrote a book saying women's magazines are run by liberals and the *Times* gave it a snippy review—written by the daughter of Clinton's White House counsel.

Liberals never argue with one another over substance; their only dispute is how to prevent the public from figuring out what they really believe. Meanwhile, it is a source of constant alarm to conservatives that the public will *not* understand what they really believe. After the spectacular success of Ronald Reagan's presidency, white-shoe WASPs took a look at Reagan's legacy and said, "That's enough of that. Now we're going to make liberals love us." Vice President George Bush promised conservatism with a smiley face. To show how nice he was, Bush even raised taxes. Unfortunately, that made the rest of the country hate him and liberals weren't voting for him. That's our well-oiled political machine!

Until a few years ago, there was no alternative media that allowed conservatives to make themselves clear. This generated terrific defensiveness. As an upstart insurgency fighting all organs of elite opinion, a lot of conservatives talk in the stilted, paranoid manner of people who believe they will be shot by the Nazi SS if their words are somehow misconstrued.

> *Don't mention the blacks!*
> But I just said Lincoln freed the slaves.
> *People will misunderstand.*
>
> *Don't mention the Jews!*
> I just said I supported Israel.
> *Shhhh! Liberals will say that's anti-Semitic.*

I never got the hang of being scared of liberals. The technical term for conservatives who are not afraid of liberals is: "unpublished." But my columns won't be put in a lockbox! The following columns are what editors didn't want you to see. Perhaps these columns are not as good as I thought they were. But on rereading them, I still think they're better than they are! So here it is—a right-wing Lollapalooza, Ann Coulter's Private Stock.

NATIONAL REVIEW

Far from a right-wing cabal greasing the wheels for young conservatives, *National Review* would not even publish my article on "Feminist Legal Theory" in 1991 after soliciting the piece. I was a year out of law school and had about as much interest in "Feminist Legal Theory" as I did in handicrafts or gardening, but that's what editor John O'Sullivan wanted. He gave me a 1988 symposium on "Women in Legal Education—Pedagogy, Law, Theory, and Practice" in the *Journal of Legal Education* and asked me to write about it. (I didn't grasp the concept of "word limit" yet, so this is basically the first half.)

☞ Call Me Ms.

1991

At a party on the Lower East Side last night I happened to glance up at the video screen as it was showing a man slitting the throat of a beautiful naked woman lying face-up on a table. I was in a cab headed back uptown approximately sixty seconds later, and it occurred to me: I'm pretty sure that, even in her wild youth, Mother never attended parties that included video displays of women's throats being erotically slit. This naturally led me to wonder: Just why is it that my generation is constantly being harangued into paying obeisance to the dazzling triumphs of the feminists?

We are now more frequently raped, pimped, divorced, cheated on, and—if one's dating proclivities run toward Democrats—expected to spring for dinner. But at least no sane man would dare speak the word "Miss." Freedom at last! It's not just because bras burned while men fiddled that I hate the feminists. The real reason I loathe and detest feminists is that real feminists, the core group, the Great Thinkers of the movement, which I had until now dismissed as the invention of a frat boy on a dare, have been at the forefront in tearing down the very institutions that protect women: monogamy, marriage, chastity, and chivalry. And surveying the wreckage, the best they have to offer is: "Call me Ms."

No, wait, that's not entirely fair. They can also credibly lay claim to an entire complex of idiot rules that can only be explained as a pathetic effort to recapture the power women once had. But frankly, chastity, virtue, and the affectation of weakness were nuclear weapons in the area of social control. "Nonsexist" phraseology doesn't rise to the level of a peashooter. Where we once had chivalry and protectiveness, feminists now promote a "duty to rescue." Where the crime of seduction once protected our reputations, feminists offer only "date rape." And where the concept of virtue once prevented "unwanted" pregnancies, they give us our precious legal right to knock off the fetus.

I'd like to mention at the outset that roughly 90 percent of women who call themselves feminists haven't a clue what the Grand Wizards of the movement are up to, nor do they particularly behave like good feminists. Many do, of course, presume deep primal malevolence on the part of the male of the species, quickly take offense at courteous gestures from men, and call themselves "Ms." But I have yet to meet a female who could respect any man who tries to split the check with her. We pretty much emerge from the womb with an instinctive understanding that all research and development costs fall to the male.

I definitely sympathize with the impulse to ignore feminist source material. Of all the ludicrous victim groups debuting every five minutes in this country, Rich White Women From Scarsdale is responsible for more rolled eyeballs than the rest combined. Having delved into the Womyn's white papers, I'm here to report that it's what I imagine alternating between Quaaludes and nitrous oxide would be like—and for the record, I have no actual experience with this little experiment. On one hand, you get absolutely ox-sedating sentences like these: "People are decontextualized from the analysis, yet no one really lives an acontextural life." But then you get real howlers like "We especially attach ourselves to such categories as male/female because of our own psychological development in a culture that has made gender matter." (Boy, think of all the neato articles *Cosmopolitan* magazine would run but for the importance our "culture" has placed on gender:

"How to Weld Sprockets with a Socket Wrench." Let me just say, I am on tenterhooks awaiting the coming of this revolution!) Having read the stellar compendium of feminist writings about the "law," I present the following not as an account of substance abuse but as a report on feminist "legal" "theory."

One scholarly piece on "Women in Legal Education" begins cheerfully with this long self-description: "Feminism is a dirty word. I never fail to be amazed at the strength of the hostility the word generates. . . . Feminists are portrayed as bra-burners, man haters, sexists . . . castrators, [lesbians] . . . bitchy, demanding, aggressive, confrontational and uncooperative, as well as overly sensitive and humorless."

I would add to this that feminists are also marauding, bloodthirsty vipers—but more on that later. Considering the number of otherwise sane and apparently heterosexual men who openly call themselves "feminist men," regularly employ the convoluted "he or she" phraseology, and will endure tongue-lashings for such high crimes as opening doors for distaff ingrates, I would say this description tends toward the self-indulgent.

Be that as it may, what, really, is the most open of possible minds to make of this: "There is substantial ferment within the feminist community . . . over whether a reasonably clear line can be drawn between forced sexual encounters, which should be criminalized as rape, and all mutually chosen heterosexual encounters." Of course, it would be narrow-minded stereotyping to leap to the conclusion that these girls, as it used to be phrased, "wear comfortable shoes." They could just be really dumb.

But even brains with improperly firing neurons could be expected to occasionally hit upon some positive aspect of heterosexuality. Not the feminist "legal theorists." Heterosexuality for these gals is just another form of oppression—the "heterosexist assumption" is right in there with racism and sexism as an oppression that must be eradicated. Thus, one feminist law professor provides examples of classroom exercises to "help us guard against the presumption of race, the presumption of class, and that one presumption that seemed to occur more than all the others: the heterosexist assumption."

She delightedly describes the effect these exercises worked upon her students: By the end of the course, students were able to call each other on their own biases.

Consider the following student dialogue:

> FIRST STUDENT: It isn't fair, men never worry about birth control. I mean don't they even care? Finally I asked one of them, "Why don't you ever ask?" And he said it was because he knew I wouldn't risk it. Really, how could he know? . . . That leaves women with only two choices: take full responsibility or claim celibacy!
> *[Slight pause, second student looks at professor before speaking.]*
> SECOND STUDENT: Only two choices? Don't you want to reconsider that statement?
> FIRST STUDENT *[in a defeated whisper]*: The heterosexist assumption again. [38 *Journal of Legal Education*, March/ June 1988, 169–70.]

One wonders if extra credit was offered to students who went whole-hog and proclaimed themselves lesbians by the end of the semester.

While men generically are termed "patriarchs" and "oppressors," and feminism is described as an attempt "to have access to everything men have always kept for themselves" and "to get this foot off our necks," gay men are described as, I quote, "friend of women." Now, I have no dispute with gay men, but I consider an evening out sorely incomplete if it does not include at least one heterosexual member of the opposite sex.

And when I start thinking about these evenings out with heterosexual members of the opposite sex, I realize that the feminist "legal theorists" do not have my interests in mind. Dating, if not my life, is at least my hobby. So when feminists start yammering about "exposing patriarchy" and the "ambiguous phenomenon of male domination and hierarchy," I feel I am in an authoritative position to say: Huh? Are the patriarchs the ones who pay for our food and entertainment, send flowers and chocolate, and enable us to go through our entire lives without the tiresome exertion of opening a door?

I hate to give the game away, but men were essentially put on earth to serve women. It was much better when everyone pretended all their little projects—philosophy, math, science, world government, and so on—were much more important than carrying on the human race. Back in the prelapsarian fifties, women worked if they happened to fall into the .01 percent of the population who are able to have interesting jobs or they retired in their twenties to raise children and, incidentally, do what all serious people would like to do anyway—be a dilettante in many subjects. As far as I'm concerned this was a division of labor nothing short of perfect. Men worked, women didn't. So when our benefactors come under attack as "patriarchs" and "oppressors," I realize, someone has to put in a kind word for the oppressors. For cocktails alone, I figure I owe the male population several thousand dollars. So I will be the one to step forward and say: To the extent one gender is oppressing the other, it's not women who should be complaining.

The one solid defense feminists have to the man-hating accusation is that compared with what they think of women, their description of men is a bowl of cherries, a picnic in the sun, a day at the beach. Feminist "legal" "theory" places women somewhere around lawnmowers in the free-will/individual-responsibility department. Not only can women not be expected to voice an objection to having sex with a man—the man is apparently expected to sort of intuit that his companion is not in the mood—but neither can she be expected to intervene should her boyfriend decide to beat her children to death. It is yet another unfortunate example of white male patriarchy to hold women responsible for the murder of their children, at least during the first year of the child's life. Legal doctrine that holds otherwise—that is to say, that treats women as rational beings—"reveal[s] that the doctrinal law ignores the realities of women's lives."

The "realities of women's lives" mantra is used to excuse women from responsibility for little things, like not being able to say, "Not tonight dear, I've got a headache," as well as bigger things, like crimes against man and God. One legal theorist writes that "[a]nother example of lack of knowledge of women's lives occurs with the failure of act cases," and goes on to describe a woman who was convicted of assault for allowing her boyfriend to beat up her child. "It may never have crossed counsel's mind to try to construct a duress or diminished capacity defense for Walden based on her fear" (Id at 110–11).

A sewer rat does better than this to protect her offspring. So why is it that the Hedda Nussbaums of the world are considered feminist heroes rather than the pitiable creatures that they are?

Even if I were to concede, which I don't, that the role of the criminal defense attorney is to offer up any half-baked arguments that are beamed into his head and which he is capable of making without giggling—including the Twinkie defense, insanity pleas, and bedwetting theories—it is not clear why legal arguments in defense of women who allow their children to be beaten should be categorized as "pro-woman" rather than "pro-criminal." Am I to consider this a great triumph for womankind because the defendant in such cases is a woman as am I? It seems to me that by the same logic, men would be within their rights to root for rapists, all of whom are men. (Feminists have become so crazed in demanding equal representation in all walks of life that this fact inevitably distresses them to the point that they will proudly cite the efforts of two or three noble equality-seeking females who *assisted* rapes and thus are technically brought up on rape charges. But the idea that it would take a threat of violence to get a man to have sex is so ludicrous, I refuse to acknowledge the concept of a female rapist.) In fact, maybe I should be pro-rapist because rapists and I are all part of the personhood family. The urge to have sex is at least a normal human impulse. I know of no mother not on crack, who would not exert herself just a little bit—say, throwing herself in front of an oncoming train—to protect her child.

In the feminist worldview, women are more likely to be throwing their children in front of trains. Not to worry though—it's just one of those "realities of women's lives" most women have never heard of until reading feminist legal theory, in this case, "postpartum depression." Inasmuch as many women suffer depression after giving birth, feminist legal theorettes would give them pretty much a free shot at their child's life for one year, because "the doctrinal law ignores the realities of women's lives." The author described a case of a woman who was convicted of killing her three-month-old child, explaining, "The mother, however, stated that she was depressed. Is it possible that she was suffering from postpartum depression?" (Id at 109). For a more humane approach, the Legal Theoress cites British law, "where a woman cannot be charged with the murder of her infant in the first twelve months after she gives birth . . . [but only] manslaughter, on the theory of diminished responsibility because "the balance of the mother's mind was disturbed by reason of her not having fully recovered from the effect of giving birth" (Id at 109–10).

If women are so gaga insane as to be very likely to murder their offspring for one full year after giving birth, is it really wise to allow them to cast votes in important national elections in which the leader of the free world is chosen? Or for that matter, in stupid irrelevant local dogcatcher elections? If they manage to resist murdering their children during that first year, maybe we could just send them a lifetime supply of Tupperware or handsome designer luggage or something.

Where did this fixation on what is a fairly unusual phenomenon come from anyway? Really, you would think the principal female hobbies were shopping, dieting, and murdering their children. Moreover, the victims aren't even our white male patriarchal oppressor friends. They're children, babies, and at the risk of pointing out the obvious, some of them are even going to be female children. Don't at least the girl babies figure into an allegedly pro-female legal movement? Have the feminists no faith that some of these pink-cheeked, cooing baby girls could blossom into dour, hateful lesbians someday? Finally, it's bad enough to think about any person reaching a point at which he is capable of viciously beating or killing a child. That there are mothers who would do that to their own flesh and blood is really disturbing. Feminist legal theorists may credit themselves with this much: They have demonstrated that there is something still worse than that. And that is privileged academics sitting in their comfortable offices thinking up Twinkie defense theories to exculpate infanticidal mothers as part of an ideological cause.

————

O'Sullivan wrote back, in part:

> Greatly simplifying, I would like to suggest that the structure of the article (which would include most of what you have but this time ON VALIUM) would be as follows:
>
> a) What is the purpose of the law? (To create an orderly society in which people can pursue their own interests without coercion, interference, etc.)
>
> b) How in particular, does the law achieve this for women?
>
> c) From what general social and political theories to these criticisms spring? What view of men, women, children and the relationships between the sexes do they imply?
>
> d) What legal proposals flow from such theories? What obligations would be placed on women, what lifted, etc.?

There was obviously nothing to be done. Confusing "feminist legal theory" with an article about "the law" is like confusing *Plessy v. Ferguson* with Sarah Ferguson, former Duchess of York and current Weight Watchers spokesman. ■

CIGAR AFICIONADO

On the basis of a recommendation from George Will, *Cigar Aficionado* (popularly known as *Cigar, Fishing, and Auto*) asked me to write a column on campaign-finance reform a few years ago. This is what I submitted.

☞ This Congressman Bought for You by the *New York Times*

MAY 27, 2000

I'm toying with the idea of becoming an outlaw. You would too, if your representative in Congress were Chris Shays (Republican, of the *New York Times*). I won't bore you with his entire tedious and pathetic career, but just for starters, Shays was one of only five Republicans to vote against the impeachment of a lying, felonious president.

I'm hopping mad about it, to the point that I want to commit an act of free speech against him.

In a country that enshrined the right of free speech—political speech in particular (also known among constitutional cognoscenti as "core First Amendment speech")—this would be easy. I could take out television, radio, and newspaper ads detailing Mr. Shays's perfidy, or—if, say, I had a life—I could pay his political opponents to do it for me.

But in this country it's impossible for me to do that without becoming a lawbreaker or, at the very least, a suspect. Even if I hire a band of lawyers to advise me on navigating the narrow legal path to engaging in core First Amendment speech, I will undoubtedly be investigated, audited, and publicly accused of being a scofflaw. In the end, I might even be found to have broken a campaign-finance law or two.

The catch is that the whole point of my free speech would be, in a sense, to help Mr. Shays's opponent get elected. If Mr. Shays were pumping gas somewhere, I wouldn't feel compelled to run radio ads denouncing him for his political views. I want him to lose his job as my representative. The only way for that to happen is for his opponent to win. If his opponent is Mickey Mouse, I'm for Mickey Mouse.

If I were to run ads attacking Shays, those ads would inevitably help Mickey Mouse, and my free speech would be portrayed as a "thinly disguised campaign contribution" to the Mouse campaign. Campaign contributions, you see, are strictly limited to $2,000 per person. (Otherwise we might end up with idiots in Congress, like Chris Shays.)

This is what happened when Texas businessman Sam Wyly ran television ads attacking John McCain just before the New York primary earlier this year. The *New York Times* immediately demanded an investigation by the Federal Election Commission of Mr. Wyly's "subterfuge" and "secret sponsorship" of the ads. (Political speech should be left in the hands of responsible *New York Times* editorial writers.)

The *Times* identified such wanton free speech by a private citizen as a menace to the "integrity of politics" and "a serious threat to the integrity of future elections." There was evidence, you see, that Mr. Wyly actually wanted McCain's opponent, George Bush, to win (!) —and "equally intriguing news that the ads were placed through an advertising agency with ties to Gov. George Pataki." (Also believed by law-enforcement officials to be a Bush supporter.)

So if you're tempted to engage in political speech, the only safe course is to run a wholly ineffective ad campaign that could not possibly persuade anyone to vote one way or another. Any indication, for example, that I actually want Chris Shays to lose, or any communication with his political opponents, no matter how indirect, will constitute evidence of "coordination"—a secret campaign contribution to his opponent!

Meanwhile, let's say I don't care about my country, politics, or civic affairs. All I want to do is make porno movies. Without limitation or consultations with fancy lawyers, I could spend a million dollars producing speech of the *Debbie Does Dallas* variety. But if I want to engage in speech of the "Vote Against Chris Shays" variety, I can only spend $2,000. It is easier to pander obscenity in this country than it is to engage in core First Amendment speech.

Advocates for campaign-finance reform claim they have no problem with political speech, it's just the "horrifying" amounts of money being spent on campaign speech that bother them. ("Horrifying" was the technical term used by one "specialist" quoted in a recent *Washington Post* article on campaign-finance reform.) But saying you have a right to do something, and the government is merely placing limits on how much money you can spend doing it, isn't even a clever ruse.

How about this: You have a right to engage in the free exercise of your religion but can only spend $2,000 a year on it. (Otherwise, rabbis, priests, and ministers might be bought!) We'll call it "religion-finance reform."

Yes, you're saying to yourself, but no one wants to bribe a man of the cloth. What are you going to get out of it? A quick path to salvation? Pah! Congress can screw your competitors, grant you a cartel, subsidize your business, create little welfare programs ("for the children") that will send federal booty your way, or create legal bars to people suing you.

Far be it from me to quarrel with the proposition that politicians are corrupt, but first of all, no law has ever been written that could stop the citizenry from trying to get at the $1.7 trillion of taxpayer money Congress doles out every year. Indeed, the only serious and workable solution to political corruption is for politicians to be worth substantially less. Until that time, though, even stipulating that politicians are corrupt, it still does not follow that suppressing free speech will make them any less so.

The theory of "campaign-finance reform" devotees is that if Congress would further limit speech by non–news-media-owning citizens, any taxpayers who want to get some of that $1.7 trillion would at least not be able to do it by engaging in speech. That's really the theory.

Citizens can bribe politicians by arranging favorable cattle futures trades, selling them stocks and bonds at a loss, buying their houses above market price and selling them houses below market price, building million-dollar pantheons in their names, hiring their wives and mistresses, sending them on exotic vacations—er, "fact-finding missions"—and giving to their favorite charities. But the one way you can't bribe a politician is by engaging in free speech (at a cost of more than $2,000) saying "Reelect [or Defeat] Senator Blowhard."

Of course, for bribing politicians, nothing beats owning a newspaper. Newspapers like the *New York Times* have absolutely no limitations on running editorials exhorting, "Vote for Chris Shays"—as that paper did in violation of an almost uninterrupted, century-long tradition of endorsing only Democrats. Nor are there any restrictions on how often the *Times* can run "news" articles describing Chris Shays as a "moderate."

Indeed, assuming a favorable editorial in the *New York Times* were worth only as much as a half-page paid political ad in that paper, the *New York Times* gave Shays about a million dollars in campaign donations in 1999 alone. (To put this in perspective, Shays typically spends about $500,000 on his entire reelection campaign.)

It was a wise investment. Shays voted against almost every member of his party—but with the *Times*—on the not insignificant issue of a president's impeachment. Most strikingly, he repeatedly introduces "campaign-finance reform" bills that would grant special rights to the *Times* and other newspapers to engage in political speech without contradiction by upstarts like Sam Wyly.

I'm not saying free speech can't function as a bribe. I just think private citizens ought to be able to bribe politicians as easily as the *New York Times* does.

POSTSCRIPT: My *Cigar, Fishing, and Auto* editor responded with a long e-mail suggesting that instead of making the strong argument against campaign-finance restrictions, I make the weak argument. To wit: I should complain that rich people can spend whatever they like on their own campaigns. (It is a source of endless fascination to liberals that the rich can do things poor people can't.) In retrospect, maybe it was a mistake to try to attack Bill Clinton in the pages of *Cigar Aficionado.* As I recall from the Starr Report, Mr. Clinton has been known to enjoy a good cigar.

For simplicity, e-mail exchanges of approximately one million messages are distilled to a point-by-point exchange, edited only for spelling.

CIGAR AFICIONADO: Here are a few of my thoughts. "Felonious" implies some degree of conviction. Whatever your political leanings or mine, or the implied injustice of the impeachment proceedings, he was not convicted . . . therefore, felonious becomes potentially libelous, but the jury, as they say, is still out on the lying issue. In other words, you can call a public official a liar, but to suggest he is a felon is a bit more problematic. (This may be entirely a semantic issue based on the Webster's definition, but nonetheless, I'm suggesting another modifier, or just leave it at liar.)

COULTER: Just for the record, I do disagree that speech conventions have to follow legal conventions (innocent until proven guilty), especially in egregious and obvious cases. O.J. is innocent before the law, but he's not innocent. I know a lot of newspapers won't call him a "murderer" unless he's a "convicted murderer," but I'm against that policy. By the way, several prominent federal judges—whose names I will give you in something other than an e-mail—are known to refer to the president exclusively as "that felon." But anyway, I'll change that.

CIGAR AFICIONADO: Secondly, you rail against the rules & regs but without neatly defining what they are, or what alternative you propose. While that may be implicit, I think you need to be more explicit, probably in one paragraph about exactly what the rules are, whether or not you're talking about "soft money" issue, and what exactly you mean by letting the first amendment dictate the rules here: i.e., I can spend as much money as I have to get the candidate elected that I want without any restrictions. The piece needs a graf that concisely outlines the exact issue you are tackling here. . . . It may fit after the graf, "*The Times* identified . . ." with some additional transitional work in the following graf.

COULTER: I'll put in a graf on the rules. (I just didn't want to go over my word limit.)

[Coulter off-camera: zzzzzzzzzzzzzzzzzzzzzzzzzzzzzzz]

CIGAR AFICIONADO: Finally, I find your basic argument weakened somewhat by the *New York Times* angle in the second half of the story; for better or worse, from William Randolph Hearst to Arthur Sulzberger, the Fourth Estate has been granted the territory of political endorsement on its editorial pages. You can quibble with me over the use in the news pages of the word "moderate" to describe Shays, but in his constituency I wouldn't be surprised to find the *New York Post* calling him every name under the sun on the opposing side of the ledger. Pitting individual restrictions against the established precedent of newspapers doesn't build your case. I'd find it more compelling to explore some of the inherent contradictions in the campaign financing law that, for instance, allows Jon Corzine and Steve Forbes to spend their millions on their own elections but not on others, thus building on the whole Wyly case in Texas.

I just end up feeling that the reader shouldn't be distracted by your partisan bias against the *New York Times* (which is a whole other column sometime) when what you really want them to focus on is the campaign finance issue. Full disclosure here; I used to freelance for the *New York Times*, but I would say [BLAH, BLAH, BLAH]. . . . Your comments are awaited.

COULTER: The *NYT* angle is the only edit that really goes to the heart of my argument, which is a constitutional argument, *not* a pragmatic argument. It's not just that the rules are inconsistent and have perverse consequences (e.g., Forbes and Perot examples), though that's certainly true. But that would be true even if we didn't have a First Amendment.

My argument is that the First Amendment doesn't just apply to working journalists. The First Amendment protects speech that is robust, wide open, etc. etc., and not just speech that is robust, wide open, etc. as between competing newspapers (like the *Post* and the *Times*). The First Amendment refers to "the people," not to "the newspaper editors."

Moreover, the *NYT* is my focus *not* because I hate them and their speech is contrary to mine, but because they are the ones demanding campaign-finance "reforms" that would further reduce the free-speech rights of nonmedia citizens. It's outrageous and hypocritical for the *NYT* to be incessantly promoting their own special interest in denying First Amendment rights to normal citizens while pretending to be the great protector of the First Amendment.

I can make that point more clearly in a couple sentences, so that it's clear that this IS my argument, but I'll have to go over my word limit.

CIGAR AFICIONADO: Ann, don't worry too much about the word limit.

I see your point about the *NYT,* but you do need to make that part of the argument more explicit, otherwise it just sounds like an anti-*NYT* attack. In fact, the next to last graf of the e-mail puts it pretty concisely. . . .

I guess my overall point, and the way I'm justifying putting in a column that I disagree with on some basic points, is that we have been hearing way too much about the evils of campaign finance and not enough about the opposing point of "let the people speak" that you espouse. I want that point to come through loud and clear.

After not "worry[ing] too much about the word limit" through several more drafts, pointless e-mails, and wasted weekends, I was informed that the editors at *Cigar Aficionado* decided that they definitely wanted my point "to come through loud and clear"—just not in their magazine.

In conclusion, here are some comments on my original column from two Yale Law grads:

Yale Law grad 1: "I think it's great."

Yale Law grad 2: "My one piece of advice: Make the same point in another article from a different direction. Point out that a company that wants to make a campaign contribution can make whatever contribution it wants—as long as you substitute 'labor union' for 'company.'"

And no, not *those* two Yale Law School graduates. We haven't been on speaking terms since I called him a lying felon. ■

WALL STREET JOURNAL

This was the only one of the rejected columns that was not solicited by the publication. A professor read my draft and insisted I submit it to the *Wall Street Journal*. I said the *Wall Street Journal* would sooner publish Jane Mayer—hate-mongering author of the Clarence Thomas hatchet job *Strange Justice*—than publish me. Then I remembered that the *Journal* did publish Mayer. I sent the column, and the *Journal* turned it down, explaining they just weren't interested in the topic. A few weeks later, they asked someone else to write about the exact same topic. It was a good article, except for one tiny detail: It overlooked the fact that the central charge against Thomas Jefferson was actually disproved by DNA evidence.

☞ Sally Does Monticello

JUNE 21, 2001

In a terrifically humiliating episode, Pulitzer Prize–winning historian Joseph Ellis was recently exposed by the *Boston Globe* as an exotic Walter Mitty of the Ivory Tower. For years, he claimed he had gone to Vietnam in the 101st Airborne, had served under General William Westmoreland in Saigon, had been a rider on the Freedom Trail in Mississippi (beaten up by racist cops), and had been a high school football hero, once scoring the winning touchdown, among his other fanciful claims. None of it was true. Faced with the evidence, Ellis was forced to apologize for having "let stand" the "assumption" that he had been telling the truth.

You might say Ellis had fancied himself the Thomas Jefferson of the twentieth century, except that Jefferson's reputation is shot, thanks in part to Joseph Ellis. Between 'Nam flashbacks and Freedom Rider reunions, Ellis coauthored the ground-breaking 1998 report "Jefferson Fathered Slave's Last Child." You might remember this report if you weren't on the moon when it was released—it was the Clinton defenders' giddiest "Gotcha!" moment. It was unveiled to instant acclaim—just weeks before the House impeachment vote on William "You Know Who" Clinton's impeachment stemming from his sexual affair with an intern. As Ellis put it, "It is as if Clinton had called one of the most respected character witnesses in all of U.S. history to testify that the primal urge has a most distinguished presidential pedigree." Ellis said the new testing proved "beyond any reasonable doubt that Jefferson had a long-term sexual relationship with his mulatto slave." As author of the award-winning *American Sphinx: The Character of Thomas Jefferson*—and a Vietnam veteran—Ellis spoke with some authority on the matter. (We're still waiting for the publication of *American Liar: The Joseph Ellis Story*.)

An editorial in the *Washington Post* promptly denounced Jefferson for carrying on "a private sexual relationship with an inherited young slave girl" and proclaimed that having sex with slaves smacked of racism—separate and apart, evidently, from merely holding them as property. It was as if Jefferson was morally obligated to carry on exploitative relationships with Latina, Asian, snd Caucasian chattel as well, just for the sake of appearances. *USA Today* reported, "Thomas Jefferson owned lots of slaves and had lots of sex with at least one of them, Sally Hemings.... According to new DNA tests, Jefferson sired at least one child, Eston, through that union and probably six others."

Unfortunately for the gang of harpies defending Clinton, proof of a Jefferson-Hemings liaison was as fanciful as Professor Ellis's military service. Two months after the report's "findings" had been published in every news outlet where English is spoken, a correction had to be issued. Ellis's coauthor pathologist Eugene Foster—the actual scientist—admitted to the British science journal *Nature* that they had not proved Thomas Jefferson fathered any children by Sally Hemings. "We never proved it," Foster told the *Washington Times*. "We never can. We never will." What they meant to say was "Jefferson *could have* fathered slave's last child." (And it was also *not* true that Jefferson met Hemings while serving in the 101st Airborne during the Vietnam War.) The press was not as interested in the "we lied" correction as it had been in the original inflammatory (and false) charge. Less than a half dozen newspapers admitted that the report had traced the paternity of Hemings's last child to any one of several Jefferson males.

Besides Jefferson, there were twenty-five Jefferson adult males alive when Hemings conceived her last son, seven of them at Monticello. Many scholars consider Jefferson's younger brother, Randolph, a more likely suspect, on account of his frequent socializing with the slaves. While Jefferson was busy entertaining prominent international visitors in the main house, Randolph would generally retire to the slave quarters. As Randolph was described by one slave, "Old Master's brother, Mass Randall, was a mighty simple man: used to come out among black people, play the fiddle and dance half the night; hadn't much more sense than Isaac" (Isaac was one of the slaves evidently not known for his intellectual prowess. Today we would say, "He hadn't much more sense than Justice Souter.")

Stunningly, the Ellis study actually exonerated Jefferson on the principal charge against him. The Hemings rumor was based on two sources: The contemporaneous attacks of a political enemy and the "oral history" passed down through Hemings's descendants—and lovingly promoted by twentieth-century Clinton-defenders. In 1802, muckraking, alcoholic journalist James Callender, who had earlier served prison time for his particular brand of journalism, tried to blackmail Jefferson into appointing him postmaster at Richmond. When blackmail failed, Callender publically accused Jefferson of miscegenation with Sally Hemings—or as Callender put it, "a slut as common as pavement." He wrote of Jefferson, "It is well known that the man . . . keeps and for many years has kept, as his concubine, one of his slaves. Her name is Sally. The name of her eldest son is Tom. His features are said to bear a striking,

though sable resemblance to those of the president himself." Thus
began the rumor of "President Tom," as Callender called Jefferson's
putative illegitimate son. The "oral history," passed down through
Hemings's children, also pointed to Tom as Jefferson's child. From
there, it was simply assumed that if Tom was Jefferson's son, the
rest of Hemings's children were his, too.

Now here's the crescendo: The preimpeachment, get-Jefferson
study specifically proved that Tom, at least, was *not* fathered by
Jefferson. After testing six different genetic lines from "President
Tom," the DNA tests ruled out *any* Jefferson as the father. The
study that allegedly proved "JEFFERSON FATHERED CHILD WITH
SLAVE" had scientifically disproved the centerpiece of the accusation! But that wasn't the title of Professor Ellis's report. Nor was it
mentioned in the blanket news coverage of the report's false accusation against Jefferson. In fact, there was no news coverage—not
a single article—on the amazing fact that the DNA study had actually exonerated Jefferson of fathering Tom. To repeat: The famous
Tom, the Tom who got the whole reputation-blackening ball rolling, was proved by DNA tests not to be fathered by any Jefferson.

The preimpeachment report had to fall back on an entirely
new suspect in order to smear Jefferson: Hemings's last-born son,
Eston, whose claims to paternity are far more incredible. Eston,
the only Hemings child who could be tied by DNA to some Jefferson, was born in 1808, when Thomas Jefferson was sixty-four
years old. Randolph—the Jefferson fiddling and dancing with the
slaves—was twelve years younger. But more significant, Eston was
conceived five years *after* Callender made his scurrilous accusation
against Jefferson! In order to implicate President Jefferson, the
theory must be that he waited five years to start engaging in the
depraved conduct Callender accused him of back in 1802.

Amazingly, a few years after the principal charge against Jefferson was disproved, the Thomas Jefferson Memorial Foundation
issued a "report" purporting to acknowledge that Jefferson fathered all six of Hemings's illegitimate children. (Katie Couric is

one of the renowned historians on the board of the Monticello Foundation.) Guided tours of Monticello today include the provably false information that Jefferson fathered all of Hemings's children. The Monticello Association, a group of Jefferson descendants, invited the Hemings descendants to join Jefferson family reunions at Monticello.

Apparently there are limits to "oral history." For example, most people would prefer to be descendants of a former president, rather than, say, descendants of his halfwit brother. If anyone ought to have recognized the possibility of self-aggrandizement in such "oral histories," you'd think it would have been Professor Ellis. ∎

GOOD HOUSEKEEPING

For about a year after each one of these happy experiences in publishing, I would refuse to waste one second writing anything for any publication without an ironclad promise that whatever I submitted would be published, even if it was twenty pages of "All work and no play makes Ann a dull girl." But time would pass, a new opportunity would arise, and I'd tell myself, *This time it will be different!* And then the same thing would happen all over again. To put it in terms comprehensible to a women's magazine editor, I was like a battered wife, clinging to a series of abusive publications.

The last time was in the fall of 2003, when *Good Housekeeping* asked me to write about a proverb. Inasmuch as their proverbs were the kinds of sayings that make you want to kill yourself—"A friend in need is a friend indeed" and "The early bird catches the worm"—this assignment was not exactly my cup of tea. But it was no less heinous than writing about "feminist legal theory," and at least this column would be published. Or so I thought. Now that I had three best-sellers under my belt, I figured magazine editors were finally willing to throw caution to the wind and publish Ann Coulter! Not only that, but at about the same time I was writing my proverb column, British *Good Housekeeping* ran a consumer review of vibrators. Could I say anything racier than that?

Why yes I could! Here's the column that was too hot for *Good Housekeeping*.

☞ If You Sup with the Devil, Use a Long Spoon

FALL 2003

A few years ago, when I was on radio promoting my book about the Clinton scandals, *High Crimes and Misdemeanors,* a woman called in with the standard DNC talking point informing me that "everybody does it"—to wit, all men cheat on their wives. People who say "everybody does it" are announcing nothing more than the implacable fact that *they* do it. As Edmund Burke said, "He who accuses all of mankind convicts only one." But this caller didn't have the glib, vaguely contemptuous tone of the typical Clinton defender. She was on the verge of tears. The pain in this woman's voice made clear that the "everybody" was not her, but her spouse.

I'm not clinically trained to deal with despair, but I did tell the caller that she was wrong and she needed to start hanging with a new crowd. In fact, according to the only serious, long-term scientific study of the sexual behavior of Americans ever performed, 75 percent of married men and 85 percent of married women have never been unfaithful. (John Gagnon, Robert Michael, and Stuart Michaels, *The Social Organization of Sexuality* [Chicago: University of Chicago Press, 1994]). *Never.* And consider that that figure includes couples who are separated or headed toward divorce court. (And further consider that residents of Manhattan and Malibu were included in the category "Americans.")

But you can be sure that in any town, the 20 percent of adulterers will know one another. Alcoholics hang around alcoholics, drug addicts hang around drug addicts, liars hang around liars. Vices of a feather flock together. This is a great tip for figuring out which of your friends are liars and cheats: They are the ones who seem to know a curiously large number of people who lie and cheat. But it's also a warning to keep those friends at a distance.

It's hard enough to resist temptation—the one thing Oscar Wilde said he could not resist—without also feeling like you are the only person on earth being asked to engage in the Herculean task of not committing a mortal sin. When every fiber of your being wants to do something and the only thing stopping you is the knowledge that it would be wrong, it's not going to make it easier to know that a lot of your friends apparently do not care that it is wrong. It's especially not going to be easy if the ones who do not care seem no worse for the wear.

This is part of what is so corrupting about television shows and Hollywood movies that show gorgeous people with an endless supply of witty lines and fabulous clothes engaging in wildly promiscuous behavior. Americans' friends are NBC's *Friends*. If you think people can distinguish between TV characters and real-life friends and neighbors, consider the firestorm of indignation Dan Quayle ignited when he made the incontrovertibly true point that the scriptwriters for the fictional television character Murphy Brown were not performing a public service by portraying the heroine as having a child out of wedlock. Apparently a lot of people believed Murphy Brown was a real person and Dan Quayle had just cruelly insulted her. A decade later, when the writers for *Friends* wrote in an out-of-wedlock pregnancy for a popular character, no one made a peep.

Perhaps the greater disservice of Hollywood movies is their

cartoonish villains. In real life, I promise you, the devil will look more like Julia Roberts than Snidely Whiplash. Evil does not arrive with a flashing neon sign: MEPHISTOPHELES! LUCIFER! SATAN! FOR ETERNAL DAMNATION, APPLY HERE. Evil arrives packaged as a winsome movie about a long-legged brunette who manages to marry a rich, handsome bachelor and live happily ever after—all by turning tricks on Hollywood Boulevard! There's a reason Beelzebub is known as the prince of lies.

Evil presents itself like a beautiful banquet. That's why Adam and Eve were tempted with a delicious-looking apple instead of a spoonful of castor oil. Satan takes the form of gorgeous actresses, successful politicians, and pop icons cavorting across the gossip columns, subliminally exhorting the reader: *Be like me! Don't be a prude! This is how the glamorous people live!* But as in Wilde's *Picture of Dorian Gray,* the sinner's beauty conceals a soul growing uglier by the minute.

People don't commit acts of great evil or great courage out of thin air. Character is developed out of a lifetime of choices. Almost every decision you make, however small, will be a step closer to God or a step closer to the devil. When you are unkind to a clumsy shop clerk, you are taking a step closer to the devil. When you snap at your mother, you are taking a step closer to the devil. When you gossip enviously about a friend, you are taking a step closer to the devil. When you go along with the in crowd and don't speak out against liars, against promiscuity, against abortion, you are taking a step closer to the devil. But it's never too late to stop and begin taking steps toward God. It's a lot easier to make that journey with companions who know the way.

———

POSTSCRIPT: *Good Housekeeping* kept telling me to make it more "personal," which was like telling a dog to make a soufflé. I'm a Republican. That column is as personal as it gets. Moreover, I consider a person's view of God, right, wrong, and eternity as eminently "personal." What could be more personal than that? In *Good Housekeeping*-ese, "personal" seems to mean "something involving victimhood and tragedy" or "something having more to do with bodily functions." How about: "My Secret Shame: Why I Became a Conservative" or "How Inappropriate Touching Led Me to Believe in Elimination of the Capital Gains Tax."

Alas, I can't write magazine essays about being abused or neglected, because I never had those opportunities. (By contrast, Naomi Wolf has them all indexed: *Sexual harassment? I got that. The curse and tragedy of being beautiful? I wrote a book about it. How awful men are? Got it right here. The trauma of motherhood? Hold on to your hats!*) My father wasn't a racist, my mother was never arrested, and my brother wasn't a cross-dresser. In other words, I come from a disadvantaged, minority background: I am the product of an intact and loving family. My parents are Caucasian, native-born, English-speaking, happily married, monogamous, and self-supporting. The best word to describe my early family life would be "functional." Thus, I had no one to blame but myself when I didn't succeed at something, which in turn led me to the dreaded, upward spiral known as "achievement." Having no one to blame, I had nothing to fall back on my whole life but my native talents. Then again, nobody ever said that life was supposed to be fair. I'm a survivor.

Several months after my proverb column was rejected, I came across a *Good Housekeeping* magazine in a waiting room and immediately looked up the proverb column to see exactly what the editors meant by "personal." The proverb was "You can lead a horse to water, but you can't make him drink." The story illustrating this proverb was as follows: The author's son refused to practice his piano lessons, so the author told him he didn't have to take piano lessons anymore, and now he takes harpsichord lessons. Truth be told, that story did create a deep, emotional reaction in me: *Who do I sue to get that five minutes of my life back?* At least now I know what "personal" means: really, really boring. That may work for *Good Housekeeping*, but I'm afraid such columns would not make "Ann Coulter: The Director's Cut." ■

Afterword for the Paperback Edition

Gigolos, Document Forgers, Food Throwers, Sodomy Worshipers, and Other Distinguished Liberals

———■———

Say what you will about liberals, one has to admire their savage energy. They never rest. Only since the hardcover of this book came out, liberals have:

- run obviously dummied National Guard documents on CBS News in a failed attempt to unseat a sitting president.
- ignored, and then viciously attacked, the Swift Boat Veterans for Truth.
- lost a presidential election.
- tried to cheer themselves up by lashing out at the blacks and killing a disabled girl in Florida.

- modified their debating techniques from calling Republicans Nazis to throwing food and then went back to calling Republicans Nazis anyway.
- altered Senate rules to require the minority party to choose judicial nominees with the advice and consent of the president.

On the bright side, John Kerry is gone. Dan Rather is gone. Air America is gone. (I can't be absolutely sure about that last one.) So we have liberals on the run, except in the U.S. Senate, where there are at least seven Republicans who prefer chasing their tails (and being hailed for their "bipartisanship") to getting anything done. Here are some of the happy memories of arguing with liberals, covering the election, the courts, the media, and the intriguing question of why liberals throw like girls.

POLITICAL DEBATE, THREE STOOGES STYLE

☞ It's Only Funny Until Someone Loses a Pie

APRIL 13, 2005

Liberals enjoy claiming that they are intellectuals, thrilled to engage in a battle of wits. This, they believe, distinguishes them from conservatives, who are religious fanatics who react with impotent rage to opposing ideas. As one liberal, Jonathan Chait, put the cliché in *The New Republic*: Bush is an "instinctive anti-intellectual" and his administration hostile to "fact-driven debate." In a favorable contrast, Clinton is "the former Rhodes scholar who relished academic debates." Showing his usual reverence for fact-checking, the *New York Times*'s Paul Krugman says the Republican Party is "dominated by people who believe truth should be determined by revelation, not research."

I'm not sure how these descriptions square with the fact that liberals keep responding to conservative ideas by throwing food. (Remember the good old days when liberals' "fact-driven" ideas only meant throwing money at their problems?)

Last October, two liberals responded to my speech at the University of Arizona—during question and answer, no less—by charging the stage and throwing two pies at me from a few yards away. Fortunately for me, liberals not only argue like liberals, they also throw like girls. (Apologies in advance to the Harvard biology professors who walked out on Larry Summers in a demonstration of their admiration of "research," not "revelation"—but this may account for the dearth of female pitchers in Major League Baseball.)

Unfortunately for them, Republican men don't react favorably to two *Deliverance* boys trying to sucker-punch a 110-pound female in a skirt and heels. The geniuses ended up with bloody noses and broken bones.

It's really outrageous how conservatives respond to liberals who are just trying to engage in a "fact-driven debate." How typical of Republicans to go on the offensive just because a female has been physically attacked. Instead of capturing and subduing my attackers, those strong Republican men should have been trying to understand *why* they threw the pies.

In the five months following the liberal ass-whupping in Arizona—I mean "fact-driven debate"—all was quiet on the Eastern Front. College liberals still couldn't formulate a coherent argument, but they seemed to want to avoid ending up in jail having to explain to their cellmates that they were in for trying to hit a girl (and missing).

Then on March 19, all charges were dismissed against the *De-*

liverance boys—including a felony charge for $3,000 worth of damage to school property. Inexplicably, this outcome did not instantly lead to widespread rioting and looting in South Central Los Angeles.

Democrat Barbara LaWall is the Pima County attorney who allowed the liberal debate champions to walk. LaWall brags on her website about "holding criminals accountable." She didn't say anything about liberals, however. Be forewarned, conservatives: Do not expect the law to protect you in Pima County.

In the three weeks following the dismissal of all charges against my attackers, three more conservatives were attacked on college campuses.

On March 29, liberals' intellectual retort to a speech by William Kristol at Earlham College was to throw a pie. On March 31, liberals enjoyed the hurly-burly of political debate with Pat Buchanan at Western Michigan University by throwing salad dressing. On April 6, liberals engaged David Horowitz on his ideas at Butler University by throwing a pie at him.

If you close your eyes, it's almost like you're listening to Ludwig Wittgenstein!

If there had been that many attacks on Muslims in the weeks following the 9/11 attack, we'd still be watching Showtime specials about it. (In liberals' defense, this is what they must resort to when there are no student newspapers with conservative editorials to burn.)

At the risk of provoking one of those brainy liberals to throw more food, here's an idea: In order to reduce physical assaults on conservative speakers, maybe we should increase the price. But, to the contrary, when conservative speakers are physically attacked on college campuses, university administrators ignore the attacks, Democratic prosecutors somehow manage to get the charges dismissed, and Democratic flacks like Chait and Krugman pretend they missed the news that day.

What might work better is some form of disincentive to liberals who engage in violent behavior whenever they hear an idea they don't like but can't come up with words to dispute. The punishment doesn't have to be severe—just a small fraction of the wailing and healing that occurs every time there's a hoax "hate crime" on a college campus. (But which still serve a valuable function by calling attention to the issue of hate crimes.)

Last year, classes were canceled and demonstrations held at Claremont College after a white, Catholic visiting professor claimed her car had been vandalized with racist and anti-Semitic slurs. This—at the very moment she was giving a talk on intolerance!

It was just a little too ironic. The incident had all the exquisite timing of an "ABC After-School Special" about hate crimes. But as one student angrily told the *Los Angeles Times,* the suggestion that it was a hoax is "so sick. They are in denial. People don't want to accept that a well-educated, liberal community can have hate." Needless to say, the vandalism turned out to have been perpetrated by the professor herself.

Or maybe physical attacks on conservatives could merit a small slice of the rage and indignation directed at the display of racist symbols. Last year, a white student at a high school in Washington State was accused of taunting a black student with a noose. In response, the white student was immediately expelled from school. He was charged with a felony. There was a series of town-wide discussions. The U.S. Justice Department sent in mediators. And two more years were suddenly added to Whoopi Goldberg's career.

I think Kristol, Buchanan, Horowitz, and I would be perfectly happy if college liberals merely brandished symbols at us. Speaking for myself, I would be unhappy if they didn't. But these Rhodes scholar geniuses with a taste for "fact-driven debate" can't even achieve the level of argument practiced by the average juvenile delinquent. They're still stuck at the intellectual level of two-year-olds in high chairs throwing food. ■

After *How To Talk To a Liberal (If You Must)* went to
print, including a chapter of columns commissioned
and then rejected by mainstream publications, I accepted
another writing assignment with a mainstream news outlet,
USA Today, writing a daily opinion column on the Democratic National Convention.

When my first column landed on the editors' desks at
USA Today headquarters, I imagine the editors throwing
my column down in disgust, saying, "This sounds like that
crazy blonde on TV!" During a six-hour conference with
the editors regarding my first column, the principal objection to my column boiled down to my "tone." Apparently
no one at *USA Today* had ever read Ann Coulter before.
Inasmuch as *USA Today* intended to run my byline on the
piece, I took the position that it should be my column.

I left Boston the next morning, having told the editors
the night before that if they didn't like my first column,
they definitely weren't going to like the next four. Those
Democrats sure have the Midas touch when it comes to
the economy—I was at their convention less than a day
before I lost my job. I was sad I wouldn't be published in
USA Today, as it's one of my favorite papers, especially the
Purple Section. This right-wing media I keep hearing
about never seems to work out for me.

Below is the column too hot for the Purple Section.
Editors' comments in caps.

☞ Put the Speakers in a Cage

JULY 26, 2004

Here at the Spawn of Satan convention in Boston, conservatives
are deploying a series of covert signals to identify one another,

much like gay men do. My allies are the ones wearing crosses or American flags. The people sporting shirts emblazoned with the "F-word" are my opponents. Also, as always, the pretty girls and cops are on my side, most of them barely able to conceal their eye-rolling.

USA Today: EYE ROLLING? AT WHAT?

Democrats are constantly suing and slandering police as violent, fascist racists—with the exception of Boston's police, who'll be lauded as national heroes right up until the Democrats pack up and leave town on Friday, whereupon they'll revert to their natural state of being fascist, racist pigs.

USA Today: WHAT DEMOCRATS SUE THE POLICE? BUT THEY WON'T ACTUALLY REVERT TO BEING FASCIST PIGS, DON'T YOU MEAN THE DEMS WILL THINK THEY HAVE REVERTED TO BEING FASCIST PIGS?

A speaker at the Democratic National Convention this year, Al Sharpton, accused white police officers of raping and defacing Tawana Brawley in 1987, lunatic charges that eventually led to a defamation lawsuit against Sharpton and even more eventually, to Sharpton paying a jury award to the defamed plaintiff Steve Pagones. So it's a real mystery why cops wouldn't like Democrats.

USA Today: IS THAT LAST SENTENCE SARCASTIC? IF SO, YOU SURE LOST ME.

As for the pretty girls, I can only guess that it's because liberal boys never try to make a move on you without the UN Security Council's approval. Plus, it's no fun riding around in those dinky little hybrid cars. My pretty-girl allies stick out like a sore thumb amongst the corn-fed, no makeup, natural-fiber, no-bra-needing, sandal-wearing, hirsute, somewhat fragrant hippie chick pie wagons they call "women" at the Democratic National Convention.

USA Today: NOT FUNNY, I DON'T GET IT.

Apparently, the nuts at the Democratic National Convention are going to be put in cages outside the convention hall. Sadly, they won't be fighting to the death as is done in WWF caged matches. They're calling this the "protestors' area," although I suppose a better name would be the "truth-free zone."

USA Today: CLARIFY WHICH NUTS.

I thought this was a great idea until I realized the "nut" category did not include Sharpton, Al Gore, Bill Clinton, and Teddy Kennedy—all featured speakers at the convention. I'd say the actual policy is only untelegenic nuts get the cages, but little Dennis Kucinich is speaking at the convention, too. So it must be cages for "nuts who have not run for president as serious candidates for the Democratic Party."

Looking at the lineup of speakers at the Convention, I have developed the 7-11 challenge: I will quit making fun of, for example, Dennis Kucinich, if he can prove he can run a 7-11 properly for eight hours. We'll even let him have an hour or so of preparation before we open up. Within eight hours, the money will be gone, the store will be empty, and he'll be explaining how three eleven-year-olds came in and asked for the money and he gave it to them.

USA Today: I DON'T GET IT.

For twenty years, the Democrats wouldn't let Jimmy Carter within a hundred miles of a convention podium. The fact that Carter is now their most respectable speaker tells you where that party is today. Maybe they just want to remind Americans who got us into this Middle East mess in the first place. We've got millions of fanatical Muslims trying to slaughter Americans while shouting "Allah Akbar!" Yeah, let's turn the nation over to these guys.

With any luck, Gore will uncork his speech comparing Republicans to Nazis. Just a few weeks ago, Gore gave a speech accusing the Bush administration of deploying "digital Brown Shirts" to intimidate journalists and pressure the media into writing good things about Bush—in case you were wondering where all those glowing articles about Bush were coming from.

The last former government official to slake his thirst so deeply with the Kool-Aid and become a far-left peacenik was Ramsey Clarke, and it took him a few years to really blossom. Clinton must have done some number on Gore. Then again, with his yen for earth tones in a man's wardrobe, maybe Gore's references to "Brown Shirts" was intended as a compliment.

Only one major newspaper—the *Boston Herald*—reported Gore's "Brown Shirt" comment, though a Bush campaign spokesman's statement quoting the "Brown Shirt" line made it into the very last sentence of a *Los Angeles Times* article. The *New York Times* responded with an article criticizing "both" Republicans and Democrats for using Nazi imagery. Democrats call Republicans Nazis, the Republicans quote the Democrats calling Republicans Nazis, and "both" are using Nazi imagery. (It's a cycle of violence!)

The nuts in the cages are virtual Bertrand Russells compared to the official speakers at the Democratic convention. On the basis of their placards, I gather the caged-nut position is that they love the troops so much, they don't want them to get hurt fighting. "Support the troops," the signs say, "bring them home."

That's my new position on all government workers, except the 5 percent who aren't useless, which is to say cops, prosecutors, firemen, and U.S. servicemen. I love bureaucrats at the National Endowment of the Arts funding crucifixes submerged in urine so much—I think they should go home. I love public school teachers punishing any mention of God and banning Christmas songs so much—I think they should go home.

Walking back from the convention site I chatted with a normal

Bostonian for several blocks—who must have identified me through our covert system of signals. He was mostly bemused by the Democrats' primetime speakers and told me he used to be an independent, but for the last twenty years found himself voting mostly Republican. Then he corrected himself and said he votes for the "American."

I'd say I love all these Democrats in Boston so much I want them to go home, but I don't. I want Americans to get a good long look at the French Party and keep the 7-11 challenge in mind.

USA Today: WHAT DO YOU MEAN BY "THE FRENCH PARTY"? I DON'T GET IT.

––––––

POSTSCRIPT: In keeping with *USA Today*'s unique contributions to the craft of journalism, here's a pie chart summarizing its reasons for pulling my column. ■

■ Editors didn't get it, 34%

□ *USA Today* doesn't "do" irony, 26%

■ Editors liked Dennis Kucinich's idea for a "Peace Department," 19%

■ Pro-Kerry editors had a bug up their ass, 12%

□ Other, 9%

––––––

THE MEDIA: SOME DISSEMBLY REQUIRED

If only our totally objective, unbiased media had been as dubious about a foaming-at-the-mouth Bush-hater as they were of 254 Swift Boat Veterans, Dan Rather would still be on air, rather than the disgraced pathetic loser he is now. Alas, to the swift (boat veteran) goes the (presidential) race.

☞ Brothers Band Together Against Kerry

AUGUST 11, 2004

Democrats haven't been this upset about an American engaging in free speech since Juanita Broaddrick opened her yap.

Two hundred fifty-four Swift Boat Veterans have signed a letter saying John Kerry is not fit to be commander in chief, a point developed in some detail in the blockbuster new book by John O'Neill, aptly titled *Unfit for Command*. At the 2003 reunion of Swift Boat Veterans, about three hundred men showed up: 85 percent of them think Kerry is unfit to be president. (On the bright side, Kerry was voted, in absentia, "Most Likely to Run for President on His Phony War Record.") Fewer than 10 percent of all Swift Boat Veterans contacted refused to sign the letter.

Kerry was in Vietnam for only four months, which, coincidentally, is less than the combined airtime he's spent talking about it. It takes a special kind of person to get that many people to hate your guts in so little time. In fact, I think the last time this many people hated one person after only four months was when Margaret Cho had her own sitcom.

But our young Eddie Haskell managed to annoy other servicemen even before he came home and called them war criminals. About sixty eyewitnesses to Kerry's service are cited in the book, describing Kerry fleeing comrades who were under attack, disregarding orders, putting others in danger, sucking up to his commanders, creating phony film footage of his exploits with a home-movie camera, and recommending himself for medals and Purple Hearts in vainglorious reports he wrote himself. (This was apparently before the concept of "fragging" put limits on such behavior.)

After three months of combat, Kerry had collected enough film footage for his political campaigns, so he went home. He even shot three different endings to the episode where he chases down a VC guy after test audiences thought Kerry shooting a wounded teenager in the back was too much of a "downer." After filming his last staged exploit, Kerry reportedly told a buddy, "That's a wrap. See you at the convention in about thirty-five years."

Kerry is demanding to be made president on the basis of spending four months in Vietnam thirty-five years ago. And yet the men who know what he did during those four months don't think he's fit to be dogcatcher. That seems newsworthy to me, but I must be wrong since the media have engineered a total blackout of the Swift Boat Veterans.

In May, the Swiftees held a spellbinding press conference in Washington, D.C. In front of a photo being used by the Kerry campaign to tout Kerry's war service, the officers stood up, one by one, pointed to their own faces in the campaign photo, and announced that they believed Kerry unfit for command. Only one officer in the photo supports Kerry for president. Seventeen say he is not fit to be president.

The press covered it much as they covered Paula Jones's first press conference.

With the media playing their usual role as Truth Commissar for the now-dead Soviet Union, the Swiftees are having to purchase ad time in order to be heard. No Tim Russert interviews, no *Today* show appearances, no *New York Times* editorials or *Vanity Fair* hagiographies for these heretics against the liberal religion. The only way Swift Boat Veterans for Truth could get less attention would be to go on Air America Radio.

If the 254 veterans against Kerry got one-tenth as much media coverage for calling Kerry a liar as Clown Joe Wilson did for calling Bush a liar, the veterans wouldn't need to buy ad time to get their message out. (Wilson, you'll recall, was a media darling for six or seven months before being exposed as a fantasist by Senate investigators.)

With their commitment to free speech and a robust exchange of ideas (i.e., "child pornography" and "sedition"), the Democratic National Committee is threatening to sue TV stations that run the

Swift Boat Veterans' paid ads. Sue? Can you tell already that there are two lawyers at the top of the Democratic ticket? These are the same people who accuse John Ashcroft of shredding the Bill of Rights. WHY ISN'T THE PRESS COVERING THIS??? Wait, now I remember. Okay, never mind.

The threat to sue is absurd, but will allow the very same TV stations that are already censoring the Swiftees to have an excuse to censor even purchased airtime.

Leave aside the fact that Kerry is a presidential candidate and—judging by the ads being run against George Bush—I gather there's nothing you can't say about a presidential candidate, including calling him Hitler. After reading *Unfit for Command,* I am pretty sure Kerry doesn't want a neutral tribunal deciding who's telling the truth here.

The Swift Boat Veterans provide detailed accounts from dozens and dozens of eyewitnesses to Kerry's Uriah Heep–like behavior—which *Unfit for Command* contrasts with Kerry's boastful descriptions of the exact same incidents.

By contrast, Kerry's supporters have their usual off-the-rack denunciations of any witness against a Democrat. The veterans are: liars, bigots, idiots, politically motivated, and I was never alone in a hotel with Paula Jones.

Ron Brownstein, *Los Angeles Times* reporter and Bill Clinton's favorite reporter, compared the Swift Boat Veterans' ad to a "snuff film." He claimed the veterans have "strong Republican ties."

Apparently, before being permitted to engage in free speech against Democrats in this country you have to: (1) prove that you are not a Republican, (2) take a vow of poverty, and (3) purchase the right to speak in a TV ad. On the basis of Clown Wilson, Michael Moore, George Soros, MoveOn.org, etc., etc., etc., I gather the requirements for engaging in free speech against a Republican are somewhat less rigorous. Hey! Maybe John Edwards is right: There really are two Americas!

O'Neill, the author of *Unfit for Command* and founder of Swift Boat Veterans for Truth, can be heard on the Nixon tapes—unaware that he was being taped—telling Nixon that he came from a family of Democrats and voted for Hubert Humphrey in the prior election. Unlike Joe Wilson, Anita Hill, Richard Clarke, Woodward and Bernstein, et al., O'Neill has said he will take no royalties on his book but will donate all his profits to the Navy. So I think even under liberals' rules, O'Neill is allowed to have an opinion.

Before the book was released and O'Neill could appear to defend it, liberals were on television denouncing the book. If memory serves, the last book Democrats tried this hard to suppress was the Bible. When Democrats are this terrified of a book, it's not because they have a good answer. Howard Dean can accuse Ashcroft of book-burning all he wants, but it's the Democrats who are doing everything in their power to prevent you from reading *Unfit for Command*. In bookstores beginning this week. ■

☞ Dan Rather: Fairly Unbalanced

SEPTEMBER 22, 2004

I believe we now have conclusive proof that:

(1) Dan Rather is not an honest newsman who was simply duped by extremely clever forgeries; and

(2) We could have won the Vietnam War.

A basic canon of journalism is not to place all your faith in a lunatic stuck on something that happened years ago who hates the target of your story and has been babbling nonsense about him for years. And that's true even if you yourself are a lunatic stuck on something that happened years ago (an on-air paddling from Bush 41) who hates the target of your story and has been babbling nonsense about him for years, Dan.

CBS's sole source authenticating the forged National Guard documents is Bill Burkett, who's about as sane as Margot Kidder was when they dragged her filthy, toothless butt out of somebody's shrubs a few years back. Burkett has compared Bush to Hitler and

Napoleon, and rambles on about Bush's "demonic personality shortcomings." (This would put Burkett on roughly the same page as Al Gore.)

According to *USA Today*, an interview with Burkett ended when he "suffered a violent seizure and collapsed in his chair"—an exit strategy Dan Rather has been eyeing hungrily all week, I'm sure. Burkett admits to having nervous breakdowns and having been hospitalized for depression.

At a minimum, the viewing public should have been informed that CBS's sole "unimpeachable" source of the forged anti-Bush records was textbook crank Bill Burkett in order to evaluate the information—"Oh no, not that guy again!" The public would know to use the same skeptical eye it uses when watching the *CBS Evening News* itself.

Whoever forged these documents should not only be criminally prosecuted, but should also have his driver's license taken away for the stupidity of using Microsoft Word to forge 1971 documents.

And yet this was the evidence CBS relied on to accuse a sitting president of a court martial-level offense fifty days before a presidential election.

As of September 20, Dan Rather says he still believes the documents are genuine and says he wants to be the one to break the story if the documents are fake. (Dan might want to attend to that story after his exclusive report on the Japanese attack on Pearl Harbor.) Rather is also eagerly awaiting some other documents Burkett says he has that prove Bush is a brainwashed North Korean spy.

By now, the only possibilities are: (1) Dan Rather knew he was foisting forgeries on the nation to try to change a presidential election or (2) "Kenneth" inflicted some real brain damage when he hit Rather in the head back in 1986.

Liberals keep telling us to "move on" from the CBS scandal—which means we're really onto something. They act surprised and insist this incident was a freak occurrence—an unfortunate mistake in the twilight of a great newsman's career.

To the contrary, such an outrageous fraud was inevitable given the mendacity and outright partisanship of the press.

Burkett didn't come to CBS; CBS found Burkett. Rather's producer, Mary Mapes, called Joe Lockhart at the Kerry campaign and told him he needed to talk to Burkett. Lockhart himself is the apotheosis of the media-DNC complex, moving in and out of Democratic campaigns and jobs with the mainstream media, including at ABC, NBC, and CNN.

CBS was attempting to manipulate a presidential election in wartime. What if CBS had used better forgeries? What if—like Bush's thirty-year-old DUI charge—the media had waited seventy-two hours before the election to air this character assassination?

There is one reason CBS couldn't wait until just before the election to put these forgeries on the air: It would be too late. Kerry was crashing and burning—because of the Swift Boat Veterans for Truth. (Funny that the Swift Boat veterans haven't been able to get on Kerry PR agency CBS News.)

Despite a total blackout on the Swift Boat Veterans in the mainstream media, the Swifties had driven Kerry's poll numbers into the dirt long before the Republican National Convention—proving once again that it's almost impossible for liberals to brainwash people who can read.

Even the *New York Times* had to stop ignoring the number one book on its own best-seller list, *Unfit for Command,* in order to run front-page articles attacking the Swift Boat Veterans.

The *Today* show has given Kitty Kelley a chair next to Katie Couric until Election Day. (At least they're more likely to get the truth in Kitty Kelley's book than in Doug Brinkley's *Tour of Duty.*) But Katie hasn't had time to interview the Swift Boat Veterans.

CBS showcased laughable forgeries obtained from a man literally foaming at the mouth in order to accuse the president of malfeasance. But CBS would never put a single one of the 254 Vietnam veterans on the air to say what they knew about Kerry.

The Swift Boat Veterans for Truth show the role of the individual in history. It wasn't Karl Rove or Republican strategists who finished Kerry off two months before the election; it was the Swift Boat Veterans. The Swifties came along and kicked Kerry in the shins and no matter how much heat they took, they were brave and wouldn't give up. Veterans who served with Kerry told the truth and the American people listened (as soon as they managed to locate a copy of *Unfit for Command* hidden on one of the back shelves at their local bookstores).

CBS was forced to run a fake story so early in the campaign that it was exposed as a fraud—only because of the Swift Boat Vets. These brave men, many of them decorated war heroes, have now not only won the election for Bush, they have ended Dan Rather's career.

It's often said that we never lost a battle in Vietnam, but that the war was lost at home by a seditious media demoralizing the American people. Ironically, the leader of that effort was Rather's predecessor at CBS News, Walter Cronkite, president of the Ho Chi Minh Admiration Society.

It was Cronkite who went on air and lied about the Tet offensive, claiming it was a defeat for the Americans. He told the American people the war was over and we had lost. Ronald Reagan said CBS News officials should have been tried for treason for those broadcasts.

CBS has already lost one war for America. The Swift Boat Vets weren't going to let CBS lose another one. ∎

☞ 2004: Highlights and Lowlifes

DECEMBER 29, 2004

The single biggest event of 2004 was the Election Day exit poll, which, like John Steinbeck's *The Short Reign of Pippin IV,* made John Kerry the president for a few moments. But in a move that stunned the experts, American voters chose "moral values" over an

America-bashing trophy husband and his blow-dried, ambulance-chasing sidekick.

The second biggest event in 2004 came on Sunday, December 26, when the *New York Times* referred to an organization as a "liberal research group." (I think it may have been the Communist Party USA, Trotskyite wing, but still, it's progress.)

CBS eminence Dan Rather was driven off the air in disgrace after he tried to take down a sitting president by brandishing Microsoft Word documents he claimed were authentic Texas Air National Guard memos from the '70s. By liberals' own account, the pompous blowhard was exposed by people sitting around their living rooms in pajamas.

John Kerry's meal ticket, Teresa Heinz, continually made remarks that were wildly inappropriate, such as when she strangely referred to the "seven-year itch" in relation to herself and John Kerry, creating at least three images I didn't want in my head. On the other hand, for any voters who considered the most important campaign issue to be whether the first lady was an earthy, condescending foreigner who had traveled extensively and spoke several languages, Teresa was a huge asset.

Somewhat surprisingly, Teresa never became a major campaign issue. It turned out that supporters of a phony war hero who preyed on rich widows were also okay with the notion of a first lady who might use the F-word during Rose Garden press conferences. By the same token, anyone who was put off by the not-so-affable Eva Peron of American politics already didn't like John Kerry—thanks largely to John O'Neill and the Swift Boat Veterans.

Like the archers of Agincourt, O'Neill and the 254 Swift Boat Veterans took down their own haughty Frenchman.

Meanwhile, San Francisco mayor Gavin Newsom is nipping at O'Neill's heels as the man second-most responsible for Bush's re-election. Thanks largely to Newsom's hard work, gay marriage was big news all year.

In retrospect, the Democrats would have been better off if they had found every gay guy in America who actually wanted to get married and offered each one a million dollars in exchange for the Democrats not having to talk about gay marriage. (Finally, a problem that could have been solved by throwing money at it!)

On the basis solely of media coverage, Abu Ghraib was the biggest story of 2004, maybe the biggest story ever. And for good reason: An American soldier was caught on film not only humiliating Iraqi prisoners—but smoking!

The *New York Times* even had to drop its coverage of Augusta National Golf Course to give Abu Ghraib due prominence. Only the Rumsfeld autopen scandal was big enough to knock Abu Ghraib off the front page.

I personally haven't been so singularly disturbed by an atrocity since I had to sit through all of *The Matrix: Reloaded.*

By contrast, the least important story—again, judging by media coverage—was the peculiar development of a Clintonite caught trying to get into his own pants. Sandy Berger was spotted by National Archives staff repeatedly stuffing top-secret documents into his undergarments in preparation for defending the Clinton administration's record on fighting terrorism before the 9/11 Commission. If you happened to take a long nap the day the Berger story broke, you would have missed it entirely.

On the bright side, the *New York Times* has adopted an all-new standard for covering the extramarital affairs of public figures. With no fanfare, the *Times* quickly abandoned its earlier position that a U.S. president molesting White House staff—including while on the phone discussing sending troops into battle—is not news. The new rule rolled out for Bernie Kerik makes extramarital affairs major front-page news deserving of nonstop coverage, even after the public figure has withdrawn his name from consideration for any government office.

American hero Pat Tillman won a Silver Star this year. But unlike Kerry, he did not write his own recommendation or live to throw his medals over the White House fence in an antiwar rally.

Tillman was an American original: virtuous, pure, and masculine like only an American male can be. The stunningly handsome athlete walked away from a three-year, $3.6 million NFL contract with the Arizona Cardinals to join the U.S. military and fight in Afghanistan, where he was killed in April.

He wanted no publicity and granted no interviews about his decision to leave pro football in the prime of his career and join the Army Rangers. (Most perplexing to Democrats, he didn't even take a home movie camera to a war zone in order to create fake footage for future political campaigns in which he would constantly palaver about his military service and drag around his "Band of Brothers" for the media.)

Tillman gave only an indirect explanation for his decision on the day after 9/11, when he said, "My great-grandfather was at Pearl Harbor, and a lot of my family has gone and fought in wars, and I really haven't done a damn thing as far as laying myself on the line like that." He said he wanted to "pay something back" to America.

He died bringing freedom and democracy to 28 million Afghans—pretty much confirming Michael Moore's view of America as an imperialist cowboy predator. There is not another country in the world—certainly not in continental Europe—that could have produced a Pat Tillman.

On the anniversary of D-Day, as Americans like Pat Tillman risked their lives to liberate 50 million Iraqis and Afghans, in a year when Americans poured into theaters to see a movie about Christ and reaffirmed their support for moral values at the polling booth, America's greatest president died. Ronald Reagan appealed to what is best about America and so transformed the nation that we are now safe to carry on without him. ∎

☞ Liar, Liar, Now You're Fired

JANUARY 12, 2005

If CNN doesn't hire them, Dan Rather and his producers can always get a job teaching at the Columbia School of Journalism. The Columbia Journalism Review recently defended the CBS report on George Bush using forged National Guard documents with the Tawana Brawley excuse: The documents might be "fake but accurate."

Dan Rather and his crack investigative producer Mary Mapes are still not admitting the documents were fakes. Of course, Dan Rather is still not admitting Kerry lost the election or that a woman named Juanita Broaddrick credibly accused Bill Clinton of rape.

Responding to Bill O'Reilly's question in a May 15, 2001, interview on *The O'Reilly Factor* about why CBS News had mentioned crackpot rumors of George Bush's drug use on air seven times, but the name "Juanita Broaddrick" had never crossed Dan Rather's lips (and was only mentioned twice on all of CBS News), Rather replied, "Juanita Broaddrick, to be perfectly honest, I don't remember all the details of Juanita Broaddrick. But I will say that—and you can castigate me if you like. When the charge has something to do with somebody's private sex life, I would prefer not to run any of it."

If only the press had extended that same courtesy to Mike Tyson! Rape has as much to do with "somebody's private sex life" as Bush's National Guard service does.

Admittedly, Juanita Broaddrick's charge against Clinton—that Bill Clinton raped her so brutally that her clothing was torn and her lip was swollen and bleeding, hence his parting words of "you'd better put some ice on that"—was not a story on the order of Augusta National Golf Course's exclusion of women members. But, unlike the Bush drug-use charge, which remains unsupported to this day, Broaddrick's allegations had been fully corroborated by NBC News—which then refused to air Lisa Myers's report until after Clinton's acquittal in the Senate.

Fortunately for Ms. Mapes, Rather also described Bill Clinton as "honest," explaining to O'Reilly, "I think you can be an honest person and lie about any number of things." This must have come as great comfort to Mapes, as she based an entire story about Bush's outrageous behavior in the National Guard on one Lieutenant Colonel Bill Burkett.

Among the issues that might have raised questions about relying on Burkett as your source before accusing a sitting president of having disobeyed direct military orders are:

- Burkett had a long-standing grudge against the National Guard for failing to pay for his medical treatment for a rare tropical disease he claims he contracted during Guard service in Panama.
- He blamed Bush, who was governor at the time, for the Guard's denial of medical benefits because, as everyone knows, the Texas governor's main job is processing medical claims from former National Guard members.
- After leaving the Guard, Burkett suffered a nervous breakdown and was hospitalized for depression.
- At the meeting where he was supposed to give Mapes the National Guard documents, Burkett brought "two binders full of depositions and other documents that were apparently from his litigation with the National Guard over health benefits"—apparently he forgot the two shoeboxes full of UFO photos he'd collected over the years.
- He had compared Bush to Hitler—which admittedly could have been just his way of establishing that he was serious to Democrats.

- He had told a number of stories over the years about Bush's National Guard service, all of which had collapsed under conflicting evidence and even his own contradictory accounts—which is to say the stories were both made up and inaccurate.
- In exchange for the National Guard documents, Burkett demanded money, "relocation assistance" if the story put him or his family in danger (perhaps oceanfront property for a quick getaway), and direct contact with the Kerry campaign.

Even before the story aired, Burkett's description of his own source for the documents kept changing. He said he received the documents anonymously in the mail. He said he was given the documents by someone who would "know what to do with [the documents] better than" he would. He said his source was Chief Warrant Officer George Conn—amid copious warnings that CBS "should not call Chief Warrant Officer Conn because he would deny it" and further that "Conn was on active duty and could not be reached at his Dallas home."

Burkett needn't have worried about crack investigator Mary Mapes getting in touch with his alleged source. Even though a three-second search on Google would have revealed that (1) Burkett was crazy, and (2) he had tried to use Conn as a source before and Conn had vehemently denied Burkett's claims, Mapes told the investigating committee "she did not consider Chief Warrant Officer Conn's denial to be reliable."

It seems Burkett had told Mapes that "Conn was still in the military and that his wife threatened to leave him if he spoke out against President Bush." That was good enough for Mapes. She concluded that Conn—the only person who could have corroborated Burkett's story but denied it—was not to be trusted. Instead, Mapes placed all her faith in the disgruntled, paranoid nut with a vendetta against Bush, an extensive psychiatric history, and an ever-growing enemies list. I'm referring to Bill Burkett here, not Dan Rather.

Finally, Burkett claimed a woman named Lucy Ramirez had passed the documents to him at a livestock show in Houston. It is believed that this account marks the exact day that Burkett's lithium prescription ran out. Despite the fact that no one at CBS was able to locate Ramirez, CBS stuck to the story.

This isn't a lack of "rigor" in fact-checking, as the CBS report suggests. It's a total absence of fact-checking. CBS found somebody who told the story they wanted told—and they ran with it, wholly disregarding the facts.

Curiously, though Mapes trusted Burkett implicitly, she was very careful not to reveal his name to anyone at CBS, probably because she would have been laughed out of the room.

Instead, Mapes described Burkett in the abstract as: "solid," "without bias," "credible," "a Texas Republican of a different chromosome," a "John McCain supporter," "reliable," and "a maverick"—leaving out only "Burkett is convinced he can communicate with caterpillars" and "his best friend is a coffee table." His name was not important. It's not as if he was the sole source for a highly damaging story about the president eight weeks before the election or anything. Oh wait . . .

At a meeting with CBS lawyers the day the story would air, Mapes "did not reveal the source's name or anything negative about the source," but "expressed 'enormous confidence' in her source's reliability and said that he was solid with no bias or credibility issues." She described Burkett as a "moralistic stickler." The subject of UFOs simply never came up.

Mapes trusted Burkett on the basis of the following:

- "Mapes told the panel that she spoke to a mainstream media reporter, who had known Lt. Col. Burkett since

2001, and she stated that he viewed Lt. Col. Burkett as reliable." At least it was a "mainstream media reporter" and not one of those unreliable bloggers throwing anything up on the Net and ruining reputations!

- "Mapes told the panel that she informed the Burketts that she was worried the documents might be a 'political dirty trick.' Mapes said that the Burketts appeared 'genuinely shocked' at the suggestion and this reaction gave her comfort." (You could tell they were really shocked because they had the same look on their faces that Condi Rice had when Richard Clarke first told her about al-Qaeda.)
- Mapes really hated George Bush and would do anything to make him lose the election.

Actually, Mapes did not put her last reason in writing, which created a real mystery for the CBS investigating committee. Proving once again how useless "moderate Republicans" are, the CBS Report—co-authored by moderate Republican Dick Thornburgh—found no evidence of political bias at CBS.

If Fox News had come out with a defamatory story about Kerry based on forged documents, liberals would be demanding we cut power to the place. (Fortunately, the real documents on Kerry were enough to do the trick.) But the outside investigators hired by CBS could find no political agenda at CBS.

By contrast, the report did not hesitate to accuse the bloggers who exposed the truth about the documents of having "a conservative agenda." As with liberal attacks on Fox's "fair and balanced" motto, it is now simply taken for granted that "conservative bias" means "the truth." ■

☞ Ever Have One of Those Millennia?

MAY 11, 2005

It's always important to get liberals to stop complaining long enough to make a hard prediction. This week we will review liberal predictions on bringing democracy to Iraq.

When they weren't claiming the Iraq elections would not take place at all—and, even if they did, the people wouldn't participate—liberals were telling us that if we let those crazy Arabs vote, the Iraqi people would elect extremist Islamic mullahs hostile to the United States.

Well, the Iraq National Assembly completed filling out the cabinet this week, and it can now be said that this was liberals' laughably wrong prediction No. 9,856. (Or No. 9,857 if you count their predictions of ruinous global cooling back in the 1970s, which I don't because that could still happen.)

Iraq's first democratically elected government in half a century has a Shia prime minister and a Kurdish president and several Sunni cabinet ministers. In fact, toss in a couple of dowdy lesbians from the Green Party and it would look a lot like Vermont's state house.

Fat Muqtada al-Sadr saw his radical Shiite movement humiliated in the January elections. According to a recent poll by the International Republican Institute, two-thirds of Iraqis say Iraq is on the right track.

The minority Sunnis, who once held sway under Saddam Hussein and were told by American liberals to expect major payback from the Shiites under a democracy, were chosen by the majority

Shia government for four cabinet positions, including the not insignificant position of defense minister. Plus, the Sunnis might get a fifth if they can convince Representative Ali Abu Jeffords to switch parties.

One of the Sunnis picked for a cabinet post turned it down on the grounds that he thought he was chosen simply to fill a Sunni quota. "I don't believe in sectarianism," he said, "I believe in democracy." So I'll be moving to Iraq soon to live in a country that forcefully rejects quotas.

Also this week, Prime Minister Ibrahim al-Jaafari said he would like a woman as his fourth deputy prime minister. It's as if the Taliban has risen from the dead!

Apparently—like John Kerry and the Democrats—the Muslim extremists just didn't get their message out. Although "Green Zone Veterans for Truth" were also a factor.

What we've learned from this is: Talking to liberals is much more fun now that we have LexisNexis.

In a November 9, 2003, news article, the *New York Times* raised the prospect that "democracy in the Middle East might empower the very forces that the United States opposes, like Islamic fundamentalists in Saudi Arabia and Egypt."

Democracy in the United States might have put John Kerry in the White House, too, but you'll notice we didn't abandon the idea.

One difference is that the Islamic fundamentalists in Saudi Arabia and Egypt were not democratically elected. Still, the *Times* said that "something similar" happened in Iran when "domestic pressures" installed the Ayatollah Ruhollah Khomeini. By "domestic pressures" in Iran, I gather the *Times* meant "the Carter presidency."

Philadelphia Inquirer columnist Trudy Rubin claimed to be talking about "grim Iraq realities," explaining to her readers that if elections were held, the new Iraqi government "will likely be dominated by religious parties. If the economy stays bad, radical Islamic parties could do well." So you can see how leaving the tyrannical Hussein dynasty (slogan: "We're the rape room people!") in place was preferable to that.

Winning the category of Most Wrong Predictions in the Fewest Words, Joe Conason predicted in the September 27, 2004, *New York Observer*: "a series of horrifically violent confrontations in Iraq's cities, a postponement of the January elections, a wider call-up of National Guard and Reserve units, or even a renewed military draft." And if Bush won a second term, Conason said: "Beware the 'November surprise' that will begin to bring home the true costs of his feckless adventure."

Conason's feeble litany of harebrained predictions reads like a haiku of bum steers. No increase in "horrific" violence, no postponement of elections, no draft, no "November surprise." (Okay, there was one "November surprise"—but only for the Democrats. It happened on November 2.)

Winning the category of Most Wrong Predictions, Lifetime Achievement Award, Katrina vanden Heuvel (Queen of the May at the fun-loving *Nation* magazine) said invading Iraq would lead to "more terrorist retaliation, undermine the fight against al-Qaida and make America less secure and possibly unleash those very weapons of mass destruction into the hands of rogue terrorists in Iraq."

What weapons, Katrina? (Katrina lied, kids died!) Hey! Wait a minute! How can rogue terrorists in Iraq detonate bombs? They're all too busy flying kites with their children! Hasn't she seen *Fahrenheit 9/11*?

After we invaded Iraq, Katrina predicted the United States would stay in Iraq as a colonial power—as the only nonimperialist superpower in the history of the world is wont to do. As we paved the way for elections, she said, "You know, if there are elections in Iraq, it's very likely it will not be secular democracy."

But it's not fair to quote Katrina. She still thinks the Soviet Union's planned economy failed because the farmers had seventy years of bad weather. Liberals' current prediction is that Hillary will be able to do a planned economy right. ■

☞ Where's That Religious Fanatic We Elected?

JANUARY 27, 2005

Maybe he is an idiot. On the thirty-second anniversary of *Roe v. Wade* this past Monday—I was going to say "birthday of *Roe v. Wade*," but that would be too grimly ironic even for me—President Bush told a pro-life rally in Washington that a "culture of life cannot be sustained solely by changing laws. We need, most of all, to change hearts."

Actually, what we need least of all is to "change hearts." Maybe it's my law background, but I think it's time we changed a few laws.

The "changing hearts" portion of the abortion debate is over. ATTENTION, PASSENGERS: We're now entering the "minds" portion of the "hearts and minds" journey on abortion. We've been talking about abortion for thirty-two years. All the hearts that can be changed have been changed. By some estimates, 35 million human hearts (and counting) have been "changed" by abortion.

Judging by her comments this week calling abortion a "sad, even tragic choice," we've even changed Hillary Clinton's heart. (And who would know better than the sad, even tragic, choice offered to New York voters in 2000 herself?)

Hillary went so far as to say she had "respect" for those who believe that "there are no circumstances under which any abortion should ever be available."

I've never heard of anyone who thinks abortion should not be "available" to save the life of the mother. There was never a law in any state that prohibited abortion to save the life of the mother. If Hillary "respects" even this (nonexistent) lunatic fringe of the pro-life movement, she must adore the rest of us!

The only thing we need to do now is to start "changing laws." A culture of life cannot even begin—much less be sustained—until we change the law and repeal *Roe v. Wade*. Only then can we tally up how many hearts have been changed.

If, right now, pro-lifers had already succeeded in changing the hearts of every last person in America—including Hillary Clinton!—abortion would still be legal in every state of the union. It's a "constitutional right"—taking its place alongside all those other "sad," "tragic" rights guaranteed by the Constitution, such as religious expression, free speech, freedom of assembly, and so on. (Who was it who said, "Free speech should be safe, legal, and rare"?)

Only when at least five members of the Supreme Court stop pretending to see a secret, hidden clause in the Constitution, discernible only to members of the ACLU, and repeal *Roe* can Americans finally vote on abortion. This is a right we have been denied for thirty-two years. In effect, a thirty-two-year gag rule has been imposed on those of us who respect every stage of life.

NARAL Pro-Choice America—formerly the National Abortion Rights Action League—claims that if *Roe* were overturned, nineteen states would immediately outlaw abortion, and nineteen more would soon follow suit. This is the one issue on which NARAL and I agree: Pro-lifers already have changed the hearts of Americans about abortion!

Abortion was not terribly popular when *Roe v. Wade* was first concocted in 1973—by seven male justices and their mostly male law clerks. Abortion—like other liberal priorities over the years including forced busing, gay marriage, and removing "under God" from the Pledge of Allegiance—is an issue liberals believe is best voted on by groups of nine or fewer.

We know it wasn't popular with actual Americans back then because forty-six states had outlawed abortion in a once-common procedure known as "representative democracy." Reflect on the fact that among the things more popular than abortion even back in 1973 were white-guy afros, lime-green leisure suits, and earth shoes.

In the intervening thirty-two years, abortion has only become less popular. People have seen sonograms of smiling fetuses, they've seen the mangled remains of aborted babies, they've heard the ghastly arguments from NARAL termagants, and they've seen untold women marking the birth dates of their terminated children with weeping and despair.

In a *Los Angeles Times* poll a few years ago, 57 percent of respondents said they believed abortion was "murder." Seventy-two percent of women and 58 percent of men said they thought abortion should be illegal after the first trimester. (Among men currently listed on NBA rosters, the figure was even lower.)

Note that men in the poll were more supportive of abortion than women, which is perfectly in keeping with the pro-abortion orthodoxy that men should have no say in this matter, unless they're saying "yes, dear." Once again, NARAL and I are in agreement! It's a "woman's issue"; could you men please just butt out?

Despite the fact that feminists cry and try to make people feel guilty about opposing a "woman's right" to abortion, men always support abortion more than women—no matter who takes the poll or how the questions are asked. Curiously, single men aged eighteen to thirty-four are the cohort most dearly devoted to a woman's "right to choose."

Until *Roe* is overturned, telling pro-lifers they need to be "changing hearts" is like telling the New England Patriots they need to practice more—while never, ever letting them play in the Super Bowl. We've been changing hearts for thirty-two years—I think we're ready for the big match now. I think Americans would support massive restrictions on abortion. And NARAL agrees with me! How about it, liberals? Prove me wrong! Let Americans vote. ■

☞ Starved for Justice

MARCH 24, 2005

Democrats have called out armed federal agents in order to: (1) prevent black children from attending a public school in Little Rock, Arkansas (National Guard); (2) investigate an alleged violation of federal gun laws in Waco, Texas (Bureau of Alcohol, Tobacco, and Firearms); and (3) deport a small boy to Cuba (Immigration and Naturalization Service).

So how about a Republican governor sending in the National Guard to stop an innocent American woman from being starved to death in Florida? Republicans like the military. Democrats get excited about military force only when it's going to be used against Americans.

In two of the three cases mentioned above, the Democrats' use of force was in direct contravention of court rulings. Admittedly, this was a very long time ago—back in U.S. history when the judiciary was only one of the three branches of our government. Democratic Governor Orval Faubus called out the Arkansas National Guard expressly for purposes of defying rulings of the U.S. Supreme Court and lower federal courts.

The decadent buffoon Bill Clinton sent armed agents from the INS to seize a small boy from an American family—despite rulings by the majestic and infallible Florida courts granting custody of the boy to that very family.

None of these exercises of military force has gone down in history as a noble moment, but that's because of the underlying purpose of the force, not the fact that force was used.

To the contrary, what has gone down in history as a glorious moment for the republic was when President Dwight Eisenhower (Republican) called out military force of his own. In response to Governor Faubus's abuse of the National Guard, Eisenhower simultaneously revoked Faubus's control of the National Guard and ordered the 101st Airborne Division to escort black students to school. (Minutes later, Democrats pronounced the Arkansas public schools a "hopeless quagmire" and demanded to know what Ike's exit strategy was.)

As important as it was to enforce the constitutional right to desegregated schools, isn't it also important to enforce Terri Schiavo's right to due process before she is killed by starvation?

Liberals' newfound respect for "federalism" is completely disingenuous. People who support a national policy on abortion are prohibited from ever using the word *federalism*.

I note that whenever liberals talk about "federalism" or "states' rights," they are never talking about a state referendum or a law passed by the duly elected members of a state legislature—or anything voted on by the actual citizens of a state. What liberals mean by "federalism" is: a state court ruling. Just as "choice" refers to only one choice, "the rule of law" refers only to "the law as determined by a court."

As a practical matter, courts will generally have the last word in interpreting the law because courts decide cases. But that's a pragmatic point. There is nothing in the law, the Constitution, or the concept of "federalism" that mandates giving courts the last word. Other public officials, including governors and presidents, are sworn to uphold the law, too.

It would be chaotic if public officials made a habit of disregarding court rulings simply because they disagreed with them. But a practice borne of practicality has led the courts to greater and greater flights of arrogance. Sublimely confident that no one will ever call their bluff, courts are now regularly discovering secret legal provisions requiring abortion and gay marriage and prohibiting public prayer and Ten Commandments displays.

Just once, we need an elected official to stand up to a clearly incorrect ruling by a court. Any incorrect ruling will do, but my vote is for a state court that has ordered a disabled woman to be starved to death at the request of her adulterous husband.

Florida state court judge George Greer—last heard from when he denied an order of protection to a woman weeks before her husband stabbed her to death—determined that Terri would have wanted to be starved to death based on the testimony of her husband, who was then living with another woman. (The judge also took judicial notice of the positions of O.J. Simpson, Scott Peterson, and Robert Blake.) The husband also happened to be the only person present when the oxygen was cut off to Terri's brain in the first place. He now has two children with another woman.

Greer has refused to order the most basic medical tests for brain damage before condemning a woman to death. Despite all those years of important, searching litigation we keep hearing about, Terri has yet to receive either an MRI or a PET scan—although she may be allowed to join a support group for women whose husbands are trying to kill them.

Greer has cut off the legal rights of Terri's real family and made her husband (now with a different family) her sole guardian, citing as precedent the landmark *Fox v. Henhouse* ruling of 1893. Throughout the process that would result in her death sentence, Terri was never permitted her own legal counsel. Evidently, Florida lawyers were all tied up defending the right to life of child-molesting murderers.

Given the country's fetishism about court rulings, this may be a rash assumption, but I presume if Greer had ordered that Terri Schiavo be shot at her husband's request—a more humane death, by the way—the whole country would not sit idly by, claiming to be bound by the court's ruling because of the "rule of law" and "federalism." President Bush would order the FBI to protect her and Governor Bush would send in the state police.

What was supposed to be the "least dangerous" branch has become the most dangerous—literally to the point of ordering an innocent American woman to die, and willfully disregarding congressional subpoenas. Judges can't be stopped—solely because the entire country has agreed to treat the pronouncements of former ambulance-chasers as the word of God. The only power courts have is that everyone jumps when they say "jump." (Also, people seem a little intimidated by the black robes. From now on we should make all judges wear lime-green leisure suits.)

President Andrew Jackson is supposed to have said of a Supreme Court ruling he opposed: "Well, John Marshall has made his decision, now let him enforce it." The court's ruling was ignored. And yet, somehow, the republic survived.

If Governor Jeb Bush doesn't say something similar to the Florida courts that have ordered Terri Schiavo to die, he'll be the second Republican governor disgraced by the illiterate ramblings of a state judiciary. Governor Mitt Romney will never recover from his acquiescence to the Massachusetts Supreme Court's miraculous discovery of a right to gay marriage. Neither will Governor Bush if he doesn't stop the torture and murder of Terri Schiavo. ■

POSTSCRIPT: Months later, in the summer of 2005, liberals were gloating when an autopsy showed that Terri was severely disabled. No "liquid" brain, as her husband's lawyer had claimed, but severely disabled. I thought everyone already knew that, but I guess not. In any event, I believe the question was about due process of law. Based on the Schiavo precedent, how about we immediately execute all convicted murderers, without appeal, and *then* investigate to see if they were guilty? ■

☞ Drag Liberals into the Light

APRIL 28, 2005

Democrats are in an incomprehensible rage over the filibuster. DON'T STOP READING! I AM NOT GOING TO DISCUSS THE HISTORY OF THE FILIBUSTER! Republicans have got to learn to stop getting into technicalities with the

Democrats. They win in the dark; we win in the light. And it doesn't get much darker than a discussion of the Senate filibuster.

It's no excuse that the Democrats are lying. They do that all the time. Republicans have got to learn to let it go.

In one sentence Republicans should state that the so-called nuclear option means: "Majority vote wins." (This is as opposed to the Democrats' motto, which is "Our side always wins.")

I am supremely confident that normal Americans will not be shocked to learn that a Republican Senate plans to confirm the judicial nominees of a Republican president. Democrats believe that they should win all disputes on the basis of their being the minority in the Senate, the minority in the House, the loser in the last two presidential races, the minority in state governorships, and the minority in all but a tiny number of very small but densely populated enclaves in this country that need to tax Rush Limbaugh, even though he lives in another state, just to keep all their little socialist programs afloat.

The question Republicans need to start loudly asking is: Why do the Democrats want to keep judicial nominees like Janice Rogers Brown and Priscilla Owen off the federal bench? As I understand it, the reason Democrats are in a blind rage about Priscilla Owen is that, as a state court judge in Texas, Owen interpreted a law passed by the Texas legislature requiring parental consent for fourteen-year-old girls to have abortions to mean that parental consent was required for fourteen-year-old girls to have abortions. I think Americans need to hear Democrats explain that.

Democrats oppose Janice Rogers Brown because she's black. One cartoon on Blackcommentator.com shows President Bush introducing Brown to Clarence Thomas, Colin Powell, and Condoleezza Rice, with Bush saying, "Welcome to the bench, Ms. Clarence—I mean, Ms. Rogers Brown. You'll fit right in!"

Let's see, what do those four have in common? Two secretaries of state, a former general, a former professor, and a Supreme Court justice . . . What's the common thread? I know there's something—but what is it? There's a whole array of groups opposed to Brown: People for the American Way, the National Women's Law Center, NARAL Pro-Choice America, the Feminist Majority, the Aryan Nation, and so on.

But their actual objections to Brown are opaque. The website of "People for a Small Slice of the Upper West Side Way" contains a lengthy diatribe on Brown's nightmarish extremism while managing never, ever to give one specific example. In fact, if you take out "Janice Rogers Brown" and replace it with "Tom DeLay," it makes just as much sense when you read it.

This is what we get by way of explanation on the horror show that is Janice Rogers Brown:

- "ideological extremism"
- "aggressive judicial activism"
- "even further to the right than the most far-right justices"
- "prone to inserting conservative political views into her appellate opinions"
- "many disturbing dissents"
- "a disturbing tendency to try to remake the law"
- "extreme states' rights and anti-federal-government positions"
- "working to push the law far to the right"
- "doesn't hate America and all that it stands for"

Okay, I made up that last one.

Conservatives never attack liberal judges this way. We simply say: He found the Pledge of Allegiance unconstitutional. . . . He found a right to gay marriage in a state constitution written in 1780 by John Adams. . . . He ruled that smelly homeless people have a constitutional right to stink up public libraries and scare patrons. . . . He excluded eighty pounds of cocaine found in the defendant's car on the grounds that it was reasonable to run from the police when the police are viewed as "corrupt, violent, and abusive."

Democrats want to terrify people by claiming Bush's judicial nominees are nutcase extremists hell-bent on shredding the Constitution—as opposed to liberals' preferred method of simply rewriting it on a daily basis—but they're terrified that someone might ask them what they mean by "extremist." Let's ask!

If liberals could win in the court of public opinion, they wouldn't need the federal courts to hand them their victories in the first place. The reason liberals refuse to elaborate on "extremist right-wing ideologue" is that they need liberal courts to give them gay marriage, a godless Pledge of Allegiance, abortion on demand, nude dancing, rights for pederasts, and everything else they could never win in America if it were put to a vote.

Republicans are letting them get away with it by allowing the debate on judges to consist of mind-numbing arguments about the history of the filibuster. Note to Republicans: Of your six minutes on TV, use thirty seconds to point out the Democrats are abusing the filibuster and the other five-and-a-half minutes to ask liberals to explain why they think Bush's judicial nominees are "extreme." ∎

☛ Seven "Extraordinary" Idiots

JUNE 1, 2005

Let's not put the seven Republican senators who engineered the "compromise" deal with the Democrats in charge of negotiations with North Korea. I would sooner trust the North Koreans to keep their word than the Democrats.

The North Koreans at least waited for the ink to dry on Clinton's 1996 "peace" deal before they set to work violating it by feverishly building nuclear weapons. After hoodwinking seven Republicans into a "compromise" deal, Senate Democrats waited exactly seven seconds before breaking it.

The deal was this: Senate Republicans would not use their majority status to win confirmation votes. In return, the Democrats promised to stop blocking nominees supported by a majority of senators—except in "extraordinary circumstances." Thus, a minority of senators in the party Americans keep trying to throw out of power will now be choosing federal judges with the advice and consent of the president.

The seven Republicans we're not leaving in charge of the national treasury believed they could trust the Democrats to interpret "extraordinary circumstances" fairly. And why not? It's not as if the Democrats have behaved outrageously for the past four years using their minority status to block Bush's nominees. Oh, wait— no, I have that wrong. The Democrats *have* behaved outrageously for the past four years using their minority status to block Bush's nominees.

Hmmm. Well, at least the Democrats didn't wait until Trent Lott foolishly granted them an equal number of committee chairmanships following the 2000 election to seize illegitimate control of the Senate by getting future Trivial Pursuit answer Jim Jeffords to change parties after being elected as a Republican. Oops, no— they did that, too.

The seven Republican "mavericks," as the *New York Times* is wont to call them, had just signed off on this brilliant compromise when the Democrats turned around and filibustered John Bolton, Bush's nominee to be ambassador to the United Nations.

At least it wasn't an important job. But even so, didn't we win the last election? Why, yes, we did! And didn't we win a majority in the Senate? Yes, we did! To be precise, Republicans have won a majority of Senate seats the past six consecutive elections. (And the last six consecutive elections in the House of Representatives, too!)

I think that means Republicans should win. Republican senators support Bush's nominees and Democratic senators oppose them. The way disagreements like this are ordinarily sorted out in a democracy is that a vote is taken among our elected representatives, and majority vote wins.

But sometime after 1993—which, by eerie coincidence, was the last time Democrats had a majority in the Senate—a new rule developed, requiring that the minority party win all contested votes. The Democrats—the same people the seven mavericks are relying on to play fair now—began using procedural roadblocks to prevent the majority vote from prevailing by simply preventing votes from taking place at all. (Senate Democrats do this by voting not to vote, whereas Texas Democrats do it by boarding a Greyhound bus bound for Oklahoma.)

Democrats tried "Count All the Votes (Until I Win)"—Al Gore, 2000. They tried "Vote or Die!"—P. Diddy, 2004. Those failed, so now the Democrats' motto is: "No Voting!"

The Senate majority leader, Bill Frist, thought the party with the most votes should be able to win. (Boy, talk about out of touch! And this guy wants to be president?)

The seven "maverick" Republicans thought a better idea would be to crawl to the minority party and plead for crumbs. If the "maverick" Republicans had a slogan, it would be: "Always surrender from a position of strength."

The deal they struck, this masterful Peace of Westphalia, simply put into writing the rule that the minority party controls the Senate, which will remain the rule until the Democrats aren't the minority party anymore.

Chuck Schumer could be the last Democrat in the Senate and the new rule would be: Unanimous votes required for all Senate business. But at least we could count on Senators Lindsey Graham, Mike DeWine, John McCain, John Warner, Olympia Snowe, Susan Collins, and Lincoln Chafee to strike a deal forcing Schumer to agree not to block the ninty-nine other senators except in "extraordinary circumstances."

No wonder Democrats were so testy about bringing democracy to Iraq: They don't like democracy in America. Liberals' beef with Iraq's new government was that the Sunnis—the minority sect whose reign of terror controlled Iraq for almost thirty years—wouldn't be adequately represented. Obviously, this did not bode well for the Democrats—a minority party whose reign of terror controlled the U.S. House for forty years.

The only way for Americans to get some vague semblance of what they voted for is to elect mammoth Republican majorities—and no "mavericks." Fortunately, for the sake of civilization and the republic, that process seems to be well under way. ■

AT LEAST THEIR MOTHERS ARE STILL LISTENING

☞ Come Back, Liberals!

MARCH 9, 2005

Liberals have been completely intellectually vanquished. Actually, they lost the war of ideas long ago. It's just that now their defeat is so obvious, even they've noticed. As new DNC Chairman Howard Dean might say, it's all over but the screaming.

In an editorial last week, the *New York Times* gave President Bush credit for democracy sweeping through the Middle East or, as the *Times* put it, "a year of heartening surprises." Yes, the Middle East's current democratization would come as quite a surprise to anyone who puts his hands over his ears and hums during the president's speeches.

Rolling Stone magazine is making fun of MoveOn.org for having no contact with normal Americans. Their Bush-hating cause has become so hopeless that MoveOn.org is on the verge of actually moving on.

Marking the first time Walter Cronkite and I have agreed on anything, Cronkite is ridiculing Dan Rather, saying he should have retired a long time ago.

No one, not even Chris Matthews, is defending the Italian Communist who claims American forces intentionally shot at her in Iraq. (But to be fair, Keith Olbermann has been on vacation this week.) She may have lost some credibility when she backed her claim that Americans were targeting her by quoting her kidnappers. She said her kidnappers had warned her to stay away from the Americans because they would only hurt her. And then my rapist said, "Whatever you do, don't cry out for the police! They won't help you!"

Consider that less than twenty years ago, ABC's Peter Jennings and CBS's Mike Wallace announced at an "Ethics in America" panel that they would not intervene to prevent the slaughter of American troops while on duty as journalists—especially during sweeps. Wallace said, "You don't have a higher duty. No. No. You're a reporter!" It almost makes you wonder if U.S. troops have ever targeted American journalists in the field during wartime. Maybe Eason Jordan would know something about that.

Now liberal journalists are pretending to support the troops. They hardly ever call them "baby killers" anymore, at least to their faces.

Democrats are even pretending to believe in God—you know, as they understand Her.

The only liberals putting up a fight these days are ex-Klanners and other assorted nuts.

There's former KKK "Kleagle" and Democratic Senator Bob Byrd, who compared the Republicans to Hitler last week. Byrd having been a charter member of a fascist organization himself, no one was sure if this was intended as a critique or a compliment.

Aspiring first lady Teresa Heinz claims the election was stolen through the machinations of a vast conspiracy involving Republican polling machine manufacturers. We eagerly await a Michael Moore documentary to flesh out the details. It's only a matter of time before Heinz announces that anti-Bush insurgents control most of the Red States, and that the sooner the U.S. pulls out of those quagmires, the better.

Howard Dean—chairman of the party that supports murder, adultery, lying about adultery, coveting other people's money, stealing other people's money, mass-producing human embryos for spare parts like an automotive chop shop, and banning God—has called the Republican Party "evil." One Democrat in the audience, a preschool teacher no less, complained that Dean was soft-pedaling his message.

Teddy Kennedy's big new idea is to wheel out his eighteenth proposal to raise the minimum wage. He's been doing this since wages were paid in Spanish doubloons (which, coincidentally, are now mostly found underwater). Kennedy refuses to countenance any risky schemes like trying to grow the economy so people making minimum wage get raises because they've been promoted. Kennedy's going down and he's taking the party with him! (Recognize the pattern?)

I keep expecting the real Democrats to appear and drag these nuts out of the room, saying, *Oh sorry, he's escaped again—don't worry, he does this all the time,* and then Howard Dean will stand up and have no pants on.

So now, the entire country is ignoring liberals. As proof, I note that twenty-six congressmen have signed a letter denouncing me for a column I wrote two weeks ago; for the past two weeks, I've been attacked on MSNBC and CNN, in the *Detroit Free-Press,* and on every known liberal blog and radio show. (I especially want to thank Pacifica Radio in this regard.) I personally have shouted their complaints from the rooftops. Liberals had fallen into my trap!

But there was no point in responding because no one had heard about the liberal denunciations in the first place. It was like explaining a joke: *Okay, and then they said, "Call me a cab," and then I said, "Okay! You're a cab!" Are you following this? . . . Sorry, let me start over again.*

This is like beating Dennis Kucinich in an untelevised presidential debate. That and $8.50 will get you a cup of coffee at Starbucks. I'm tired of helping liberals publicize their attacks on me. Liberals are going to have to do better than that if they want a response from me.

It's not just that we're a divided nation, with liberals watching only CNN and conservatives watching only Fox News. I'm pretty sure liberals are aware of me, and I haven't appeared on CNN for months. It's liberals the country is ignoring. No one knows or cares what they're carrying on about in their media outlets. I'm the canary in the coal mine: Liberals can't get arrested. They're even letting Martin Sheen off with a warning now.

I hate to sound selfish at such a great moment for the country, but this is nothing short of calamitous for completely innocent right-wing polemicists. Liberals are too pathetic to write about. I have nothing to do; my life is over. Where have all the flowers gone?

I'm confident they'll stage a comeback someday. In lieu of common sense, liberals have boundless energy. But I'm getting bored waiting. In the interest of good sportsmanship, I have some proposals for liberals. I think Democrats might want to drop the contract all Democrats apparently have to sign pledging to pretend to believe insane things. Also, if you could just get the base of your party to not participate anymore and maybe be a little less crazy, people might listen to you. Barring that, Howard Dean is just going to have to scream a little louder. ∎

Acknowledgments

I have a lot of careers to jeopardize here.

Luckily for me, I have a posse of smart friends who are absurdly generous with their time. Two must be singled out for special mention. First, the funniest man I know, Ned Rice, is a joke-writing machine who has given me more lines than I care to admit and breaks it to me gently when my jokes are "hacky." Second, Merrill Kinstler is my main talking partner and general consigliere. He probably would be a professional joke writer, too, except he doesn't have time because he's on the phone with me.

As for the rest, I have been blessed with so many brilliant friends, I will not attempt to describe their individual contributions, but will simply thank them: Hans Bader, Jon Caldera, Robert Caplain, George Conway, Jim Downey, Miguel Estrada, Steve Gilbert, Melanie Graham, John Harrison, James Higgins, Jim Hughes, Gary Lawson, David Limbaugh, Jay Mann, Jim Moody, Jeremy Rabkin, and Younis Zubchevich. Also, Gene Meyer performs an invaluable service by regularly placing nervous phone calls to me pleading with me not to use a certain line, which is how I know what the most popular line of the column is going to be. So I want to thank him for that. (And please don't let my mentioning it deter you, Gene!)

The original editor for much of the material in this book was Greg Melvin at Universal Press Syndicate—who is also a friend from his days singing in a rock band. *Human Events* has been my longtime home and, inasmuch as it is run by men like Tom Winter and Terry Jeffrey, published me when no one else would. In addition, I was lucky enough to have two Crown editors on this book, which would normally constitute sarcasm coming from me, but not in the case of Jed Donahue and Doug Pepper. Jed was called in to pinch-hit for my longstanding editor, Doug—

who was so good, now he's running a publishing house in Canada. I am indebted to all my editors, and that's coming from someone who, as a rule, detests editors.

I remain eternally grateful to my publisher, Steve Ross, and my sainted agent, Joni Evans, who together unleashed me on liberal America. Also thanks to my publicist, Diana Banister, who works tirelessly on each new book. Most of all, I thank my family for their unwavering support: my parents, Jack and Nell; my brothers, John and Jim; my sisters-in-law, Pam and Diane; and my nieces, Kimberly and Christina.

Index

ABA, 179–84
Abbas, Abul, 59
abortion, 447–49
Abraham, S. Daniel, 144
Abu Ghraib prison, 14–15, 81, 437
Abu-Jamal, Mumia, 34
Achille Lauro hijacking, 23, 59–60
adultery, 64, 413–15
Afghanistan, 29
Against All Enemies (Clarke), 150–52
Ailes, Roger, 219–21
air travel, 87–112
    armed pilots, 101–3
    federal laws and, 87–91
    racial profiling and, 6–7, 103–12
    security procedures, 91–100
al-Jaafari, Ibrahim, 445
al-Jazeera, 58–59
Al Noor School, 44–45
al Qaeda. *See* Qaeda, al
Albasti, Tarek, 68–69
ALCU, 106–7
Aldrich, Gary, 150
Alhazmi, Nawaf, 103–4
Allende, Salvador, 227
Almihdhar, Khalid, 103–4
Alzheimer's disease, 202
Amar, Akhil, 167
Amar, Vikram David, 366
Ambrose, Stephen, 74, 208
American Airlines, 107
American Dreamer (Culver and
    Hyde), 175
The American President (movie), 5
anti-Semitism, 242–45

Arctic National Wildlife Refuge
    (ANWR), 164–66
Arming America (Bellesiles), 167
Ashcroft, John, 67–70, 103–5,
    166–68, 176–77
asylum laws, 325–26
ATF (Bureau of Alcohol, Tobacco,
    and Firearms), 100–101
Atkins, Daryl Renard, 265–66
Atta, Mohammed, 40
Augusta National Golf Club,
    230–32, 437
Aziz, Tariq, 62
Aznar, José Maria, 78

Baker, Jim, 365
Beamer, Todd, 45–46
beauty pageant, in Nigeria, 46–48
Beidler, Mike, 217–18
Bellesiles, Michael, 167
The Bell Curve (Murray and Hern-
    stein), 265–68
Ben-Veniste, Richard, 103, 110–12
Berger, Sandy, 437
Berry, Halle, 138–39
Bias (Goldberg), 231
Biden, Joseph, 9, 49, 121, 299
bin Laden, Osama. *See* Laden,
    Osama bin
Bing, Stephen, 145, 146–47
Blair, Jayson, 215–17, 221–25
Blumenthal, Sidney, 19
Blyth, Myrna, 390
Bob Roberts (movie), 6
Boies, David, 360

Bolton, John, 457
Boorstin, Daniel, 39–40
Bork, Robert, 180
Bowman, Pasco, 179
Bradlee, Ben, 219
Braun, Carol Moseley, 121, 204
Brawley, Tawana, 425
Brinkley, Doug, 434
Broaddrick, Juanita, 11, 439–40
Broadus, Kayla, 188
Brock, David, 17, 18
Broder, David, 300
Brooklyn Museum of Art, 284–89
Brown, Janice Rogers, 454–55
Brown, Jerry, 233
Buchanan, Pat, 213–14, 422
Buckley, James, 180
Burkett, Bill, 432–34, 440–43
Burton, Dan, 301
Bush, George H.W., 24
Bush, George W.
    2003 State of the Union address,
        85
    accomplishments of, 25–26
    accused of Abu Ghraib abuse,
        14–15
    Chinese plane incident, 301
    financial investments, 156–57
    fundraising, 145
    National Guard service, 246–47
    proposed tax cuts, 302–3
    ultimatum to Hussein, 54–55,
        65–66
Bush, Jeb, 358, 452–53
Bushnell, George, 183–84
butterfly ballots, 347–48, 360
Byrd, Robert C., 11, 147–50,
    329–30, 460

Caesarean sections, 135, 137
California, 158–60

Callender, James, 410–11
campaign-finance reform, 401–4
campaign fundraising, 144–47
Campbell, Jennifer, 136
Campbell, Jim, 372–73
Caner, Emir Fethi, 45
Caner, Ergun Hehmet, 45
capitalism, 153–56, 160
Caputo, Phil, 208
Carlson, Margaret, 297–98
Carter, Jimmy, 22, 140, 426
Castro, Fidel, 311
CBS News, 231–32, 432–35,
    442–43
Central Park rape case, 268–79
cerebral palsy, 135, 137
Chamberlain, Joshua, 206
Chemerinsky, Erwin, 338
Cheney, Dick, 73–74, 156–57
Chile, 227–28
China, 301
Christianity, 194–99
Churchill, Winston, 207
CIA (Central Intelligence Agency),
    9, 334–35
The Cider House Rules (movie), 4–5
cigarette deaths, 376
Citizen Soldiers (Ambrose), 208
civil unions, 190–94
Civil War, 205–11
Claiborne, Harry E., 180
Clancy, Tom, 199
Clark, Wesley, 14, 57, 73, 116–18,
    122, 127
Clarke, Ramsey, 427
Clarke, Richard, 150–52
Cleland, Max, 246–61
Clift, Eleanor, 201
Clinton, Bill
    affair with Lewinsky, 4, 280–83
    book by, 306–9

impeachment proceedings, 306–8
major speech by, 10
opinion polls about, 289–91
presidential pardon from, 298–300
rape charges against, 439–40
role in 9/11 timeline, 24–25
standards of, 157–58
White House furniture and, 295–98
Clinton, Hillary Rodham
    on abortion, 447–48
    book by, 303–6
    ethnic slurs by, 291–95
    on Jewish ancestry, 122
    on Mahood's detention, 111–12
    opinion polls about, 289–90, 305
    reaction to husband's affair, 27, 303
    Senate campaign, 238, 283–89
    on slavery, 313
    on World Trade Center, 38
Cockburn, Alexander, 19
Collins, Gail, 293
Collins, Robert F., 180–81
Columbia space shuttle explosion, 51–52
Columbia University, 226, 227
Columbine High School, 189
Coming Home (movie), 4
Conason, Joe, 446
Confederate flag, 203–7
Conn, George, 441
Continental Airlines, 87–88, 108
Contract with America, 183
Coors, Pete, 212
Corzine, Jon, 145
Coughlin, Charles, 213–14
Coughlin, Paula, 60–61
Couric, Katie, 235, 236–37
The Creators (Boorstin), 39–40
criminals
    confessions by, 275–79

death penalty for, 271–75
DNA evidence from, 268–70
IQ tests and, 265–68
police treatment of, 262–65
Cronkite, Walter, 232, 435
Cuba, 85, 310–12
Cuban Missile Crisis, 85–86
The Cultural Life of Modern America (Hamsun), 56
Cuomo, Kerry Kennedy, 15–16
Cuomo, Mario, 233

Daoud, Abu, 33
Daschle, Tom, 54–55, 85, 331
dating scene, 379–82
Dave (movie), 5
Davis, Angela, 374–75
Davis, Gray, 161–63
Davis, John, 87–88
Day After Tomorrow (movie), 4
Dean, Charlie, 121
Dean, Howard
    on brother's death, 121
    on civil unions, 191–92
    on Confederate flag, 203–4
    Democratic nomination race, 70, 76, 113, 126–27
    on Madrid bombings, 79
    on religion, 124–25
    on Republican Party, 461
    on Super Bowl halftime show, 132
    on war and terrorists, 118
Death by Government (Rummel), 290
death penalty, 271–75
DeLay, Tom, 18
Democratic Leadership Council, 123
Democratic National Convention, 424–28
Democratic nomination campaign, 113–37
    family tragedy stories, 119–23

Democratic nomination campaign
  (continued):
  newsworthy quotes during, 132–34
  political views, 127–29
  religious views, 123–26
Dershowitz, Alan, 7, 186, 233, 237,
  365
desegregation, 176–79
DiBagio, Thomas M., 216
discrimination
  anti-Semitism, 291–95
  ethnic, 291–95
  gender, 230–32
  racial, 6–7, 41, 103–12, 174, 242–45
Dixiecrat Party, 174
DNA tests, 268–70
Dodd, Chris, 329–30
Dohrn, Bernardine, 183–84
Donahue, Phil, 234
Dowd, Maureen, 225–26
Drudge, Matt, 18
Drudge Report, 212
drug legalization, 373–79

Earnhardt, Dale, 242
Easterbrook, Frank, 180
Edwards, John, 68, 73, 120–21,
  134–36, 203
Edwards, Wade, 120
Eisenhower, Dwight, 74, 450–51
electoral college, 348–50
electricity crisis (California), 158–60
Ellis, Joseph, 408–10
Eltantawi, Sarah, 7
Emancipation Proclamation, 205
energy policy, 164–66
Enron, 153–56
Equal Protection Clause, 343–45
Estrada, Miguel, 181–82
Ex Parte Milligan, 31
Ex Parte Quirin, 31, 32

Falwell, Jerry, 125
fathers'-rights laws, 313–14, 316–20
Faubus, Orval, 450–51
FBI (Federal Bureau of Investiga-
  tion), 40–42, 103, 110–11,
  334–35
"federalism," 451–53
feminism, 392–400
Field, Martha, 365
First Amendment, 369, 370
Flinn, Kelly, 176
Florida Supreme Court, 351–67
Flynt, Larry, 285
Fonda, Jane, 145
Fouad, Esshassah, 69
Fox News, 219–21
France, 32–35
Frank, Barney, 157, 299
Franken, Al, 9, 239–45
Fray, Mary Lee, 293
Fray, Paul, 293
free market economy, 153–56, 160
Friedman, Thomas, 243–44
Friends (TV show), 4
Frist, Bill, 458
fundraising, 144–47

Galloway, George, 62
gay marriage, 190–94, 436–437
gay rights, 201
gays, media portrayal of, 170–73
Geneva Convention, 35–37
George magazine, 383–86
Gephardt, Dick, 68, 118–19, 119,
  120, 128
Gibson, Mel, 18, 194, 196–97
Ginsberg, Ruth Bader, 333
Giuliani, Rudolph, 238, 283–84, 287
Giuliani, Rudolph W., 264
Goddard, H.H., 266
Goebbels, Joseph, 56

Goldberg, Bernard, 231
Gonzáles, Elián, 310–28
Gonzáles, Juan Miguel, 316, 317–18
Gonzáles, Lázaro, 321–22
Good Housekeeping magazine,
    412–13, 415–17
Gordon, John, 206
Gore, Al
    antiwar speech, 86
    aviation-security commission, 111
    "Brown Shirt" comment by,
      427
    family tragedies, 120
    fundraising by, 144–46
    presidential campaign, 141–47,
      335, 337–67
Gorelick, Jamie, 103–5
Graham, Bob, 118
Graham, Lindsey, 14
Grant, Ulysses S., 206–7
Greer, George, 452
Greinsky, Charles, 305
Grossman, Andrew, 236, 238
Guantánamo detainees, 35–37
Gulf War, 49
gun laws, 8, 101–3, 166–69, 368–72

Halliburton, 156
Hamsun, Knut, 55–56
Harken Energy, 156
Harkin, Tom, 13
Harris, Katherine, 353–54, 357–58
Hart, Gary, 233
Harvard University, 226
Hastings, Alcee L., 180, 181
hate crimes, 43–46
Haupt, Herbert Hans, 31
Heinz, Teresa, 115–16, 131, 436,
    460
Hell to Pay (Olson), 27
Hemings, Sally, 408–12

Hernandez, Pedro, 276
Hernstein, Richard, 265
heterosexuality, 394–95
Heuvel, Katrina vanden, 446
Hewitt, Don, 232
Heymann, Philip, 347
High Crimes and Misdemeanors
    (Coulter), 388
Hightower, Jim, 234
Hill, Anita, 219, 332
Hitchens, Christopher, 18, 19
Hitler, Adolf, 55–56, 197–98
Homeland Security Bill, 248–49
homosexuality, 64
homosexuals, 18
Hoover, J. Edgar, 18
Horowitz, David, 422
Hubbell, Webster, 182
Hunt, Al, 250, 251
The Hunting of the President (movie),
    5–6
Hurley, Elizabeth, 147
Hussein, Saddam
    African uranium and, 9, 11
    capture of, 76–78
    speech by, 58
    threat posed by, 49–51
    ties with bin Laden, 62
    ultimatum to, 54–55, 65–66
    weapons held by, 64–67
Hussein, Uday, 54

immigration, 311–28
Independence Day (movie), 4
IQ tests, 265–68
Iran, Shah of, 22
Iraq war, 51–59, 70–72, 81–86,
    445–46
Iraqi democracy, 444–46
Isaacoff, Dana, 114
Islamic "crash course," 190

Islamic terrorists
   Achille Lauro hijacking, 59–60
   attacks in Nigeria, 46–48
   9/11 attacks, 22–26, 103–5,
      111–12
   support from France, 33
Ivins, Molly, 251

Jackson, Janet, 132
Jackson, Jesse, 245
Jefferson, Thomas, 408–12
Jeffords, Jim, 457
Jennings, Peter, 460
Jewish religion, 122, 291–95
Johnson, Gary, 376, 378
Jong, Kim, II, 80
Jospin, Lionel, 33
journalism, 213–45
   discrimination in, 230–32
   misquotes in, 236–45
   New York Times articles, 212,
      215–32
   talk shows, 233–35
judges, federal, 179–84, 433–35, 457

Karbala, 82
Kayyem, Juliette, 7
Keller, Bill, 74–75, 85
Kelley, Kitty, 434
Kelso, Frank, 23, 60–61
Kennedy, Edward, 7, 11, 15, 73, 128,
     175, 176–77, 461
Kennedy, John F., 336, 390
Kennedy, John F., Jr., 383–86
Kennedy, Mark, 2
Kerik, Bernie, 437
Kerry, John H.
   ancestry of, 53–54, 122
   on ANWR drilling, 166
   choice of running mate, 134, 137
   on civil rights, 68

   on gay marriage, 192, 193
   on Hussein's capture, 76
   marriages of, 130–32, 436
   North Korean support for, 80
   presidential campaign, 113–16,
     118, 124, 127, 129–32, 133–34,
     203, 435–36
   Vietnam duty, 429–32, 434–35
   on war, 48–50, 70–71, 73
Kinnock, Neil, 121
Kirsch, Steven, 144
Klein, Joe, 250, 251
Klinghoffer, Leon, 59
Koran, The, 45
Kosovo, 117
Kramer, Michael, 337
Kristof, Nicholas, 53, 66–67, 82–83
Kristol, William, 422
Ku Klux Klan, 210, 329–30, 460
Kucinich, Dennis, 119, 132, 203,
     426, 461
Kyl, Jon, 13

Laden, Osama bin, 26, 62
Larry King Live (TV show), 13
Law & Order (TV show), 3–4
LaWall, Barbara, 422
lawsuits, personal injury, 135–37
Leahy, Patrick, 29, 181, 298–99
Lebranchu, Marylise, 34
LeDuff, Charlie, 217–18
Lee, Robert E., 205, 206–7
Lehman, Arnold, 284
Lehman, John, 103
Levinson, Sam, 167, 169
Lewinsky, Bernard, 282–83
Lewinsky, Monica, 4, 19, 27, 140,
     280–83
Libertarian Party, 373–75, 377–79
Lieberman, Joe, 54, 73, 122, 128, 132
Limbaugh, David, 187

Limbaugh, Rush, 184–87
Lincoln, Abraham, 205, 207
Living History (Clinton), 303–6
Lopez, Nancy, 230
Lott, John, 8
Lott, Trent, 173–76, 329–30, 457
Lynn Lucas Middle School, 188–89

MacArthur, Douglas, 71
Madonna, 12
Madrid bombings, 78–80
Magaw, John, 100–103
Mahmood, Ansar, 111–12
Making the Corps (Ricks), 113
Mandela, Nelson, 304–5
Manion, Daniel, 181
Mapes, Mary, 439–43
Markey, Ed, 164, 165, 166
marriage, same-sex, 190–94, 437
Marshall Plan, 72
Matthews, Chris, 459
McAuliffe, Terry, 125, 248
McCain, John, 401
McCarthy, Joseph, 18
McCray, Antron, 270, 273
McGovern, George, 175
McGrory, Mary, 298
Meet the Press (TV show), 9
Menendez, Robert, 86
metal detectors, 92
Milgram, Stanley, 99
military tribunals, 29–32
Mineta, Norman, 100–102, 106–10
minimum wage, 461
Miringoff, Lee M., 288
Miss World beauty pageant, 46–48
Mnookin, Seth, 224
Moore, Michael, 2
Morgenthau, Robert M., 278
Moss, Mitchell L., 288
Moussaoui, Zacarias, 34, 41, 110–12

MTV half-time show, 132
Muhammad, John, 215–17
Murray, Charles, 265, 267
Muslim terrorists
    Achille Lauro hijacking, 59–60
    attacks in Nigeria, 46–48
    9/11 attacks, 22–26, 103–5,
        111–12
    support from France, 33
My Life (Clinton), 306–9

NARAL Pro-Choice America,
    448–49
National Endowment of the Arts,
    284–89
National Guard documents, 246–47,
    436, 432–34, 439–41
National Public Radio, 235
National Review, 391–92
Nesbitt, Eric, 265–66
New York Times, 153–55, 212,
    215–32
Newsom, Gavin, 436
Newsweek magazine, 224
Nigeria, 46–48
Nightline (TV show), 213–15
9/11 terrorist attack
    blame for, 334–35
    Commission on, 103–5, 112, 437
    media coverage of, 26–28
    timeline of, 22–26
Nixon, Richard M., 336–37
Nixon, Walter L., 180
North, Oliver, 23, 52, 59–60
North Korea, 456
Norton, Gale, 164

Obasanjo, Olusegun, 46–47
O'Hanlon, Michael, 81
oil drilling, 164–66
Olson, Barbara, 26–28

O'Neill, John, 429, 436, 432
O'Neill, Paul, 147–49
Oppenheimer, Jerry, 291
Opperman, Vance, 144
O'Reilly Factor (TV show), 7
Owen, Priscilla, 454
Owens, Major, 298

Palestinian Authority, 33
Palmer, A. Mitchell, 67
Pan Am Flight 103, 24
Parker, Elizabeth Rindskopf, 7–8
Parker, Sarah Jessica, 172
The Passion of the Christ (movie), 18, 194–99
Patriot Act, 310
Pearl Harbor, 74
Persecution (Limbaugh), 187–88
personal injury cases, 135–37
Pinochet, Augusto, 227–28
police enforcement, 262–65
polygamy, 64
Posner, Richard, 179–80
Powell, Colin, 35–36
Progressive Party, 174
Prohibition, 377
Promiscuities (Wolf), 142, 144
Prudhoe Bay, 165
Puerto Rican Day Parade, 262–65

Qaeda, al, 25–26, 78–80
Quarls, Richard, 209

racial profiling, 6–7, 41, 103–12, 243–44
radio talk shows, 233–35
Raines, Howell, 74, 223–24, 225–26
Raines, Raymond, 188
Rakove, Jack, 167–68
Ramirez, Lucy, 442
Ramo, Roberta, 183

rape, of Central Park jogger, 268–79
Rather, Dan, 235, 432–35, 436, 439, 440
Reagan, Nancy, 201–2
Reagan, Ronald, 23–24, 60, 231
Reagan, Ronald, Jr., 199–202
Redish, Martin, 366
Reid, Richard, 109
religion, 122, 187–90, 194–99, 283–84
Reno, Janet, 310, 314–15, 319, 320, 321
Reyes, Matias, 269, 272–74, 276–77
Rice, Condoleezza, 150–52
Rich, Denise, 145
Rich, Frank, 197
Rich, Marc, 145, 298–300
Richardson, Kevin, 275–76
Ricks, Thomas, 113
Rights of the Child Treaty, 313
Ritter, Scott, 53, 62
Rivera, Geraldo, 237
Roberts, Julia, 140
Robeson, Paul, 12
Roe v. Wade, 447–49
Roosevelt, Franklin D., 67, 74
Rowley, Coleen, 40–42
Rubin, Trudy, 445
Ruby Ridge, 101–2
Rummel, R.J., 290
Rumor of War (Caputo), 208
Rumsfeld, Donald, 86
The Rush Limbaugh Show (radio show), 233

Safire, William, 198, 239
Salaam, Yusef, 268, 271, 273
Santana, Raymond, 273
Santorum, Rick, 64
Scalia, Antonin, 181
Schafly, Phyllis, 230–31

Schama, Simon, 55–56

Schiavo, Terri, 451–53

school desegregation, 176–79

schools, religion in, 187–90

Schroeder, Gerhard, 118

Schroeder, Patricia, 61

Schumer, Charles, 29, 38, 111–12, 181, 458

Schwarzenegger, Arnold, 163

Second Amendment, 166–69, 369–71

segregation, 173–79

sex, in the media, 170–73

Sex and the City (TV show), 171–72

Sharpton, Al, 122, 132, 203, 425

Shays, Christopher, 299, 372–73, 400–404

Sheen, Martin, 12

Sherman, William Tecumseh, 75

Shiite movement, 444

Silberman, Laurence, 180

Slander (Coulter), 241–42, 266, 388

slavery, 205, 210, 313

Smith, Jerry, 180

Somalia, 72

Souter, David, 180

Spain, 78–80

Special Forces, 10

Specter, Arlen, 299

Stahl, Leslie, 232

Star, Darren, 173

Starr, Ken, 283, 300

State of a Union (Oppenheimer), 291

stem-cell research, 201–2

Stephanopoulos, George, 4, 150

Stern, Nat, 366

Sternberg, Robert, 266

Stohlberg, Sheryl Gay, 257–61

Sulzberger, Arthur "Pinch," 221, 223, 225, 227, 230

Summers, Larry, 421

The Sum of All Fears (Clancy), 199

Sunnis, 445

Super Bowl half-time show, 132

Supreme Court appointments, 179–84, 453–456, 456–457

Swift Boat Veterans, 428–32, 434–35, 436

Tailhook, 60–61

talk shows, 233–35

tax cuts, 302–3

Teamsters, 128, 165

terrorism, 22–86

  Achille Lauro hijacking, 59–60

  civil liberties and, 68–70

  FBI's role in, 40–42

  France and, 32–25

  Hussein's capture, 76–78

  Iraq war and, 51–53, 56–59, 70–72, 83–86

  Kerry's view on, 48–50

  Madrid bombings, 78–80

  military tribunals and, 29–32

  9/11, 22–29

  patriotic lesson plans for, 43–46

  "plan" for, 73–75

  ties between Hussein and bin Laden, 62

  treatment of detainees, 35–37

  weapons of mass destruction, 64–67

Tet offensive, 81, 435

Texas Air National Guard documents, 246–47, 432–34, 436, 439, 440–41

Thatcher, Margaret, 24

There's My Bush (movie), 4

Thomas, Clarence, 178, 180, 331–32

Thomas, Evan, 186–87, 242

Thomas, Norman, 242

Thorne, Julia, 130

Thurmond, Strom, 173–75, 238, 329–30

Tillman, Pat, 437–38

Time magazine, 254–57

Tisch, Jon, 145

torture, 7–8

Totenberg, Nina, 219

Tour of Duty (Brinkley), 434

Treason (Coulter), 388

Tribe, Larry, 167

Tripp, Linda, 282, 290

"trusted traveler" program, 100, 102

UN Human Rights Commission, 33–34

UN Weapons Inspection Team, 11

Unfit for Command (O'Neill), 429, 431–32, 434

United Airlines, 107

United States v. Miller, 168–69

Unlimited Access (Aldrich), 150

Unveiling Islam (Caner and Caner), 45

U.S. Department of Transportation, 91–94, 107–9

Valhouli, Christina, 236

Wade Edwards Learning Lab, 120

Wallace, Henry, 174–75

Wallace, Mike, 460

Walters, Barbara, 303–4

War on Poverty, 75

Warner, John, 13

Warren, Earl, 67

Warren, Michael, 278–79

Washington, Denzel, 140

Wasserman, Debbie, 361–62

weapons of mass destruction, 64–67

Weaver, Randy, 101–2

Weicker, Lowell, 233

Wellstone, Paul, 299

What Not To Wear (TV show), 4

White House furniture, 295–98

Wiehl, Lis, 366–67

Wilder, Doug, 233

Williams, Stephen, 180

Wilson, Woodrow, 67

Wise, Kharey, 276

Wolf, Naomi, 141–44

Wolfowitz, Paul, 84, 85

World Trade Center, 24, 38–40

Wyly, Sam, 401

Wyman, Thomas, 231

Zapatero, José Luis Rodríguez, 79–80

Zemin, Jiang, 301

Zuckman, Jill, 252–53

About the Author

ANN COULTER is the author of three *New York Times* best-sellers: *Treason, Slander,* and *High Crimes and Misdemeanors.* She is the legal correspondent for *Human Events* and a syndicated columnist for Universal Press Syndicate. A frequent guest on many TV shows, she was named one of the top 100 public intellectuals by federal judge Richard Posner in 2001. Coulter is a Connecticut native and a graduate of Cornell University and University of Michigan Law School.